MCTS 70-643

Windows Server 2008 Applications Infrastructure, Configuring

Patrick Regan

MCTS 70-643 Exam Cram: Windows Server 2008 Applications Infrastructure, Configuring

Copyright © 2009 by Pearson Education, Inc.

All rights reserved. No part of this book shall be reproduced, stored in a retrieval system, or transmitted by any means, electronic, mechanical, photocopying, recording, or otherwise, without written permission from the publisher. No patent liability is assumed with respect to the use of the information contained herein. Although every precaution has been taken in the preparation of this book, the publisher and author assume no responsibility for errors or omissions. Nor is any liability assumed for damages resulting from the use of the information contained herein.

ISBN-13: 978-0-7897-3819-6
ISBN-10: 0-7897-3819-8

Library of Congress Cataloging-in-Publication Data

Regan, Patrick E.

    MCTS 70-643 exam cram : Windows server 2008 applications infrastructure, configuring / Patrick Regan. — 1st ed.

        p. cm.

    ISBN 978-0-7897-3819-6 (pbk. w/cd)

    1. Electronic data processing personnel—Certification—Study guides. 2. Microsoft software—Examinations—Study guides. 3. Microsoft Windows server—Examinations—Study guides. I. Title.

    QA76.3.R4556 2009

    005.4'476—dc22

                                        2008033895

Printed in the United States of America

First Printing: September 2008

Bulk Sales

Que Publishing offers excellent discounts on this book when ordered in quantity for bulk purchases or special sales. For more information, please contact

    U.S. Corporate and Government Sales
    1-800-382-3419
    corpsales@pearsontechgroup.com

For sales outside of the U.S., please contact

    International Sales
    international@pearson.com

Associate Publisher
Dave Dusthimer

Acquisitions Editor
Betsy Brown

Development Editor
Box Twelve
Communications

Managing Editor
Patrick Kanouse

Project Editor
Amanda Gillum

Copy Editor
Margo Catts

Indexer
WordWise
Publishing Services
LLC

Proofreader
Suzanne Thomas

Technical Editor
Chris Crayton

**Publishing
Coordinator**
Vanessa Evans

**Multimedia
Developer**
Dan Scherf

Designer
Gary Adair

Composition
TnT Design, Inc

Contents at a Glance

Table of Contents

About the Author

Patrick Regan has been a PC technician, network administrator/engineer, design architect, and security analyst for the past 16 years after graduating with a bachelor's degree in physics from the University of Akron. He has taught many computer and network classes at local Sacramento colleges (Heald Colleges and MTI Colleges) and participated in and led many projects (Heald Colleges, Intel Corporation, Miles Consulting Corporation, and Pacific Coast Companies). For his teaching accomplishments, he received the Teacher of the Year award from Heald Colleges, and he has received several recognition awards from Intel. Previously, he worked as a product support engineer for the Intel Corporation Customer Service, as a senior network engineer for Virtual Alert supporting the BioTerrorism Readiness suite, and as a senior design architect/engineer and training coordinator for Miles Consulting Corp (MCC), a premiere Microsoft Gold partner and consulting firm. He is currently a senior network engineer at Pacific Coast Companies supporting a large enterprise network.

He holds many certifications, including the Microsoft MCSE, MCSA, MCITP, MCT; CompTIA's A+, Network+, Server+, Linux+, Security+ and CTT+; Cisco CCNA; and Novell's CNE and CWNP Certified Wireless Network Administrator (CWNA).

Over the last several years, he has written several textbooks for Prentice Hall Publisher, including *Troubleshooting the PC, Networking with Windows 2000 and 2003, Linux, Local Area Networks, Wide Area Networks*, and the Acing Series (*Acing the A+, Acing the Network+, Acing the Security+,* and *Acing the Linux+*). He has also co-authored the *ExamCram 70-290 MCSA/MCSE Managing and Maintaining a Microsoft Windows Server 2003 Environment, 2nd Edition ExamCram* and written *70-620 MCSA/MCSE TS: Microsoft Windows Vista, Configuring* and the *Exam Cram 70-642: Windows Server 2008 Network Infrastructure, Configuring*. In addition, he has completed the study guides for the A+ certification exams for Cisco Press.

You can write with questions and comments to the author at Patrick_Regan@hotmail.com. (Because of the high volume of mail, every message might not receive a reply.)

Dedication

I dedicate this book to Lidia, a wonderful and beautiful woman that I love very much.

We Want to Hear from You!

As the reader of this book, *you* are our most important critic and commentator. We value your opinion and want to know what we're doing right, what we could do better, what areas you'd like to see us publish in, and any other words of wisdom you're willing to pass our way.

As an associate publisher for Que Publishing, I welcome your comments. You can email or write me directly to let me know what you did or didn't like about this book—as well as what we can do to make our books better.

Please note that I cannot help you with technical problems related to the topic of this book. We do have a User Services group, however, where I will forward specific technical questions related to the book.

When you write, please be sure to include this book's title and author as well as your name, email address, and phone number. I will carefully review your comments and share them with the author and editors who worked on the book.

Email: feedback@quepublishing.com

Mail: Dave Dusthimer
Associate Publisher
Que Publishing
800 East 96th Street
Indianapolis, IN 46240 USA

Reader Services

Visit our website and register this book at www.quepublishing.com/register for convenient access to any updates, downloads, or errata that might be available for this book.

Introduction

Welcome to the 70-643 Exam Cram! Whether this book is your first or your 15th *Exam Cram* series book, you'll find information here that will help ensure your success as you pursue knowledge, experience, and certification. This book aims to help you get ready to take and pass the Microsoft certification exam "TS: Windows Server 2008 Applications Infrastructure, Configuring" (Exam 70-643). After you pass this exam, you will earn the Microsoft Certified Technology Specialist: Windows Server 2008 Applications certification.

This introduction explains Microsoft's certification programs in general and talks about how the *Exam Cram* series can help you prepare for Microsoft's latest certification exams. Then Chapters 1 through 9 are designed to remind you of everything you'll need to know to pass the 70-643 certification exam. The two sample tests at the end of the book (Chapters 10 through 13) should give you a reasonably accurate assessment of your knowledge and, yes, we've provided the answers and their explanations for these sample tests. Read the book, understand the material, and you'll stand a very good chance of passing the real test.

Exam Cram books help you understand and appreciate the subjects and materials you need to know to pass Microsoft certification exams. *Exam Cram* books are aimed strictly at test preparation and review. They do not teach you everything you need to know about a subject. Instead, the author streamlines and highlights the pertinent information by presenting and dissecting the questions and problems he's discovered that you're likely to encounter on a Microsoft test.

Nevertheless, to completely prepare yourself for any Microsoft test, we recommend that you begin by taking the "Self Assessment" that is included in this book, immediately following this introduction. The self-assessment tool helps you evaluate your knowledge base against the requirements for becoming a Microsoft Certified Technology Specialist (MCTS) and will be the first step in earning more advanced certifications, including Microsoft's IT Professional and Professional Developer (MCITP and MCPD) and Architect (MCA).

Based on what you learn from the self assessment, you might decide to begin your studies with classroom training or some background reading. On the other hand, you might decide to pick up and read one of the many study guides available from Microsoft or third-party vendors. We also recommend that you supplement your study program with visits to http://www.examcram.com to receive additional practice questions, get advice, and track the Windows certification programs.

This book also offers you an added bonus of access to Exam Cram practice tests online. This software simulates the Microsoft testing environment with similar types of questions to those you're likely to see on the actual Microsoft exam. We also strongly recommend that you install, configure, and play around with the Microsoft Windows Vista and Windows Server 2008 operating systems. Nothing beats hands-on experience and familiarity when it comes to understanding the questions you're likely to encounter on a certification test. Book learning is essential, but without a doubt, hands-on experience is the best teacher of all!

The Microsoft Certification Program

Microsoft currently offers multiple certification titles, each of which boasts its own special abbreviation. (As a certification candidate and computer professional, you need to have a high tolerance for acronyms.)

The certification for end-users is

> ▶ **Microsoft Office Specialists:** For professionals recognized for demonstrating advanced skills with Microsoft desktop software (including Microsoft Office).

The older certifications associated with the Windows Server 2003 operating system and related network infrastructure are

> ▶ **Microsoft Certified Professional (MCP):** For professionals who have the skills to successfully implement Microsoft products (such as Windows XP or Windows Server 2003) or technology as part of a business solution in an organization.
>
> ▶ **Microsoft Certified Desktop Support Technician (MCDST):** For professionals who have the technical and customer service skills to troubleshoot hardware and software operation issues in Microsoft Windows environments.
>
> ▶ **Microsoft Certified Systems Administrators (MCSA):** For professionals who administer network and systems environments based on the Microsoft Windows operating systems. Specializations include MCSA: Messaging and MCSA: Security.
>
> ▶ **Microsoft Certified Systems Engineer (MCSE):** For professionals who design and implement an infrastructure solution that is based on the Windows operating system and Microsoft Windows Server System software. Specializations include MCSE: Messaging and MCSE: Security.

The newer certifications that are based on Windows Vista, Windows Server 2008, and related server products are

► **Microsoft Certified Technology Specialist (MCTS):** For professionals who target specific technologies and distinguish themselves by demonstrating in-depth knowledge and expertise in the various Microsoft specialized technologies. The MCTS is a replacement for the MCP program.

► **Microsoft Certified IT Professional (MCITP):** For professionals who demonstrate comprehensive skills in planning, deploying, supporting, maintaining, and optimizing IT infrastructures. The MCITP is a replacement for the MCSA and MCSE programs.

► **Microsoft Certified Architect (MCA):** For professionals who are identified as top industry experts in IT architecture and who use multiple technologies to solve business problems and provide business metrics and measurements. Candidates for the MCA program are required to present to a review board—consisting of previously certified architects—to earn the certification.

For those who want to become or who are database professionals, the following certifications are based on the Microsoft SQL Server products:

► **Microsoft Certified Database Administrators (MCDBA):** For professionals who design, implement, and administer Microsoft SQL Server databases.

For developers and programmers, the following certifications are based on the Microsoft .NET Framework and Visual Studio products:

► **Microsoft Certified Professional Developer (MCPD):** For professionals who are recognized as expert Windows Application Developers, Web Application Developers, or Enterprise Applications Developers. They demonstrate that you can build rich applications that target a variety of platforms such as the Microsoft .NET Framework 2.0.

► **Microsoft Certified Application Developers (MCAD):** For professionals who use Microsoft technologies to develop and maintain department-level applications, components, web or desktop clients, or back-end data services.

For trainers and curriculum developers, the following certifications are available:

- **Microsoft Certified Trainer (MCT):** For qualified instructors who are certified by Microsoft to deliver Microsoft training courses to IT professionals and developers.

- **Microsoft Certified Learning Consultant (MCLC):** Recognizes MCTs whose job roles have grown to include frequent consultative engagements with their customers and who are experts in delivering customized learning solutions that positively affect customer return on investment (ROI).

In 2008, Microsoft introduced two advanced certifications. The Master certifications identify individuals with the deepest technical skills available on a particular Microsoft product such as Windows Server 2008, Exchange 2007, and SQL Server 2008. To achieve Master certification, candidates must attend several required sessions, successfully complete all in-class (written and lab) exams, and successfully complete a qualification lab exam.

The highest level certification is the Microsoft Certified Architect (MCA) program focusing on IT architecture. Microsoft Certified Architects have proven experience with delivering solutions and can communicate effectively with business, architecture, and technology professionals. These professionals have three or more years of advanced IT architecture experience and possess strong technical and leadership skills. Candidates are required to pass a rigorous Review Board interview conducted by a panel of experts.

The best place to keep tabs on all Microsoft certifications is the following website:

http://www.microsoft.com/learning/default.mspx

Microsoft changes their website often, so if this URL does not work in the future, you should use the Search tool on Microsoft's site to find more information on a particular certification.

Microsoft Certified Technology Specialist

Technology Specialist certifications enable professionals to target specific technologies and to distinguish themselves by demonstrating in-depth knowledge and expertise in their specialized technologies. Microsoft Technology Specialists are consistently capable of implementing, building, troubleshooting, and debugging a particular Microsoft technology.

At the time of the writing of this book, there are 28 Microsoft Certified Technology Specialist (MCTS) certifications:

Technology Specialist: SQL Server 2008, Business Intelligence Development and Maintenance

Technology Specialist: SQL Server 2008, Database Development

Technology Specialist: SQL Server 2008, Implementation and Maintenance

Technology Specialist: .NET Framework 3.5, Windows Presentation Foundation Applications

Technology Specialist: .NET Framework 3.5, Windows Communication Foundation Applications

Technology Specialist: .NET Framework 3.5, Windows Workflow Foundation Applications

Technology Specialist: .NET Framework 2.0, Web Applications

Technology Specialist: .NET Framework 2.0, Windows Applications

Technology Specialist: .NET Framework 2.0, Distributed Applications

Technology Specialist: SQL Server 2005

Technology Specialist: SQL Server 2005, Business Intelligence

Technology Specialist: BizTalk Server 2006

Technology Specialist: Microsoft Office Project Server 2007, Enterprise Project Management

Technology Specialist: Microsoft Office Project 2007, Project Management

Technology Specialist: Microsoft Office Live Communications Server 2005

Technology Specialist: Microsoft Exchange Server 2007, Configuration

Technology Specialist: Microsoft Office SharePoint Server 2007, Configuration

Technology Specialist: Microsoft Office SharePoint Server 2007, Application Development

Technology Specialist: Windows Mobile 5.0, Applications

Technology Specialist: Windows Mobile 5.0, Implementation and Management

Technology Specialist: Windows Server 2003, Hosted Environments, Configuration, and Management

Technology Specialist: Windows Server 2008, Active Directory Configuration

Technology Specialist: Windows Server 2008, Network Infrastructure Configuration

Technology Specialist: Windows Server 2008, Applications Infrastructure Configuration

Technology Specialist: Windows SharePoint Services 3.0, Application Development

Technology Specialist: Windows SharePoint Services 3.0, Configuration

Technology Specialist: Windows Vista and 2007 Microsoft Office System Desktops, Deployment and Maintenance

Technology Specialist: Windows Vista, Configuration

Microsoft Certified IT Professional

The new Microsoft Certified IT Professional (MCITP) credential lets you highlight your specific area of expertise. Now, you can easily distinguish yourself as an expert in database administration, database development, business intelligence, or support. At the time of this writing, the following Microsoft Certified IT Professional certifications exist:

IT Professional: Database Developer

IT Professional: Database Administrator

IT Professional: Business Intelligence Developer

IT Professional: Enterprise Support Technician

IT Professional: Consumer Support Technician

IT Professional: Database Developer 2008

IT Professional: Database Administrator 2008

IT Professional: Enterprise Messaging Administrator

IT Professional: Enterprise Project Management with Microsoft Office Project Server 2007

IT Professional: Enterprise Administrator

IT Professional: Server Administrator

The MCTS on Windows Server 2008 helps you and your organization take advantage of advanced server technology with the power to increase the flexibility of your server infrastructure, save time, and reduce costs. Transition certifications are available today for Windows Server 2003 certified professionals, while full certification paths will be available soon after the Windows Server 2008 product release. For more details about these certifications, visit the following website:

http://www.microsoft.com/learning/mcp/windowsserver2008/default.mspx

If the URL is no longer available, don't forget to search for MCTS and Windows Server 2008 with the Microsoft search tool found on the Microsoft website.

Microsoft Certified Technology Specialist: Windows Server 2008 Applications Infrastructure

The Microsoft Certified Technology Specialist certifications enable professionals to target specific technologies and distinguish themselves by demonstrating in-depth knowledge and expertise in their specialized technologies. A Microsoft

Certified Technology Specialist in Windows Vista, Configuration possesses the knowledge and skills to configure Windows Vista for optimal performance on the desktop, including installing, managing, and configuring the new security, network, and application features in Windows Vista.

To earn the Microsoft Certified Technology Specialist: Windows Vista, Configuration, you must pass one exam that focuses on supporting end-user issues about network connectivity, security, applications installation and compatibility, and logon problems that include account issues and password resets:

Exam 70-643: TS: Windows Server 2008 Applications Infrastructure, Configuration

If you decide to take Microsoft recognized class, you would take several classes to cover all of the material found on this exam. The preparation guide (including exam objectives) for Exam 70-643 TS: Windows Server 2008 Applications Infrastructure, Configuration can be found at

http://www.microsoft.com/learning/exams/70-643.mspx

Taking a Certification Exam

After you prepare for your exam, you need to register with a testing center. At the time of this writing, the cost to take exam 70-643 is (U.S.) $125, and if you don't pass, you can take each again for an additional (U.S.) $125 for each attempt. In the United States and Canada, tests are administered by Prometric. Here's how you can contact them:

> ▶ **Prometric:** You can sign up for a test through the company's website, http://www.2test.com or http://www.prometric.com. Within the United States and Canada, you can register by phone at 800-755-3926. If you live outside this region, you should check the Prometric website for the appropriate phone number.

To sign up for a test, you must possess a valid credit card or contact Prometric for mailing instructions to send a check (in the United States). Only when payment is verified, or a check has cleared, can you actually register for a test.

To schedule an exam, you need to call the appropriate phone number or visit the Prometric websites at least one day in advance. To cancel or reschedule an exam in the United States or Canada, you must call before 3 p.m. Eastern time the day before the scheduled test time (or you might be charged, even if you don't show up to take the test). When you want to schedule a test, you should have the following information ready:

▶ Your name, organization, and mailing address.

▶ Your Microsoft test ID. (In the United States, this means your Social Security number; citizens of other countries should call ahead to find out what type of identification number is required to register for a test.)

▶ The name and number of the exam you want to take.

▶ A method of payment. (As mentioned previously, a credit card is the most convenient method, but alternate means can be arranged in advance, if necessary.)

After you sign up for a test, you are told when and where the test is scheduled. You should arrive at least 15 minutes early. You must supply two forms of identification—one of which must be a photo ID—to be admitted into the testing room.

Tracking Certification Status

As soon as you pass a qualified Microsoft exam and earn a professional certification, Microsoft generates transcripts that indicate which exams you have passed. You can view a copy of your transcript at any time by going to the MCP secured site (this site may change as the MCP is retired) and selecting the Transcript Tool. This tool enables you to print a copy of your current transcript and confirm your certification status.

After you pass the necessary set of exams, you are certified. Official certification is normally granted after six to eight weeks, so you shouldn't expect to get your credentials overnight. The package for official certification that arrives includes a Welcome Kit that contains a number of elements (see Microsoft's website for other benefits of specific certifications):

▶ A certificate that is suitable for framing, along with a wallet card and lapel pin.

▶ A license to use the related certification logo, which means you can use the logo in advertisements, promotions, and documents, and on letterhead, business cards, and so on. Along with the license comes a logo sheet, which includes camera-ready artwork. (Note that before you use any of the artwork, you must sign and return a licensing agreement that indicates you'll abide by its terms and conditions.)

▶ Access to the *Microsoft Certified Professional Magazine Online* website, which provides ongoing data about testing and certification activities, requirements, changes to the MCP program, and security-related information on Microsoft products.

Many people believe that the benefits of MCP certification go well beyond the perks that Microsoft provides to newly anointed members of this elite group. We're starting to see more job listings that request or require applicants to have Microsoft and other related certifications, and many individuals who complete Microsoft certification programs can qualify for increases in pay and responsibility. As an official recognition of hard work and broad knowledge, a certification credential is a badge of honor in many IT organizations.

About This Book

Each topical *Exam Cram* chapter follows a regular structure and contains graphical cues about important or useful information. Here's the structure of a typical chapter:

- ▶ **Opening hotlists:** Each chapter begins with a list of the terms, tools, and techniques that you must learn and understand before you can be fully conversant with that chapter's subject matter. The hotlists are followed with one or two introductory paragraphs to set the stage for the rest of the chapter.

- ▶ **Topical coverage:** After the opening hotlists and introductory text, each chapter covers a series of topics related to the chapter's subject. Throughout that section, we highlight topics or concepts that are likely to appear on a test, using a special element called an Exam Alert:

> **EXAM ALERT**
>
> This is what an Exam Alert looks like. Normally, an alert stresses concepts, terms, software, or activities that are likely to relate to one or more certification-test questions. For that reason, we think any information in an Exam Alert is worthy of unusual attentiveness on your part.

You should pay close attention to material flagged in Exam Alerts; although all the information in this book pertains to what you need to know to pass the exam, Exam Alerts contain information that is really important. You'll find what appears in the meat of each chapter to be worth knowing, too, when preparing for the test. Because this book's material is very condensed, we recommend that you use this book along with other resources to achieve the maximum benefit.

In addition to the Exam Alerts, we provide tips that will help you build a better foundation for Windows Server 2008 knowledge. Although the tip information might not be on the exam, it is certainly related and it will help you become a better-informed test taker.

> **TIP**
>
> This is how tips are formatted. Keep your eyes open for these, and you'll become a Windows Server 2008 guru in no time!

> **NOTE**
>
> This is how notes are formatted. Notes direct your attention to important pieces of information that relate to Windows Server 2008 and Microsoft certification.

▶ **Exam prep questions:** Although we talk about test questions and topics throughout the book, the section at the end of each chapter presents a series of mock test questions and explanations of both correct and incorrect answers.

▶ **Details and resources:** Every chapter ends with a section titled "Need to Know More?" That section provides direct pointers to Microsoft and third-party resources that offer more details on the chapter's subject. In addition, that section tries to rank or at least rate the quality and thoroughness of the topic's coverage by each resource. If you find a resource you like in that collection, you should use it, but you shouldn't feel compelled to use all the resources. On the other hand, we recommend only resources that we use on a regular basis, so none of our recommendations will be a waste of your time or money (but purchasing them all at once probably represents an expense that many network administrators and Microsoft certification candidates might find hard to justify).

The bulk of the book follows this chapter structure, but we'd like to point out a few other elements. Chapters 10 to 13—two practice exams and their answers (with detailed explanations)—help you assess your understanding of the material presented throughout the book to ensure that you're ready for the exam.

Finally, the tear-out Cram Sheet attached next to the inside front cover of this *Exam Cram* book represents a condensed collection of facts and tips that we think are essential for you to memorize before taking the test. Because you can dump this information out of your head onto a sheet of paper before taking the exam, you can master this information by brute force; you need to remember it only long enough to write it down when you walk into the testing room. You might even want to look at it in the car or in the lobby of the testing center just before you walk in to take the exam.

We've structured the topics in this book to build on one another. Therefore, some topics in later chapters make the most sense after you've read earlier chapters. That's why we suggest that you read this book from front to back for your initial test preparation. If you need to brush up on a topic or if you have to bone up for a second try, you can use the index or table of contents to go straight to the topics and questions that you need to study. Beyond helping you prepare for the test, we think you'll find this book useful as a tightly focused reference to some of the most important aspects of Windows Vista.

The book uses the following typographical conventions:

▶ Command-line strings that are meant to be typed into the computer are displayed in monospace text, such as

    net use lpt1: *print_server_name**printer_share_name*

▶ *New terms* are introduced in italics.

Given all the book's elements and its specialized focus, we've tried to create a tool that will help you prepare for and pass Microsoft Exam 70-643. Please share with us your feedback on the book, especially if you have ideas about how we can improve it for future test takers. Send your questions or comments about this book via email to feedback@quepublishing.com. We'll consider everything you say carefully, and we'll respond to all suggestions. For more information on this book and other Que Certification titles, visit our website at http://www.quepublishing.com. You should also check out the new Exam Cram website at http://www.examcram.com, where you'll find information, updates, commentary, and certification information.

Exam Layout and Design

Historically, there have been six types of question formats on Microsoft certification exams. These types of questions continue to appear on current Microsoft tests, and they are discussed in the following sections:

▶ Multiple-choice, single answer

▶ Multiple-choice, multiple answers

▶ Build-list-and-reorder (list prioritization)

▶ Create-a-tree

▶ Drag-and-connect

▶ Select-and-place (drag-and-drop)

The Single-Answer and Multiple-Answer Multiple-Choice Question Formats

Some exam questions require you to select a single answer, whereas others ask you to select multiple correct answers. The following multiple-choice question requires you to select a single correct answer. Following the question is a brief summary of each potential answer and why it is either right or wrong.

1. You have three domains connected to an empty root domain under one contiguous domain name: tutu.com. This organization is formed into a forest arrangement, with a secondary domain called frog.com. How many schema masters exist for this arrangement?

   ○ **A.** 1

   ○ **B.** 2

   ○ **C.** 3

   ○ **D.** 4

1. The correct answer is A because only one schema master is necessary for a forest arrangement. The other answers (B, C, and D) are misleading because they try to make you believe that schema masters might be in each domain or perhaps that you should have one for each contiguous namespace domain.

This sample question format corresponds closely to the Microsoft certification exam format. The only difference is that on the exam, the questions are not followed by answers and their explanations. To select an answer, you position the cursor over the option button next to the answer you want to select. Then you click the mouse button to select the answer.

Let's examine a question for which one or more answers are possible. This type of question provides check boxes rather than option buttons for marking all appropriate selections.

2. What can you use to seize FSMO roles? (Choose two.)

   ○ **A.** The ntdsutil.exe utility

   ○ **B.** The Active Directory Users and Computers console

   ○ **C.** The secedit.exe utility

   ○ **D.** The utilman.exe utility

2. Answers A and B are correct. You can seize roles from a server that is still running through the Active Directory Users and Computers console, or in the case of a server failure, you can seize roles with the ntdsutil.exe utility. You use the secedit.exe utility to force group policies into play; therefore, Answer C is incorrect. The utilman.exe tool manages accessibility settings in Windows Server 2003; therefore, Answer D is incorrect.

This particular question requires two answers. Microsoft sometimes gives partial credit for partially correct answers. For Question 2, you have to mark the check boxes next to Answers A and B to obtain credit for a correct answer. Notice that to choose the right answers you also need to know why the other answers are wrong.

The Build-List-and-Reorder Question Format

Questions in the build-list-and-reorder format present two lists of items—one on the left and one on the right. To answer the question, you must move items from the list on the right to the list on the left. The final list must then be reordered into a specific sequence.

These questions generally sound like this: "From the following list of choices, pick the choices that answer the question. Arrange the list in a certain order." Question 3 shows an example of how these questions would look.

3. From the following list of famous people, choose those who have been elected president of the United States. Arrange the list in the order in which the presidents served.

- ► Thomas Jefferson

- ► Ben Franklin

- ► Abe Lincoln

- ► George Washington

- ► Andrew Jackson

- ► Paul Revere

3. The correct answer is

1. George Washington

2. Thomas Jefferson

3. Andrew Jackson

4. Abe Lincoln

On an actual exam, the entire list of famous people would initially appear in the list on the right. You would move the four correct answers to the list on the left and then reorder the list on the left. Notice that the answer to Question 3 does not include all the items from the initial list. However, that might not always be the case.

To move an item from the right list to the left list on the exam, you first select the item by clicking it, and you click the Add button (left arrow). After you move an item from one list to the other, you can move the item back by first selecting the item and then clicking the appropriate button (either the Add button or the Remove button). After you move items to the left list, you can reorder an item by selecting the item and clicking the up or down arrow buttons.

The Create-a-Tree Question Format

Questions in the create-a-tree format also present two lists—one on the left side of the screen and one on the right side of the screen. The list on the right consists of individual items, and the list on the left consists of nodes in a tree. To answer the question, you must move items from the list on the right to the appropriate node in the tree.

These questions can best be characterized as simply a matching exercise. Items from the list on the right are placed under the appropriate category in the list on the left. Question 4 shows an example of how they would look.

4. The calendar year is divided into four seasons:

    1. Winter

    2. Spring

    3. Summer

    4. Fall

Identify the season during which each of the following holidays occurs:

    ○ Christmas

    ○ Fourth of July

    ○ Labor Day

    ○ Flag Day

    ○ Memorial Day

    ○ Washington's Birthday

    ○ Thanksgiving

    ○ Easter

4. The correct answers are

    1. Winter

        ▶ Christmas

        ▶ Washington's Birthday

    2. Spring

        ▶ Flag Day

        ▶ Memorial Day

        ▶ Easter

    3. Summer

        ▶ Fourth of July

        ▶ Labor Day

    4. Fall

        ▶ Thanksgiving

In this case, you use all the items in the list. However, that might not always be the case.

To move an item from the right list to its appropriate location in the tree, you must first select the appropriate tree node by clicking it. Then, you select the item to be moved and click the Add button. After you add one or more items to a tree node, the node appears with a + icon to the left of the node name. You can click this icon to expand the node and view the items you have added. If you have added any item to the wrong tree node, you can remove it by selecting it and clicking the Remove button.

The Drag-and-Connect Question Format

Questions in the drag-and-connect format present a group of objects and a list of "connections." To answer the question, you must move the appropriate connections between the objects.

This type of question is best described with graphics. For this type of question, it isn't necessary to use every object, and you can use each connection multiple times.

The Select-and-Place Question Format

Questions in the select-and-place (drag-and-drop) format display a diagram with blank boxes and a list of labels that you need to drag to correctly fill in the blank boxes. To answer such a question, you must move the labels to their appropriate positions on the diagram. This type of question is best described with graphics.

Special Exam Question Formats

Starting with the exams released for the Windows Server 2003 MCSE track, Microsoft introduced several new question types in addition to the more traditional types of questions that are still widely used on all Microsoft exams. These innovative question types have been highly researched and tested by Microsoft before they were chosen to be included in many of the "refreshed" exams for the MCSA/MCSE on the Windows 2000 track and for the new exams on the Windows Server 2003 and Windows Server 2008 track. These special question types are as follows:

- Hot area questions
- Active screen questions
- Drag-and-drop–type questions
- Simulation questions

Hot Area Question Types

Hot area questions ask you to indicate the correct answer by selecting one or more elements within a graphic. For example, you might be asked to select multiple objects within a list.

Active Screen Question Types

Active screen questions ask you to configure a dialog box by modifying one or more elements. These types of questions offer a realistic interface in which you must properly configure various settings, just as you would within the actual software product. For example, you might be asked to select the proper option within a drop-down list box.

Drag-and-Drop Question Types

New drag-and-drop questions ask you to drag source elements to their appropriate corresponding targets within a work area. These types of questions test your knowledge of specific concepts and their definitions or descriptions. For example, you might be asked to match a description of a computer program to the actual software application.

Simulation Question Types

Simulation questions ask you to indicate the correct answer by performing specific tasks, such as configuring and installing network adapters or drivers, configuring and controlling access to files, or troubleshooting hardware devices. Many of the tasks that systems administrators and systems engineers perform can be presented more accurately in simulations than in most traditional exam question types.

Microsoft's Testing Formats

Currently, Microsoft uses three different testing formats:

- Fixed length
- Short form
- Case study

Other Microsoft exams employ advanced testing capabilities that might not be immediately apparent. Although the questions that appear are primarily multiple choice, the logic that drives them is more complex than that in older Microsoft tests, which use a fixed sequence of questions, called a *fixed-length test*. Some questions employ a sophisticated user interface, which Microsoft calls a *simulation*, to test your knowledge of the software and systems under consideration in a more-or-less "live" environment that behaves just like the real thing. You should review the Microsoft Learning, Reference, and Certification Web pages at http://www.microsoft.com/learning/default.mspx for more detailed information.

In the future, Microsoft might choose to create exams using a well-known technique called *adaptive testing* to establish a test taker's level of knowledge and product competence. In general, adaptive exams might look the same as fixed-length exams, but they discover the level of difficulty at which an individual test taker can correctly answer questions. Test takers with differing levels of knowledge or ability therefore see different sets of questions; individuals with high levels of knowledge or ability are presented with a smaller set of more difficult questions, whereas individuals with lower levels of knowledge are presented with a larger set of easier questions. Two individuals might answer the same percentage of questions correctly, but the test taker with a higher knowledge or ability level will score higher because his or her questions are worth more. Also, the lower-level test taker will probably answer more questions than his or her more knowledgeable colleague. This explains why adaptive tests use ranges of values to define the number of questions and the amount of time it takes to complete the test.

NOTE

Microsoft does *not* offer adaptive exams at the time of this book's publication.

Most adaptive tests work by evaluating the test taker's most recent answer. A correct answer leads to a more difficult question, and the test software's estimate of the test taker's knowledge and ability level is raised. An incorrect answer leads to a less difficult question, and the test software's estimate of the test taker's knowledge and ability level is lowered. This process continues until the test targets the test taker's true ability level. The exam ends when the test taker's level of accuracy meets a statistically acceptable value (in other words, when his or her performance demonstrates an acceptable level of knowledge and ability) or when the maximum number of items has been presented. (In which case, the test taker is almost certain to fail.)

Microsoft has also introduced a short-form test for its most popular tests. This test delivers 25 to 30 questions to its takers, giving them exactly 60 minutes to complete the exam. This type of exam is similar to a fixed-length test in that it allows readers to jump ahead or return to earlier questions and to cycle through the questions until the test is done. Microsoft does not use adaptive logic in short-form tests, but it claims that statistical analysis of the question pool is such that the 25 to 30 questions delivered during a short-form exam conclusively measure a test taker's knowledge of the subject matter in much the same way as an adaptive test. You can think of the short-form test as a kind of "greatest hits exam" (that is, it covers the most important questions) version of an adaptive exam on the same topic.

Because you won't know which form the Microsoft exam might take, you should be prepared for either a fixed-length or short-form exam. The layout is the same for both fixed-length and short-form tests—you are not penalized for guessing the correct answer(s) to questions, no matter how many questions you answer incorrectly.

The Fixed-Length and Short-Form Exam Strategy

One tactic that has worked well for many test takers is to answer each question as well as you can before time expires on the exam. Some questions you will undoubtedly feel better equipped to answer correctly than others; however, you should still select an answer to each question as you proceed through the exam. You should click the Mark for Review check box for any question that you are unsure of. In this way, at least you have answered all the questions in case you run out of time. Unanswered questions are automatically scored as incorrect; answers that are guessed at have at least some chance of being scored as correct. If time permits, after you answer all questions you can revisit each question that you have marked for review. This strategy also enables you to possibly gain some insight into questions that you are unsure of by picking up some clues from the other questions on the exam.

> **TIP**
>
> Some people prefer to read over the exam completely before answering the trickier questions; sometimes, information supplied in later questions sheds more light on earlier questions. At other times, information you read in later questions might jog your memory about facts, figures, or behavior that helps you answer earlier questions. Either way, you could come out ahead if you answer only those questions on the first pass that you're absolutely confident about. However, be careful not to run out of time if you choose this strategy!

Fortunately, the Microsoft exam software for fixed-length and short-form tests makes the multiple-visit approach easy to implement. At the top-left corner of each question is a check box that permits you to mark that question for a later visit.

Here are some question-handling strategies that apply to fixed-length and short-form tests. Use them if you have the chance:

▶ When returning to a question after your initial read-through, read every word again; otherwise, your mind can miss important details. Sometimes, revisiting a question after turning your attention elsewhere lets you see something you missed, but the strong tendency is to see only what you've seen before. Avoid that tendency at all costs.

▶ If you return to a question more than twice, articulate to yourself what you don't understand about the question, why answers don't appear to make sense, or what appears to be missing. If you chew on the subject awhile, your subconscious might provide the missing details, or you might notice a "trick" that points to the right answer.

As you work your way through the exam, another counter that Microsoft provides will come in handy—the number of questions completed and questions outstanding. For fixed-length and short-form tests, it's wise to budget your time by making sure that you've completed one-quarter of the questions one-quarter of the way through the exam period and three-quarters of the questions three-quarters of the way through.

If you're not finished when only five minutes remain, use that time to guess your way through any remaining questions. Remember, guessing is potentially more valuable than not answering. Blank answers are always wrong, but a guess might turn out to be right. If you don't have a clue about any of the remaining questions, pick answers at random or choose all As, Bs, and so on. (Choosing the same answer for a series of question all but guarantees you'll get most of them wrong, but it also means you're more likely to get a small percentage of them correct.)

EXAM ALERT

At the very end of your exam period, you're better off guessing than leaving questions unanswered.

Question-Handling Strategies

For those questions that have only one right answer, usually two or three of the answers will be obviously incorrect and two of the answers will be plausible. Unless the answer leaps out at you (if it does, reread the question to look for a trick; sometimes those are the ones you're most likely to get wrong), begin the process of answering by eliminating those answers that are most obviously wrong.

You can usually immediately eliminate at least one answer out of the possible choices for a question because it matches one of these conditions:

▶ The answer does not apply to the situation.

▶ The answer describes a nonexistent issue, an invalid option, or an imaginary state.

After you eliminate all answers that are obviously wrong, you can apply your retained knowledge to eliminate further answers. You should look for items that sound correct but refer to actions, commands, or features that are not present or not available in the situation that the question describes.

If you're still faced with a blind guess among two or more potentially correct answers, reread the question. Picture how each of the possible remaining answers would alter the situation. Be especially sensitive to terminology; sometimes the choice of words (for example, "remove" instead of "disable") can make the difference between a right answer and a wrong one.

You should guess at an answer only after you've exhausted your ability to eliminate answers and you are still unclear about which of the remaining possibilities is correct. An unanswered question offers you no points, but guessing gives you at least some chance of getting a question right; just don't be too hasty when making a blind guess.

Numerous questions assume that the default behavior of a particular utility is in effect. If you know the defaults and understand what they mean, this knowledge will help you cut through many of the trickier questions. Simple "final" actions might be critical as well. If you must restart a utility before proposed changes take effect, a correct answer might require this step as well.

Mastering the Test-Taking Mindset

In the final analysis, knowledge breeds confidence, and confidence breeds success. If you study the materials in this book carefully and review all the practice questions at the end of each chapter, you should become aware of the areas where you need additional learning and study.

After you've worked your way through the book, take the practice exams in the back of the book. Taking these tests provides a reality check and helps you identify areas to study further. Make sure you follow up and review materials related to the questions you miss on the practice exams before scheduling a real exam. Don't schedule your exam appointment until after you've thoroughly studied the material and you feel comfortable with the whole scope of the practice exams. You should score 80% or better on the practice exams before proceeding to the real thing. (Otherwise, obtain some additional practice tests so that you can keep trying until you hit this magic number.)

TIP

If you take a practice exam and don't get at least 80% of the questions correct, keep practicing. Microsoft provides links to practice-exam providers and also self-assessment exams at http://www.microsoft.com/learning/mcpexams/prepare/default.asp.

Armed with the information in this book and with the determination to augment your knowledge, you should be able to pass the certification exam. However, you need to work at it, or you'll spend the exam fee more than once before you finally pass. If you prepare seriously, you should do well.

The next section covers other sources that you can use to prepare for Microsoft certification exams.

Additional Resources

A good source of information about Microsoft certification exams comes from Microsoft itself. Because its products and technologies—and the exams that go with them—change frequently, the best place to go for exam-related information is online.

Microsoft offers training, certification, and other learning-related information and links at the http://www.microsoft.com/learning web address. If you haven't already visited the Microsoft Training and Certification website, you should do so right now. Microsoft's Training and Certification home page resides at http://www.microsoft.com/learning/default.mspx.

Coping with Change on the Web

Sooner or later, all the information we've shared with you about the Microsoft Certified Professional pages and the other web-based resources mentioned throughout the rest of this book will go stale or be replaced by newer information. In some cases, the URLs you find here might lead you to their replacements; in other cases, the URLs will go nowhere, leaving you with the dreaded "404 File not found" error message. When that happens, don't give up.

(continues)

(continued)

There's always a way to find what you want on the web if you're willing to invest some time and energy. Most large or complex websites—and Microsoft's qualifies on both counts—offer search engines. All of Microsoft's web pages have a Search button at the top edge of the page. As long as you can get to Microsoft's site (it should stay at http://www.microsoft.com for a long time), you can use the Search button to find what you need.

The more focused (or specific) that you can make a search request, the more likely the results will include information you can use. For example, you can search for the string

```
"training and certification"
```

to produce a lot of data about the subject in general, but if you're looking for the preparation guide for Exam 70-643, *Windows Server 2008 Applications Infrastructure, Configuring*, you'll be more likely to get there quickly if you use a search string similar to the following:

```
"Exam 70-643" AND "preparation guide"
```

Likewise, if you want to find the Training and Certification downloads, you should try a search string such as this:

```
"training and certification" AND "download page"
```

Finally, you should feel free to use general search tools—such as http://www.google.com, http://www.yahoo.com, http://www.excite.com, and http://www.ask.com—to look for related information. Although Microsoft offers great information about its certification exams online, there are plenty of third-party sources of information and assistance that need not follow Microsoft's party line. Therefore, if you can't find something where the book says it lives, you should intensify your search.

Thanks for making this *Exam Cram* book a pivotal part of your certification study plan; best of luck on becoming certified!

Self-Assessment

We include a self-assessment to help you evaluate your readiness to tackle Microsoft certifications. It should also help you to understand what you need to know to master the 70-643 exam. You might also want to check out the Microsoft Skills Assessment Home web page http://www.microsoft.com/learning/assessment on the Microsoft Training and Certification website. But, before you tackle this self-assessment, let's talk about concerns you might face when pursuing a Microsoft certification credential on Windows and what an ideal Microsoft certification candidate might look like.

Microsoft Certification in the Real World

In the next section, you'll learn about the ideal Microsoft certified candidate, knowing full well that only a few candidates meet that ideal. In fact, our description of those ideal candidates might seem downright scary, especially with the changes that have been made to the Microsoft certifications to support Windows. But take heart: Although the requirements to obtain the advanced Microsoft certification might seem formidable, they are by no means impossible to meet. However, you need to be keenly aware that getting through the process takes time, involves some expense, and requires real effort.

Increasing numbers of people are attaining Microsoft certifications. You can get all the real-world motivation you need from knowing that many others have gone before, so you will be able to follow in their footsteps. If you're willing to take the process seriously and do what it takes to obtain the necessary experience and knowledge, you can take and pass all the certification tests involved in obtaining the credentials. In fact, at Que Publishing, we've designed the Exam Cram series and the Exam Prep series to make it as easy for you as possible to prepare for these exams. We've also greatly expanded our website, http://www.examcram.com, to provide a host of resources to help you prepare for the complexities of the Windows exams.

The Ideal Microsoft Certification Candidate

To give you an idea of what an ideal Microsoft certification candidate is like, here are some relevant statistics about the background and experience such an individual might have:

> **NOTE**
>
> Don't worry if you don't meet these qualifications or even come very close. This world is far from ideal, and where you fall short is simply where you have more work to do.

▶ Academic or professional training in network theory, concepts, and operations. This area includes everything from networking media and transmission techniques through network operating systems, services, and applications.

▶ Two or more years of professional networking experience, including experience with Ethernet, DSL routers, cable modems, and other networking media. This experience must include installation, configuration, upgrading, and troubleshooting experience.

> **NOTE**
>
> Although all certifications really need some hands-on experience if you want to become certified, some of the more advanced exams require you to solve real-world case studies and network design issues—so the more hands-on experience you have, the better.

▶ Two or more years in a networked environment that includes hands-on experience with Windows Server 2008, Windows Vista, Windows Server 2003, Windows 2000 Server, or Windows 2000/XP Professional. A solid understanding of the system's architecture, installation, configuration, maintenance, and troubleshooting is essential.

▶ Knowledge of the various methods for installing Windows Vista, including manual and unattended installations, features of the different editions of Vista, and overcoming installation problems.

▶ Knowledge of how to resolve post-installation issues, including configuring Windows Aero, administrative versus standard user accounts, and configuring permissions.

▶ A good working understanding of optimizing performance for and configuration of Windows Media Player, Media Center, and connectivity with mobile devices.

▶ A thorough understanding of key networking protocols, addressing, and name resolution, including Transmission Control Protocol/Internet Protocol (TCP/IP), TCP/IP utilities and services, Dynamic Host Configuration Protocol (DHCP), and Domain Name System (DNS), and remote Desktop Connection.

▶ An understanding of how to implement security for the Windows Vista operating system and home office network, including IE security, Windows Firewall, Windows Defender, Parental Controls, User Account Control, and Windows Backup.

▶ A good working understanding of disaster recovery techniques, including Safe Mode, Last Known Good Configuration, Restore Points and System Restore, Complete PC Backup and Restore, System File Checker, and the BDCEdit and RegEdit utilities.

To meet all of these qualifications, you would need a bachelor's degree in computer science plus three year's work experience in PC networking design, installation, administration, and troubleshooting. Don't be concerned if you don't have all of these qualifications. Fewer than half of all Microsoft certification candidates meet these requirements. This self-assessment chapter is designed to show you what you already know and to prepare you for the topics that you need to learn.

Put Yourself to the Test

The following series of questions and observations is designed to help you figure out how much work you must do to pursue Microsoft certification and what kinds of resources you can consult on your quest. Be absolutely honest in your answers, or you'll end up wasting money on exams that you're not yet ready to take. There are no right or wrong answers—only steps along the path to certification. Only you can decide where you really belong in the broad spectrum of aspiring candidates. Two things should be clear from the outset, however:

▶ Even a modest background in computer science is helpful.

▶ Hands-on experience with Microsoft products and technologies is an essential ingredient in certification success.

Educational Background

The following questions concern your level of technical computer experience and training. Depending upon your answers to these questions, you might need to review some additional resources to get your knowledge up to speed for the types of questions that you will encounter on Microsoft certification exams:

1. Have you ever taken any computer-related classes? (Yes or No)

   If Yes, proceed to Question 2; if No, proceed to Question 3.

2. Have you taken any classes on computer operating systems? (Yes or No)

   If Yes, you will probably be able to handle Microsoft's architecture and system component discussions. If you're rusty, you should brush up on basic operating system concepts, especially virtual memory, multitasking regimes, user-mode versus kernel-mode operation, and general computer security topics.

   If No, you should consider doing some basic reading in this area. We strongly recommend a good general operating systems book on Windows Vista, such as *Sams Teach Yourself Microsoft Windows Vista All in One* by Greg Perry (Sams). If this book doesn't appeal to you, check out reviews for other similar books at your favorite online bookstore.

3. Have you taken any networking concepts or technologies classes? (Yes or No)

   If Yes, you will probably be able to handle Microsoft's networking terminology, concepts, and technologies. (But brace yourself for frequent departures from normal usage.) If you're rusty, you should brush up on basic networking concepts and terminology, especially networking media, transmission types, the Open System Interconnection (OSI) reference model, and networking technologies, such as Ethernet, Token Ring, Fiber Distributed Data Interface (FDDI), and Wide Area Network (WAN) links.

   If No, you might want to read one or two books in this topic area. The three best books that we know are *Computer Networks* by Andrew S. Tanenbaum (Prentice-Hall), *Computer Networks and Internets* by Douglas E. Comer and Ralph E. Droms (Prentice-Hall), and *Local Area Networks* by Patrick Regan (Prentice-Hall).

Hands-On Experience

The most important key to success on all the Microsoft tests is hands-on experience, especially when it comes to Windows Server 2008, and the many features and add-on services and components around which so many of the Microsoft certification exams revolve. If we leave you with only one realization after you take this self-assessment, it should be that there's no substitute for time spent installing, configuring, and using the various Microsoft products on which you'll be tested. The more in-depth understanding you have of how these software products work, the better your chance in selecting the right answers on the exam. Therefore, ask yourself if you have installed, configured, and worked with the following:

1. Windows Server 2003 or Windows Server 2008? (Yes or No)

    If No, you might want to obtain one or two machines and a copy of Windows Server 2008. (A trial version is available on the Microsoft website.) Pick up a well-written book to guide your activities and studies (such as *MCSE Windows Server 2008 Exam Cram*), or you can work straight from Microsoft's exam objectives, if you prefer.

> **NOTE**
>
> You can download objectives, practice exams, and other data about Microsoft exams from the Training and Certification page at http://www.microsoft.com/traincert. You can use the "Exams" link to obtain specific exam information.

2. Windows XP Professional? (Yes or No)

    If No, you might want to obtain a copy of Windows XP Professional and learn how to install, configure, and maintain it. Pick up a well-written book to guide your activities and studies (such as *MCSE Windows XP Professional Exam Cram*), or you can work straight from Microsoft's exam objectives, if you prefer.

3. Windows Vista? (Yes or No)

    If No, you should obtain a copy of Windows Vista and learn how to install, configure, and maintain it. Carefully read each page of this book while working in your copy of Windows Vista, and review the Microsoft's exam objectives.

Use One Computer to Simulate Multiple Machines

If you own a powerful enough computer—one that has plenty of available disk space, a lot of RAM (at least 512MB), and a Pentium 4–compatible processor or better—you should check out the VMware and Virtual PC virtual-machine software products that are on the market. These software programs create an emulated computer environment within separate windows that are hosted by your computer's main operating system— Windows Server 2008, Windows Vista, Windows Server 2003, Windows XP, Windows 2000, and so on. With this tool, on a single computer you can have several different operating systems running simultaneously in different windows! You can run everything from DOS to Linux, from Windows 95, XP, or Vista to Windows Server 2008. Within a virtual-machine environment, you can "play" with the latest operating systems, including beta versions, without worrying about "blowing up" your main production computer and without having to buy an additional PC. VMware is published by VMware, Inc.; you can get more information from its website at http://www.vmware.com. Virtual PC is published by Microsoft Corporation; you can find out more information from the Virtual PC 2007 website at www.microsoft.com/windows/products/winfamily/virtualpc/ default.mspx.

TIP

For any and all of these Microsoft operating systems exams, the Resource Kits for the topics involved always make good study resources. You can purchase the Resource Kits from Microsoft Press (you can search for them at http://microsoft.com/mspress), but they also appear on the TechNet CDs, DVDs, and website (http://www.microsoft.com/ technet). Along with the Exam Cram books, we believe that the Resource Kits are among the best tools you can use to prepare for Microsoft exams. Take a look at the Windows Deployment and Resource Kits web page for more information: http://www.microsoft.com/windows/reskits/default.asp.

Before you even think about taking any Microsoft exam, you should make sure you've spent enough time with the related software to understand how to install and configure it, how to maintain such an installation, and how to troubleshoot the software when things go wrong. This time will help you in the exam—and in real life!

TIP

If you have the funds, or if your employer will pay your way, you should consider taking a class at a Microsoft Certified Training and Education Center (CTEC). In addition to class-room exposure to the topic of your choice, you get a copy of the software that is the focus of your course, along with a trial version of whatever operating system it needs, as part of the training materials for that class.

How to Prepare for an Exam

Preparing for any Microsoft certification test (including Exam 70-643) requires that you obtain and study materials designed to provide comprehensive information about the product and its capabilities that will appear on the specific exam for which you are preparing. The following list of materials can help you study and prepare:

▶ The Windows Server 2008 product DVD-ROM. This disk includes comprehensive online documentation and related materials; it should be one of your primary resources when you are preparing for the test.

▶ The exam preparation materials, practice tests, and self-assessment exams on the Microsoft Training and Certification site, at http://www. microsoft.com/learning/default.mspx. The Exam Resources link offers samples of the new question types on the Microsoft Certification track series of exams. You should find the materials, download them, and use them!

▶ The exam preparation advice, practice tests, questions of the day, and discussion groups on the http://www.examcram.com.

In addition, you might find any or all of the following materials useful in your quest for Windows Vista expertise:

▶ **Microsoft training kits:** Microsoft Learning offers a training kit that specifically targets Exam 70-643. For more information, visit http://www.microsoft.com/learning/books/. This training kit contains information that you will find useful in preparing for the test.

▶ **Microsoft TechNet CD or DVD and website:** This monthly CD- or DVD-based publication delivers numerous electronic titles that include coverage of Windows operating systems and related topics on the Technical Information (TechNet) series on CD or DVD. Its offerings include product facts, technical notes, tools and utilities, and information on how to access the Seminars Online training materials for Windows operating systems and the Windows line of products. Visit http://technet.microsoft.com and check out the information for TechNet subscriptions. You can utilize a large portion of the TechNet website at no charge.

▶ **Study guides:** Several publishers—including Que Publishing—offer Windows Server 2008, Windows Server 2003, Windows Vista, and Windows XP titles. Que Publishing offers the following:

> ► **The Exam Cram series:** These books give you the insights about the material that you need to know to successfully pass the certification tests.

> ► **The Exam Prep series:** These books provide a greater level of detail than the *Exam Cram* books and are designed to teach you everything you need to know about the subject covered by an exam. Each book comes with a CD-ROM that contains interactive practice exams in a variety of testing formats.

> Together, these two series make a perfect pair.

> ► **Classroom training:** CTECs, online partners, and third-party training companies (such as Wave Technologies, New Horizons, and Global Knowledge) all offer classroom training on Windows Server 2008, Windows Server 2003, Windows Vista, and Windows XP. These companies aim to help you prepare to pass Exam 70-643, as well as several others. Although this type of training tends to be pricey, most of the individuals lucky enough to attend find this training to be quite worthwhile.

> ► **Other publications:** There's no shortage of materials available about Windows Vista. The "Need to Know More?" resource sections at the end of each chapter in this book give you an idea of where we think you should look for further discussion.

This set of required and recommended materials represents an unparalleled collection of sources and resources for Windows Vista and related topics. We anticipate that you'll find this book belongs in this company.

Studying for the Exam

Although many websites offer suggestions on *what* to study for a particular exam, few sites offer any on *how* you should study for an exam. The study process can be broken down into various stages. However, key to all these stages is the ability to concentrate. Concentration, or the lack thereof, plays a big part in the study process.

To be able to concentrate, you must remove all distractions. While you should plan for study breaks, it is the unplanned breaks caused by distractions that do not allow you to concentrate on what you need to learn. Therefore, first, you need to create an environment that's conducive to studying or seek out an existing environment that meets these criteria, such as a library.

First, do not study with the TV on and do not have other people in the room. It is easy for the TV to break your concentration and grab your attention. In addition, if you have people in the room, you have to pretend that you are not there and that they are not causing distractions, including talking with other people. Lastly, there are varying opinions on whether it is better to study with or without music playing. Although some people need to have a little white noise in the background to study, if you do choose to have music, you should keep the volume on a low level and you should listen to music without vocals in it.

After you find a place to study, you must schedule the time to study. This should take into consideration not studying on an empty stomach. You should also not study on a full stomach because it tends to make people drowsy. You may also consider having a glass of water near to sip on.

In addition, make sure that you are well rested so that you don't start dozing off when you start. Next, make sure that you find a position that is comfortable and that the furniture that you are using is also comfortable. Lastly, make sure that your study area is well lit. Natural light is best for fighting fatigue.

The first thing that you should do when you study is to clear your mind of distractions. So take a minute or two, close your eyes and empty your mind.

When you prepare for an exam, the best place to start is to take the list of exam objectives and study them carefully for its scope. During this time, you then organize your study, keeping these objectives in mind. This narrows your focus area to individual topic or subtopic. In addition, you need to understand and visualize the process as a whole. This helps in addressing practical problems in real environments as well as some unexpected questions.

In a multiple-choice–type exam, you do have one advantage: The answer or answers are already there and one has to simply choose the correct ones. Because the answers are already there you can start eliminating the incorrect answers by using your knowledge and some logical thinking. One common mistake is to select the first obvious-looking answers without checking the other options, so always examine *all* the options, then think and choose the correct answer. Of course, with multiple-choice questions, you have to be exact and should be able to differentiate between very similar answers. This is where a peaceful place to study without distractions helps so that you can read between the lines and not miss key points.

Testing Your Exam Readiness

Whether you attend a formal class on a specific topic to get ready for an exam or use written materials to study on your own, some preparation for the Microsoft certification exams is essential. At $125 a pop—whether you pass or fail—you'll want to do everything you can to pass on your first try. That's where studying comes in.

We include two practice tests in this book, so if you don't score very well on these tests, you can study the practice exams more and then tackle the test again. We also have practice questions for which you can sign up online through http://www.examcram.com. The MeasureUp CD-ROM in the back of this book has sample questions to quiz you; you can purchase additional practice questions from http://www.measureup.com. If you still don't hit a score of at least 80% after practicing with these tests, you should investigate the other practice test resources that are mentioned in this section.

For any given subject, you should consider taking a class if you've tackled self-study materials, taken the test, and failed anyway. The opportunity to interact with an instructor and fellow students can make all the difference in the world, if you can afford that luxury. For information about Microsoft classes, visit the Training and Certification page at http://www.microsoft.com/traincert/training/find/findcourse.asp to locate training courses offered at Microsoft CTECs.

If you can't afford to take a class, you can visit the Training and Certification pages anyway because they include pointers to free practice exams and to Microsoft-approved study guides and other self-study tools. And even if you can't afford to spend much money at all, you should still invest in some low-cost practice exams from commercial vendors. The Microsoft Training and Certification "Assess Your Readiness" page at http://www.microsoft.com/traincert/assessment offers several skills-assessment evaluations that you can take online to show you how far along you are in your certification preparation.

The next question deals with your personal testing experience. Microsoft certification exams have their own style and idiosyncrasies. The more acclimated that you become to the Microsoft testing environment, the better your chances will be to score well on the exams:

1. Have you taken a practice exam on your chosen test subject? (Yes or No)

   If Yes, and if you scored 80% or better, you're probably ready to tackle the real thing. If your score isn't above that threshold, you should keep at it until you break that barrier.

   If No, you should obtain all the free and low-budget practice tests you can find and get to work. You should keep at it until you can break the passing threshold comfortably.

> **TIP**
>
> When it comes to assessing your test readiness, there is no better way than to take a good-quality practice exam and pass with a score of 80% or better. When we're preparing ourselves, we shoot for 80% or higher, just to leave room for the "weirdness factor" that sometimes shows up on Microsoft exams.

Assessing Readiness for Exam 70-643

In addition to the general exam-readiness information in the previous section, there are several things you can do to prepare for the Exam 70-643. As you're getting ready for the exam, you should visit the Exam Cram website at http://www.examcram.com. We also suggest that you join an active MCSE/MCSA email list and email newsletter. Some of the best list servers and email newsletters are managed by Sunbelt Software. You can sign up at http://www.sunbelt-software.com.

Microsoft exam mavens also recommend that you check the Microsoft Knowledge Base (available on its own CD as part of the TechNet collection, and on the Microsoft website at http://support.microsoft.com) for "meaningful technical support issues" that relate to your exam's topics. Although we're not sure exactly what the quoted phrase means, we have also noticed some overlap between technical-support questions on particular products and troubleshooting questions on the exams for those products.

Day of the Exam

Before you take an exam, eat something light, even if you have no appetite. If your stomach is actively upset, try mild foods such as toast or crackers. Plain saltine crackers are great for settling a cranky stomach. Keep your caffeine and nicotine consumption to a minimum; excessive stimulants aren't exactly conducive to reducing stress. Plan to take a bottle of water or some hard candies such as lozenges with you to combat dry mouth.

Arrive at the testing center early. If you have never been to the testing center, make sure that you know where it is. You may even consider taking a test drive. If you arrive between 15 and 30 minutes early for any certification exam, it gives you:

- ▶ Ample time for prayer, meditation, and/or breathing.

- ▶ Time to scan glossary terms, quick access tables, and the cram sheet before taking the exam so that you can get the intellectual juices flowing and to build a little confidence.

▶ Time to practice physical relaxation techniques.

▶ Time to visit the washroom.

But don't arrive too early. Of course, when you take the exam, you should also dress comfortably.

When you are escorted into the testing chamber, you will be usually given two sheets of paper (or laminated paper) with pen (or wet erase pen). As soon as you hear the door close behind you, immediately unload bits of exam information that you need to quickly recall onto the paper. Then throughout the exam, you can refer to this information easily without thinking about it. This way, you can focus on answering the questions and use this information as reference. Then before you actually start the exam, close your eyes and take a deep breath to clear your mind of distractions.

Typically, the testing room is furnished with anywhere from one to six computers, and each workstation is separated from the others by dividers designed to keep anyone from seeing what's happening on someone else's computer screen. Most testing rooms feature a wall with a large picture window. This layout permits the exam coordinator to monitor the room, to prevent exam takers from talking to one another, and to observe anything out of the ordinary that might go on. The exam coordinator will have preloaded the appropriate Microsoft certification exam—for this book, that's Exam 70-643 TS: Windows Server 2008 Applications Infrastructure, Configuring—and you are permitted to start as soon as you're seated in front of the computer.

EXAM ALERT

Always remember that the testing center's test coordinator is there to assist you in case you encounter some unusual problems, such as a malfunctioning test computer. If you need some assistance not related to the content of the exam itself, feel free to notify one of the test coordinators—after all, they are there to make your exam-taking experience as pleasant as possible.

All exams are completely closed book. In fact, you are not permitted to take anything with you into the testing area, but you receive a blank sheet of paper and a pen or, in some cases, an erasable plastic sheet and an erasable pen. We suggest that you immediately write down on that sheet of paper all the information you've memorized for the test. Then throughout the exam, you can refer to this information easily without thinking about it. This way, you can focus on answering the questions and use this information as reference. In *Exam Cram* books, this information appears on the Cram Sheet inside the front cover of the book. You are given some time to compose yourself, record this information, and take a sample orientation exam before you begin the real thing. We suggest that you take the orientation test before taking your first exam, but because all the certification exams are more or less identical in layout, behavior, and controls, you probably don't need to do so more than once. Lastly, before you actually start the exam, close your eyes and take deep breath to clear your mind of distractions.

All Microsoft certification exams allow a certain maximum amount of testing time. (This time is indicated on the exam by an onscreen timer clock, so you can check the time remaining whenever you like.) All Microsoft certification exams are computer generated. In addition to multiple choice, most exams contain select–and-place (drag-and-drop), create-a-tree (categorization and prioritization), drag-and-connect, and build-list-and-reorder (list prioritization) types of questions. Although this format might sound quite simple, the questions are constructed not only to check your mastery of basic facts and figures about Windows Vista, but also to require you to evaluate one or more sets of circumstances or requirements. Often, you are asked to give more than one answer to a question. Likewise, you might be asked to select the best or most effective solution to a problem from a range of choices—all of which are technically correct. Taking the exam is quite an adventure, and it involves real thinking and concentration. This book shows you what to expect and how to deal with the potential problems, puzzles, and predicaments.

Dealing with Test Anxiety

Because taking a certification exam costs money and preparation time, and failing an exam can be a blow to self-confidence, most people feel a certain amount of anxiety when they are about to take a certification exam. It is no wonder that most of us are a little sweaty in the palms when taking the exam. However, certain levels of stress can actually help you to raise your level of performance when taking an exam. This anxiety usually serves to help you focus your concentration and think clearly through a problem.

But for some individuals, exam anxiety is more than just a nuisance. For these people, exam anxiety is a debilitating condition that affects their performance with a negative impact on the exam results.

Exam anxiety reduction begins with the preparation process. The first thing that you should consider is that if you know the material, there should not be anything to be nervous about. It goes without saying that the better prepared you are for an exam, the less stress you will experience when taking it. Always give yourself plenty of time to prepare for an exam; don't place yourself under unreasonable deadlines. But again, make goals and make every effort to meet those goals. Procrastination and making excuses can be just as bad.

There is not hard and fast rule for how long it takes to prepare for an exam. The time required varies from student to student and depends on a number of different factors, including reading speed, access to study materials, personal commitments, and so on. In addition, don't compare yourself to peers, especially if doing so has a negative effect on your confidence.

For many students, practice exams are a great way to shed some of the fears that arise in the test center. Practice exams are best used near the end of the exam preparation, and be sure to use them as an assessment of your current knowledge, not as a method to try to memorize key concepts. When reviewing these questions, be sure you understand the question and to understand all answers (right and wrong). Also be sure to set time limits on the practice exams.

If you know the material, don't plan on studying the day of your exam. You should end your studying the evening before the exam. In addition, don't make it a late night so that you can get a full good night's rest. Of course, you should be studying on a regular basis for at least a few weeks prior to the evening of the exam so that you should not need the last-minute cramming.

1

CHAPTER ONE

Managing Windows Server 2008

Terms you'll need to understand:

✓ server roles

✓ Windows features

✓ Server Core

✓ Control Panel

✓ Administrative Tools

✓ Computer Management console

✓ Server Manager console

✓ Windows Reliability and Performance Monitor

✓ Initial Configuration Tasks window

✓ Microsoft Management Console (MMC)

Techniques/concepts you'll need to master:

✓ How to install roles and features in Windows Server 2008.

✓ Manage and configure Windows Server 2008 with common configuration tools, including the Control Panel and the Administrative tools (including the Computer Management Console and the Server Management Console).

✓ Manage and configure Windows Server 2008 Core Server.

Windows Server 2008 is a network operating system and server that is successor to the Windows Server 2003. The client version of Windows Server 2008 is Windows Vista, on which Windows Server 2008 is partially based. Because it shares the same architecture of Windows Vista, it also has

- A new, improved rewritten network stack (native IPv6, native wireless, improved performance, and improved security)

- Improved diagnostics and monitoring

- Improved security, including BitLocker and improved Windows Firewall

- .NET Framework 3.0

- Memory and file system improvements

- Windows Internet Explorer 7

- Vista Aero themes

- An improved Internet Information Server (IIS) 7.0

- Server Core

- Greatly improved Windows Terminal Services

- Windows Server Virtualization

- Self-healing NTFS

- A Windows Server 2008 Server Manager

- Windows PowerShell

Server Roles

A server is designed to provide services. Therefore, Windows Server 2008 has organized the most common services into *server roles*, whereby a server role describes the server's function. When you define a server role in Windows Server 2008 (see Table 1.1), you are installing and configuring a set of software programs that enable a computer to perform a specific function for multiple users or other computers within a network. To install roles, you would use the Initial Configuration Tasks window or the Server Manager console.

TABLE 1.1 Available Roles in Windows Server 2008

Role Name	Description
Active Directory Certificate Services	Provides service for creating and managing public key certificates used in software security systems that employ public key technologies to prove the identity of a person, device, or service, which can be used by secure mail, secure wireless networks, virtual private networks (VPN), Internet Protocol Security (IPSec), Encrypting File System (EFS), smart card logon, and others. For ease of use, the digital certificates interface with Microsoft's Active Directory.
Active Directory Domain Services	To transform a server into a domain controller to provide a directory service via Microsoft's Active Directory (AD), which stores information about users, computers, and other devices on the network. Active Directory helps administrators securely manage this information and facilitates resource sharing and collaboration between users. Active Directory is required for directory-enabled applications such as Microsoft Exchange Server (email server) and to apply other Windows Server technologies such as Group Policy.
Active Directory Federation Services	Provides web single-sign-on (SSO) technologies to authenticate a user with a single user account to multiple web applications.
Active Directory Lightweight Directory Services (AD LDS)	For applications that require a director for storing application data as a data store, without installing Active Directory domain services. Because this runs as a non-operating-system service, it enables multiple instances of AD LDS to run concurrently on a single server, and each instance can be configured independently for servicing multiple applications.
Active Directory Rights Management Services (AD RMS)	Technology that works with Active Directory RMS–enabled applications to help safeguard digital information from unauthorized use by specifying who can use the information and what they can do with it (open, modify, print, forward, and/or take other actions with the information).
Application Server	Provides a complete solution for hosting and managing high-performance distributed business applications built around Microsoft .NET Framework 3.0, COM+, Message Queuing, web services, and Distributed Transactions.
Dynamic Host Configuration Protocol (DHCP) Server	Enables servers to assign, or lease, IP addresses to computers and other devices that are enabled as DHCP clients.
Domain Name System (DNS) Server	Provides naming service that associates names with numeric Internet addresses. This makes it possible for users to refer to network computers by using easy-to-remember names instead of a long series of numbers. Windows DNS services can be integrated with Dynamic Host Configuration Protocol (DHCP) services on Windows, eliminating the need to add DNS records as computers are added to the network.

(continues)

TABLE 1.1 *Continued*

Role Name	Description
Fax Server	Sends and receives faxes, and enables you to manage fax resources such as jobs, settings, reports, and fax devices on this computer or on the network.
File Services	Provides technologies for storage management, file replication, distributed namespace management, fast file searching, and streamlined client access to files.
Network Policy and Access Services	Delivers a variety of methods (including using VPN servers, dial-up servers, routers, and 802.11 protected wireless access points) to provide users with local and remote network connectivity, to connect network segments, and to enable network administrators to centrally manage network access and client health policies.
Print Services	Enables users to print to and manage centralized printers that are connected directly or indirectly to print servers.
Terminal Services	Enables users to connect to a Terminal Server to remotely run programs, use network resources, and access the Windows desktop on that server.
Universal Description, Discovery, and Integration (UDDI) Services	Provides capabilities to share information about web services within an organization's intranet, between business partners on an extranet, or on the Internet.
Web Server (IIS)	Enables sharing of information on the Internet, an intranet, or an extranet via a unified web platform that integrates Internet Information Server (IIS) 7.0 to provides web pages, File Transfer Protocol (FTP) services or newsgroups, ASP.NET, Windows Communication Foundation, and Windows SharePoint Services.
Windows Deployment Services	Used to install and configure Microsoft Windows operating systems remotely on computers with Pre-boot Execution Environment (PXE) boot ROMs.
Windows SharePoint Services	Helps organizations increase productivity by creating websites where users can collaborate on documents, tasks, and events and easily share contacts and other information. The environment is designed for flexible deployment, administration, and application development.
Windows Server Virtualization	Provides the services that you can use to create and manage virtual machines (virtualized computer system that operates in an isolated execution environment, which enables you to run multiple operating systems simultaneously) and their resources.

Windows Features

Windows Features are software programs that are not directly part of a role or they can support or augment the functionality of one or more roles, or enhance the functionality of the entire server. The features that are included in Windows Server 2008 are shown in Table 1.2. To install Windows Features, use the Initial Configuration Tasks window or the Server Manager console.

TABLE 1.2   Features Available in Windows Server 2008

Feature Name	Description
.NET Framework 3.0 Features	Combines .NET Framework 2.0 Application Programming Interface (API) to build applications with appealing user interfaces and provide various forms of security for those services.
BitLocker Drive Encryption	Helps protect data on disks by encrypting the entire volume.
BITS Server Extension	Short for Background Intelligence Transfer Service, allows a client computer to transfer files in the foreground or background asynchronously so that the responsiveness of other network applications is preserved.
Connection Manager Administration	Customizes the remote connection experience for users on your network by creating pre-defined connections to remote servers and networks via a Virtual Private Network (VPN) server.
Desktop Experience	Includes features of Windows Vista such as Windows Media Player, desktop themes, and photo management.
Failover Clustering	Allows multiple servers to work together to provide high availability of services and applications. If one server fails, a second server is available to take over its work.
Group Policy Management	A Microsoft Management Console snap-in that allows easy management of Active Directory Group Policies to secure or standardize a network environment.
Internet Printing Client	Enables clients to use Internet Printing Protocol (IPP) to connect and print to printers on the network or Internet.
Internet Storage Name Server	Provides discovery services for Internet Small Computer System Interface (iSCSI) storage area networks.
LPR Port Monitor	Enables the computer to print to printers that are shared via a Line Printer Daemon (LPD) service. LPD service is commonly used by UNIX-based computers and printer-sharing devices.

(continues)

TABLE 1.2 *Continued*

Feature Name	Description
Message Queuing	Provides guaranteed message delivery, efficient routing, security, and priority-based messaging between applications.
Multipath I/O	Along with the Microsoft Device Specific Module (DSM) or a third-party DSM, provides support for using multiple data paths to a storage device on Windows.
Network Load Balancing	Distributes traffic across several servers, using the TCP/IP networking protocol. NLP is particularly useful for ensuring that stateless applications such as web servers running IIS are scalable by adding additional servers as the load increases.
Peer Name Resolution Protocol	Enables applications to register and resolve names on your computer so that other computers communicate with these applications.
Quality Windows Audio Video Experience	A networking platform for audio and video streaming applications on IP home networks.
Remote Assistance	Enables you or a support person to offer assistance to users with computer issues or questions.
Remote Differential Compression	Computes and transfers the differences between two objects over a network, using minimal bandwidth.
Remote Server Administration Tools	Includes an MMC snap-in and a command-line tool to remotely manage roles and features.
Removable Storage Manager	Manages and catalogs removable media and operates automated removable media devices.
RPC over HTTP Proxy	Relays RPC traffic from client applications over HTTP to the server as an alternative to clients accessing the server over a VPN connection.
Simple TCP/IP Services	Supports Character Generator, Daytime, Discard, Echo, and Quote of the Day TCP/IP services.
SMTP Server	Supports the transfer of email messages between email systems.
SNMP Services	Includes the SNMP service and SNMP WMI provider. SNMP is used in network management systems to monitor network-attached devices for conditions that warrant administrative attention.
Storage Manager for SANs	Helps create and manage logical unit numbers (LUN) on Fibre Channel and iSCSI disk drive subsystems that support Virtual Disk Service (VDS).

(continues)

TABLE 1.2 *Continued*

Feature Name	Description
Subsystem for UNIX-based Applications	Enables you to run UNIX-based programs and compile and run custom UNIX-based applications in the Windows environment.
Telnet Client	Uses the Telnet protocol to connect to a remote Telnet server and run applications on that server.
Telnet Server	Allows remote users, including UNIX-based clients, to use a Telnet client to perform command-line administration and run programs.
TFTP Client	Enables users to read files or write files to a remote Trivial FTP (TFTP) server.
Windows Internal Database	A relational data store that can be used by only Windows roles and features.
Windows PowerShell	A command-line shell and scripting language.
Windows Process Activation Service	Generalizes the IIS process model, removing the dependency on HTTP.
Windows Recovery Disc	Enables you to use the system recovery options to restore your computer if you do not have a Windows installation disc or cannot access recovery options provided by your computer's manufacturer.
Windows Server Backup Features	Enables you to back up and recover your operating system, applications, and data.
Windows System Resource Manager	An administrative tool that can control how CPU and memory resources are allocated.
WINS Server	WINS, short for Windows Internet Naming Service, provides a distributed database for registering and querying dynamic mappings of NetBIOS names for computers and groups used on your network.
Wireless LAN Service	Configures and starts the WLAN AutoConfig service, regardless of whether the computer has any wireless adapters.

One feature that is included with Windows Server 2008 is the subsystem for UNIX-based Applications (SUA). It provides a complete UNIX-based environment that includes supporting case-sensitive file names, job control, compilation tools, and the use of over 300 UNIX commands, utilities, and shell scripts. It also provides a source-compatibility subsystem for compiling and running custom UNIX-based applications on the server that are based on Portable Operating System Interface (POSIX). You can make your UNIX applications fully interoperable with Windows in SUA with little or no change to your original source code. Because the subsystem installs separately from the Windows kernel, it offers true UNIX functionality without emulation. You can also download a package from Microsoft that includes a comprehensive set of scripting utilities and a software development kit (SDK) designed to fully support the development capabilities of SUA. Last, the subsystem also includes a database (OCI/ODBC) library that supports connectivity to Oracle and SQL Server from database applications by using the Oracle Call Interface (OCI) and the Open Database Connectivity (ODBC) standard. It also supports 64-bit applications.

Another feature worth mentioning is the Simple Network Management Protocol (SNMP), which is a network management standard widely used in TCP/IP networks. With SNMP, you can manage and monitor network hosts such as workstation or server computers, routers, bridges, and hubs from a centrally located computer running network management software. The SNMP service provides an SNMP agent that allows remote, centralized management of computers running modern Windows operating systems, including Windows Server 2008, Windows Server 2003, Windows Vista, and Windows XP computers. It also allows the management of Windows Internet Name Service (WINS), Dynamic Host Configuration Protocol (DHCP), Internet Information System (IIS), and LAN Manager (file and print sharing).

NOTE

To access the information that the SNMP agent service provides, you need at least one SNMP management system software application. Microsoft Windows does not include SNMP management software. SNMP management software must be running on the host that acts as the management system.

Configuring and Managing Windows

To configure and manage Windows, you still use the standard tools that you find in Windows XP, Windows Vista, and Windows Server 2003. They include the Control Panel and Administrative tools (which include the Computer Management and Server Manager consoles).

Control Panel

The *Control Panel* is a graphical tool used to configure the Windows environment and hardware devices. To access the Control Panel, you can click Start on the taskbar and select Control Panel. You can also display the Control Panel in any Windows Explorer view by clicking the leftmost option button in the Address bar and selecting Control Panel (see Figure 1.1).

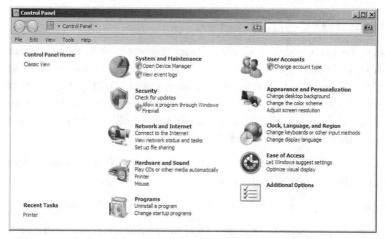

FIGURE 1.1 Windows Server 2008 Control Panel in Category view.

Of the 10 categories that are listed, each category includes a top-level link, and under this link are several of the most frequently performed tasks for the category. Clicking a category link provides a list of utilities in that category. Each utility listed within a category includes a link to open the utility, and under this link are several of the most frequently performed tasks for the utility.

As with Windows XP and Windows Vista, you can change from the default category view to classic view. Control Panel in Windows Server 2008 has two views:

▶ Category view is the default view, which provides access to system utilities by category and task.

▶ Classic view is an alternative view that provides the look and functionality of Control Panel in Windows 2000 and earlier versions of Windows (see Figure 1.2).

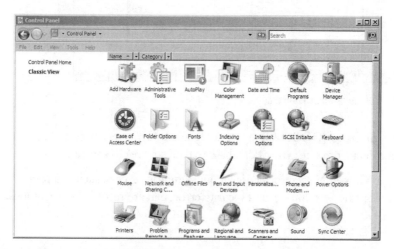

FIGURE 1.2 Windows Server 2008 Control Panel in Classic view.

Administrative Tools

Administrative Tools is a folder in Control Panel that contains tools for system administrators and advanced users. Many of the tools in this folder, such as Computer Management, are *Microsoft Management Console (MMC)* snap-ins that include their own help topics. To view specific help for an MMC tool, or to search for an MMC snap-in that you do not see in the following list, open the tool, click the Help menu, and then click Help Topics.

Open Administrative Tools by clicking Start, Control Panel, System and Maintenance, Administrative Tools. You can also find it on the Start menu.

Some common administrative tools in this folder include the following:

▶ **Computer Management:** Manage local or remote computers by using a single, consolidated desktop tool. Using *Computer Management*, you can perform many tasks, such as monitoring system events, configuring hard disks, and managing system performance (see Figure 1.3).

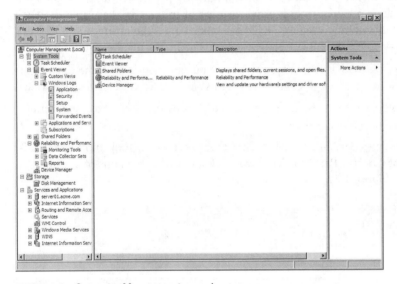

FIGURE 1.3   Computer Management console.

▶ **Data Sources (ODBC):** Use Open Database Connectivity (ODBC) to move data from one type of database (a data source) to another.

▶ **Event Viewer:** View information about significant events, such as a program starting or stopping, or a security error, that are recorded in event logs.

▶ **iSCSI Initiator:** Configure advanced connections between storage devices on a network.

▶ **Local Security Policy:** View and edit Group Policy security settings.

▶ **Memory Diagnostics Tool:** Check your computer's memory to see whether it is functioning properly.

▶ **Print Management:** Manage printers and print servers on a network and perform other administrative tasks.

▶ **Reliability and Performance Monitor:** View advanced system information about the central processing unit (CPU), memory, hard disk, and network performance.

▶ **Services:** Manage the different services that run in the background on your computer.

▶ **System Configuration:** Identify problems that might be preventing Windows from running correctly.

▶ **Task Scheduler:** Schedule programs or other tasks to run automatically.

▶ **Windows Firewall with Advanced Security:** Configure advanced firewall settings on both this computer and remote computers on your network.

▶ **Windows Server Backup:** Use to back up and restore the server.

Server Manager

New to Windows Server 2008 is the *Server Manager console* (see Figure 1.4), which is designed to simplify the task of managing and securing server roles. It enables you to manage the server's identity, display current server status, identify problems with server role configuration, and manage all roles designated for the server. To simplify these tasks, it often uses integrated wizards that step through adding and configuring server functions. While using these wizards, the Server Manager console performs all the necessary dependency checks and conflict resolutions so the server is stable, reliable, and secure. It also has event viewer, performance and reliability monitors, device manager, task scheduler, services, local user and group administration, Windows server backup, and disk management.

Windows Server 2008 includes a Security Configuration Wizard (SCW), which can help you secure Windows. For example, when you install a role or change a role's components, run the Security Configuration Wizard to reduce the surface attack (disable unneeded services based on the server role, remove unused firewall rules and constrain existing firewall rules, and define restricted audit policies).

> **NOTE**
>
> In Windows Server 2008, when you right-click My Computer and select Manage, you open the Server Manager. This is different from Windows Server 2003, Windows XP, and Windows Vista, which open the Computer Management console.

FIGURE 1.4 Server Manager console.

Windows Reliability and Performance Monitor

Windows Reliability and Performance Monitor is a Microsoft Management Console snap-in that provides tools for analyzing system performance. From a single console, you can monitor application and hardware performance in real time, customize what data you want to collect in logs, define thresholds for alerts and automatic actions, generate reports, and view past performance data in a variety of ways.

An important feature in Windows Reliability and Performance Monitor is the Data Collector Set (DCS), which groups data collectors into reusable elements. After a Data Collector Set is defined, you can schedule the collection of data with the DCS or see it in real time.

Windows Reliability and Performance Monitor consists of three monitoring tools:

► Resource Overview

► Performance Monitor

► Reliability Monitor

Windows Reliability and Performance Monitor starts with the Resource Overview display (see Figure 1.5), which enables you to monitor the usage and performance of the major system subcomponents: processors, disks, network, and memory resources in real time. You can then click Detail to see which processes are using which resources.

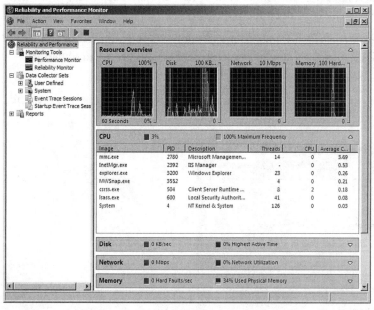

FIGURE 1.5 Reliability and Performance Monitor showing the Resource Overview display.

Performance Monitor provides a visual display of built-in Windows performance counters, either in real time or as a way to review historical data. You can add performance counters to Performance Monitor by dragging and dropping, or by creating custom DCSs. It features multiple graph views that enable you to visually review performance log data. You can create custom views in Performance Monitor that can be exported as DCSs for use with other systems with performance and logging features.

Besides combing through the Event Viewer, you can use Reliability Monitor to give you an overview of the system stability and to view individual events that affect overall stability. Some of the events shown are software installation, operating system updates, and hardware failures.

Initial Configuration Tasks

The *Initial Configuration Tasks window* (see Figure 1.6) is a new feature in Windows Server 2008, launched automatically after the installation of Windows Server 2008. As the name implies, it is designed to finish the setup and configuration of a new server, including performing many security-related tasks, such as setting the Administrator password, changing the name of the Administrator account, running Windows Updates, and configuring the Windows Firewall. It also enables you to add roles and features.

Some changes you should make to the settings include the following:

► You should change the Administrator account password because it is set initially to blank by default.

► Servers are usually assigned static IP addresses, so you need to configure the IP addresses because all network connections are set to obtain IP addresses automatically through DHCP.

► If you need to, join the server to a domain. By default, it is joined to the common workgroup named WORKGROUP.

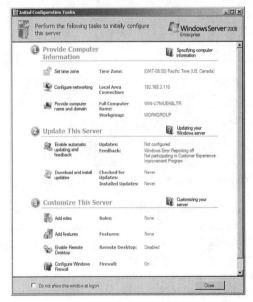

FIGURE 1.6 Initial Configuration Tasks window.

Microsoft Remote Server Administration Tools (RSAT)

Microsoft Remote Server Administration Tools (RSAT) enables administrators to remotely manage roles and features in Windows Server 2008 from a computer that is running Windows Vista with Service Pack 1 (SP1). It includes support for remote management of computers that are running either a Server Core installation option or a full installation option of Windows Server 2008. It provides similar functionality to the Windows Server 2003 Administration Tools Pack.

Windows Server 2008 Administration Tools for Roles

Here's a list of Windows Server 2008 Administration Tools for Roles:

- ► **Active Directory Certificate Services Tools:** Includes the Certification Authority, Certificate Templates, Enterprise PKI, and Online Responder Management snap-ins. Active Directory Certification Authority Tools includes the Certification Authority, Certificate Templates, and the Enterprise PKI snap-ins. Online Responder Tools includes the Online Responder Management snap-in.

- ► **Active Directory Domain Services (AD DS) Tools:** Includes Active Directory Users and Computers, Active Directory Domains and Trusts, Active Directory Sites and Services, and other snap-ins and command-line tools for remotely managing Active Directory Domain Services. Server for Network Information Service (NIS) Tools includes an extension to the Active Directory Users and Computers snap-in and the Ypclear.exe command-line tool.

- ► **Active Directory Lightweight Directory Services (AD LDS) Tools:** Includes Active Directory Sites and Services, Active Directory Services Interfaces (ADSI) Edit, Schema Manager, and other snap-ins and command-line tools for managing Active Directory Lightweight Directory Services.

- ► **DHCP Server Tools:** Includes the DHCP snap-in.

- ► **DNS Server Tools:** Includes the DNS Manager snap-in and the Dnscmd.exe command-line tool.

- ► **File Services Tools:** Includes the Storagemgmt.msc snap-in, the Distributed File System (DFS) Tools, and File Server Resource Manager Tools.

- **Network Policy and Access Services Tools:** Includes the Routing and Remote Access snap-in.

- **Terminal Services Tools:** Includes the Remote Desktops and Terminal Services Manager snap-ins.

- **Universal Description, Discovery, and Integration (UDDI) Services Tools:** Includes the UDDI Services snap-in.

Windows Server 2008 Administration Tools for Features

Here's a list of Windows Server 2008 Administration Tools for Features:

- **BitLocker Drive Encryption Tools:** Includes the `Manage-bde.wsf` script.

- **Failover Clustering Tools:** Includes the Failover Cluster Manager snap-in and the `Cluster.exe` command-line tool.

- **Group Policy Management Tools:** Includes Group Policy Management Console, Group Policy Management Editor, and Group Policy Starter GPO Editor.

- **Network Load Balancing Tools:** Includes the Network Load Balancing Manager utility and the `Nlb.exe` and `Wlbs.exe` command-line tools.

- **SMTP Server Tools:** Includes the SMTP snap-in.

- **Storage Manager for SANs Tools:** Includes the Storage Manager for SANs snap-in, and the `ProvisionStorage.exe` command-line tool.

- **Windows System Resource Manager Tools:** Includes the Windows System Resource Manager snap-in and the `Wsrmc.exe` command-line tool.

Server Core

One of the notable new features of Windows Server 2008 is the introduction of the Server Core. *Server Core* installation provides a minimal environment with no Windows Explorer shell for running specific server roles and no Start button. Just about the only thing that you can see is a command-prompt window to type in commands (see Figure 1.7). Because the system has a minimal environment, the system runs more efficiently, reduces the maintenance and management requirements, and reduces the attack surface for those server roles.

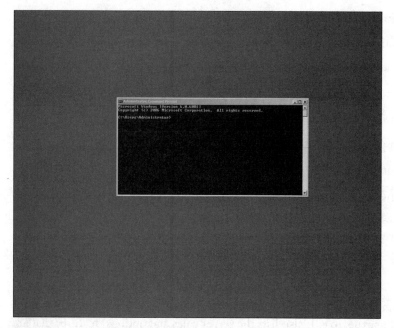

FIGURE 1.7 Windows Server 2008 Server Core.

A Server Core machine can be configured for the following roles:

- Active Directory Lightweight Directory Services (AD LDS)
- DHCP Server
- DNS Server
- Domain controller/Active Directory Domain Services
- File Services (including DFSR and NFS)
- IIS 7 web server (but does not include ASPNET, .Net Framework, IIS Management Console, IIS Legacy Snap-In, and IIS FTP Management)
- Print Services
- Streaming Media Services
- Terminal Services including Easy Print, TS Remote Programs, and TS Gateway
- Windows Server Virtualization

A Server Core machine can be configured for the following features:

- Backup
- BitLocker Drive Encryption

- ▸ Failover Clustering

- ▸ Multipath IO

- ▸ Network Load Balancing

- ▸ Removable Storage

- ▸ Simple Network Management Protocol (SNMP)

- ▸ Subsystem for UNIX-based applications

- ▸ Telnet client

- ▸ Windows Internet Name Service (WINS)

To discover the available server roles, open a command prompt and type the following:

```
oclist
```

This command lists the server roles and optional features that are available for use with `Ocsetup.exe`. It also lists the server roles and optional features that are currently installed.

Shutting and Restarting Server Core

To shut down or restart Windows Server 2008 Server Core, you need to use the `shutdown.exe` file. To shut down the computer, use the following command:

```
shutdown /s
```

To restart the computer, use the following command:

```
shutdown /r /t 0 or shutdown /r
```

The `/r` specifies reboot, whereas the `/t  0` (short for 0 seconds) indicates a reboot immediately.

To logoff, use the following command:

```
shutdown /l
```

Available Control Panel Applets

All configuration and maintenance is done entirely through command-line interface windows or by connecting to the machine remotely with Microsoft Management Console. A few basic tools are available (including Notepad) and some Control Panel applets are available (such as Regional Settings). Server Core does not include .NET Framework and Internet Explorer.

To open the Data and Time applet, type the following command at the command prompt:

```
control timedate.cpl
```

To change the International settings, including changing your keyboard for different layouts, type the following at the command prompt:

```
control intl.cpl
```

EXAM ALERT

> The only control panel applets that are available in the Server Core are the Date and Time applet and the International Settings applet.

Changing Computer Names and Joining Domains

To change the computer name, you must first know the current computer name. To find the current name, you can fuse the hostname or `ipconfig` command. Then use the following command to change the computer name:

```
netdom renamecomputer <ComputerName> /NewName:<NewComputerName>
```

Then restart the computer.

To join a domain, use the following command:

```
netdom join <ComputerName> /domain:<DomainName>
➥/userd:<Admin_UserName> /passwordd:*
```

You will then be prompted for the admin password.

If you need to add a domain user account to the local Administrators group, type the following command:

```
net localgroup administrators /add <DomainName>\<UserName>
```

Then restart the computer.

Configuring the Network Connection

Configuring IP configuration is a little bit more complicated because it is done entirely at the command prompt. To view the IP configuration, you can execute the following command:

```
ipconfig /all
```

To view your interfaces, execute the following command:

```
netsh interface ipv4 show interfaces
```

When you view the output of the `netsh` command, you need to note the number shown in the Idx column for your network adapter.

To set a static IP address and default gateway, you would use the following command:

```
netsh interface ipv4 set address name <ID from interface list>
```

➥`source=static address=<preferred IP address>`

➥`gateway=<gateway address>`

To set the static DNS address, use the following command:

```
netsh interface ipv4 add dnsserver name=<name of primary DNS server>
```

➥`address=<IP address of the primary DNS server> index=1`

For each DNS server you want to set, increment the `index=` number each time. Therefore, for the first DNS server, the index would be 1. For the second DNS server, the index would be 2.

To change a server to the DHCP-provided IP address from a static IP address, use the following command:

```
netsh interface ipv4 set address name=<IP address of local system>
```

➥`source=DHCP`

Running the Administrative Tools

Many of the administrative tools on a Server Core server can be accessed remotely, including those tools that are based on the Microsoft Management Console. To manage a Server Core server using a MMC snap-in, follow these steps:

1. Log on to a remote computer.

2. Start an MMC snap-in, such as Computer Management.

3. In the left pane, right-click the top of the tree and click Connect to Another Computer. For example, in the Computer Management, you would right-click Computer Management (Local).

4. On Another Computer, type the computer name or IP address of the server running a Server Core installation and click OK (see Figure 1.8).

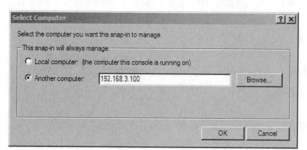

FIGURE 1.8 Initial configuration tasks.

You can now use the MMC snap-in to manage the server running a Server Core installation as you would any other computer running a Windows Server operating system.

NOTE

To use the Disk Management MMC snap-in remotely on a Server Core computer, you must start the Virtual Disk Service on the Server Core computer by typing the `net start VDS` command at the command prompt.

Other Useful Tools and Options

Before finishing this chapter let's discuss some important tools that are found on the Server Core. You can still access Notepad by executing the `notepad.exe` command at the command prompt. This always comes in handy when you have to modify a text file such as those found as configuration files.

You can also execute the Task Manager by executing the `taskmgr.exe` command or by using Ctrl+Alt+Del. If you close all command prompts, you can open a new command prompt by using Ctrl+Alt+Del to start the Task Manager. Then click File, Run and type **cmd.exe**. Alternatively, you can log off and log back on again.

You also have the Registry Editor and the System Information programs still available. To open the Registry editor, execute the `regedit.exe` command. To start the System Information program, execute the `msinfo32.exe` command.

Lastly, `cscript.exe` is a command-line version of the Windows Script Host that provides command-line options for setting script properties while requiring little memory. With `Cscript.exe`, you can run scripts by typing the name of a script file at the command prompt.

One example of using `cscript` on a Core Server computer is to configure automatic updates. To verify the current automatic settings, execute the following command:

```
cscript scregedit.wsf /AU /v
```

To enable automatic updates, execute the following command:

```
cscript scregedit.wsf /AU /4
```

To disable automatic updates, execute the following command:

```
cscript scregedit.wsf /AU /1
```

EXAM ALERT

To configure automatic updates, you must execute the `scregedit.wsf` script with the `cscript` command.

Exam Prep Questions

1. Which of the following would enable you to provide network services?

   ○ **A.** Server roles

   ○ **B.** Windows features

   ○ **C.** Control Panel

   ○ **D.** Server Manager

2. What provides a bare minimum system that focuses on providing a particular network service?

   ○ **A.** Windows Explorer

   ○ **B.** Services console

   ○ **C.** Windows Power Shell

   ○ **D.** Server Core

3. Which tool was added to Windows Server 2008 that enables you to manage and secure the server roles?

   ○ **A.** Computer Management console

   ○ **B.** Server Management console

   ○ **C.** Reliability and Performance monitor

   ○ **D.** Hyper-V

4. If you have a UNIX application that you would like to run in Windows Server 2008, what Windows feature would you install?

   ○ **A.** Windows Power Shell

   ○ **B.** .NET Framework

   ○ **C.** Subsystem for UNIX-based applications

   ○ **D.** Windows Internal Database

5. What would SNMP be used for?

   ○ **A.** To provide a simple mail delivery system.

   ○ **B.** To allow you to read and write to a Trivial File Transfer Protocol server.

   ○ **C.** To allow you to activate Windows on your network.

   ○ **D.** To monitor network-attached devices for conditions that warrant administrative attention in network management systems.

6. You have a Windows Server 2008 Server Core computer. You need to change the International settings. What do you need to do?

   ○ **A.** Execute the `control timezone.cpl` command.

   ○ **B.** Execute the `control intl.cpl` command.

   ○ **C.** Execute the `cscript int.wsf` command.

   ○ **D.** Execute the `cscript control.cpl` command.

7. You have installed several Windows Server 2008 Server Core computers. What do you need to do to make sure that they have used automatic updates to receive the latest security updates?

   ○ **A.** Open Regedit on the server and configure the WSUS options.

   ○ **B.** Run the `cscript scregedit.wsf /cs 0` command.

   ○ **C.** Run the `cscript scregedit.wsf /AU /4` command.

   ○ **D.** Run the `cscript scregedit.wsf /AU /1` command.

8. You have a Windows Server 2008 Server Core loaded on a server. You just installed DHCP on the server. How do you configure the DHCP scopes?

   ○ **A.** Run the `cscript dhcp.wsf` script.

   ○ **B.** Modify the `C:\windows\system32\etc\hosts` file with Notepad.

   ○ **C.** Connect to the DHCP server with a DHCP MMC console that connects to the DHCP server.

   ○ **D.** You don't need to configure DHCP because it is self configuring.

9. What command do you use to restart Windows Server 2008 Server Core?

   ○ **A.** `shutdown /r`

   ○ **B.** `reboot /now`

   ○ **C.** `shutdown /now`

   ○ **D.** `start /r`

10. You have a Windows Server 2008 Server Core computer. You log on as a domain admin on your Windows Vista computer and open the Computer Management console on your Windows Vista computer. You then use the Computer Management console to connect to the Server Core computer. However, you are having trouble accessing the Disk Management MMC snap-in. What is the problem?

○ **A.** You are not running the updated Windows Server 2008 MMC on the Windows Vista computer.

○ **B.** You need to execute the `net start` VDS command at the command prompt on the Windows Server 2008 Server Core computer.

○ **C.** You are not logged in as an administrator for the Windows Server 2008 Server Core computer.

○ **D.** The Server Core computer needs to be added to the same domain as that to which the Windows Vista computer belongs.

Answers to Exam Prep Questions

1. Answer A is correct. Server roles are those network applications that provide network services. Answer B is incorrect because Windows features are software programs that are not directly part of a role. Answer C is incorrect because the Control Panel is used to configure the Windows environment. Answer D is incorrect because the Server Manager is a tool used to install and configure Server Roles and features and administer many of the server/network services.

2. Answer D is correct. The Server Core installation provides a minimal environment with no Windows Explorer shell for running specific server roles. Answer A is the shell that provides file management for Windows. Answer B is incorrect because the Services console is used to enable or disable services running on a Windows computer. Answer C is incorrect because the Windows Power Shell is a powerful scripting language.

3. Answer B is correct. The Server Management console is used to manage and secure server roles. The Computer Management console can be used to manage some server roles but it is not new to Windows Server 2008, so answer B is incorrect. Answer C is incorrect because the Reliability and Performance monitor is used to monitor the reliability and performance of your Windows Server 2008 system. Answer D is incorrect because Hyper-V is the technology that provides virtualization to Windows Server 2008.

4. Answer C is correct. The subsystem for UNIX-based applications provides a kernel that enables the UNIX applications to run. Answer A is incorrect because the Windows Power Shell is a powerful command prompt/scripting environment. Answer B is incorrect because the .NET Framework provides an interface for programming applications. Answer D is incorrect because the Windows Internal Database provides a relational data store that can be used for Windows roles and features.

5. Answer D is correct. Simple Network Management Protocol (SNMP) enables you to manage and monitor network hosts such as workstation or server computers, routers, bridges, and hubs from a centrally located computer running network management software. Answer A is incorrect because a simple mail delivery system is provided by Simple Mail Transfer Protocol (SMTP), not SNMP. Answer B is incorrect because a TFTP client enables you to read and write to a TFTP server. Answer C is incorrect because SNMP has nothing to do with activating Windows.

6. Answer B is correct. To change the international settings of a computer running a Server Core, you need to run the `control intl.cpl` command. Answer A is incorrect because the `control timezone.cpl` command does not exist. The closest is the `control timedate.cpl` command, which changes the date, time, and time zone. Answer C is incorrect because `int.wsf` is a made-up command for the `cscript` to run. Answer D is incorrect because you don't use `cscript` to open the control panel, which is not available in Server Core.

7. Answer C is correct. The `cscript scregedit.wsf /AU /4` command enables automatic updates on the Server Core installation computers via a WSUS server. Answer A is incorrect because Regedit is not available on a Server Core installation. Answer B is incorrect because `cscript scregedit.wsf /cs 0` is used to turn off the higher security level for compatibility with earlier versions of the RDP-client. Answer D is incorrect because the `cscript scregedit.wsf /AU /1` command is used to disable automatic updates.

8. Answer C is correct. You would have to load administrative tools on your local PC or another server. You would then connect to the Windows Server 2008 Server Core. Answer A is incorrect because there is no `dhcp.wsf` script on the server. Answer B is incorrect because the host file is used for name resolution (hostname to IP addresses) but not to configure the DHCP scopes. Answer D is incorrect because DHCP is not self configuring.

9. Answer A is correct. You use the `shutdown.exe` command with the `/r` option. Answer B is incorrect because the `reboot` command is not included with the Server Core. Answer C is incorrect because there is no `/now` option with the `shutdown` command. Answer D is incorrect because the `start` command is used to run programs in a separate window.

10. Answer B is correct. You must run the `net start VDS` command at the command prompt on the Windows Server 2008 Server Core. Answer A is incorrect because you can still access disk management with a Windows Vista MMC. Answer C is incorrect because you are logged in as a domain admin. Although that computer may not be part of the domain, you can still access the computer management from other computers that are not in the same domain or as part of a workgroup. Answer D is incorrect because the computer does not have to be part of the same domain to access it.

Need to Know More?

To find out more information about Windows Server 2008, visit the following websites:

http://www.microsoft.com/servers/home.mspx

http://www.microsoft.com/windowsserver2008/en/us/
product-information.aspx

To find more information about the configuring Server Core, open the Server Core Installation Option of the Windows Server 2008 Step-By-Step Guide, which can be found at:

http://technet2.microsoft.com/windowsserver2008/en/library/
47a23a74-e13c-46de-8d30-ad0afb1eaffc1033.mspx?mfr=true

CHAPTER TWO

Windows Deployment and Activation

Terms you'll need to understand:

✓ security identifier (SID)
✓ System Preparation Tool (Sysprep)
✓ Windows Imaging Format (WIM) file
✓ Windows System Image Manager (Windows SIM)
✓ Windows Deployment Services (WDS)
✓ Windows Preinstallation Environment (Windows PE or WinPE)
✓ pre-boot execution environment (PXE)
✓ Key Management Service (KMS)
✓ Multiple Activation Key (MAK)
✓ Product Activation
✓ Volume Activation Management Tool (VAMT)

Techniques/concepts you'll need to master:

✓ Use the System Preparation (Sysprep) utility to deploy Windows.
✓ Install Windows using Windows System Image Manager.
✓ Deploy images by using Windows Deployment Services.
✓ Activate Windows using the KMS Server and the Volume Activation Management Tool.

When you first installed Windows, you most likely used the Windows Setup that was started when you booted from the Windows installation disk. If you have to install Windows on many computers, booting each computer from the installation disk and going through the installation wizard is not always the most efficient way to install, configure, and customize Windows. Microsoft has made available several methods to install and configure Windows Server 2008, using disk images, answer files, and a Windows deployment server.

Disk Cloning and the System Preparation Tool

One way to install Windows is to use disk cloning software such as Norton Ghost to create an image file. To use the disk cloning software, you use the installation disk to install Windows onto a master computer, update and patch the computer, customize Windows, and install any additional software. You then use the cloning software to copy the contents of a hard drive to a file. You use the disk cloning software to copy the contents of the image to a target computer.

If you create a cloned copy of Windows and apply the cloned copy to multiple computers, each copy of Windows cloned to a target computer using the same image has the same parameters, such as the same computer name and *security identifier (SID)*. Unfortunately, for these computers to operate properly on a network, these parameters have to be unique.

To overcome this problem, you run the *System Preparation Tool (Sysprep)*, which removes the security identifiers and all other user-specific or computer-specific information from the computer before you run the disk cloning software to make the cloned disk image. When you copy the cloned image to the disk image, a small wizard runs that enables you to specify the computer name and other computer specific information. The SID and other information is re-created automatically. The Sysprep utility is located in the c:\Windows\System32\sysprep or the c:\Windows\SysWOW64\sysprep folder.

The following command-line options are available for Sysprep:

```
sysprep.exe [/oobe | /audit] [/generalize] [/reboot | /shutdown | /quit]
[/quiet] [/unattend:answerfile]
```

▶ /audit: Restarts the computer into audit mode. Audit mode enables you to add additional drivers or applications to Windows. You can also test an installation of Windows before it is sent to an end user. If an unattended Windows setup file is specified, the audit mode of Windows Setup runs the auditSystem and auditUser configuration passes.

▶ /generalize: Prepares the Windows installation to be imaged. If this option is specified, all unique system information is removed from the Windows installation. The SID resets, any system restore points are cleared, and event logs are deleted. The next time the computer starts, a specialize configuration pass runs. A new SID is created, and the clock for Windows activation resets, if the clock has not already been reset three times.

▶ /oobe: Restarts the computer into Windows Welcome mode. Windows Welcome enables end users to customize their Windows operating system, create user accounts, name the computer, and other tasks. Any settings in an answer file's oobe system configuration pass are processed immediately before Windows Welcome starts.

▶ /reboot: Restarts the computer. Use this option to audit the computer and to verify that the first-run experience operates correctly.

▶ /shutdown: Shuts down the computer after Sysprep completes.

▶ /quiet: Runs Sysprep without displaying onscreen confirmation messages. Use this option if you automate Sysprep.

▶ /quit: Closes Sysprep after running the specified commands.

▶ /unattend:answerfile: Applies settings in an answer file to Windows during unattended installation. The answerfile specifies the path and filename of the answer file to use.

EXAM ALERT

If you are using a single image to install onto multiple computers, you need to use the Sysprep command to strip the computer name and SID and create a new computer name and SID when you first start a computer with an image that was prepped.

Deploying Windows with WIM Images

The Windows installation files can be distributed within a *Windows Imaging Format (WIM) file*. WIM is the file-based imaging format that Windows Server 2008 uses for rapid installation on a new computer. WIM files store copies (known as images) of the operating systems, such as Windows PE, Windows Vista, or Windows Server 2008. Maintaining an operating system in a WIM file is easy because you can add and remove drivers, updates, and Windows components offline, without ever starting the operating system.

The following are the benefits of using a file-based image format over the typical sector-based image format:

▶ A single WIM file deals with different hardware configurations.

▶ WIM can store multiple images within a single file.

▶ WIM enables compression and single instancing of files. Single instancing enables multiple images to share a single copy of a file.

▶ WIM allows images to be serviced offline. You can add or remove drivers, files, and patches.

▶ A WIM image can be installed on partitions of any size, unlike sector-based image formats.

▶ WIM enables you to boot Windows PE from a WIM file.

You can do the following with WIM files:

▶ When installing Windows Vista or Windows Server 2008 using Windows Deployment Server (WDS), you first boot the system with Windows PE. You then install Windows Vista or Windows Server 2008 from a WIM file that contains the Windows image.

▶ You can mount the WIM image as a new volume under Windows with a drive letter associated to facilitate easier extraction.

▶ You can mount the WIM image as a new volume and convert the WIM image to an ISO image.

▶ WIM images can be made bootable, as is the case with Windows Vista's setup DVD. In this case, `BOOT.WIM` contains a bootable version of Windows PE from which the installation is performed. Other setup files are contained in the file `INSTALL.WIM`.

▶ Because Windows PE can be contained within a WIM file, you can start Windows PE directly from a WIM file without copying it to a hard disk.

To create and manage a WIM file, you use the ImageX command-line tool, which is available in several of Microsoft's deployment tools, such as in the Windows Automated Installation Kit (WAIK), Windows OEM Preinstallation Kit (OPK), or in Business Desktop Deployment 2007. ImageX allows you to do the following:

▶ View the contents of a WIM file

▶ Capture desktop images

▶ Mount images for offline image editing

▶ Store multiple images in a single file

▶ Compress image files

▶ Implement scripts for image creation

The `imagex` command uses the following syntax:

```
imagex [flags] {/append ¦ /apply ¦ /capture ¦ /delete ¦ /dir ¦ /export
➥¦ /info ¦ /mount ¦ /mountrw ¦ /split ¦ /unmount} [parameters]
```

▶ **/append**: Adds a volume image to an existing WIM file and create a single instance of the file.

▶ **/apply**: Applies a volume image to a specified drive.

▶ **/capture**: Captures a volume image from a drive to a new WIM file.

▶ **/delete**: Removes the specified volume image from a WIM file.

▶ **/dir**: Displays a list of the files and folders within a specified volume image.

▶ **/export**: Exports a copy of the specified .wim to another .wim file. If you use the /ref splitwim.swm option, it enables you to reference a split .wim file (*.swm).

▶ **/info**: Returns information about the WIM file.

▶ **/mount**: Mounts a WIM file with Read-only permission.

▶ **/mountw**: Mounts a WIM file with Read/Write permission, thereby allowing the contents of the file to be modified.

▶ **/split**: Splits an existing .wim file into multiple read-only split .wim files (*.swm).

▶ **/unmount**: Unmounts an image from a specified directory.

Installing Windows Using Windows System Image Manager

Windows System Image Manager (Windows SIM) provides a GUI interface to create unattended Windows Setup answer file. The answer files, which are XML-based files, are then used to configure and customize the default Windows installation. You create an answer file by using information from a Windows image (.wim) file and a catalog (.clg) file. Component settings are added to a configuration pass in the answer file. You can also add packages to be installed during Windows Setup.

Using Windows SIM, you can

▶ Create or update existing unattended answer files.

▶ Validate the settings of an existing answer file against a WIM file.

▶ View all the configurable component settings in a WIM file.

▶ Create a configuration set.

▶ Add third-party drivers, applications, or other packages to an answer file.

To install Windows SIM, you first need to download and install Windows Automated Installation Kit (AIK) for Windows Vista SP1 and Windows Server 2008 from the Microsoft website. To start Windows SIM, you then click the Start button, select Microsoft Windows AIK, and select Windows System Image Manager (see Figure 2.1).

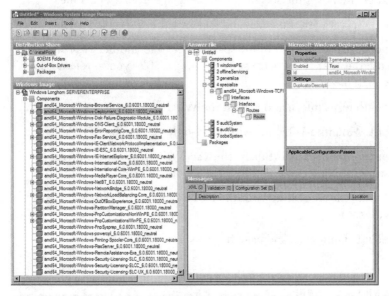

FIGURE 2.1 Windows System Image Manager.

To deploy a Windows operating system, follow these steps:

1. Create an answer file by using SIM. To do so, follow these steps:

   A. Build a catalog and then create a new blank answer file.

   B. Add components and configure Windows settings.

   C. Validate the answer file and then save it to removable media.

2. Build a master installation by using the product DVD and your answer file. A master installation is a customized installation of Windows, which you can duplicate on one or more destination computers.

3. Create an image of the master installation by using Windows PE and ImageX technologies. Follow these steps to create an image of the master installation:

   A. Create a CD that you can use to start Windows PE.

   B. Start the master installation by using Windows PE media.

   C. Capture the installation image by using ImageX.

   D. Store the image on a network share.

4. Deploy the image from a network share onto a destination computer by using Windows PE and ImageX technologies. Follow these steps to deploy the image from a network share:

   A. Start the computer by using Windows PE media.

   B. Format that hard drive.

   C. Connect to your network share and copy the custom image down to the destination computer's local hard drive.

   D. Apply the image by using ImageX.

Windows Deployment Services

The successor to Remote Installation Services (RIS) found in Windows Server 2003 is *Windows Deployment Services (WDS)*, which is used to deploy Windows Vista and Windows Server 2008. It is also available for Windows Server 2003 and included with Windows Server 2003 SP2. By booting a computer with Windows PE 2.0, you can connect to the WDS server and install Windows from a configured image.

Image Types

The main image types used in Windows Deployment Services are the following:

▶ **Install images:** Install images are the operating system images that you deploy to the client computer. You can use the default install image (install.wim) located in the \Sources directory on the Windows Vista or Windows Server 2008 DVDs. In addition, you can build custom install images from reference computers and deploy them to client computers. First, you boot a computer (which has been prepared with Sysprep) into a capture image, and then the capture image creates an install image of the computer.

▶ **Boot images:** Boot images are the images into which you boot a client computer before installing the operating system image. The boot image presents a boot menu that contains the images that users can install onto their computers. These images contain Windows PE 2.0 and the Windows Deployment Services client. You can use the default boot image (boot.wim) that is included in the \Sources directory of the Windows Server 2008 installation media.

In addition, you can create two types of images from boot images:

▶ **Capture images:** Capture images are boot images that launch the Windows Deployment Services Capture Utility instead of Setup. When you boot a reference computer (that has been prepared with Sysprep) into a capture image, a wizard creates an install image of the reference computer and saves it as a .wim file. You can also create media (such as a CD, DVD, or USB drive) that contains a capture image, and then boot a computer from the media. After you create the install image, you can add the image to the server for PXE boot deployment. These images provide an alternative to the command-line utility, ImageX.exe.

▶ **Discover images:** Discover images are boot images that force Setup.exe to launch in Windows Deployment Services mode and then discover a Windows Deployment Services server. These images are typically used to deploy images to computers that are not PXE enabled or that are on networks that do not allow PXE.

When you create a discover image and save it to media (such as a CD, DVD, or USB drive), you can then boot a computer with the media. The discover image on the media locates a Windows Deployment Services server, and the server deploys the install image to the computer.

Connecting to a WDS Server

Windows Preinstallation Environment (Windows PE or WinPE) is a lightweight version of Windows XP, Windows Server 2003, or Windows Vista that is booted from a network disk, a CD, or a USB flash drive. Windows PE can be used to deploy workstations and servers, restore Windows back to manufacturing specifications, and fix and troubleshoot a wide variety of problems.

The newest version of Windows PE is Windows PE 2.0, which is built from Windows Vista and Windows PE 2.1, which is built from Windows Server 2008 (the same code-based as Windows Vista SP1). The whole process of creating the bootable environment from WinPE 2.0 is made much easier compared to older versions of WinPE, partly because in WinPE 2.0 you do not need to use command-line tools.

To install Windows Vista or Windows Server 2008 with a Windows Deployment Server, follow these steps:

1. Turn on your computer and boot from the network card (PXE).

2. By booting using PXE, you connect to the Windows Deployment Service server and download the customized Windows PE image across the network.

3. The new computer loads Windows PE into memory and launches the configuration script. The script verifies the computer's configuration and hardware requirements.

4. If necessary, the script backs up the user's data to a shared folder on another computer.

5. The script runs the Diskpart tool to partition and format the disk.

6. The script connects to a shared folder containing the Windows Setup files and runs the Windows Setup program to install the operating system fully unattended.

Installing Windows Deployment Services

Like any other standard role that comes with Windows Server 2008, you install Windows Deployment Services by using the Initial Configuration Wizard or Server Manager. During the installation, you have the following two role services to choose from (see Figure 2.2):

▶ **Deployment Server:** Install both the Deployment Server and Transport Server, which provides the full functionality of Windows Deployment Services. With Windows Deployment Services, you can create and customize images and then use them to re-image computers.

▶ **Transport Server:** If you deselect Deployment Server on the second installation wizard screen, you have a subset of the functionality of Windows Deployment Services that contains only the core networking parts. You can use Transport Server to create multicast namespaces that transmit data (including operating system images) from a standalone server.

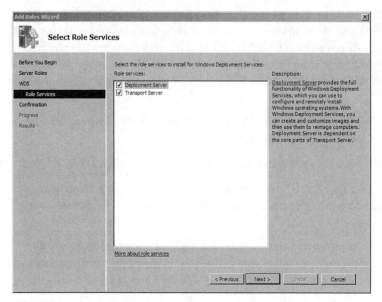

FIGURE 2.2   Windows System Image Manager.

If you chose to install the Deployment Server, the following prerequisites must be available on your network:

▶ Active Directory Domain Services

▶ Dynamic Host Configuration Protocol (DHCP) server

▶ Dynamic Name Services (DNS) server

Configuring Windows Deployment Services

With Windows Deployment Services you can create and modify boot images and install images. After WDS is installed, you can configure WDS by using the Windows Deployment Services MMC snap-in or by using WDSUTIL at the command prompt. When configuring WDS, you complete the following:

▶ You create a shared folder that contains the initial bootstrap program and files for booting Windows PE into RAMDISK, Windows PE boot images, and install images.

▶ You configure the answer settings of the PXE listener to control whether and how the server services incoming client boot requests.

▶ If Microsoft DHCP is installed on the same physical computer as Windows Deployment Services, the configuration wizard adds DHCP option tag 60, with the PXE client setting selected, to all DHCP scopes (as a DHCP global option), so that a booting PXE client can be notified that there is a listening PXE server on the network. It also selects the Do Not Listen on Port 67 option so that the booting clients can find the DHCP server on the network. If you configure Windows Deployment Services by using WDSUTIL, you have to make these changes manually.

Windows Deployment Services requires interaction with Active Directory Domain Services for several critical functions. Therefore, you have to authorize WDS servers in AD by using the DHCP or WDS snap-in. To authorize in the DHCP snap-in, just right-click your server name and choose Authorize. The red down arrow on the server changes to a green up arrow (you may need to press F5 to refresh). To authorize the WDS server, choose Properties. Then in the Advanced tab, choose Yes, I Want to Authorize the WDS Server in DHCP. When you authorize from the WDS snap-in, you have to restart the DHCP server service.

EXAM ALERT

Don't forget that you need to authorize WDS severs in AD.

To configure Windows Deployment Services, follow these steps:

1. Click Start, click Administrative Tools, and then click Windows Deployment Services.

2. In the left pane of the Windows Deployment Services MMC snap-in, click to expand the server list (see Figure 2.3).

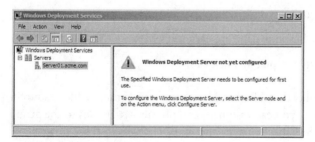

FIGURE 2.3 Windows Deployment Services.

3. Right-click the server and click Configure Server.

4. On the Welcome page, click Next.

5. Specify the location of the Remote Installation folders that will be used to store your images. Note: This must be an NTFS volume. It is also not recommended to put it on the system partition. Click Next.

6. If a DHCP server is running on the Windows Deployment Services server, you must configure Windows Deployment Services not to list on port 67 and you must add a DHCP option Tab 60 to all DHCP scopes. After making the appropriate selections, click Next.

   Pre-boot execution environment (PXE) client computers may be pre-staged (pre-configured) in Active Directory or they may be unknown. If you will only have pre-staged computers, select Respond Only to Known Client Computers. If you plan to use unknown computers, select Respond to All (Known and Unknown) Client Computers. For added security, you can select For Unknown Clients, Notify Administrator and Respond After Approval. Click Finish.

7. When the configuration is complete, click to clear the check box beside Add Images to Windows Deployment Services Now and then click Finish.

8. Specify the full path to the Windows images (install and boot images). Install images are the operating system images that you deploy to the client computer. A default install image (`install.wim`) is located in the \sources directory on the Windows Vista and Windows Server 2008 DVDs. Boot images are the images into which you boot a client computer before installing the operating system image. The default boot image (`boot.wim`) is included in the \Sources directory of the Windows Server 2008 installation media. Click Next.

9. Specify an image group. Click Next.

10. When the Review Settings page appears, click Next.

11. When the tasks are completed, click Finish.

An image group is a collection of `.wim` files that share common file resources and security. For example, you can assign several physical `.wim` files to the group and specify who can access these images and make changes to these images.

To add the default boot image included in the product installation DVD, follow these steps:

1. Click the server to which you want to add the boot image.

2. Right-click the Boot Images node, and then click Add Boot Image.

3. Browse to choose the default boot image (`boot.wim`) located on the Windows Server 2008 DVD, in the \Sources directory.

NOTE

If you are using the standard boot images (`boot.wim`) from the media, it must match (or be newer than) the operating system of the install image. For example, if you are installing Windows Server 2008, you must use the `Boot.wim` from the Windows Server 2008 media—you cannot use the `Boot.wim` from the Windows Vista media.

---

4. Click Open, and then click Next.

5. Specify the name of the image and click Next.

6. When the summary screen appears, click Next.

7. When the images are created, click Finish.

To add the default install image(s) included in the product installation DVD, follow these steps:

1. Click the server to which you want to add the install image.

2. Right-click the Install Images node, and then click Add Install Image.

3. Specify a name for the image group, and then click Next.

4. Browse to select the default install image (`install.wim`) located on the Windows Vista or Windows Server 2008 DVD, in the \Sources directory, and then click Open.

5. To add a subset of the images included in `install.wim`, then clear the check boxes for the images that you do not want to add to the server. You should add only the images for which you have licenses. If you want to change the default names, uncheck Use Default Name and Description for Each of the Selected Images. Click Next (see Figure 2.4).

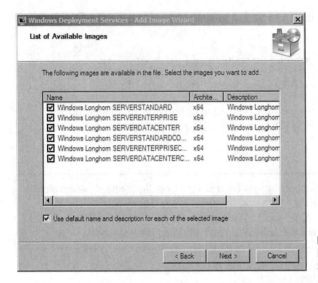

FIGURE 2.4 Adding images in Windows Deployment Services.

6. When the summary is displayed, click Next.

7. When finished, click Finish.

The `wdsutil` command is a command-line utility used for managing your Windows Deployment Services server. For example, to use the `wdsutil` command to configure Windows Deployment Services, do the following:

1. Click Start, right-click Command Prompt, and then click Run as Administrator.

2. Type the following command where *<driveletter>* is the name of the NTFS formatted drive and *<foldername>* is the name of the directory where you want to create the shared folder:

   ```
   WDSUTIL /initialize-server /reminst:"<driveletter>\<foldername>"
   ```

3. To set the answer policy to answer all clients, run

   ```
   WDSUTIL /Set-Server /AnswerClients:all
   ```

4. If you are installing Windows Deployment Services on a computer with Microsoft DHCP installed, run

   ```
   WDSUTIL /Set-Server /UseDHCPPorts:no /DHCPoption60:yes
   ```

5. To add a boot image, run the following command where *<bootimage>* is the full path to the boot image:

   ```
   WDSUTIL /Add-Image /ImageFile:<bootimage> /ImageType:boot
   ```

6. To add an install image, run the following command where
   <installimage> is the full path to the install image and *<name>* is the name
   of the image group to create. (You can append /SingleImage:*<imagename>*
   to add only one of the images included in the install.wim.)

   ```
   WDSUTIL /add-image /ImageFile:<installimage> /ImageType:install
   ➥/ImageGroup:<name>
   ```

To add an additional boot image at a command prompt, follow these steps:

1. Click Start, right-click Command Prompt, and then click Run as
   Administrator.

2. Run the following command to add an additional boot image, where
   <bootimage> is the full path to the boot image on the server. The image
   can be the same or a different architecture.

   ```
   WDSUTIL /Add-Image /ImageFile:<bootimage> /ImageType:boot
   ```

3. When you have completed this procedure and you PXE boot a client
   computer, a boot menu appears that shows both boot images.

When you PXE boot a computer, the Windows Deployment Services client
presents a boot menu. The boot menu allows Windows Deployment Services to
support separate boot architectures and a choice of boot images for each architecture type. If you want to make changes to the boot menu, use the
bcdedit.exe command to edit the default.bcd file located at
%REMINST%\boot\<architecture>. You can run bcdedit /? at the command
prompt to see the options available for bcdedit.

Creating a Captured Image

You can also use the WDS to prepare a configured computer with installed
applications, capture the computer setup to an image, and apply that image to
other computers, using CDs, DVD, USB drives, and network drives.

When creating a capture image, the first steps are to install Windows on a computer, install drivers and applications, and configure the computer. You must
then use Sysprep, which prepares an operating system for disk cloning and
restoration via a disk image. Using Sysprep on the prepared computer strips the
computer down, including removing the computer name and SID so that the
computer is uniquely identifiable. When you first boot the computer that has
had the Sysprep utility used on it, it starts a minisetup wizard that enables you
to define the computer name, define the administrator password, and generate
a security identifier.

To run Sysprep on a Windows Vista or Windows Server 2008 computer, follow these steps:

1. Open a command prompt.

2. Execute the following command:

   `C:\Windows\System32\sysprep\sysprep.exe`

3. At the Windows System Preparation Tool dialogue box, click OK.

4. At the System Preparation Tool window, enable the MiniSetup and Pre-activated check boxes. Ensure that Shutdown is selected from the Shutdown drop-down menu and click Reseal.

5. At the prompt To Continue with Current Settings and Regenerate the SIDs, click the OK button.

Sysprep starts to prepare the computer for duplication and shutdown of the system when duplication is completed. After the minisetup wizard is executed, the system is rebooted and is then ready for use.

NOTE

You must always run the version of Sysprep that was included in that version of Windows and you must always run Sysprep from the sysprep folder.

Now that you have the reference computer prepared, use WDS to create an image:

1. Restart the master machine by booting to a WinPE.

2. Launch the WDSCapture utility (included in a WinPE by default).

3. The WDSCapture utility launches the WDS Image Capture Wizard. Click Next on the Welcome page and you see the Image Capture Source page.

4. Select the volume you want to capture. Give the new image a name and description and click Next.

5. When prompted for credentials to connect to the WDS server, type an administrative account and password. On the Image Capture Destination page, you have to enter a name and location to store the image locally.

6. Next, check Upload Image to WDS Server. Under server name, enter either the WDS server's name or IP address. After the WDSCapture utility has authenticated to the WDS server, a list of Image Groups appears in the drop-down box. Choose your image group and click Finish.

You can modify images to add files or drivers without having to create a new image, using the tools in the Windows Automated Installation Kit (AIK).

To upload the image to the WDS server, follow these steps:

1. In the Windows Deployment Services MMC snap-in, expand the Boot Images node.

2. Right-click the image to use it as a capture image.

3. Click Create Capture Boot Image.

4. Type a name, description, and the location to save a local copy of the file. You must specify a location in case there is a problem with the network when you deploy the capture image.

5. Continue to follow the instructions in the wizard, and when it is complete, click Finish.

6. Right-click the boot image folder.

7. Click Add Boot Image.

8. Browse and select the new capture image, and then click Next.

9. Follow the instructions in the Windows Deployment Services Capture Utility.

Multicast Support in WDS

One of the advantages of running WDS on Windows Server 2008 over running WDS on Windows Server 2003 is that WDS on Windows Server 2008 supports multicast. Multicast is defined as the communication between a single sender and multiple receivers on a network. Although multicast is used to send an audio or video stream to multiple users, it can also be used to install multiple computers at the same time, allowing for a much more efficient use of the network.

To implement multicast in WDS, you need to have the following:

▶ Routers that support multicasting, particularly the Internet Group Management Protocol (IGMP) to properly forward multicast traffic. Without the IGMP, multicast packets are treated as broadcast packets, which can lead to network flooding.

▶ At least one install image that you want to transmit on the server.

▶ The Boot.wim file from the Windows Server 2008 media (located in the \Sources folder).

▸ IGMP snooping enabled on all devices. This causes your network hardware to forward multicast packets only to those devices that are requesting data. If IGMP snooping is turned off, multicast packets are treated as broadcast packets, and are sent to every device in the subnet.

To enable multicasting for an image, you must create a multicast transmission for it. In Windows, you have two options for creating a multicast transmission:

▸ Right-click the Multicast Transmission node, and then click Create Multicast Transmission.

▸ Right-click an image, and then click Create Multicast Transmission.

Discover Images

A discover image is a boot image that has been modified to start Windows Deployment Services and discover a valid server (it is generally used in non-PXE boot scenarios). These images enable a computer that cannot perform a PXE boot from a Windows Deployment Services server to locate such a server and use it to install an image. These images must be started with the /WDSDiscover option. The discovery functionality has two configuration options:

▸ **Static discovery:** This means specifying the server that the computer should use. Static discovery works well in data center environments or branch offices where DHCP may not be available.

▸ **Dynamic discovery:** With this option, the Windows Deployment Services client emulates a PXE request from within Windows PE. Based on the responses to that PXE request, the client can locate a valid server and continue the installation process. If you do not specify the server when you create the discover image, the image uses this method to locate a server.

In most cases, you can use the Boot.wim file included on the Windows Server 2008 DVD to create your image. To create a discover image, right-click the image in the MMC snap-in, and then click Create Discover Boot Image. You can also create a discover image by using the tools provided in the Windows AIK.

Prestage Client Computers

Prestaging takes place when a computer account is created before the computer is installed and can be used to provide a measure of security. Unauthorized clients cannot receive WDS images. By prestaging client computers, you can do the following:

- Assign computers to a specific known client computer policy on the PXE Response Settings tab

- Control to which computers Windows Deployment Services will deploy and image

- Control where the computer account will be placed in Active Directory

To prestage client computers by using the Windows interface, follow these steps:

1. To open Active Directory Users and Computers, click Start, click Run, type **dsa.msc**, and then click OK.

2. In the console tree, right-click the organizational unit that will contain the new client computer.

3. Click New, and then click Computer.

4. Type the client computer name, click Next, and then click This Is a Managed Computer.

5. In the text box, type the client computer's MAC address or globally unique identifier (GUID), and then click Next. If you specify a MAC address, you must precede it with 20 zeros (0).

6. Click one of the following options to specify which server or servers will support this client computer:

   - Any available remote installation server

   - The following remote installation server

7. Click Next, and then click Finish.

To prestage client computers by using a command line, follow these steps:

1. Click Start, right-click Command Prompt, and then click Run as Administrator.

2. Type the following, where *<devicename>* is the name,
<GUIDorMACAddress> is the identifier of the new computer, and
<options> are any optional settings:

```
WDSUTIL /add-device /device:<devicename> /ID:<GUIDorMACAddress>
➥/options
```

If you use a MAC address with the /ID option, you must precede it with
20 zeros (0).

To configure the server to prestage clients by using their MAC address instead
of their GUID, follow these steps:

1. Open an elevated Command Prompt window.

2. Run WDSUTIL /Set-Server /PrestageUsingMAC:Yes.

Windows Activation

After you install Windows Vista or Windows Server 2008, you need to activate
it. Microsoft *Product Activation* is an anti-piracy technology designed to verify
that software products are legitimately licensed.

Microsoft provides two types of customer-specific keys used for license-enrolled
customers under their volume licensing agreement:

▶ The *Key Management Service (KMS)* key is used to establish a local activation enablement service (the Key Management Service or KMS) that is
hosted locally in the customer's environment.

▶ The *Multiple Activation Key (MAK)* is used for one-time activation with
Microsoft's hosted activation services. Each MAK key has a predetermined number of allowed activations dependent upon the volume license
agreement that the customer has. Each MAK activation with Microsoft's
hosted activation service counts towards the predetermined activation
limit. MAK activations can be reclaimed.

Activation Overview

Product Activation works by verifying that a software program's product key has
not been used on more computers than intended by the software license. After
you install Windows and apply the product key, an installation ID number is
generated and shown. The installation ID is then provided to Microsoft through
a secure transfer over the Internet or by telephone. After Microsoft verifies the

installation ID with the software license, a confirmation ID is sent back to your server, which activates your product.

The software activation status does not affect the services running on the server and remote administration, even if the hardware goes out of tolerance and you are asked to reactivate it. Services continue to run if the software is not reactivated. If you do not reactivate, you receive persistent notifications reminding you to activate the server. Services and remote administration are not affected.

The installation ID number includes an encrypted form of the product ID and a hardware hash, or checksum. It does not include any information that can be used to identify you or contact you. The confirmation ID is used only as an unlocking code for Windows Server 2008.

If you overhaul your server by replacing a substantial number of hardware components, the operating system may think it is on a different system. Therefore, you need to reactivate Windows Server 2008 within three days to continue to log on and avoid the activation notifications. After 60 days of not activating Windows, you will not be able to log on until it is activated.

If you choose to activate your product over the Internet, the activation wizard detects your Internet connection and securely connects to a Microsoft server to transfer your installation ID when you submit it. A confirmation ID is passed back to your computer, automatically activating Windows Server 2008. This process typically takes just a few seconds to complete. No personally identifiable information is required to activate Windows Server 2008.

To activate Windows Server 2008 over the telephone, you can simply call a toll-free number displayed on your screen. A customer service representative asks for the installation ID number displayed on the same screen, enters that number into a secure database, and returns a confirmation ID to you. After you have typed the confirmation ID, the activation process is complete.

Key Management Services

The Key Management Services (KMS) establishes a local activation service that is hosted locally in your environment. With the use of KMS, individual machines running Windows Vista or Windows Server 2008 do not have to connect to Microsoft to connect. Instead, KMS installs the KMS key and activates the computers running Windows Vista or Windows Server 2008.

To use a KMS Activation, you need the following:

> ▶ You must install a KMS server or host with the appropriate Volume License media.

▶ The KMS clients must also have the appropriate Volume License media to activate against the KMS host.

▶ KMS clients must be able to access the KMS host. Of course, if the host and clients are separated by firewalls, you have to allow the default TCP port 1688 for KMS to function.

EXAM ALERT

The default port for KMS is TCP port 1688.

Before you activate the KMS host, you should consider the following:

▶ To activate Windows Vista, you must have at least 25 computers running Windows Vista or Windows Server 2008 that are connected together; for Windows Server 2008, the minimum is five computers.

▶ Computers that are activated through KMS must be reactivated every six months by connecting to your organization's network.

EXAM ALERT

You must have at least five Windows Server 2008 computers to use KMS.

To install the KMS host, follow these steps:

1. Choose and install the desired volume licensed media. No product key is required during setup.

2. Start the computer, log on, and launch an elevated Command Prompt.

3. Install your KMS key by running the following script:

   ```
   cscript C:\windows\system32\simgr.vbs /<KMS Key>
   ```

NOTE

You should always use the KMS key from the highest product group your organization has licensed. Do not use the Windows Change Product key wizard to install a KMS key.

4. Activate the KMS host with Microsoft, either with online activation or telephone activation.

To activate the KMS host using the Internet, run the following commands from an elevated Command Prompt:

```
Slmgr.vbs /ipk <New_KMS_Key>
Slmgr.vbs /ato
```

To activate over the phone, use the following commands from an elevated Command Prompt:

```
Slmgr.vbs /ipk <New_KMS_Key>
Slui 4
```

You can verify the KMS host is set up correctly by observing the KMS count and by reviewing the KMS event log entries. You can also run the `slmgr.vbs /dli` command on the KMS host to obtain the current KMS count. The KMS Event Log 12290 entries show the name of the computer and the time-stamp for each activation request. If you have an existing volume license and then purchase a new volume license for a Windows edition in a higher product group, you should upgrade your existing KMS hosts.

KMS Publishing to DNS

KMS publishing enables clients to automatically locate a KMS, using DNS SRV records to find KMS hosts if they have already been registered to use a specific KMS. The KMS SRV Resource Records define the hostname that corresponds to the FQDN of the KMS host and the port. Again, the default port is 1688.

Clients query DNS and retrieve a KMS SRV record. The client then selects a KMS host randomly from the list and attempts to use the information to connect to the KMS. If the connection is successful, the KMS location is cached for subsequent connections. If the host is not available, the process is repeated until a KMS host is found or the list is exhausted.

Enabling and Disabling KMS DNS entries

DNS publishing is enabled by default. You can disable publishing by using

```
cscript c:\windows\system32\slmgr.vbs /cdns
```

or by setting the Registry value `DisableDnsPublishing`. The network administrators can also create a list of DNS domains that a KMS host uses to automatically publish its SRV records.

If KMS is uninstalled, DNS records are not automatically removed by KMS. Run `slmgr /cdns` to disable DNS publishing and then manually delete the appropriate KMS SRV records from DNS. If DNS scavenging is enabled on the

DNS server, the SRV records are eventually removed after the server determines they have become stale.

If you are using only one KMS host, you do not need to configure any permissions in DNS. However, if you have more than one KMS, the other host is not able to update the SRV record unless SRV default permissions are changed. Therefore, to configure the security for KMS publishing to DNS, you would

1. Create a global group in Active Directory that will be used for your KMS hosts.

2. Add each of your KMS hosts to this group. Be sure that they are in the same domain.

3. As soon as the first KMS host is created, it creates the original SRV record and sets the permissions for the SRV group to allow updates by members of the global security group.

EXAM ALERT

It may take several minutes before the SRV records are automatically registered. If you want the DNS records to be displayed more quickly, you can stop and restart the Netlogon service by running the `net stop netlogon` and `net start netlogon` commands.

If you need to create the KMS SRV record on the Microsoft DNS Server manually, follow these steps:

1. Open the DNS Manager.

2. Select the DNS server in which the SRV will be created. Expand Forward Lookup Zones.

3. Expand the first domain that will contain the SRV resource record.

4. Right-click the Domain and choose Other New Records.

5. Scroll down and select Service Location (SRV).

6. Click [Create Record].

7. Enter the following information, typing over any existing text:

   ▶ `Service: _VLMCS`

   ▶ `Protocol: _TCP`

   ▶ `Port Number: 1688`

   ▶ `Host offering the service: <FQDN_of_KMS_Host>`

8. Click OK and then Done.

Of course, if you are not using the default port of 1688, change the port to the appropriate number.

Supporting KMS in Multiple Domains

By default, only the DNS domain to which the KMS host belongs is registered in an SRV record. If you have more than one DNS domain name, you can create a list of DNS domains for a KMS host to use when publishing its SRV record.

To automatically publish KMS in multiple DNS domains, follow these steps:

1. Log on to a KMS host.

2. Open an elevated command prompt. To do this, click Start, All Programs, Accessories and then right-click Command Prompt and click Run as Administrator.

3. At the command prompt, type `Regedit.exe` and then press Enter.

4. Navigate to HKEY_LOCAL_MACHINE\SOFTWARE\Microsoft\Windows NT\CurrentVersion\SL.

5. In the tree pane, click SL. Right-click in the details pane, point to New, and then click Multi-String Value.

6. Type `DnsDomainPublishList` as the name for the new value, and then press Enter.

7. Right-click the new DnsDomainPublishList value, and then click Modify.

8. In the Edit Multi-String dialog box, type each DNS domain suffix to which KMS should publish on a separate line. When you are finished, click OK.

9. Restart the Software Licensing Service, using the Service application. The SRV records are then created.

You then export the Registry key and import it into additional KMS hosts.

Activating Clients Using KMS Activation

After the KMS hosts are installed, you are ready to activate your clients. To install KMS clients for KMS Activation, follow these steps:

1. Choose and install the desired volume licensed media. No product key is required during setup.

2. If you use DNS auto-discovery, no further configuration is required.

> ▶ For domain-joined computers, the DNS auto-discovery of KMS requires that the DNS zone corresponding to either the primary DNS Suffix of the computer or the Active Directory DNS domain contain the SRV resource record for a DNS.

> ▶ For workgroup computers, DNS auto-discovery of KMS requires that the DNS zone corresponding to either the primary DNS suffix of the computer or the DNS domain name assigned by DHCP contain the SRV resource record for a KMS.

If you need to override DNS auto-discovery and perform direct registration with a KMS host, you can run the following script manually or through group policies:

```
cscript \windows\system32\slmgr.vbs /skms <KMS_FQDN>[:<port>]
```

To re-enable auto-discovery for a client computer that was registered to use a specific KMS, run the following built-in-script:

```
cscript \windows\system32\slmgr.vbs /ckms
```

You can also activate a KMS client manually in the Windows interface:

1. Open the Control Panel and open the System Properties. If you are prompted for permission, click Allow.

2. Click Click Here to Activate Windows Now. If you are prompted for permissions, click Allow.

If your computer has access to the network and a KMS, Windows reports that activation was successful.

To activate a KMS client manually (including activating Server Core using a script), follow these steps:

1. Launch an elevated Command Prompt.

2. Run the following script:

```
cscript \windows\system32\slmgr.vbs /ato
```

The script then reports activation success or failure, along with a result code.

Deploying KMS Clients

You can also use the `slmgr.vbs` option to run `sysprep.exe`. The `/generalize` parameter for `Sysprep.exe` resets the activation timer, security identifier, and other important parameters. Resetting the activation timer prevents the image's grace period from expiring before the image is deployed. Running Sysprep.exe does not remove the installed product key and you are not prompted for a new key during minisetup.

If running Sysprep.exe causes changes that complicate your deployment, you can run the Slmgr.vbs script with the /Rearm parameter instead. This script resets the activation timer, but makes no other changes to the system. You can reset the activation timer three times for Windows Vista and Windows Server 2008 computers. You can reset the activation timer for computers running Enterprise editions of Windows Server 2008 five times.

Volume Activation Management Tool

The *Volume Activation Management Tool (VAMT)* enables you to automate and centrally manage the Microsoft Windows volume activation process for Windows Vista and Windows Server 2008 machines. It does not allow you to manage your Windows XP or Windows Server 2003 activations. The VAMT can manage volume activation with Multiple Activation Keys (MAK) or the Windows Key Management Service (KMS). You can install this tool as a stand-alone application on any computer that has one of the following Windows operating systems: Windows XP, Windows Server 2003, Windows Vista, or Windows Server 2008.

Installing the Volume Activation Management Tool

Search for and download the Volume Activation management Tool (VAMT) from the Microsoft Download Center. To install VAMT, follow these steps:

1. Double-click on VAMTInstall.msi.

2. When the VAMT Setup Wizard opens, click Next.

3. Click the check box to Accept the End User License Agreement and click Next.

4. Type or browse to indicate a new path for the installation, or click Next to accept the default.

5. Click Install to confirm the installation.

6. The User Account Control window appears. Click Allow for the Installation to Continue.

7. The status window appears. Click Cancel at any time to stop the installation.

8. Click Finish when the Installation Wizard is complete.

Adding Computers to VAMT

To add computers to the VAMT, you use the following procedure:

1. Open the VAMT console (see Figure 2.5).

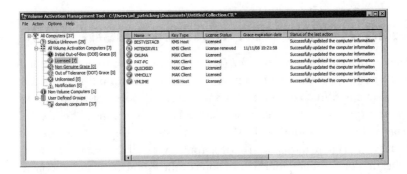

FIGURE 2.5 VAMT Console.

2. Click Action, and then click Add Computers to display the Add Computers dialog.

3. Enter a Computer Group name. If you are creating a new group, type a descriptive name for the group, such as Core Network Group. Each specified group creates a node in the tree view pane, which can be selected for further actions. A computer can be a member of only one user-defined group at a time. If you are adding new computers to an existing group, select the group from the drop-down list.

4. Click the drop-down list to select a search option. You can search for computers in a workgroup, in an Active Directory domain, or by individual computer name or IP address. If you are searching by individual computer name or IP address, enter the full name or IP address in the text box below the drop-down list. Separate multiple entries with a comma, a semicolon, or a space. If you are searching Active Directory or a work-

group, select the domain or workgroup from the additional drop-down list displayed for those search options. Use the Filter by Computer Name field to search for a specific computer within the domain or workgroup. This filter supports the asterisk (*) wildcard. For example, typing **a*** causes only computer names that start with the letter *a* to be displayed.

5. (Optional) Select Gather Computer Information for All Discovered Computers to perform a license status query on each discovered computer.

6. (Optional) Select Provide Alternate Credentials if the computers you are adding to the CIL will require an administrator username and password other than the ones you are currently using. VAMT requires administrator-level access to each target computer. For domain-joined computers, a domain administrator account satisfies this requirement. However, for computers in a workgroup, a local computer administrator name and password are required for each computer.

7. Click OK.

8. The VAMT searches for the specified computers and adds them to the CIL. If you are creating a new group, the VAMT creates a new node for that group in the tree view pane. To cancel the search, click Cancel.

To retrieve license status, the VAMT must have administrative permissions on all selected computers, and Windows Management Instrumentation (WMI) must be accessible through the Windows firewall. To refresh the license status of a computer or group, follow these steps:

1. Open the VAMT console.

2. To refresh the status of an individual computer, select it in the computer list view pane. To refresh the status of a group, select the group in the tree view pane.

3. Right-click the computer or group to display the context-sensitive Action menu.

4. On the menu, select Refresh Computer Status and choose a credential option. Choose Alternate Credentials only if you are refreshing a computer that requires administrator credentials different from the ones you are currently using.

5. (For alternate credentials only) At the prompt, type the appropriate username and password, and then click OK.

6. The VAMT displays the Collecting Computer Information dialog while it collects the status of all selected computers. When the process is finished, the refreshed status of each computer appears in the computer list view pane of the VAMT console.

Performing MAK Independent Activation

To enable Windows Multiple Activation Key to one or more connected computers within a network, and to instruct those computers to activate over the Internet, you must make sure all computers are on a common network managed by Active Directory. The VAMT is installed on a central computer with network access to all client computers. Both the VAMT host and client computers have Internet access.

To perform MAK Independent activation, follow these steps:

1. Open the VAMT console.

2. Select the computers to be activated, either by clicking a group in the tree view pane or by selecting individual computers in the list view pane.

3. Right-click the selected group or computer(s) to display the context-sensitive Action menu.

4. On the menu, click MAK Independent Activate to display the MAK Independent Activate dialog.

5. Select the appropriate MAK from the Install MAK drop-down list.

6. Select Install MAK (Overwrite Existing) and Activate Now. This instructs the selected computers to activate immediately by contacting Microsoft Windows Activation over the Internet. If an asterisk (*) appears next to the text for these check boxes, the action applies only to applicable computers. For example, a computer installed with Windows Vista Retail Edition cannot be activated with a MAK.

7. If you are activating computers that require administrator credentials different from the ones you are currently using, select Use Alternate Credentials.

8. Click OK.

9. The VAMT displays the Assigning Product Keys dialog and then displays the Activating Computers dialog until it completes the requested action. If you selected Use Alternate Credentials, you are prompted to enter the credentials prior to these dialogs.

If you select the Install MAK (Overwrite Existing) force option, it will install a MAK on a client computer. This must be done with care.

Performing MAK Proxy Activation

To perform volume activation for client computers that do not have Internet access, you can use MAK Proxy Activation. The VAMT host computer distributes a Windows Multiple Activation Key (MAK) to one or more client computers and collects the installation ID (IID) from each computer. The VAMT host sends the IIDs to Microsoft on behalf of the client computers and obtains the corresponding Confirmation IDs (CID). The VAMT host then installs the CIDs on the client computer to complete the activation. With this activation method, only the VAMT host computer needs Internet access.

> **EXAM ALERT**
>
> If you have computers that don't have direct access to the Internet, you need to use Multiple Activation Key (MAK) Proxy Activation to install a Multiple Activation Key (MAK).

For workgroups that are completely isolated from any larger network, you can still perform MAK proxy activation. This requires installing a second VAMT on a computer within the isolated group and using removable media to transfer activation data between that computer and another VAMT host that has Internet access.

Before performing MAK proxy activation, ensure that the VAMT is installed on a computer that has Internet access. Then add computers that need to be activated to the VAMT. Of course, you need to have administrative permissions on all computers and the VAMT/Windows Management Instrumentation (WMI) must be accessible through the firewall. For workgroup computers, a Registry key must be created to enable remote administrative actions under User Account Control (UAC).

To perform MAK Proxy Activation, follow these steps:

1. Open the VAMT console.

2. Select the computers to be activated, either by clicking a group in the tree view pane or by selecting individual computers in the list view pane.

3. Right-click the selected group or computer(s) to display the context-sensitive Action menu.

4. On the menu, click MAK Proxy Activate to display the MAK Proxy Activate dialog.

5. Select the appropriate MAK from the Install MAK drop-down list.

6. Select Install MAK (Overwrite Existing), Get Confirmation ID from Microsoft, and Apply Confirmation ID and Activate. If an asterisk (*) appears next to the text for these check boxes, the action applies only to applicable computers. For example, a computer installed with Windows Vista Retail Edition cannot be activated with a MAK.

7. If you are activating computers that require administrator credentials different from the ones you are currently using, select Use Alternate Credentials.

8. Click OK.

9. The VAMT displays three status dialogs while it completes the proxy activation: Assigning Product Keys, Acquiring Confirmation ID Online, and finally Assigning Confirmation IDs. If you selected Use Alternate Credentials, you are prompted to enter the credentials before you see these dialogs.

Configure Computers for KMS Activation

The KMS Client keys are the default product keys used by Volume License editions of Windows Vista and Windows Server 2008. You can use the VAMT to install and activate KMS Client keys on computers accessible to the VAMT. For you to do this, you must make sure of three things:

▶ The computers to be activated and the VAMT computer are part of the same Active Directory structure.

▶ VAMT/Windows Management Instrumentation (WMI) is accessible through the network.

▶ The computers to be activated have been added to the VAMT.

To configure computers for KMS Activation, follow these steps:

1. Open the VAMT console.

2. Select the computers to be activated, either by clicking a group in the tree view pane or by selecting individual computers in the list view pane.

3. Right-click the selected group or computer(s) to display the context-sensitive Action menu.

4. On the menu, click Configure for KMS Activation to display the KMS Configuration dialog.

5. Select Install KMS Client Key (Overwrite Existing). This instructs the VAMT to install a KMS client key on a client computer.

6. Select either Auto-Discover KMS Host Using DNS or Use Specific KMS Host and Port. The Auto-Discover KMS Host Using DNS option first clears any previously configured KMS host on the target computer and then instructs the computer to query the Domain Name Service (DNS) to locate a KMS host and attempt activation. The Use Specific KMS Host and Port option sets the specified KMS hostname and KMS host port on the target computer and then instructs the computer to attempt activation with that specific KMS host.

7. If you are activating computers that require administrator credentials different from the ones you are currently using, select the Use Alternate Credentials check box.

8. Click OK.

9. The VAMT displays the Assigning Product Keys dialog, and then displays the Activating Computers dialog until it completes the requested action. If you selected Use Alternate Credentials, you are prompted to enter the credentials before these dialogs appear.

Perform Local Reactivation

If you reinstall Windows on a computer that was initially activated through MAK proxy activation, and have not made significant changes to the hardware, you can use the following procedure to reactivate Windows on that computer:

1. Open the VAMT console.

2. In the tree view pane, select the group that contains the computer to be reactivated, and then select the individual computer in the list view pane.

3. Right-click the selected computer to display the context-sensitive Action menu.

4. In the menu, click Reapply Confirmation ID to display the MAK Proxy Reactivate dialog.

5. If you reapplied the Windows image on the computer, uncheck Install MAK (Overwrite Existing). The image includes the MAK. If you installed a different (for example, retail) version of Windows and are going to activate it with a MAK, leave this box checked and select the correct MAK from the drop-down list.

6. Leave Reapply Confirmation ID and Reactivate checked to apply the stored CID (pending CID) from the currently loaded VAMT CIL file to the computer.

7. Leave Require Exact IID Match checked if the hardware has not changed since the initial MAK Proxy activation and you are using the same MAK to reactivate. If the computer's hardware has changed since initial activation, or if you are using a different MAK than the one used for initial activation, uncheck Require Exact IID Match. Note that Windows might not be successfully reactivated in this scenario.

8. If you are activating a computer that requires administrator credentials different from the ones you are currently using, select Use Alternate Credentials.

9. Click OK.

Before you can use a Windows MAK, you must add it to the VAMT.

Adding Windows Multiple Activation Keys

To add MAK keys to the VAMT, use the following procedure:

1. Open the VAMT console.

2. Click Options and then click Manage MAKs to open the Manage MAK Keys dialog.

3. Click Add to open the Add a MAK Key dialog.

4. Type the 25-character MAK and click Validate. You do not need to type the hyphens; the dialog inserts them automatically. After validation, the Edition field automatically populates.

5. Type a description for the MAK such as Core Network Group MAK and click Add. The VAMT displays the MAK in the Manage MAK Keys dialog.

6. Click Exit to close the dialog.

If you are activating a large number of computers, you should refresh the MAK's activation count to ensure that the MAK can support the required number of activations. In the Manage MAK Keys dialog, select the MAK and click Refresh Remaining Count to retrieve the number of remaining activations for the MAK from Microsoft. This step requires Internet access.

Managing VAMT Data

The VAMT is used to import, export, and merge data primarily in MAK proxy activation scenarios, where the target computers are to be activated with a MAK and have no Internet access. The following procedure summarizes these VAMT data operations:

1. Launch the VAMT in a test environment with no Internet access.

2. Perform a discovery of all computers in the test environment.

3. Install a MAK to all computers in the environment and retrieve the installation IDs (IID).

4. Click File and then Save. Save the VAMT Computer Information List (CIL) in the local VAMT host computer.

5. Click File and then Export to export the CIL to removable media. Use either the standard or secure export.

6. Import the CIL into a VAMT host that has Internet access.

7. Obtain the Confirmation IDs (CID) for all computers in the CIL from the Microsoft Web-based Windows activation service.

8. Export the CIL back onto the removable media.

9. Load the standard-save CIL back into the VAMT host.

10. Import the CIL (which now contains the CIDs acquired from Microsoft) into the VAMT.

11. The VAMT merges the CIDs with their corresponding computer IIDs.

12. Click Action, select MAK Proxy Activate, and choose Apply Confirmation ID and Activate to activate all computers in the environment.

Exam Prep Questions

1. What would you use to boot a computer to install Windows over the network or to troubleshoot Windows?

   ○ **A.** Windows Server 2008 Installation DVD

   ○ **B.** WinPE

   ○ **C.** DOS bootable disk

   ○ **D.** PXE-floppy disk

2. What is the default port used for KMS?

   ○ **A.** 80

   ○ **B.** 443

   ○ **C.** 1688

   ○ **D.** 4343

   ○ **E.** 6523

3. You need to deploy Windows Vista on 20 computers within your company. You prepare a reference Windows Vista computer with all the software loaded and configured. What should you do next?

   ○ **A.** You should discover the image with a WDS server.

   ○ **B.** You should install the image to the WDS server.

   ○ **C.** You should capture the image with a WDS server.

   ○ **D.** You should copy the Windows PE image to the reference computer.

4. You have a Windows Vista image that you just finished creating from a reference computer. Unfortunately, you discover that the WIM file is too large. How do you divide the file into small files?

   ○ **A.** Execute the `imagex /split d:\VistaImage.wim 700` command.

   ○ **B.** Execute the `imagex /capture d:\VistaImage.wim /Split 700` command.

   ○ **C.** Execute the `imagex /mountrw d:\VistaImage.wim 700` command.

   ○ **D.** Execute the `imagex /mount d:\VistaImage.wim 700` command.

5. You have just created a reference computer running Windows vista. You want to deploy this reference computer to new computers using WDS. What should you do next?

- ○ **A.** Run the `WDSUTIL` `/add-image` `/imagefile:image` `/imagetype:` `boot` command

- ○ **B.** Run the `sysprep` `/OOBE` `/Generalize` `/Reboot` command.

- ○ **C.** Run the `riprep` `/pnp` `/Reboot` command

- ○ **D.** Run the `imagex` `/capture` `C:\` `image.wim` command.

6. You have just installed Windows Vista on five machines. Because of your security policy, these computers do not have access to the Internet. However, you have a Windows Server 2008 computer on which the Volume Activation Management Tool (VAMT) is loaded. What is the best way to activate these computers?

- ○ **A.** Use MAK Independent Activation.

- ○ **B.** Use MAK Proxy Activation.

- ○ **C.** Use KMS Activation process.

- ○ **D.** Use System Center Operations Manager (SCOM).

7. You have installed a Key Management Service (KMS) on your domain and you want to manually configure the clients to locate the KMS server with a direct connection. Your KMS server is configured to use port 2897 for activation. What should you do?

- ○ **A.** Run the `cscript` `C:\windows\system32\slmgr.vbs` `-cnds:2897` command on the KMS host.

- ○ **B.** Run the `cscript` `C:\windows\system32\slmgr.vbs` `-sdns:2897` command on the KMS host.

- ○ **C.** Run the `cscript` `C:\windows\system32\slmgr.vbs` `-skms` `host1.acme.com:2897` command on each client.

- ○ **D.** Run the `cscript` `C:\windows\system32\slmgr.vbs` `ckms:2897` command on each client.

8. You have four domains in your forest. You configure a KMS service for all of your domains. However, the KMS server is registering its SRV record only in its home domain but not in the other domains. What do you need to do to get the KMS server to register the SRV records in the other domains?

   - ○ **A.** Reboot the KMS server.

   - ○ **B.** On each client, open the HKLM\SOFTWARE\Microsoft\Windows NT\CurrentVersion\SL Registry key and create a key named DnsDomainPublishList and populate its value for each of the domain names.

   - ○ **C.** On each KMS server, open the HKLM\SOFTWARE\Microsoft\Windows NT\CurrentVersion\SL Registry key and create a key named DnsDomainPublishList and populate its value for each of the domain names.

   - ○ **D.** Run net stop netlogon and net start netlogon on the KMS server.

9. You have a company with several Windows 2000 Servers with SP5 and several Windows Server 2003 computers. You want to use one of these servers to deploy Windows Vista to your clients. What should you do?

   - ○ **A.** Install RIS on a Windows Server 2003 computer.

   - ○ **B.** Install WDS on a Windows Server 2003 computer.

   - ○ **C.** Upgrade a Windows Server 2003 computer to Windows Server 2008 and install the WDS role.

   - ○ **D.** Install WDS on two Windows 2000 Server computers.

10. You just replaced a network administrator for your organization. You find an ImageX image split into several small images with the extension .swm. You need to combine these into one large image. How do you do this?

   - ○ **A.** Use the imagex command with the /export option.

   - ○ **B.** Use the imagex command with the /capture option.

   - ○ **C.** Use the imagex command with the /mountrw command.

   - ○ **D.** use the imagex command with the combine option.

Answers to Exam Prep Questions

1. Answer B is correct. The WinPE is a bootable disk that enables you to boot from a network disk, a CD, or a USB flash drive. Windows PE can be used to deploy workstations and servers, restore Windows back to manufacturing specifications, and fix and troubleshoot a wide variety of problems. Answer A is incorrect because the Windows Server 2008 Installation DVD would not enable you to install over the network. Answer B is incorrect because the DOS bootable disk would not give you network access and would not allow you to access NTFS volumes. Answer D is incorrect because PXE technology is used to boot directly over the network, not with a floppy disk.

2. Answer C is correct. The default port for KMS is 1688. Therefore, Answers, A, B, D, and E are wrong because they do not list port 1688.

3. Answer C is correct. If you capture an image of a reference computer after it has been prepared, WDS uses the Sysprep option to remove the SID and other computer-specific information and copy the install image to the WDS server. Answer A is incorrect because when you discover an image, WDS launches and discovers a valid WDS to acquire an image. Answer D is incorrect because copying the Windows PE image is used to boot a computer. Therefore, copying the Windows PE to the reference computer does not give you the desired result.

4. Answer A is correct. The `imagex /split d:\VistaImage 700` command splits the existing `.wim` file into smaller 700MB `.swm` files. If necessary, you can then copy these to CDs for easy distribution. Answer B is incorrect because the `/capture` option is used to capture a volume image from a drive and to create a new `.wim` file. This does not split the current image file. Answers C and D are incorrect because you do not need to mount the images.

5. Answer B is correct. You need to use the `sysprep` command to assign a new security ID and other unique computer information. The Answer A is incorrect because the WDSUTILI command is used to add a boot image called `image`. Answer C is incorrect because the `ripprp` command is used to capture the Windows 2000 Professional and Windows XP Professional images from a reference computer to a Remote Installation Services (RIS) server. Answer D is incorrect because the `imagex` command is used to capture an image. But you need to first run the `sysprep` command before you create an image because it needs to pull the unique information, such as the security ID, first.

6. Answer B is correct. You need to use MAK Proxy Activation for those clients who do not have direct access to the Internet. Answer A is incorrect because MAK Independent Activation does not work if you do not have direct access to the Internet. Answer C is incorrect because KMS activation requires at least five physical machines before activation occurs. Answer D is incorrect because SCOM is not used to activate Windows.

7. Answer C is correct. You should run the `cscript c:\windows\system32\`
   `slmgr.vbs -skms host1.acme.com:2897` on each client. This command specifies the FQDN and port to the KMS server. Answer A is incorrect because the `-cdns`
   option disables the automatic registration of SRV records for the KMS service in DNS.
   Answer B is incorrect because the `-sdns` option is used to enable the automatic registration of SRV records. Answer D is incorrect because the `ckms` option enables auto-
   discovery on the clients.

8. Answer C is correct. You must create a `DnsDomainPublishList` on each KMS
   server if you have multiple domains in your forest. Answer A is incorrect because
   rebooting does nothing to fix the problem. Answer B is incorrect because you do not
   have to configure each client, just the KMS servers. Answer D is incorrect because
   restarting the netlogon services does not fix the problem.

9. Answer C is correct. To install Vista, you need to use WDS, which can be installed only
   on a Windows Server 2003 with SP2 or a Windows Server 2008. Answer A is incorrect
   because RIS does not support Windows Vista installations. Answer B is incorrect
   because for WDS to run on a Windows Server 2003 computer, you need to have SP2.
   Answer D is incorrect because WDS cannot be installed on Windows Server 2000.

10. Answer A is correct. `imagex` is the command used to create, mount, and manage
    Windows image files. The `/export` option allows you to copy an existing `.wim` file
    into a new `.wim` file, and if you use the `/ref` parameter, it can combine split image
    files. Answer B is incorrect because the `capture` option captures a volume image
    from a drive to a new `.wim` file. Answer C is incorrect because the `/mount` and
    `/mountrw` options are used to mount a `.wim` file. Answer D is incorrect because the
    `combine` option does not exist with the `imagex` command.

Need to Know More?

For more information about the system preparation tool (Sysprep), visit the following website:

> http://technet2.microsoft.com/WindowsVista/en/library/bb068119-
> 1ba6-48c7-9ad7-3ed3f72592e91033.mspx

For more information about the Windows System Image Manager, visit the following website:

> http://technet2.microsoft.com/WindowsVista/en/library/d9f7c27e-
> f4d0-40ef-be73-344f7c7626ff1033.mspx

For more information about the Windows Deployment Services, visit the following website:

> http://technet2.microsoft.com/windowsserver2008/en/servermanager/
> windowsdeploymentservices.mspx

For more information about using the `wsdutil.exe` command, visit the following website:

> http://technet2.microsoft.com/windowsserver2008/en/library/a2d6bf06-
> c99e-4c30-aa94-baf8319b3ce21033.mspx?mfr=true

For more information about Volume Activation, download the Volume Activation 2.0 Technical guide, which can be found at the following website:

> http://www.microsoft.com/downloads/details.aspx?FamilyId=9893F83E-
> C8A5-4475-B025-66C6B38B46E3&displaylang=en

CHAPTER THREE

Windows Server 2008 Storage

Terms you'll need to understand:

- ✓ Virtual Disk Specification (VDS)
- ✓ IDE Drives
- ✓ SCSI Drives
- ✓ Redundant Arrays of Inexpensive Disks (RAID)
- ✓ network-attached storage (NAS)
- ✓ storage area network (SAN)
- ✓ iSCSI
- ✓ fibre channel
- ✓ Storage Manager
- ✓ iSCSI initiator
- ✓ partition

- ✓ Master Boot Record (MBR)
- ✓ GUID partition table (GPT)
- ✓ basic disks
- ✓ dynamic disks
- ✓ diskpart.exe command
- ✓ simple volumes
- ✓ spanned volumes
- ✓ striped volumes
- ✓ mirrored volumes
- ✓ RAID-5 volumes
- ✓ mount points

Techniques/concepts you'll need to master:

- ✓ Connect to a NAS and SAN, using Windows Server 2008.
- ✓ Use Storage Explorer to view and manage Fibre Channel and ISCSI Fabrics.

- ✓ Manage disks using the Disk Management console and diskpart.exe command.
- ✓ Enable and configure RAID, using Windows Server 2008.

When working with Windows, you have to work with disks. Although simple servers have you install Windows Server 2008 on a local IDE (parallel and serial) or SCSI hard drive, more complex systems may use an attached remote computer storage device such as a storage area network (SAN) or network-attached storage (NAS). Therefore, you need to know what options are available and how to configure a server's physical and virtual disk drives so that the server can meet the needs of network applications while providing reliability.

The *Virtual Disk Specification (VDS)* protocol provides a mechanism for remote configuration of disks, *partitions*, volumes, and *iSCSI initiators* on a server. Through the VDS protocol, a client can change the configuration of disks into partitions, partitions into volumes, and volumes into file systems. In the VDS protocol, two entities are involved: the server whose storage is configured and the client who needs to change the server storage configuration.

IDE and SCSI Drives

Today's hard drives are either integrated drive electronics (IDE) or small computer system interface (SCSI, pronounced "skuzzy") drives. *IDE drives* are designed as fast, low-cost drives. Traditional IDE drives were based on the parallel AT attachment (ATA) standard that used a parallel 40-pin connector. Today's IDE drives follow the serial ATA standard (SATA), which uses a connector that is attached with only four wires and a smaller power connector. Although the serial ATA uses fewer wires/connectors, it provides faster throughput then parallel ATA IDE drives.

Servers and high-performance workstations typically use *SCSI drives*. SCSI drives typically offer faster performance and throughput than IDE drives and SCSI drives support a larger number of drives to be attached through the same interface.

Redundant Arrays of Inexpensive Disks (RAID)

To help with data protection and system reliability, there are *redundant arrays of inexpensive disks (RAID)* that use two or more drives in combination to create a fault tolerance system to protect against physical hard drive failure and to increase hard drive performance. A RAID can be accomplished with either hardware or software and is usually used in network servers. Hardware RAID offers better performance and is transparent to the operating system. However, it costs more to implement because you need a RAID controller. Software RAID is inexpensive and easy to configure because it has no special hardware requirements other than multiple disks.

There are several levels of RAID. The first one is RAID 0. RAID 0 stripes data across all drives. With striping, all available hard drives are combined into a single large virtual file system, with the file system's blocks arrayed so they are spread evenly across all the drives. For example, if you have three 500MB hard drives, RAID 0 provides for a 1.5GB virtual hard drive. When you store files, they are written across all three drives. When a large file is written, a part of it may be written to the first drive, the next chunk to the second drive, more to the third drive, and perhaps more wrapping back to the first drive to start the sequence again. Unfortunately, with RAID 0 there is no parity control or fault tolerance, so it really is not a true form of RAID. If one drive fails, you lose all data on the array. However, RAID 0 does have several advantages because it has increased performance through load balancing.

A common RAID used in networked PCs and servers is RAID 1, known as disk-mirroring. Disk-mirroring copies a partition onto a second hard drive. As information is written, it is written to both hard drives simultaneously. If one of the hard drives fails, the PC still functions because it can access the other hard drive. You can then replace the failed drive, and data is copied from the remaining good drive to the replaced drive.

> **NOTE**
>
> This book focuses on RAID 0, 1, and 5 because that is the software RAID that is supported by Windows Server 2008. There are other levels of RAID, but RAID 0, 1, and 5 are the most popular and are the only software RAID supported by Windows Server 2008.

Another common RAID is RAID 5 (sometimes referred to as striped volume with parity), which is similar to striping, except one of the hard drives is used for parity (error-correction) to provide fault tolerance. To increase performance, the error-correction is spread across all hard drives in the array to avoid having one drive do all the work in calculating the parity bits. If one drive fails, you still keep working because the missing data can be filled in by doing parity calculations with the remaining drives. When the failed drive is replaced, the missing information is rebuilt. However, if two drives fail, you do loose all data on the array. RAID-5 has better performance than RAID 1. RAID 5 usually requires at least three drives, with more preferable. If you have 3×500GB drives, you will have 2×500GB=1000GB of disk space because one of the drives must be used for parity. If you have 6×500GB drives, you have 5×500GB=2500GB of disk space.

RAID can be implemented through the use of a hardware RAID controller or through software. Windows Server 2003 and Windows Server 2008 offers software RAID that supports RAID 0, RAID 1, and RAID 5. Typically, for better performance and reliability, it is recommended that you use hardware RAID.

Network-Attached Storage (NAS) and Storage Area Networks (SAN)

Network-attached storage (NAS) is a file-level computer data storage device that is connected to a computer network to provide shared drives or folders. To make NAS fault tolerant, NAS systems usually contain one or more hard disks, often arranged as RAIDs. NAS units also usually have a web interface as opposed to keyboard/video/mouse.

A *storage area network (SAN)* is an architecture that attaches remote computer storage devices (such as disk arrays, tape libraries, and optical jukeboxes) to servers in such a way that, to the operating system, the devices appear as locally attached. They are typically used in larger organizations where the SAN acts as a central disk repository that services multiple servers and network applications. The SAN usually contains multiple hard drives that use RAID or other technology to make the system redundant against drive failure and to offer high performance.

Most SANs use the SCSI protocol for communication between servers and disk drive devices. But instead of using the same SCSI interface used in local hard drives, it uses network interfaces, such as

- Fibre Channel
- iSCSI

A fabric is a network topology where devices are connected to each other through one or more high-efficiency data paths. In the case of a *Fibre Channel* fabric, the network includes one or more Fibre Channel switches that enable servers and storage devices to connect to each other through virtual point-to-point connections. For *iSCSI* fabrics, the network includes one or more Internet Storage Name Service (iSNS) servers that provide discoverability and partitioning of resources.

Fibre Channel

Fibre Channel is a gigabit-speed network technology primarily used for storage networking. Fibre Channel is standardized in the T11 Technical Committee of the InterNational Committee for Information Technology Standards (INCITS), an American National Standards Institute (ANSI)–accredited standards committee. Despite its name, Fibre Channel signaling can run on both twisted pair copper wire and fiber-optic cables. Fibre Channel Protocol (FCP) is the interface protocol of SCSI on the Fibre Channel.

In a Fibre Channel switched fabric (FC-SW), Fibre Channel switches connect devices together. When a host or device communicates with another host or device, the source and target create a point-to-point connection between themselves and communicate directly with each other. The fabric itself routes data from the source to the target. In an FC-SW, the media is not shared. Therefore, any device can communicate with any other device, assuming it is not busy, and communication occurs at full bus speed regardless of whether other devices and hosts are communicating at the same time.

A port in Fibre Channel is any entity that actively communicates over the network. Port is usually implemented in a device such as disk storage, an HBA on a server, or a Fibre Channel switch. There are three major Fibre Channel topologies, describing how a number of ports are connected together:

- ▶ **Point-to-Point (FC-P2P):** Two devices are connected back to back. This is the simplest topology, with limited connectivity.

- ▶ **Arbitrated loop (FC-AL):** In this design, all devices are in a loop or ring, similar to token ring networking. Adding or removing a device from the loop causes all activity on the loop to be interrupted. The failure of one device causes a break in the ring. Fibre Channel hubs exist to connect multiple devices together and may bypass failed ports. A loop may also be made by cabling each port to the next in a ring. A minimal loop containing only two ports, while appearing to be similar to FC-P2P, differs considerably in terms of the protocol.

- ▶ **Switched fabric (FC-SW):** All devices or loops of devices are connected to Fibre Channel switches, similar conceptually to modern Ethernet implementations. The switches manage the state of the fabric, providing optimized interconnections.

When a host or device is powered on, it must first log in to the fabric. This enables the device to determine the type of fabric (a fabric supports a specific set of characteristics) and provides a fabric address to a host or device. A given host or device continues to use the same fabric address while it is logged on to the fabric; the fabric address is guaranteed to be unique for that fabric. For a host or device to communicate with another device, it must establish a connection to that device before transmitting data. The switches route the packets in the fabric.

In a fabric topology, each device (including the HBA) is called a node. Each node has a fixed 64-bit worldwide name (WWN) assigned by the manufacturer and registered with the IEEE to ensure it is globally unique. A node can have multiple ports, each with a unique 64-bit port name and 24-bit port ID. For example, a dual-port HBA has a single worldwide name (WWN) and two world-wide port IDs used for frame routing. When a port logs in to the fabric, it registers various attributes that are stored in the fabric (usually within a switch). Zoning is a method of restricting which ports or WWN can communicate with each other.

LUNs allow SANs to break the SAN storage down into manageable pieces. The SAN then assigns each LUN to one or more servers in the SAN. If a LUN is not mapped to a given server, that server cannot see or access the LUN. LUN masking is a method of restricting which devices can view, send, and receive commands to specific LUNs on a storage controller. You need to identify only the server or cluster that is to access the LUN, and then select which HBA ports on that server or cluster will be used for LUN traffic.

When a server or cluster is identified, Storage Explorer automatically discovers the available Fibre Channel HBA ports on that server or cluster. You can also add ports manually by entering their World Wide Name (WWN).

iSCSI

iSCSI is a protocol that enables clients to send SCSI commands over a TCP/IP network using TCP port 3260. Because it uses Ethernet switches and cabling, typically Gigabit Ethernet or Fibre, it can connect a SAN to multiple servers and provide long-distance connections.

A LUN is a logical reference to a portion of a storage subsystem. A LUN can comprise a disk, a section of a disk, a whole disk array, or a section of a disk array in the subsystem. Using LUNs simplifies the management of storage resources in your SAN because LUNs serve as logical identifiers through which you can assign access and control privileges.

Because you connect to the SAN over a network, the network adapter must be dedicated to either network communication (traffic other than iSCSI) or iSCSI, not both. Therefore, if you are using iSCSI, you need two sets of network cards, one for iSCSI and one for network connections.

For a server to connect to a SAN, the server connects to a target using an iSCSI initiator. A target defines the portals/servers (IP addresses) that can be used to connect to the iSCSI device, as well as the security settings (if any) that the iSCSI device requires to authenticate the servers requesting access to its resources.

For a server to connect to an iSCSI SAN, the server uses an iSCSI initiator software to log on and connect to the SAN. After access is granted by the SAN, the server can start reading and writing to all LUNs assigned to that server. After the software initiator connects to a LUN, the iSCSI session emulates a SCSI hard disk so that the server treats the LUN just like any other hard drive.

Each iSCSI initiator can have one or more network adapters through which communication is established. Additional network adapters provide increased bandwidth and redundancy.

The iSCSI software can be built into the iSCSI host adapter (more commonly known as a Host Bus Adapter (HBA). A typical HBA is packaged as a combination of a Gigabit Ethernet NIC and a SCSI bus adapter, which is what it appears as to the operating system. The HBA contains special firmware that contains the iSCSI initiator software. Because a hardware initiator processes iSCSI and TCP processing and the Ethernet interrupts, performance can be increased over iSCSI initiator software running on the server.

For iSCSI initiators to find a storage device to connect to, the iSCSI initiator uses Internet Storage Name Service (iSNS) protocol to provide both naming and resource discovery services for storage devices on the IP network. The iSCSI initiator then uses the following to connect to the SAN:

▶ Hostname or IP address (for example, "iscsi.example.com")

▶ Port number (for example, 3260)

▶ iSCSI name (for example, the IQN "iqn.2003-01.com.ibm:00.fcd0ab21.shark128")

▶ An optional CHAP secret password

The iSCSI Name follows one of the following formats:

▶ **iSCSI Qualified Name (IQN):** IQN follows the format

iqn.yyyy-mm.{reversed domain name}

For example:

iqn.2001-04.com.acme:storage.tape.sys1.xyz

IQN addresses are the most common format.

▶ **Extended Unique Identifier (EUI):** EUI follows the format

eui.{EUI-64 bit address}

For example:

eui.02004567A425678D

EUI is provided by the IEEE Registration authority in accordance with EUI-64 standard.

▶ **T11 Network Address Authority (NAA):** NAA follows the format

naa.{NAA 64 or 128 bit identifier}

For example:

naa.52004567BA64678D

NAA is part OUI, which is provided by the IEEE Registration Authority. NAA name formats were added to iSCSI in RFC 3980, to provide compatibility with naming conventions used in Fibre Channel and SAS storage technologies.

Configuring the iSCSI Initiators

Microsoft Windows Server 2008 includes two iSCSI Initiator software interfaces. They are

▶ iSCSI Initiator applet (located in the Administrative Tools and Control Panel)

▶ `iscsicli` command interface

EXAM ALERT

For the exam, be sure you know how to connect to and configure an iSCSI volume using an iSCSI initiator.

iSCSI Initiator Applet

By using an iSCSI Initiator (located in the Administrative Tools and the Control Panel), you connect a storage array or volume of a storage array to a server and mount the array or volume as a local volume. An iSCSI initiator is the software component residing on a server or other computer that is installed and configured to connect to an iSCSI target. An iSCSI target is the actual storage array or volume.

When you open the iSCSI Initiator program, you see the following six tabs:

▶ **General:** Enables you to rename the initiator and configure the CHAP authentication and IPSec tunnel.

▶ **Discovery:** Specifies the location of the SAN and Internet Storage Name Service (iSNS) servers.

▶ **Targets:** Specifies to which storage devices the server has access and allows you to log on to those devices.

▶ **Favorite Targets:** Specifies which targets reconnect each time you start your computer.

▶ **Volumes and Devices:** Shows volumes and devices that are connected to the server.

▶ **RADIUS:** Specifies the RADIUS server to use for authentication.

Figure 3.1 shows the Discovery tab.

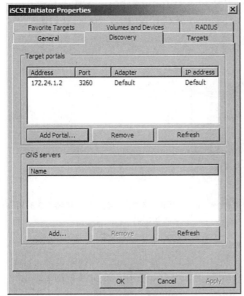

FIGURE 3.1 The iSCSI Initiator Properties dialog.

1. To connect to the iSCSI array, select the Discovery tab and click Add Portal.

2. In the Add Target Portal dialog box, provide the name or IP address of your iSCSI array. The default communication port for iSCSI traffic is 3260. If you have configured CHAP security or are using IPSec for communication between your client and the array, click Advanced and make necessary configuration changes.

3. Back in the Add Target Portal dialog box, click OK to make the initial connection to the iSCSI array.

4. To see the list of available targets (volumes to connect to and mount on the server), select the Targets tab.

5. To connect to an available target, choose the target and click Log On.

   ▶ If you want your server to connect to this volume automatically when your system boots, make sure you select Automatically Restore This Connection When The System Boots. If you do not, you need to reconnect it manually.

   ▶ To enable high availability and to boost performance, choose Enable Multi-Path. Of course, you would need to have multiple network adapters dedicated to the iSCSI connection to use multi-pathing (MPIO).

   ▶ If you are using CHAP or IPSec for communication with a target, click Advanced. After you are finished configuring the Log On options, click OK. The target status should change to Connected (see Figure 3.2).

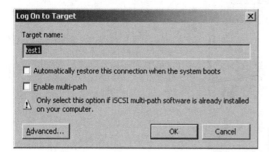

FIGURE 3.2 Log On to Target dialog box for iSCSI.

6. To bind the available iSCSI targets to the iSCSI startup process and assign them to a drive letter or mount point, select the Volumes and Devices tab. Click Add and specify the drive letter or mount point. Then Click OK.

If the iSCSI volume is a new volume that has not been mounted before, when you open the Disk Management console, it is treated as a new hard drive. At this point, you have to initialize the new drive, create a partition, and format the new volume.

iSCSICLI

iSCSICLI is a command-line tool suitable for scripting the Microsoft iSCSI initiator service. Although some of these commands may become lengthy and complex, this enables you to access all features of iSCSI. Some of the functions include:

   ▶ iscsicli AddTarget: Creates a connection to a volume or device

   ▶ iscsicli AddPersistentDevices: To make an iSCSI device persistent

- ▶ iscsicli RemovePersistentDevices: Prevents the reconnection to a specified volume

- ▶ iscsicli ClearPersistentDevices: Removes all volumes and devices from the list of persistent devices.

For more information, access the Microsoft iSCSI Software Initiator User's Guide from Microsoft:

http://www.microsoft.com/downloads/details.aspx?familyid=12CB3C1A-15D6-4585-B385-BEFD1319F825&displaylang=en

Storage Explorer

With Storage Explorer, you can view and manage the Fibre Channel and iSCSI fabrics that are available in your SAN. Storage Explorer can display detailed information about servers connected to the SAN, as well as components in the fabrics such as host bus adapters (HBA), Fibre Channel switches, and iSCSI initiators and targets (see Figure 3.3).

In addition, you can also perform many administrative tasks on an iSCSI fabric including logging onto the iSCSI targets, configuring iSCSI security, adding iSCSI target portals, adding iSNS servers, and managing Discovery Domains and Discovery Domain Sets.

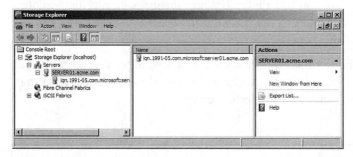

FIGURE 3.3 The Storage Explorer dialog.

Storage Manager for SANs

The *Storage Manager* for SANs, a Windows Server 2008 feature, can be used to create and manage logical unit numbers (LUN) on both Fibre Channel and iSCSI disk storage subsystems that support Virtual Disk Service (VDS).

For Fibre Channel SANs, when a server or cluster is identified, Storage Manager for SANs automatically discovers the available Fibre Channel HBA ports on that server or cluster. You can also add ports manually by typing their World Wide Name (WWN).

For iSCSI SANs, you only need to identify the server or cluster that will access the LUN, and Storage Manager for SANs automatically discovers the iSCSI initiators on that server or cluster and lists all the available adapters for those initiators. After the iSCSI initiator adapters have been discovered, you can select which adapters will be used for LUN traffic.

To add and configure a server with Fibre Channel connections, follow these steps:

1. In the console tree for Storage Manager for SANs, click LUN Management.

2. In the Actions pane, click Manage Server Connections.

3. In the Manage Server Connections dialog box, click Add.

4. In the Add Server dialog box, type the name or browse to the server that you want to add, and optionally, type a description for it.

5. Click OK. The server will now be listed in the Manage Server Connections dialog box, with all the ports that were automatically discovered on it listed on the Fibre Channel Ports tab.

6. If necessary, you can add a Fibre Channel manually by clicking Add on the Fibre Channel Ports tab and entering the WWN of the new port. Then click OK.

7. To enable Fibre Channel ports for LUN access, select a server from the server list. Then on the Fibre Channel Ports tab, select all the ports that you want to enable on the selected server.

NOTE

If you enable more than one Fibre Channel port and the server is not configured to use Multipath I/O, data corruption may occur.

8. Click OK when you have finished configuring the Fibre Channel connections.

Storage Manager for SANs includes the Provision Storage Wizard, which you can use to create a logical unit number (LUN) on a Fibre Channel or iSCSI disk storage subsystem. Before you create a LUN on a storage subsystem, verify that all the following requirements are fulfilled:

- The storage subsystem supports Virtual Disk Service (VDS).

- The VDS hardware provider for the storage subsystem is installed on your server.

- Storage space is available on the storage subsystem.

- If the server to which you will be assigning the LUN will access the LUN through more than one Fibre Channel port or iSCSI initiator, Multipath I/O has been installed and is running on that server.

To create a LUN, select LUN Management. In the Actions pane, click Create LUN. Then follow the steps in the Provision Storage Wizard pages.

If you create a LUN and do not choose to create a volume for it immediately by using the Provision Storage Wizard, the disk associated with that LUN is visible to the server to which you assign it, but it is offline. Before you can create a partition or volume on that disk, you must first use Disk Management or DiskPart to bring the disk online.

You can also use Storage Manager for SANs to assign a LUN to a server or cluster with the Assign LUN wizard. To start the Assign LUN wizard, click LUN Management in Storage Manager, and then select the LUN you want to assign in the Results pane. Then click Assign LUN in the Actions pane.

Disk Partitioning

When you prepare any drive or volume to be used by Windows Server 2008, you must first partition the disk and then format the disk. Partitioning is defining and dividing the physical or virtual disk into logical volumes called partitions. Each partition functions as if it were a separate disk drive.

Windows Server 2008 supports two types of disk partitioning styles:

- *Master Boot Record (MBR)*

- *GUID partition table (GPT)*

MBR disks have been used as standard equipment on IBM-compatible personal computers since the days of MS-DOS. MBR disks support volume sizes of up to two terabytes (TB) and allow up to four primary partitions per disk. Alternatively, MBR disks support three primary partitions, one extended partition, and an unlimited number of logical drive letters.

Windows Server 2008 includes support for global unique identifier—or GUID—Partition Table (GPT) disks in cluster storage. GPT disks were introduced with computers equipped with Intel Itanium-based processors and the Extensible Firmware Interface (EFI) as an alternative to a Basic Input/Output System (BIOS) as the interface between the computer's hardware devices, its firmware, and the operating system. GPT provides a more flexible mechanism for partitioning disks than the older MBR partitioning scheme that has been common to PCs. GPT disks support volume sizes up to 18 exabytes (EB) and can store up to 128 partitions on each disk. Eighteen exabytes are roughly equivalent to 18 billion gigabytes. Critical system files are stored on GPT partitions, and GPT disks store a duplicate set of partition tables to ensure that partitioning information is retained.

Disk Storage Management

Windows Server 2008 supports two types of hard disk storage: basic and dynamic. All disks begin as *basic disks* until a server administrator converts them to dynamic status, one physical disk at a time. The biggest advantage that *dynamic disks* offer when compared to basic disks is that you can create software-based fault-tolerant volumes via the operating system from the volumes stored on dynamic disks (*mirrored volumes*/RAID 1 and Striping with Parity/RAID-5) volumes. Of course, you can always implement a hardware RAID solution by using a RAID controller and the disks can retain their basic status, or they can be converted to dynamic status under Windows Server 2008.

Basic Disks

A basic disk under Windows Server 2008 is essentially the same as the disk configuration under earlier versions of Windows: It is a physical disk with primary and extended partitions. Prior to Windows 2000, Microsoft did not call disks *basic* because that was the only type of disk available. There were no dynamic disks. As long as you use the File Allocation Table (FAT or FAT32) file system, Windows Vista, Windows XP, Windows 2000, Windows NT, Windows 9x, and the MS-DOS operating systems can access basic disks. You can create up to three primary partitions and one extended partition on a basic disk of four primary partitions.

Management console and the Server Management console. You must be a member of the local Administrators group or the backup operators group, or else the proper authority must be delegated to you if you are working within an Active Directory environment to make any changes to the computer's disk management configuration.

For the conversion to succeed, any disks to be converted must contain at least 1MB of unallocated space. Disk Management automatically reserves this space when creating partitions or volumes on a disk, but disks with partitions or volumes created by other operating systems might not have this space available. (This space can exist even if it is not visible in Disk Management.) Windows Server 2008 requires this minimal amount of disk space to store the dynamic database, which the operating system that created it maintains. Before you convert any disks, close any programs that are running on those disks. After you convert a disk to dynamic, remember that you can have only one operating system that is bootable on each dynamic disk!

To convert a basic disk to a dynamic disk from the Disk Management console, follow these steps:

1. Open the Disk Management console.

2. Right-click the basic disk that you want to convert to a dynamic disk and click Convert to Dynamic Disk.

When you upgrade an empty basic disk to a dynamic disk, you do not need to reboot. However, if you convert a basic disk that already has partitions on it, or if the basic disk contains the system or boot partitions, you must restart your computer for the change to take effect.

NOTE

You can mount and dismount volumes from the command line with the `mountvol.exe` command. On basic disks, if you type **mountvol x: /p**, where x: represents the volume's drive letter, you can dismount a volume and take it offline. Unfortunately, the /p parameter is not supported on dynamic disks. The command `mountvol x: /l` displays the specified drive letter's volume ID. By using the syntax `mountvol x: volume_ID`, you can assign a drive letter to the volume and remount it to bring it back online. For example, the command `mountvol S: \\?\Volume{55e769f0-40d5-11d4-b223-806d6172696f}\` would assign drive letter S: to the volume ID specified. You can also use Disk Management to mount and dismount volumes from the GUI. You can mount and dismount volumes by right-clicking a volume and selecting Change Drive Letter and Paths. By removing the drive letter and any other paths (*mount points*) for the volume, you take the volume offline.

To convert a basic disk to a dynamic disk from the Windows Server 2008 command line:

1. Open a command prompt window, type **diskpart**, and press Enter.

2. Type **commands** or **help** to view a list of available commands.

3. Type **select disk 0** to select the first hard disk (**select disk 1** to select the second hard disk, and so on) and press Enter.

4. Type **convert dynamic** and press Enter.

5. Type **exit** to quit the diskpart.exe tool and then restart the computer to have the new configuration take effect.

When you convert a basic disk to a dynamic disk, any existing partitions on the basic disk become *simple volumes* on the dynamic disk. Any existing mirror sets, stripe sets, stripe sets with parity, or volume sets become mirrored volumes, *striped volumes*, dynamic *RAID-5 volumes*, or *spanned volumes*, respectively. After you convert a basic disk to a dynamic disk, you cannot change the volumes back to partitions. Instead, you must first delete all dynamic volumes on the disk, right-click the disk in Disk Management, and then select the Convert to Basic Disk option.

NOTE

Converting to a dynamic disk is a one-way process. Yes, you can convert a dynamic disk back to a basic disk, but you'll lose all your data. Obviously, this loss is a major consideration! If you find yourself needing to do it, first back up your data and then you can delete all the volumes on the disk, convert the disk to basic, and restore your data.

Because the conversion process from basic to dynamic is per physical disk, a disk has all dynamic volumes or all basic partitions; you won't see both on the same physical disk. Remember, you do not need to restart your computer when you upgrade from an empty basic to a dynamic disk from the Disk Management console. However, you do have to restart your computer if you use the diskpart.exe command-line tool for the conversion; if you convert a disk containing the system volume, boot volume, or a volume with an active paging file; or if the disk contains any existing volumes or partitions.

NOTE

When you upgrade or convert a basic disk to a dynamic disk, at least 1MB of free space must be available for the dynamic disk database. Under normal circumstances, this requirement should not be a problem.

Converting Dynamic Disks Back to Basic Disks

You must remove all volumes (and therefore all data) from a dynamic disk before you can change it back to a basic disk. After you convert a dynamic disk back to a basic disk, you can create only partitions and logical drives on that disk. After being converted from a basic disk, a dynamic disk can no longer contain partitions or logical drives, nor can older versions of Windows before Windows 2000 access the dynamic disk. To revert a dynamic disk to a basic disk, follow these steps:

1. Back up the data on the dynamic disk.

2. Open Disk Management.

3. Delete all the volumes on the disk.

4. Right-click the dynamic disk that you want to change back to a basic disk and then click Convert to Basic Disk.

5. Restore the data to the newly converted basic disk.

Converting Basic Disks to GPT Disks

You can change a disk from MBR to GPT partition style as long as the disk does not contain any partitions or volumes. You cannot use the GPT partition style on removable media, or on cluster disks that are connected to shared SCSI or Fibre Channel buses that are used by the Cluster service.

Take these steps to change a master boot record disk into a GUID partition table disk within the Windows interface:

1. Back up or move the data on the basic MBR disk you want to convert into a GPT disk.

2. If the disk contains any partitions or volumes, right-click any volumes on the disk and then click Delete Partition or Delete Volume.

3. Right-click the MBR disk that you want to change into a GPT disk and then click Convert to GPT Disk.

Take these steps to change a master boot record disk into a GUID partition table disk from a command line:

1. Back up or move the data on the basic MBR disk you want to convert into a GPT disk.

2. Open a command prompt and type **diskpart**. If the disk does not contain any partitions or volumes, skip to step 6.

3. At the diskpart prompt, type **list volume**. Make note of the volume number you want to delete.

4. At the diskpart prompt, type **select volume <*volumenumber*>**.

5. At the diskpart prompt, type **delete volume**.

6. At the diskpart prompt, type **list disk**. Make note of the disk number of the disk that you want to convert to a GPT disk.

7. At the diskpart prompt, type **select disk <*disknumber*>**.

8. At the diskpart prompt, type **convert gpt**.

Converting GPT Disks to Basic Disks

You can change a disk from GPT to MBR partition system as long as the disk is empty and contains no volumes. If it has data, you must back up your data and then delete all partitions or volumes before converting the disk.

To change a GUID partition table disk into a master boot record disk within the Windows interface, follow these steps:

1. Back up or move all volumes on the basic GPT disk you want to convert into a MBR disk.

2. If the disk contains any partitions or volumes, right-click any volumes on the disk and then click Delete Volume.

3. Right-click the GPT disk that you want to change into an MBR disk and then click Convert to MBR disk.

To change a GUID partition table disk into a master boot record disk using the command line, follow these steps:

1. Back up or move all volumes on the basic GPT disk you want to convert into a MBR disk.

2. Open a command prompt and type **diskpart**. If the disk does not contain any partitions or volumes, skip steps 3-5.

3. At the diskpart prompt, type **list volume**. Make note of the volume number you want to delete.

4. At the diskpart prompt, type **select volume <*volumenumber*>**.

5. At the diskpart prompt, type **delete volume**.

6. At the diskpart prompt, type **list disk**. Make note of the disk number of the disk that you want to convert to a GPT disk.

7. At the `diskpart` prompt, type **select disk** *<disknumber>*.

8. At the `diskpart` prompt, type **convert mbr**.

Moving Disks to Another Computer

To move disks to another computer, follow these steps:

1. Before you disconnect the disks, use Disk Management on the source computer and make sure that the status of all volumes on each of the disks is healthy. For any volumes that are not healthy, repair the volumes before you move the disks.

2. If the disks are dynamic, right-click each disk and select Remove Disk.

3. Power off the computer, remove the physical disks, and then install the physical disks on the target computer.

4. When you restart the target computer, the Found New Hardware dialog box should appear. If not, click Start, Control Panel, Add Hardware to launch the Add Hardware Wizard. Use the wizard to properly install the disks on the computer.

5. Open Disk Management on the target computer.

6. Click Action, Rescan Disks from the menu bar.

7. For any disks that are labeled Foreign, right-click them, click Import Foreign Disks, and then follow the instructions provided by the Disk Management console.

> **CAUTION**
>
> You can move dynamic disks only to Windows Server 2008, Windows Server 2003, Windows 2000, or Windows XP Professional computers.

Reactivating a Missing or Offline Disk

A dynamic disk can become "missing" or "offline" when it is somehow damaged, it suddenly loses power, or it has its data cable disconnected while still powered on. Unfortunately, you can reactivate only dynamic disks—not basic disks.

Follow these steps to reactivate a missing or offline dynamic disk:

1. Launch the Disk Management console.

2. Right-click the disk marked Missing or Offline and then select the Reactivate Disk option.

3. After the disk is reactivated, the disk should be labeled as "online."

4. Exit from the Disk Management MMC.

Basic Partitions

You can create primary partitions, extended partitions, and logical drives only on basic disks. Partitions and logical drives can reside only on basic disks. You can create up to four primary partitions on a basic disk or up to three primary partitions and one extended partition. You can use the free space in an extended partition to create multiple logical drives. You must be a member of the local Administrators group or the backup operators group, or else the proper authority must be delegated to you (if you are working within an Active Directory environment) to create, modify, or delete basic volumes.

> **NOTE**
>
> You can extend a basic partition with the `diskpart.exe` command-line utility, but it must be formatted as NTFS, it must be adjacent to contiguous unallocated space on the same physical disk, and it can be extended onto only unallocated space that resides on the same physical disk.

To create or delete a partition or logical drive, you can use the `diskpart.exe` command-line tool or the GUI and perform the following steps:

1. Open the Disk Management console.

2. Perform one of the following options:

   ▶ Right-click an unallocated region of a basic disk and click New Partition.

   ▶ Right-click an area of free space within an extended partition and click New Logical Drive.

   ▶ Right-click a partition or logical drive and select Delete Partition to remove that partition or logical drive. Click Yes to confirm the deletion.

3. When you choose to create a new partition or logical drive, the New Partition Wizard appears. Click Next to continue.

4. Click Primary Partition, Extended Partition, or Logical Drive and answer the prompts regarding disk space allocation and so on as requested by the wizard to finish the process.

You must first create an extended partition before you can create a new logical drive, if no extended partition exists already. If you choose to delete a partition, all data on the deleted partition or logical drive is lost. You cannot recover deleted partitions or logical drives. You cannot delete the system partition, boot partition, or any partition that contains an active paging file. The operating system uses one or more paging files on disk as virtual memory that can be swapped into and out of the computer's physical random access memory (RAM) as the system's load and volume of data dictate.

> **CAUTION**
>
> Windows Server 2008 requires that you delete all logical drives and any other partitions that have not been assigned a drive letter within an extended partition before you delete the extended partition itself.

Dynamic Volumes

With dynamic disks, you are no longer limited to four volumes per disk (as you are with basic disks). You can install Windows Server 2008 onto a dynamic volume; however, these volumes must contain the partition table (which means that these volumes must have been converted from basic to dynamic under Windows Server 2008, Windows Server 2003, Windows XP Professional, or Windows 2000). You cannot install Windows Server 2008 onto dynamic volumes that you created directly from unallocated space. Only computers running Windows XP Professional, the Windows 2000 family of operating systems, the Windows Server 2003 family of products, or the Windows Server 2008 can access dynamic volumes. The five types of dynamic volumes are

- ▶ Simple

- ▶ Spanned

- ▶ Mirrored

- ▶ Striped

- ▶ RAID-5

Windows Server 2008 supports all five dynamic volume types. You must be a member of the local Administrators group or the backup operators group, or you must have the proper permissions delegated to you (if you are working within an Active Directory environment) to create, modify, or delete dynamic volumes.

> **CAUTION**
>
> When you create dynamic volumes on dynamic disks using the Disk Management console, you only have the option of formatting new dynamic volumes with the NTFS file system. However, you can use the `format.exe` command at a command prompt window to format a dynamic volume using the FAT or FAT32 file system. For example, you can create a new dynamic volume using Disk Management; do not format the drive, and be sure to assign a drive letter to it. Then, at a command prompt, type **format x:** `/fs:fat32`, where `x:` represents the drive letter and `fat32` represents the file system that you want to format on the volume. You can alternatively specify `fat` or `ntfs` as the file system when you use the `format` command.

Simple Volumes

A simple volume consists of disk space on a single physical disk. It can consist of a single area on a disk or multiple areas on the same disk that are linked together. To create a simple volume, follow these steps:

1. Open Disk Management.

2. Right-click the unallocated space on the dynamic disk where you want to create the simple volume and then click New Volume.

3. Using the New Volume Wizard, click Next, click Simple, and then follow the instructions and answer the questions asked by the wizard.

Here are some guidelines about simple volumes:

▶ You can create simple volumes on dynamic disks only.

▶ Simple volumes are not fault tolerant.

▶ Simple volumes cannot contain partitions or logical drives.

▶ Neither MS-DOS nor Windows operating systems other than Windows Server 2008, Windows Server 2003, Windows XP Professional, and Windows 2000 can access simple volumes.

Spanned Volumes

A spanned volume consists of disk space from more than one physical disk. You can add more space to a spanned volume by extending it at any time. To create a spanned volume, follow these steps:

1. Open Disk Management.

2. Right-click the unallocated space on one of the dynamic disks where you want to create the spanned volume and then click New Volume.

3. Using the New Volume Wizard, click Next, click Spanned, and then follow the instructions and answer the questions asked by the wizard.

Here are some guidelines about spanned volumes:

▶ You can create spanned volumes on dynamic disks only.

▶ You need at least two dynamic disks to create a spanned volume.

▶ You can extend a spanned volume onto a maximum of 32 dynamic disks.

▶ Spanned volumes cannot be mirrored or striped.

▶ Spanned volumes are not fault tolerant.

Extending Simple or Spanned Volumes

Simple volumes are the most basic volumes on dynamic disks. If you extend a simple volume to another dynamic disk, it automatically becomes a spanned volume. You can extend a simple volume to make it a spanned volume, and you can also further extend a spanned volume to add disk storage capacity to the volume. You cannot extend a mirrored volume. Take these steps to extend a simple or a spanned volume:

1. Open Disk Management.

2. Right-click the simple or spanned volume you want to extend, click Extend Volume, and then follow the instructions and answer the questions asked by the Extend Volume Wizard.

You should be aware of the many rules about extending a simple or a spanned volume:

▶ You can extend a volume only if it contains no file system or if it is formatted using NTFS. You cannot extend volumes formatted using FAT or FAT32.

▶ After a volume is extended onto multiple disks (spanned), you cannot mirror the volume, nor can you make it into a striped volume or a RAID-5 volume.

▶ You cannot extend boot volumes, system volumes, striped volumes, mirrored volumes, or RAID-5 volumes.

▶ After a spanned volume is extended, no portion of it can be deleted without the entire spanned volume being deleted.

▶ You can extend a simple or a spanned volume only if the volume was created as a dynamic volume under Windows Server 2003 or Windows Server 2008. You cannot extend a simple or spanned volume that was originally converted from basic to dynamic under Windows 2000 or Windows XP Professional.

▶ You can extend simple and spanned volumes on dynamic disks onto a maximum of 32 dynamic disks.

▶ Spanned volumes write data to subsequent disks only as each disk volume fills up. Therefore, a spanned volume writes data to physical disk 0 until it fills up, then it writes to physical disk 1 until its available space is full, then it writes to physical disk 2, and so on. However, if just one disk fails as part of the spanned volume—all the data contained on that spanned volume is lost.

Striped Volumes

A striped volume stores data in stripes on two or more physical disks. Data in a striped volume is allocated alternately and evenly (in stripes) to the disks contained within the striped volume. Striped volumes can substantially improve the speed of access to the data on disk. Striped volumes are often referred to as RAID-0; this configuration tends to enhance performance, but it is not fault tolerant. To create a striped volume, follow these steps:

1. Open Disk Management.

2. Right-click unallocated space on one of the dynamic disks where you want to create the striped volume and select New Volume from the menu that appears.

3. Using the New Volume Wizard, click Next, select Striped, and follow the instructions and answer the questions asked by the wizard.

Here are some guidelines about striped volumes:

▶ You need at least two physical dynamic disks to create a striped volume.

▶ You can create a striped volume onto a maximum of 32 disks.

▶ Striped volumes are not fault tolerant.

- For increased volume capacity, select disks that contain similar amounts of available disk space. A striped volume's capacity is limited to the space available on the disk with the smallest amount of available space.

- Whenever possible, use disks that are the same model and from the same manufacturer.

- Striped volumes cannot be extended or mirrored. If you need to make a striped volume larger by adding another disk, you first have to delete the volume and then re-create it.

Mirrored Volumes and RAID-5 Volumes

You can create mirrored volumes and RAID-5 volumes only on dynamic disks running on Windows Server 2008, Windows Server 2003, or Windows 2000 Server computers. Both mirrored volumes and RAID-5 volumes are considered fault tolerant because these configurations can handle a single disk failure and still function normally. Mirrored volumes and RAID-5 volumes both require that an equal amount of disk space be available on each disk that will be a part of these volumes. A mirrored volume must use two physical disks—no more and no fewer than two physical hard disk drives. A RAID-5 volume must use at least three physical hard disks up to a maximum of 32 physical disks.

Many network administrators and consultants agree that hardware-based fault-tolerant solutions are more robust and reliable than software-based fault-tolerant configurations. By installing one or more RAID controller adapter cards into a server, you can set up several different types of hardware fault tolerance, such as mirroring, RAID-5, RAID 10 (mirrored volumes that are part of a striped array set), and RAID 0+1 (striped volumes that are part of a mirrored set). When you use hardware RAID, you can retain basic disks or you can convert disks to dynamic; hardware RAID is hidden to Windows Server 2008. Of course, it's less expensive to implement a software solution, such as setting up mirrored volumes or RAID-5 volumes using the Disk Management console in Windows Server 2008, but often the improved performance, reliability, and flexibility of hardware-based RAID far outweighs its extra cost.

Working with Mirrored Volumes

A mirrored volume uses volumes stored on two separate physical disks to "mirror" (write) the data onto both disks simultaneously and redundantly. This configuration is also referred to as RAID-1. If one of the disks in the mirrored configuration fails, Windows Server 2008 writes an event into the system log of the Event Viewer. The system functions normally (unless the second disk fails) until the failed disk is replaced and then the volume can be mirrored again. Mirrored volumes cost you 50% of your available storage space because of the built-in redundancy. If you mirror two 70GB disks, you are left with just 70GB of space rather than 140GB.

You can make mirrored volumes more robust by installing a separate hard disk controller for each disk; technically, this is known as disk duplexing. Disk duplexing is better than disk mirroring because you alleviate the single point of failure by having one controller for each disk. Under Windows Server 2008, disk duplexing is still referred to as disk mirroring. You can create mirrored volumes only by using dynamic disks. To create a new empty mirrored volume from unallocated space, follow these steps:

1. Open Disk Management.

2. Right-click an area of unallocated space on a dynamic disk and select New Volume.

3. Click Next for the New Volume Wizard welcome window.

4. Click Mirrored as the volume type option and click Next.

5. Select one of the available dynamic disks and click Add.

6. Enter the amount of storage space to be used (in MB) for this mirrored volume, up to the maximum available space on the first disk that you selected, and then click Next.

7. Assign the new volume a drive letter, mount the volume in an empty NTFS folder, or choose not to assign the volume a drive letter or path and click Next.

8. Choose whether to format the new mirrored volume. If you choose to format the new volume, specify the following settings:

   ▶ File system (NTFS is the only option for dynamic volumes under the Disk Management console)

   ▶ Allocation unit size

   ▶ Volume label

   ▶ Mark the check box to Perform a Quick Format (if desired)

   ▶ Mark the check box to Enable File and Folder Compression (if desired)

9. Click Next to continue.

10. Click Finish to complete the New Volume Wizard.

To create a mirrored volume from a boot or system volume, or to create a mirrored volume from an existing volume that already contains data, follow these steps:

1. Open Disk Management.

2. Right-click an existing dynamic volume and select Add Mirror.

3. Select one of the available dynamic disks on which to create the redundant volume and click Add Mirror.

You should be aware of some important issues and guidelines before you attempt to mirror system or boot volumes:

▶ When you mirror volumes stored on ATA disks, you must change the jumper switch on the nonfailed drive to the master position (on restart) if the master disk on the primary IDE channel fails, until you replace the failed disk.

▶ Microsoft does not recommend mirroring the system volume using one ATA disk and one SCSI disk because the system can encounter startup problems if one of the drives fails.

▶ If you plan to use separate SCSI controllers for each SCSI disk that you will mirror, you should use identical controllers from the same manufacturer.

▶ For a mirrored system volume, be sure to run a test to simulate a disk failure and attempt to start the system from the remaining mirrored volume. Perform this test regularly as part of your backup routine before a real failure occurs.

You can stop mirroring a volume by either breaking or removing the mirror. When you break a mirrored volume, each volume that makes up the mirror becomes an independent simple volume, and they are no longer fault tolerant. When you remove a mirrored volume, the removed mirrored volume becomes unallocated space on its disk, whereas the remaining mirrored volume becomes a simple volume that is no longer fault tolerant. All data that was stored on the removed mirrored volume is erased. To break a mirrored volume, take these steps:

1. Open Disk Management.

2. Right-click one of the mirrored volumes that you want to break and select Break Mirrored Volume.

3. Click Yes in the Break Mirrored Volume message box.

If you want to completely destroy one of the mirrored volumes and leave just one of the volumes intact, you need to perform a removal procedure instead of simply breaking the mirrored volumes. Take these steps to remove a mirrored volume:

1. Open Disk Management.

2. Right-click a mirrored volume and then select Remove Mirror.

3. At the Remove Mirror dialog box, select the disk from which you want to completely erase the mirrored volume and turn the volume into unallocated space. The remaining volume stays with all its data intact as a simple volume.

4. Click the Remove Mirror button.

5. Click Yes to confirm the removal action at the Disk Management message box that appears.

Working with RAID-5 Volumes

Windows Server 2008 supports disk striping with parity (RAID-5) volumes with the Disk Management console and through the `diskpart.exe` command-line utility. You need a minimum of three physical disks to create a RAID-5 volume. You are limited to a maximum of 32 physical disks in creating a RAID-5 volume under Windows Server 2008. In creating a fault-tolerant volume using a RAID-5 configuration, you effectively lose an amount of storage equivalent to the capacity of one of the disks because parity information gets stored across all the disks (disk striping with parity). For example, if you use three 70GB disks, your RAID-5 volume can store up to approximately 140GB of data. The remaining 70GB is used for storing the important parity data across all three disks in case of a failure—a 33% loss of available storage capacity. However, as you add disks to a RAID-5 volume, the percentage of lost storage space diminishes. For example, if you use five 70GB disks, you would again lose 70GB of available storage capacity, but that accounts only for a 20% overall loss in capacity (70GB divided by 350GB total available disk space equals .20, or 20%). In the event that one disk within the RAID-5 volume fails, the remaining disks can re-create the data stored on the failed disk as soon as a new disk is installed to replace the failed disk. To create a RAID-5 volume using Disk Management, follow these steps:

1. Open Disk Management. Be sure that the computer has three or more dynamic disks—each with unallocated space.

2. Right-click an area of unallocated space on one of the dynamic disks that you want to use for the RAID-5 volume and select New Volume.

3. Click Next for the Welcome to the New Volume Wizard window.

4. Select the RAID-5 option button and click Next.

5. Select each available disk that you want to use as part of the RAID-5 volume from within the Available list box and click Add for each one. You must select at least 3 disks and no more than 32 disks.

6. Select any disks that you do not want to use as part of the RAID-5 volume within the Selected list box, and click Remove to remove any disks that you do not want to include as a part of the RAID-5 volume.

7. Enter the storage capacity that you want for the RAID-5 volume in the Select the Amount of Space in MB spin box and click Next to continue.

8. Choose to assign the volume a drive letter, mount the volume in an empty NTFS folder, or choose to not assign a drive letter or path to the new RAID-5 volume and click Next.

9. Choose whether to format the new RAID-5 volume. If you choose to format the new volume, specify the following settings:

   ▶ File system (NTFS is the only option for dynamic volumes under the Disk Management console).

   ▶ Allocation unit size.

   ▶ Volume label.

   ▶ Mark the check box to Perform a Quick Format (if desired).

   ▶ Mark the check box to Enable File and Folder Compression (if desired).

10. Click Next to continue.

11. Click Finish to complete the New Volume Wizard.

If one disk within a RAID-5 volume is intermittently failing, you can attempt to reactivate it by right-clicking the disk and selecting Reactivate Disk. If one disk within a RAID-5 volume appears to be permanently failed, you can replace that failed disk with another dynamic disk attached to the computer or you can install a new disk. To regenerate the RAID-5 volume, right-click the RAID-5 volume on the failed disk and select Repair Volume. The replacement disk must contain at least as much unallocated space as that used by the failed disk for the RAID-5 volume.

Mount Points

When you prepare a volume in Windows Server 2008, you can assign a drive letter to the new volume or you can create a mount point with the new volume as an empty NTFS folder. By using volume mount points, you can graft, or mount, a target partition into a folder on another drive. The mounting is handled transparently to the user and applications. With the NTFS volume mount points feature, you can surpass the 26-drive-letter limitation.

To assign a mount-point folder path to a drive by using the Windows interface, follow these steps:

1. In Disk Manager, right-click the partition or volume where you want to assign the mount-point folder path, and then click Change Drive Letter and Paths.

2. To assign a mount-point folder path, click Add. Click Mount in the following empty NTFS folder, type the path to an empty folder on an NTFS volume, or click Browse to locate it (see Figure 3.4).

To remove the mount-point folder path, click it and then click Remove.

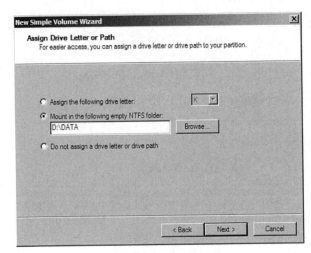

FIGURE 3.4 Mounting a volume to an NTFS folder.

Exam Prep Questions

1. You have a new Windows Server 2008 computer with multiple hard drives. You want to implement RAID1 on the server. What do you need to first?

   ○ **A.** Enable write catching on the first disk.

   ○ **B.** Enable write catching on the second disk.

   ○ **C.** Convert the basic disk to dynamic disks.

   ○ **D.** Convert the dynamic disk to basic disks.

2. You have a Windows Server 2008 computer with two hard drives. What type of RAID can you implement to provide fault tolerance?

   ○ **A.** RAID 0

   ○ **B.** RAID 1

   ○ **C.** RAID 5

   ○ **D.** RAID 1 and 5

3. Which of the following types of fault-tolerant (RAID) configurations (without using a RAID controller or third-party software) can you set up, using either Disk Management or the `diskpart.exe` command-line tool under Windows Server 2008? (Choose three.)

   ○ **A.** RAID 0

   ○ **B.** RAID 2

   ○ **C.** RAID 5

   ○ **D.** RAID 1

   ○ **E.** RAID 0+1

   ○ **F.** RAID 10

4. On which of the following hard-disk configurations can you install a fresh copy of Windows Server 2008? (Choose two.)

   ○ **A.** On a basic partition

   ○ **B.** On a dynamic volume that was created from unallocated space

   ○ **C.** On a dynamic volume that was upgraded from a basic volume

   ○ **D.** On a basic volume that is part of a removable disk

   ○ **E.** On a dynamic disk that already has Windows XP Professional installed on it

5. You have a Windows Server 2008 computer with three hard drives installed. After Windows has been installed, each disk has at least 12GB of available disk space. What can you do to provide fault tolerance data system while maximizing disk space?

   ○ **A.** Create a striped volume on the second and third disk.

   ○ **B.** Create a striped volume on all three disks.

   ○ **C.** Create a striped volume using the second and third disk.

   ○ **D.** Create a striped volume with parity using all three hard drives.

6. You have a Windows Server 2008 computer. You want to provide fault tolerance for the volume containing the operating system. Each disk is configured as a basic disk. The operating system is installed on the first disk. What should you do?

   ○ **A.** Configure a new mirrored volume using disk 0 and 1.

   ○ **B.** Convert disk 0 to a dynamic disk. Configure a new mirrored volume using disk 0 and 1.

   ○ **C.** Convert disk 1 to a dynamic disk. Configure a new mirrored volume using disk 0 and 1.

   ○ **D.** Convert disk 0 and disk 1 to dynamic disks. Configure the two disks as a striped set using disk 0 and 1.

   ○ **E.** Convert disk 0 and disk 1 to dynamic disks. Configure the two disks as a mirrored volume.

7. How many primary partitions without an extended partition can reside on a basic MBR disk under Windows Server 2003?

   ○ **A.** 3

   ○ **B.** 4

   ○ **C.** 1

   ○ **D.** 128

8. Which of the following statements are true about basic disks under Windows Server 2008? (Choose two.)

   ○ **A.** Basic disks are not supported under Windows Server 2008.

   ○ **B.** Basic disks that were configured as one disk striping with parity set under Windows NT Server 4.0 are mounted automatically after the server is upgraded to Windows Server 2003.

   ○ **C.** Basic disks can be formatted only as FAT or FAT32.

   ○ **D.** You cannot convert dynamic disks back to basic disks without deleting all data and volumes on the disks first.

   ○ **E.** IEEE 1394 disks can only be basic disks.

9. You have a Windows Server 2008 computer. What command do you use to convert a basic disk to a dynamic disk?

   ○ **A.** `diskpart basic to dynamic`

   ○ **B.** `diskpart convert dynamic`

   ○ **C.** `format c: /fs:dynamic`

   ○ **D.** `convert c: /fs:dynamic`

10. What command would you use to make an iSCSI volume connect every time you boot your system?

    ○ **A.** `iscsicli AddTarget`

    ○ **B.** `iscsicli AddPersistentDevices`

    ○ **C.** `iscsicli RemovePersistentDevices`

    ○ **D.** `iscsicli ClearPersistentDevices`

11. What command would you use to remove all iSCSI volumes so that they do not connect when you boot your system?

    ○ **A.** `iscsicli AddTarget`

    ○ **B.** `iscsicli AddPersistentDevices`

    ○ **C.** `iscsicli RemovePersistentDevices`

    ○ **D.** `iscsicli ClearPersistentDevices`

12. What command would you use to change a master boot record disk into a GUID partition table disk?

    ○ **A.** `fdisk`

    ○ **B.** `format`

    ○ **C.** `diskpart`

    ○ **D.** `convert`

13. What is the default port used by iSCSI?

    ○ **A.** TCP port 389

    ○ **B.** TCP port 443

    ○ **C.** TCP port 1433

    ○ **D.** TCP port 3260

14. You have the following address:

iqn.2534-05.com.microsoft:storage.tape.sys2.123

What type of address is this?

- ○ **A.** MAC Address
- ○ **B.** IP Address
- ○ **C.** iSCSI Qualified Name
- ○ **D.** Extended Unique Identifier

Answers to Exam Prep Questions

1. Answer C is correct. RAID 1 (disk mirroring) needs two disks to be implemented. Before you can enable RAID 1 using Windows Server 2008, you need to convert basic disks to dynamic disks, which converts the partitions into volumes. Answers A and B are incorrect because write catching improves disk performance but does not help implement RAID 1. Answer D is incorrect because to implement RAID 1 using Windows Server 2008, you must use dynamic disks.

2. Answer B is correct. RAID 1, disk mirroring, uses two disks to provide fault tolerance. In RAID 1, whatever is written to one disk is written to the other. Answer A is incorrect because RAID 0, disk striping, does enhance performance, but does not provide fault tolerance. Answers C and D are incorrect because RAID 5 (disk striping with parity) needs three disks to be implemented.

3. Answers A, C, and D are correct. Windows Server 2003 supports disk striping (RAID 0), disk striping with parity (RAID 5), and disk mirroring (RAID 1). Answer B is incorrect because Windows Server 2008 does not natively support hammering code error-correcting code (ECC) disk configurations (RAID 2). Answer E is incorrect because Windows Server 2008 does not natively support striped volumes that are part of a mirrored set (RAID 0+1). Answer F is incorrect because Windows Server 2008 does not natively support mirrored volumes that are part of a striped array set (RAID 10).

4. Answers A and C are correct. You can install a fresh copy of Windows Server 2008 onto a basic partition and onto a dynamic volume if the volume was originally a basic partition that was upgraded to dynamic because Windows Server 2008 can be installed only on a disk that contains a partition table. Answer B is incorrect because a dynamic volume that was created from unallocated space does not contain a partition table. Answer D is incorrect because Windows Server 2008 Setup does not support installation onto removable media such as USB disks or IEEE 1394 (FireWire) disks. Answer E is incorrect because you can install only one operating system per dynamic disk.

5. Answer D is correct. Of these four options, only striped volume with parity is fault tolerant. If one hard drive fails, the data will still be accessible. Answers A, B, and C are incorrect because although striped volumes do provide better performance, they do not provide fault tolerance. If one disk fails, you loose all data.

6. Answer E is correct. To use RAID provided by Windows Server 2008, you must use dynamic disks. To provide fault tolerance, you create a mirrored set using disk 0 and 1. Answers A, B, and C are incorrect because a basic disk cannot be used for mirror or RAID 5 disks. Answer D is incorrect because the striped set is not fault tolerant.

7. Answer B is correct. You can create up to four primary partitions on a basic disk without an extended partition. Answer A is incorrect because you are limited to three primary partitions only if there is an extended partition on the disk. Answer C is incorrect because you can have more than one primary partition on a basic disk. Answer D is incorrect because you are limited to a maximum of four primary partitions on a basic MBR disk; a basic GPT disk can host up to 128 partitions.

8. Answers D and E are correct. To convert dynamic disks back to basic disks, you must remove all volumes on the disk, which means that all data must be removed as well. IEEE 1394 (or FireWire) disks cannot be converted to dynamic; therefore, they can only be basic disks. Answer A is incorrect because basic disks are supported under Windows Server 2008. Answer B is incorrect because basic disk sets that were created under previous versions of Microsoft server products are not mounted by the operating system; you must use the `ftonline.exe` tool on the setup CD-ROM. Answer C is incorrect because basic disks (and dynamic disks) can be formatted as FAT, FAT32, or NTFS.

9. Answer B is correct. The command to use to convert a basic disk to a dynamic disk is `diskpart convert dynamic`. Answer A is incorrect because the command is `diskpart convert dynamic`. Answers C and D are incorrect because the `format` and `convert` commands cannot be used to convert basic to dynamic disks.

10. Answer B is correct. The `iscsicli AddPersistentDevices` command makes an iSCSI device persistent so that it connects every time the system boots. Answer A is incorrect because `iscsicli AddTarget` only creates a connection to a volume or device. If you reboot your system, it does not automatically connect. Answers C and D are incorrect because the `iscsicli RemovePersistentDevices` command prevents the reconnection to a specified volume, and the `iscsicli ClearPersistentDevices` command removes all volumes and devices from the list of persistent devices.

11. Answer D is correct. The `iscsicli RemovePersistentDevices` command prevents reconnection to a specified volume. Answer A is incorrect because `iscsicli AddTarget` only creates a connection to a volume or device. If you reboot your system, it does not automatically connect. Answer B is incorrect because the `iscsicli AddPersistentDevices` command makes an iSCSI device persistent so that it connects every time the system boots. Answer C is incorrect because the `iscsicli RemovePersistentDevices` command prevents the reconnection to a specified volume, not all volumes.

12. Answer C is correct. The `diskpart` command is a powerful disk management tool that can convert an MBR disk to a GUID partition table disk. Answer A is incorrect because `fdisk` is a partitioning tool used in older operating systems. Answer B is incorrect because the `format` command is used to format a disk, which would define FAT32 or NTFS. Answer D is incorrect because the `convert` command could be used to convert a FAT32 volume to a NTFS volume.

13. Answer D is correct. The default port for iSCSI is 3260. Answer A is incorrect because TCP port 389 is used by Lightweight Directory Access Protocol (LDAP). Answer B is incorrect because TCP port 443 is used by SSL. Answer C is incorrect because TCP port 1433 is used by SQL servers.

14. Answer C is correct. The address is an example of the iSCSI Qualified Name, which is the most commonly used iSCSI address. Answer A is incorrect because the MAC addresses used to identify network cards are 48-bits/12 hexadecimal numbers. Answer B is incorrect because an IPv4 address is a 32-bit address consisting of four 8-bit octets, each octet ranging from 0-255. Answer D is incorrect because the Extended Unique Identifier is another addressing scheme used by iSCSI, which is provided by the IEEE Registration authority in accordance with EUI-64 standard (EUI is short for extended unique identifier).

Need to Know More?

For more information about storage technologies, including NTFS and FAT file systems and Basic and Dynamic Disks, visit the following website:

http://technet2.microsoft.com/windowsserver/en/library/57282c22-30e9-4d52-9c6d-2d2db8c56adc1033.mspx?mfr=true

For more information about the `diskpart.exe` command, visit the following websites:

http://support.microsoft.com/kb/300415

http://technet2.microsoft.com/WindowsServer/en/Library/ca099518-dde5-4eac-a1f1-38eff6e3e5091033.mspx?mfr=true

For more information about iSCSI, including links to the iSCSI Software Initiator, visit the following website:

http://www.microsoft.com/windowsserver2003/technologies/storage/iscsi/default.mspx

CHAPTER FOUR

Web Services Infrastructure and Security

Terms you'll need to understand:

- ✓ Internet Information Services (IIS)
- ✓ ASP.NET
- ✓ .NET Framework
- ✓ IIS Manager
- ✓ virtual directory
- ✓ web application
- ✓ application pool
- ✓ default document
- ✓ Internet Server Application Programming Interface (ISAPI) filters
- ✓ Common Gateway Interface (CGI)
- ✓ xcopy command
- ✓ Secure Socket Layer (SSL)
- ✓ digital certificate
- ✓ Certificate Authority (CA)
- ✓ Simple Mail Transfer Protocol (SMTP)
- ✓ File Transfer Protocol (FTP)

Techniques/concepts you'll need to master:

- ✓ Create and manage websites with IIS Manager and the cmdapp.exe command.
- ✓ Add and create virtual directories in websites.
- ✓ Create and configure FTP sites.
- ✓ Add and configure SMTP on a web server.
- ✓ Back up IIS configuration and website content.
- ✓ Enable IIS websites to use digital certificates and SSL.
- ✓ Configure website authentication and permissions.

A web server is a computer that is equipped with the server software that uses Internet protocols such as Hypertext Transfer Protocol (HTTP) and File Transfer Protocol (FTP) to respond to web client requests on a TCP/IP network via web browsers. One server can service a large number of clients.

Typically, when accessing a web page you specify the web page location by using a uniform resource locator (URL). The first part of the address indicates what protocol to use; the second part specifies the IP address or the domain name where the resource is located; and the last part indicates the folder and filename. Examples of URLs would include

ftp://acme.com/files/run.exe

http://www.acme.com/index.html

Internet Information Services (IIS) is the built-in web server to Windows servers that enables you to share information with users on the Internet, an intranet, or an extranet. Although it provides the commonly used HTTP/HTTPS, FTP, and SMTP services, it also integrates ASP.NET, Windows Communication Foundation, and Windows SharePoint Services. Windows Server 2003 used IIS 6.0 while Windows Server 2008 uses IIS 7.0.

Internet Information Services 7.0 (IIS 7.0) provides a modular architecture with more than 40 feature modules that can be independently installed. This allows for greater extensibility and security so that you can enable only the modules that you need, which also reduces the server's attack surface.

> **NOTE**
>
> After Internet Information Services has been installed and you want to install additional IIS modules, open Server Manager and click Add Roles.

Web Pages

Initially, web pages are written using the Hypertext Markup Language (HTML). The web browser (such as Internet Explorer) is the client program/software that you run on a user's local machine to gain access to a web server. It receives the HTML commands, interprets the HTML, and displays the results. HTTP is called a stateless protocol because each command is executed independently, without any knowledge of the commands that came before it.

For the most part, HTML creates static and unanimated documents. After a web page is loaded into a browser window, it does not change in content or form without being reloaded. Therefore, web pages have evolved by allowing HTML to include Active Server Page (ASP) and ActiveX controls.

Active Server Pages (ASP) is Microsoft's server-side script engine that generates dynamic web pages. To simplify some of the programming of ASP websites, the ASP engineers have included various built-in objects, including Application, ASPError, Request, Response, Server, and Session. Session objects are based on cookies so that they can maintain variables from page to page, including a visitor's name or a visitor's selection on a web page. Most ASP pages are written in VBScript, but any other Active Scripting engine can be selected, including Jscript and PerlScript.

The successor to ASP is *ASP.NET*, which is a Microsoft *web application* framework used to build dynamic websites, web applications, and XML web services. It is part of Microsoft's .NET platform, which is built on the Common Language Runtime, allowing programmers to write ASP.NET code in any Microsoft .NET language.

The Microsoft .*NET Framework* is a software component that is a part of modern Microsoft Windows operating systems. It is included with Windows Server 2003, Windows Server 2008, and Windows Vista, and can be installed on most older versions of Windows, including Windows XP. The .NET Framework provides a large body of precoded solutions to common program requirements, and manages the execution of programs written specifically for the framework, much as Windows APIs provide an interface for programmers to give a program the same Microsoft Windows look and feel. Since the original release of Microsoft .NET Framework (1.0), 1.1, 2.0, 3.0, and 3.5 had all been released by the time Windows Server 2008 was released.

IIS Manager 7.0

To configure IIS, you will be using the *IIS Manager* console. Different from IIS 6.0, IIS 7.0 has a completely redesigned user interface that allows the following:

- ▶ Integrates the configuration of settings across IIS configuration files, ASP.NET configuration files, and .NET configuration files into one place.

- ▶ Incorporates an interface to install and remove IIS features.

- ▶ Controls delegation of features to nonadministrator users.

- ▶ Provides a remote administration service so that you can administer IIS remotely.

- ▶ Allows new functionality to be added or extended automatically.

Much like other roles found in Windows Server 2008, IIS Manager (see Figure 4.1) incorporates wizards that walk administrators through common tasks. Lastly, IIS 7.0 empowers you to more easily diagnose and troubleshoot problems on the web server.

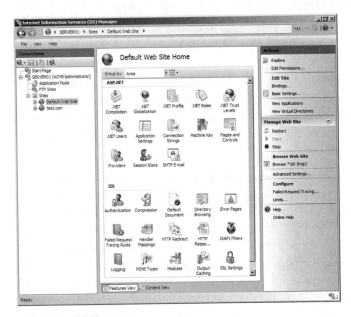

FIGURE 4.1 IIS Manager.

To open IIS Manager from the Start menu:

1. Click Start, All Programs.

2. Click Administrative Tools, Internet Information Services (IIS) Manager.

You can also execute the `inetmgr` command at a command prompt or use the run option to start the IIS Manager console.

Using the Configuration Store

The configuration of IIS 7.0 is stored in the Configuration Store, which is made of XML files. Three primary files control the operation of IIS:

▶ `Machine.config`, located in the %windir%\Microsoft.NET\ Framework\v2.0.50727\config folder, contains the .NET settings for the entire server. In Windows Vista and Windows Server 2008 this file contains all the global settings for .NET-related components and features on that server. The settings in this file are inherited by all other .NET configuration files, including IIS 7.0 configuration files.

▶ `ApplicationHost.config` contains settings for IIS and other services that have settings in common with IIS. There is one `ApplicationHost.config` file for each server. The default location for `ApplicationHost.config` is the folder systemroot\system32\inetsrv. It inherits settings from `machine.config`.

▶ The next file in the hierarchy is the root `web.config` file. The root-level `web.config` file is found in the folder %windir%\Microsoft.NET\ Framework\versionNumber\CONFIG. This file exists for each version of the .NET Framework that is present on the server. The root `web.config` file contains settings for individual websites, web applications, virtual directories, and physical directories that are inherited by all ASP.NET applications that run a specific version of the .NET Framework. This enables you to have more than one version of the .NET Framework running on the same server.

The `ApplicationHost.config` file is the root file of the IIS 7.0 configuration system. When a website is created, a site entry is created in the `ApplicationHost.config` file that specifies the definitions of all sites, applications, virtual directories, and *application pools*, as well as the global defaults for the web server settings. The `ApplicationHost.config` file is divided into two parts:

▶ The system.applicationHost group of settings contains all the settings for the application service, including security settings, HTTP compression, and logging for websites. It also contains web applications, application pools, and virtual and physical directories and files.

▶ The system.webServer group of settings contains all the settings for the web server, such as the list of modules and ISAPI filters, ASP, CGI, and others. These settings can be set in `applicationHost.config`, as well as any `web.config` file (provided the OverrideMode settings are set to `allow`).

Each application on the server has its own `web.config` file, which contains ASP.NET application elements that can be set using IIS configuration tools. The application-level `web.config` file applies configuration settings to the directory in which it resides, as well as to all child folders.

Settings in child folders can override or modify settings specified in the `web.config` file in the parent directory, unless the settings are locked at the parent `web.config` level. For example, a `web.config` file may set a particular setting to be `true` at the site level but then in application number three the setting is set to `false`. With this configuration, applications one and two have the setting set to `true`, and application three has it set to `false`. This is how the merging of configuration settings in the configuration hierarchy works.

Using the Connections Pane and Toolbar

The Connections pane (left pane) and toolbar enable you to connect to web servers, sites, and applications. When you connect to a web server, site, or application from the Connections pane, the tree loads the connection along with any children of the parent connection.

The connections toolbar includes the following buttons:

- **Create New Connection:** Starts the connection wizard to connect to a web server, a site, or an application.

- **Save Current Connections:** Saves the connection information for the current list of connections in the tree.

- **Up:** Goes up one level in the hierarchy.

- **Delete Connection:** Removes the selected connection in the tree. If you click this button when you are on a node other than the connection node, such as a physical folder, the parent connection is removed from the list.

Starting or Stopping the Web Server

From time to time, you may need to stop IIS so that you can upgrade a software package or website, or you may need to restart IIS for certain changes to take effect. To stop the web server, you must stop the Windows Process Activation Service (WAS) and the World Wide Web Publishing Service (W3SVC). When you stop WAS and W3SVC, all sessions connected to your web server are dropped and any in-memory session state is lost. All sites are unavailable until these services are restarted. Of course, you should avoid stopping and restarting your web server if you can, especially during heavy usage.

To start or stop a web server, you need to be a server administrator. You then follow these steps:

1. Open IIS Manager and navigate to the web server node in the tree.

2. In the Actions pane, click Start if you want to start the web server or Stop if you want to stop the web server.

You can also start or stop a web server at the command prompt:

1. Open an elevated command-line window.

2. At the command prompt, type **net stop WAS** and press Enter; type **Y** and then press Enter to also stop W3SVC.

3. To restart the web server, type **net start W3SVC** and press Enter to start both WAS and W3SVC.

You can also stop, start, or restart individual sites by right-clicking the site, selecting Manage Web Site, and selecting Stop, Start, or Restart.

Creating Websites

When IIS is installed, the server will have only a default website. If you want to create additional websites, you need to do the following:

1. Open IIS Manager.

2. In the Connections pane, right-click the Sites node in the tree and then click Add Web Site.

3. In the Add Web Site dialog box, type a friendly name for your website in the Web Site Name box.

4. Click Select if you want to select a different application pool than the one listed in the Application Pool box. In the Select Application Pool dialog box, select an application pool from the Application Pool list and then click OK.

5. By default, the default website is created in the \Inetpub\Wwwroot directory on the web server. In the Physical Path box, type the physical path of the website's folder, or click Browse to navigate the file system to find the folder. If the physical path that you entered is to a remote share, click Connect to specify credentials that have permission to access the path. If you do not use specific credentials, select the Application User (Pass-Thru Authentication) option in the Connect As dialog box.

6. Select the protocol for the website from the Type list.

7. The default value in the IP address box is All Unassigned. If you must specify a static IP address for the website, type the IP address in the IP Address box.

8. Type a port number in the Port text box.

EXAM ALERT

The default http port is 80 and the default https port is 443.

9. Optionally, type a host header name for the website in the Host Header box.

10. If you do not have to make any changes to the site, and you want the website to be immediately available, select the Start Web Site Immediately check box.

11. Click OK.

Bindings specify the IP addresses, ports, and host headers assigned to a website. You can assign multiple IP addresses, ports, and host headers to a website. To edit, add, or delete a binding, right-click the site and select Edit Bindings.

EXAM ALERT

The binding specifies what IP address, port, and host header are assigned to a website.

If you want the server to host multiple websites, you can assign multiple IP addresses to the network card and then specify individual IP addresses to each website. Another method is to use host header names, where you would assign the same IP address to each website and specify separate host header names to each website. Of course, the host header name must be correctly resolved to the IP address used by the websites.

NOTE

If you are using headers and you want a website to respond to www.acme.com and acme.com, you have to create two header entries.

Adding a Virtual Directory

A *virtual directory* is a directory name used in a website that corresponds to a physical directory on the server. This enables you to include directory content in a site or an application without having to move the content physically into that site or application directory. It also enables you to reuse the same folder for multiple sites.

To add a virtual directory, follow these steps:

1. Open IIS Manager.

2. In the Connections pane, expand the Sites node in the tree, and then click to select the site in which you want to create a virtual directory.

3. In the Actions pane, click View Virtual Directories.

4. On the Virtual Directories page, in the Actions pane, click Add Virtual Directory.

5. In the Add Virtual Directory dialog box, type a name in the Alias box. This alias is used to access the content from a URL.

6. In the Physical path box, type the physical path of the content folder, or click Browse to navigate through the file system to find the folder.

7. Optionally, click Connect to specify credentials that have permission to access the physical path. If you do not use specific credentials, select the Application User (Pass-Thru Authentication) option in the Connect As dialog box.

8. Optionally, click Test Settings to verify the settings that you specified for the virtual directory.

9. Click OK.

Using Applications and Application Pools

An application is a grouping of content, defined either at the root level of a website or in a separate folder under the website's root directory, which defines specific properties such as the application pool in which the application runs. Each site must have at least one application named the root application, or default application.

An application pool defines a set of resources (a worker process or a set of worker processes) used by a website or application that sets boundaries for the applications contained and prevents applications in one application pool from affecting applications running in other application pools. As a result, you have improved server and application performance, improved application availability, and improved security. If a website or application crashes or has a memory leak that consumes all the available memory, it doesn't affect the other sites and applications in other application pools.

In IIS 7.0, application pools run in one of two modes: integrated mode and classic mode. If a managed application runs in an application pool with integrated mode, the server uses the integrated, request-processing pipelines of IIS and ASP.NET to process the request. However, if a managed application runs in an application pool with classic mode, the server continues to route requests for managed code through `Aspnet_isapi.dll`, processing requests the same as if the application was running in IIS 6.0. You would want to use classic mode only when you have an application that does not run in integrated mode.

Creating Applications and Application Pools

To add an application, follow these steps:

1. Open IIS Manager.

2. In the Connections pane, expand the Sites node.

3. Right-click the site for which you want to create an application, and click Add Application.

4. In the Alias box, type a value for the application URL, such as marketing. This value is used to access the application in a URL.

5. Click Select if you want to select a different application pool than the one listed in the Application Pool box. In the Select Application Pool dialog box, select an application pool from the Application Pool list and then click OK.

6. In the Physical Path box, type the physical path of the application's folder, or click Browse to navigate the file system to find the folder.

7. Optionally, click Connect As to specify credentials that have permission to access the physical path. If you do not use specific credentials, select the Application User (Pass-Thru Authentication) option on the Connect As dialog box.

8. Optionally, click Test Settings to verify the settings that you specified for the application.

9. Click OK.

To create an application pool, follow these steps:

1. Open IIS Manager.

2. In the Connections pane, expand the server node and click Application Pools.

3. On the Application Pools page, in the Actions pane, click Add Application Pool.

4. In the Add Application Pool dialog box, type a friendly name for the application pool in the Name box.

5. From the .NET Framework version list, select the version of the .NET Framework required by your managed applications, modules, and handlers. Or select No Managed Code if the applications that you run in this application pool do not require the .NET Framework.

6. From the Managed Pipeline Mode list, select either Integrated or Classic.

7. Select Start Application Pool Immediately to start the application pool whenever the WWW service is started. By default, this is selected.

8. Click OK.

NOTE

If you create too many application pools, it can adversely affect web server performance.

If an application pool is stopped, all running processes for that application pool shut down. If you try to access a website or application with a stopped application pool, you receive a 503 Service Unavailable error.

To start or stop an application pool, follow these steps:

1. Open IIS Manager.

2. In the Connections pane, expand the server node and click Application Pools.

3. On the Application Pools page, select the application pool you want to start or stop.

4. In the Actions pane, select either Start or Stop to start or stop the application pool.

Recycling a Worker Process

By default, the WWW service establishes an overlapped recycle, in which the worker process that is to be shut down is kept running until after a new worker process is started. If the applications in an application pool cannot tolerate multi-instancing, you can optionally configure the WWW service to shut down a worker process and then start a new worker process. Use this type of recycling only if the applications in the application pool cannot tolerate multi-instancing. To turn off overlapped recycling, set the `DisallowOverlappingRotation` metabase property to `true`.

When a worker process requests a recycle, the WWW service initiates an overlapped recycle, creating a new worker process to replace the old one. While the new worker process is starting, the old process continues to serve requests. After the new process starts and initializes successfully, the WWW service instructs the old worker process to shut down. At this point, the old worker process stops accepting new requests from HTTP.sys and begins to shut down. The WWW service allows the old worker process a configured time period in which to finish processing its requests before the worker process is shut down. The WWW service terminates the worker process if it fails to shut down within the configured time.

With overlapped recycling, the old worker process remains in communication with HTTP.sys to handle requests until the new worker process is running. HTTP.sys establishes and maintains TCP/IP connections. When the WWW service recycles a worker process, it does not disconnect the existing TCP/IP connection. However, because the timeout value of a shutdown or startup is configurable, the worker process can be terminated while it is still serving requests if it does not finish servicing existing requests within the time limit.

Configuring IIS 7.0 with IIS Manager

To configure the server or website, you click the server or website in IIS manager, and the right pane displays the various ASP.NET, IIS, and management configurable features. If a configuration feature or option does not appear, it may indicate that it is not loaded as a role or feature with Server Manager.

Some of the options to configure include

- **SMTP E-mail:** Configures email address and delivery options to send email from web applications.

- **Authentication:** Configures authentication settings for sites and applications.

- **Authorization rules:** Configure rules for authorizing users for sites and applications based on user accounts and groups and the specific action (based on the action verb) allowed.

- **Compression:** Configures settings to compress responses.

- *Default document*: Configures default files to return when clients do not specify a file in a request.

- **Directory Browsing:** Configures information to display in a directory listing.

- **Error pages:** Configure information to return when an error occurs.

▸ **Handler Mappings:** Specify resources that handle responses for specific request types.

▸ **HTTP Redirect:** Specifies rules for redirecting incoming requests to another file or URL.

▸ **IPv4 Address and Domain Restrictions:** Restrict or grant access to web content based on IPv4 addresses or domain names.

▸ *ISAPI Filters*: Specify ISAPI filters that modify IIS functionality.

▸ **Logging:** Configures how IIS logs requests on the web server.

▸ **Server Certificates:** Request and manage certificates for websites that use SSL.

▸ **Worker Processes:** Show information about worker processes and about current requests inside the worker processes.

▸ **Feature Delegation:** Configures the default delegation state for features at lower levels in IIS Manager.

▸ **IIS Manager Permissions and IIS Manager Users:** Configure users who can administer sites and applications.

Compression

If your sites use lots of bandwidth, or if you want to use bandwidth more effectively, enable compression to provide faster transmission times between IIS and compression-enabled browsers. If your network bandwidth is restricted, as it is, for example, with mobile phones, compression can improve performance.

Compression of dynamic application responses can affect CPU resources because IIS does not cache compressed versions of dynamic output. If compression is enabled for dynamic responses and IIS receives a request for a file that contains dynamic content, the response that IIS sends is compressed every time it is requested. Because dynamic compression consumes significant CPU time and memory resources, use it only on servers that have slow network connections but that have CPU time to spare. Unlike dynamic responses, compressed static responses can be cached without degrading CPU resources.

To enable compression:

1. Open IIS Manager and navigate to the level you want to manage.

2. In Features View, double-click Compression.

3. Choose one or both of the following:

   ▸ Enable dynamic content compression to configure IIS to compress dynamic content.

   ▸ Enable static content compression to configure IIS to compress static content.

4. If Enable Static Content Compression is selected, under Static Compression, you can then specify the following options:

   ▸ In the Only Compress Files Larger Than (in Bytes) text box, type the minimum file size that you want IIS to compress. The default size is 256 bytes.

   ▸ In the Cache Directory text box, type the path of a local directory or click Browse to locate a directory. After a static file is compressed, it is cached in this temporary directory until it expires, or until the content changes. The temporary directory must be on a local drive on an NTFS-formatted partition. The directory cannot be compressed, and should not be shared.

   ▸ Optionally, select the box next to Per Application Pool Disk Space Limit (in MB) and type the maximum amount of space per application pool, in megabytes, you want IIS to use when it compresses static content. For example, if there are 20 application pools on the server and the disk space limit is set to 100, the maximum disk space is 2GB. If you click the Per Application Pool Disk Space Limit (in MB) option and type a number in the text box under it, IIS automatically cleans up the temporary directory according to a least recently used rule when the set limit is reached. The default is 100MB per application pool.

5. Click Apply in the Actions pane.

Default Documents and Directory Listings

When a URL is entered into a browser that does not specify a filename, the default document is generated automatically by the server or is designated by the administrator. Default documents can be a directory's home page or an index page containing a site document directory listing. For example, if the default document is configured as default.htm for http://www.acme.com, when the user types in http://www.acme.com, the http://www.acme.com/default.htm web page opens automatically.

To add a new default document, follow these steps:

1. Open IIS Manager and navigate to the level you want to manage.

2. In Features View, double-click Default Document.

3. In the Actions pane, click Add.

4. In the Name box, type the filename that you want to add to the list of default documents and then click OK. This file name will be added to the top of the default document list.

5. Optionally, select a default document in the list and in the Actions pane, click Move Up or Move Down to change the file's precedence.

6. Optionally, select a default document in the list, and in the Actions pane, click Remove to remove any filenames you do not want to use as default documents.

If you want to display a directory listing when client browsers make requests without specifying a document name, you can enable directory browsing. To enable directory browsing, follow these steps:

1. Open IIS Manager and navigate to the level you want to manage.

2. In Features View, double-click Directory Browsing.

3. On the Directory Browsing page, select or click to clear the following check boxes based on your preferences:

   ▶ Time to display the last modified time for each file.

   ▶ Size to display the size of each file.

   ▶ Extension to display the extension with the file.

   ▶ Date to display the last modified date for each file.

   ▶ Long Date to display the last modified date for each file in extended format.

4. Click Apply in the Actions pane.

Handlers and Modules

Internet Server Application Programming Interface (ISAPI) filters are programs that you can add to IIS to enhance web server behavior. ISAPI filters receive every HTTP request made to the web server to provide additional functionality for the server, such as logging request information, authenticating and authorizing users, rewriting URLs, and compressing web content to reduce bandwidth cost. In IIS 7.0, modules replace ISAPI filters, but you can still add ISAPI filters if you require the functionality that they provide.

To add an ISAPI filter in IIS 7.0:

1. Open IIS Manager and navigate to the level you want to manage.

2. In Features View, on the server or site home page, double-click ISAPI Filters.

3. On the ISAPI Filters page, in the Actions pane, click Add.

4. In the Add ISAPI Filter dialog box:

   ▶ In the Filter name box, type a friendly name for the ISAPI filter.

   ▶ In the Executable box, type the file system path of the location of ISAPI filter file, or click Browse to navigate to the folder that contains the ISAPI filter file.

5. Click OK.

First, because each module within IIS has a specific function, you need to load only the module that is required to support specific web applications. By loading only the required module, you can reduce the attack surface, in-memory footprint, running module code, and CPU load. You can also reduce patching and management requirements to the installed modules.

You can also replace the IIS modules with custom components that are developed by using the native IIS 7.0 C++ application programming interfaces (API) or the ASP.NET 2.0 APIs. You can add modules that can replace or enhance present IIS features.

Web server modules can be either of the following types:

▶ **Native modules (native .dll files):** These files are also named unmanaged modules, because they are not created within the ASP.NET model. By default, most of the features included in the web server are implemented as native modules.

▶ **Managed modules (managed types created by .NET assemblies):** These modules are created within the ASP.NET model.

When you add a module, you are not creating the module; instead, you are associating code that already exists on the computer together with the web application that is running on that computer.

You can perform this procedure by using the user interface (UI), by running Appcmd.exe commands in a command-line window, by editing configuration files directly, or by writing WMI scripts.

To add a managed module, follow these steps:

1. Open IIS Manager and navigate to the level you want to manage.

2. In Features View, on the server, site, or application home page, double-click Modules.

3. On the Modules page, in the Actions pane, click Add Managed Module.

4. In the Add Managed Module dialog box, type a name for the managed module in the Name box.

5. In the Type box, select a managed type or type a managed type.

6. Select the check box to start the module for requests to managed applications or managed handlers if you want the module to respond only to managed requests.

7. Click OK.

To edit a managed module, follow these steps:

1. Open IIS Manager and navigate to the level you want to manage.

2. In Features View, on the server, site, or application home page, double-click Modules.

3. On the Modules page, select the managed module that you want to change in the Modules list.

4. In the Actions pane, click Edit.

5. On the Edit Managed Module dialog box, edit the information that you want to change and then click OK.

Handler Mappings specify which component or module executes a web file when it is accessed through a website. For example, when you access a static file, such as an HTM or HTML file or a file that does not have a defined handler, the StaticFileModule, DefaultDocumentModule, and DirectoryListingModule modules process the files. If you execute an ASP file, it is processed by the %windir%\system32\inetsrv\asp.dll file. To view the Handler Mappings, click the site or web server and double-click Handler Mappings. If a new type of web file is introduced, you can define the component that executes it by clicking Add Managed Handler, Add Script Map, Add Wildcard Script Map, or Add Module Mapping.

For the websites, you can also define the permissions that a site can perform. The available permissions are

▸ **Read:** Allows read access to a virtual directory. You should enable read in an access policy if you want to serve static content, or want to configure default documents and directory browsing. By default, read permissions are enabled.

▸ **Scripts:** Required for script files to execute.

▸ **Execute:** Required for programs that require execute rights in a virtual directory. You should enable execute in an access policy only if you want to enable executable files, such as .exe, .dll, and .com files, to run in addition to scripts. For security and performance reasons, you should enable executable rights only for programs that you have tested and that your applications require.

EXAM ALERT

The *Common Gateway Interface (CGI)* is a standard protocol for interfacing external executable application software with IIS. Therefore, you need to enable the execute permission for CGI applications to run.

When you select an option in the Edit Feature Permissions dialog box, the State column on the Handler Mappings page displays Enabled for the handlers that are enabled by the selection. Similarly, when you clear a selection in the Edit Feature Permissions dialog box, the State column on the Handler Mappings page displays Disabled for the handlers that are disabled by the selection. You can preview the handlers that are enabled or disabled by viewing the Handler Mappings page, and then clicking OK to dismiss the Edit Feature Permissions dialog box. If you click Cancel instead of OK, the changes that you make in the dialog box are not saved.

To configure handler permissions, follow these steps:

1. Open IIS Manager and navigate to the level you want to manage.

2. In Features View, on the server, site, or application Home page, double-click Handler Mappings.

3. In the Actions pane, click Edit Feature Permissions.

4. In the Edit Feature Permissions dialog box, do the following:

   ▸ Select Read to enable handlers that require read access or clear Read to disable handlers that require read access to a virtual directory.

▶ Select Scripts to enable handlers that require script rights or clear Scripts to disable handlers that require script rights in a virtual directory.

▶ Select Execute to enable handlers that require execute rights or clear Execute to disable handlers that require execute rights in a virtual directory. The Execute option is enabled only when Scripts is selected.

5. Click OK.

> **NOTE**
>
> For security and performance reasons, you should enable executable rights only for programs that you have tested and that your applications require.

Configuring IIS Settings Using the appcmd Commands

appcmd, introduced with IIS 7.0, is a command-line management tool used to configure IIS and monitor IIS. It incorporates all the separate tools from IIS 6.0, including VBS file.

> **EXAM ALERT**
>
> The 70-643 exam puts more emphasis on using appcmd to configure IIS than on using the IIS Management console.

To start appcmd.exe, follow these steps:

1. Click Start, Run.

2. On the Run dialog box, in the Open box, type **windir%\system32\ inetsrv**.

3. Right-click Appcmd.exe, and then click Run as Administrator (see Figure 4.2).

> **NOTE**
>
> If you are logged on to the computer through the Administrator account, you can double-click Appcmd.exe.

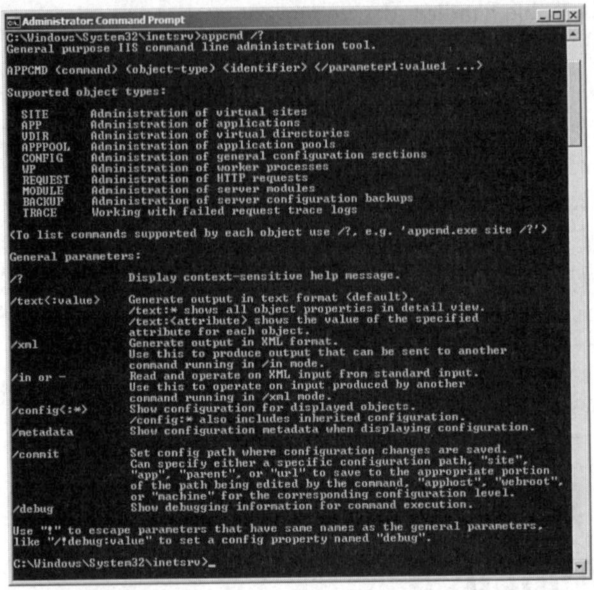

FIGURE 4.2 Using the appcmd command.

To add a site, use the following syntax:

```
appcmd add site /name:namestring /id:uint
➥/physicalPath:physicalpathstring /bindings:bindingstring
```

▶ *namestring* is the name of the site.

▶ *uint* is the unsigned integer that you want to assign to the site. The variables name string and id uint are the only variables that are required when you add a site in Appcmd.exe.

▶ *physicalpathstring* is the path of the site content in the file system.

▶ *bindingstring* contains information that is used to access the site, and it should be in the form of protocol/IP_address:port:host_header. For example, a binding of http/*:8080: enables a website to listen for HTTP requests on port 8080 for all IP addresses and domain names (also known as host headers or hostnames). A binding of http/*:8080:marketing. acme.com enables a website to listen for HTTP requests on port 8080 for all IP addresses and the domain name marketing.acme.com.

NOTE

If you add a site without specifying the values for the bindings and physicalPath attributes, the site cannot start.

To add a website named acme with an ID of 2 that has content in c:\acme, that listens for HTTP requests on port 8080 for all IP addresses, and that has a domain name of marketing.acme.com, type the following at the command prompt, and then press Enter:

```
appcmd add site /name:acme /id:2 /physicalPath:c:\acme
➥/bindings:http/*:8080:marketing.acme.com
```

To add a virtual directory to the root application in a site, use the following syntax:

```
appcmd add vdir /app.name:namestring/ /path:pathstring
➥/physicalPath:physicalpathstring
```

- ▶ *namestring* is the site name

- ▶ / following the name specifies that the virtual directory should be added to the site's root application.

- ▶ *pathstring* is the virtual path of the virtual directory, such as /photos.

- ▶ *physicalpathstring* is the physical path of the virtual directory's content in the file system.

For example, to add a virtual directory named photos with a physical location of c:\images to the root application in a site named acme, type the following at the command prompt, and then press Enter:

```
appcmd add vdir /app.name:acme/ /path:/photos /physicalPath:c:\images
```

To add a virtual directory to an application other than a site's root application, type the name of the application after / in app.namestring. For example, to add the same virtual directory used in the previous example to an application named marketing in a site named acme, type the following at the command prompt, and then press Enter:

```
appcmd add vdir /app.name:acme/marketing /path:/photos
➥/physicalPath:c:\images
```

To change the path of a virtual directory's content, use the following syntax:

```
appcmd set vdir /vdir.name:string /physicalPath:string
```

The variable vdir.name:*string* is the virtual path of the virtual directory, and physicalPath:*string* is the physical path of the application's content.

For example, to change the physical path of the location c:\images for a virtual directory named photos in an application named marketing and in a site named acme, type the following at the command prompt, and then press Enter:

```
appcmd set vdir /vdir.name:acme/marketing/photos /physicalPath:c:\images
```

EXAM ALERT

Make sure that you know to create a website and virtual directory using the appcmd command and how to change the virtual directory.

To add an application to a site, use the following syntax:

```
appcmd add app /site.name:sitenamestring /path:pathnamestring
➥/physicalPath:physicalpathstring
```

> ▸ *sitenamestring* is the name of the website to which you want to add the application.

> ▸ *pathnamestring* is the virtual path of the application, such as /application.

> ▸ *physicalPathstring* is the physical path of the application's content in the file system.

For example, to add an application named marketing to a site named acme, with content at c:\application, type the following at the command prompt, and then press Enter:

```
appcmd add app /site.name:acme /path:/marketing /physicalPath:c:\
application
```

To add an application pool to a web server by using default settings, use the following syntax:

```
appcmd add apppool /name:string
```

The variable string is the name that you want for the application pool. For example, to add an application pool named Marketing, type the following at the command prompt, and then press Enter:

```
appcmd add apppool /name:Marketing
```

By default, IIS adds an application pool that runs in integrated mode and uses .NET Framework version 2.0. If you want to add an application pool that runs a different version of the .NET Framework or that uses classic mode, you can specify the .NET Framework version with the /managedRuntimeVersion attribute and the managed request-processing mode with the /managedPipelineMode attribute.

To add an application pool to a web server by using settings different from the default settings, use the following syntax:

```
appcmd add apppool /name:namestring
➥/managedRuntimeVersion:.versionstring /managedPipelineMode:
➥Integrated ¦ Classic
```

▶ *namestring* is the name that you want for the application pool.

▶ *versionstring* is the version of the .NET Framework that you want the application pool to run. When you want to run a specific version of the .NET Framework, specify the value for versionstring as v1.0, v1.1, or v2.0, or leave the value blank if you do not want to run managed code in the application pool.

▶ You then specify either Integrated or Classic mode.

For example, to add an application pool that does not run managed code and that uses classic mode, type the following at the command prompt, and then press Enter:

```
appcmd add apppool /name:Marketing /managedRuntimeVersion:
➥/managedPipelineMode:Classic
```

To start an application pool, use the following syntax:

```
appcmd start apppool /apppool.name:namestring
```

▶ *namestring* is the name of the application pool that you want to start.

For example, to start an application pool named Marketing, type the following at the command prompt, and then press Enter:

```
appcmd start apppool /apppool.name:Marketing
```

To stop an application pool, use the following syntax:

```
appcmd stop apppool /apppool.name:namestring
```

▶ *namestring* is the name of the application pool that you want to stop.

For example, to stop an application pool named Marketing, type the following at the command prompt, and then press Enter:

```
appcmd stop apppool /apppool.name:Marketing
```

To specify what information is to be displayed in a directory listing, use the following syntax:

```
appcmd set config /section:directoryBrowse
➥/showFlags:Time¦Size¦Extension¦Date¦LongDate¦None
```

You can specify one or more of the values for the showFlags attribute, or you can specify None if you want only the filenames and directory names to be displayed in a directory listing. If you want more than one value, separate each value with a comma (,).

To enable or disable the directory browsing, use the following syntax:

```
appcmd set config /section:directoryBrowse /enabled:true¦false
```

By default, the enabled attribute is set to true, which means that directory browsing is enabled. When you set the enabled attribute to false, directory browsing is disabled.

For example, to disable directory browsing, type the following at the command prompt, and then press Enter:

```
appcmd set config /section:directoryBrowse /enabled:false
```

To specify the information to display in a directory listing, use the following syntax:

```
appcmd set config /section:directoryBrowse
➥/showFlags:Time¦Size¦Extension¦Date¦LongDate¦None
```

You can specify one or more of the values for the showFlags attribute, or you can specify None if you want only the file names and directory names to be displayed in a directory listing. If you want more than one value, separate each value with a comma (,).

For example, to display the filename extension and date in long date format, type the following at the command prompt, and then press Enter:

```
appcmd set config /section:directoryBrowse /showFlags:Extension,LongDate
```

To add a filename to the list of default documents, use the following syntax:

```
appcmd set config /section:defaultDocument /+files.[value='string']
```

The variable string is the filename that you want to add to the list. For example, to add a file named home.html to the default document list, type the following at the command prompt, and then press Enter:

```
appcmd set config /section:defaultDocument /+files.[value='home.html']
```

To remove a file named home.html from the default document list, type the following at the command prompt, and then press Enter:

```
appcmd set config /section:defaultDocument /-files.[value='home.html']
```

You can also use the appcmd to view the sites, applications, virtual directory, application pools, and worker processes by using the list parameter:

▶ Appcmd list site

▶ Appcmd list app

▶ Appcmd list vdir

▶ Appcmd list apppool

▶ Appcmd list wp

To configure request restrictions for a handler mapping, use the following syntax:

```
appcmd set config /section:handlers /[name='namestring'].attribute:string
```

▶ *namestring* is the name of the handler mapping that you want to change.

▶ *attribute* is the attribute that you want to change or add to the handler mapping.

▶ The attribute string is the value that you want to set for the attribute.

For example, to specify that a handler named ImageCopyrightHandler requires Execute rights to run, type the following at the command prompt, and then press Enter:

```
appcmd set config /section:handlers
↪/[name='ImageCopyrightHandler'].requireAccess:Execute
```

To enable logging, you can use the appcmd command to configure HTTP logging to use the default logging settings from the schema file for all websites that are configured on the web server:

```
appcmd set config /section:httpLogging /dontLog:False
↪/selectiveLogging:LogAll
```

Deploying an ASP.NET Web Application Using xcopy

xcopy is a command-prompt command that enables you to copy files from one location to another and can be used to deploy web applications on IIS servers. More powerful than the standard copy command, xcopy includes various parameters that can copy permissions and audit settings, hidden files, and sub-directories.

```
xcopy Source [Destination] [/w] [/p] [/c] [/v] [/q] [/f] [/l] [/g]
➥ [/d[:mm-dd-yyyy]] [/u] [/i] [/s [/e]] [/t] [/k] [/r] [/h] [{/a¦/m}]
➥ [/n] [/o] [/x] [/exclude:file1[+[file2]][+[file3]] [{/y¦/-y}]
```

- ▸ *Source*: Specifies the location and names of the files you want to copy. This parameter must include either a drive or a path.

- ▸ [*Destination*]: Specifies the destination of the files you want to copy. This parameter can include a drive letter and colon, a directory name, a filename, or a combination of these.

- ▸ /w—Displays the Press Any Key to Begin Copying File(s) message and waits for your response before starting to copy files.

- ▸ /p—Prompts you to confirm whether you want to create each destination file.

- ▸ /c—Ignores errors.

- ▸ /v—Verifies each file as it is written to the destination file to make sure that the destination files are identical to the source files.

- ▸ /q—Suppresses the display of xcopy messages.

- ▸ /f—Displays source and destination filenames while copying.

- ▸ /l—Displays a list of files to be copied.

- ▸ /g—Creates decrypted destination files.

- ▸ /d [:mm-dd-yyyy] —Copies source files changed on or after the specified date only. If you do not include a mm-dd-yyyy value, xcopy copies all Source files that are newer than existing Destination files. This command-line option enables you to update files that have changed.

- ▸ /u—Copies files from Source that exist on Destination only.

▶ /i—If Source is a directory or contains wildcards and Destination does not exist, xcopy assumes Destination specifies a directory name and creates a new directory. Then, xcopy copies all specified files into the new directory. By default, xcopy prompts you to specify whether Destination is a file or a directory.

▶ /s—Copies directories and subdirectories, unless they are empty. If you omit /s, xcopy works within a single directory.

▶ /e—Copies all subdirectories, even if they are empty. Use /e with the /s and /t command-line options.

▶ /t—Copies the subdirectory structure (that is, the tree) only, not files. To copy empty directories, you must include the /e command-line option.

▶ /k—Copies files and retains the read-only attribute on destination files if present on the source files. By default, xcopy removes the read-only attribute.

▶ /r—Copies read-only files.

▶ /h—Copies files with hidden and system file attributes. By default, xcopy does not copy hidden or system files.

▶ /a—Copies only source files that have their archive file attributes set. /a does not modify the archive file attribute of the source file.

▶ /m—Copies source files that have their archive file attributes set. Unlike /a, /m turns off archive file attributes in the files that are specified in the source.

▶ /n—Creates copies by using the NTFS short file or directory names. /n is required when you copy files or directories from an NTFS volume to a FAT volume or when the FAT file system naming convention (that is, 8.3 characters) is required on the destination file system. The destination file system can be FAT or NTFS.

▶ /o—Copies file ownership and discretionary access control list (DACL) information.

▶ /x—Copies file audit settings and system access control list (SACL) information (implies /o).

▶ /exclude: *filename1* [+ [*filename2*]][+ [*filename3*]]: Specifies a list of files containing strings.

▶ /y—Suppresses prompting to confirm that you want to overwrite an existing destination file.

> ▶ / -y—Prompts to confirm that you want to overwrite an existing destination file.

> ▶ /?—Displays help at the command prompt.

IIS Security

Because a website can be very important to an organization or department and may contain sensitive information, you need to know how to make the website and its content secure. You can do this by limiting who can access the website and how users authenticate, by encrypting the request associated with the website, and by delegating permissions on who can administer the website.

URL Authorization Rules

You can grant or deny specific computers, groups of computers, or domains access to sites, applications, directories, or files on your server. Authorization rules enable you to specify who can access a website based on the computer, groups of computers, or domains.

To view the URL authorization rules using IIS Manager,

1. Open IIS Manager and navigate to the level you want to manage.

2. In Features View, double-click Authorization Rules.

To view the URL authorization rules using the `appcmd` command, enter the following:

```
appcmd list config /section:authorization
```

To create a new authorization rule using IIS Manager, follow these steps:

1. Open IIS Manager and navigate to the level you want to manage.

2. In Features View, double-click Authorization Rules.

3. In the Actions pane, click Add Allow Rule.

4. In the Add Allow Authorization Rule dialog box, select one of the following types of access:

- ▶ **All Users:** Specifies that all users, whether they are anonymous or identified, can access the content.

- ▶ **All Anonymous Users:** Specifies that anonymous users can access the content.

- ▶ **Specified Roles or User Groups:** Specifies that only members of certain roles or user groups can access the content. Type the role or user group in the text box.

- ▶ **Specified Users:** Specifies that only certain users can access the content. Type the user ID in the text box.

5. Optionally, check Apply This Rule to Specific Verbs if you want to further stipulate that the users, roles, or groups allowed to access the content can use only a specific list of HTTP verbs. Type those verbs in the text box.

6. Click OK.

To create a Deny Rule, select Add Deny Rule instead of selecting Add Allow Rule.

In IIS 7.0, all Internet Protocol (IP) addresses, computers, and domains can access your site by default. To enhance security, you can limit access to your site by creating an allow rule that grants access to all IPv4 addresses, a specific IP address, a range of IP addresses, or a specific domain. For example, if you have a site on an intranet server that is connected to the Internet, you can prevent Internet users from accessing your intranet site by allowing access only to members of your intranet.

To limit access to websites by IPv4 address and domain, follow these steps:

1. Open IIS Manager and navigate to the level you want to manage.

2. In Features View, double-click IPv4 Address and Domain Restrictions.

3. In the Actions pane, click Add Allow Entry.

4. In the Add Allow Restriction Rule dialog box, select Specific IPv4 address, IPv4 address range, or Domain name, add the IPv4 address, range, mask, or domain name, and then click OK.

Use the Edit IP and Domain Restrictions dialog box to define access restrictions for unspecified clients or to enable domain name restrictions for all rules.

You can also allow or deny access to clients not specified by any IPv4 rule by clicking Edit Features Settings in the Actions pane and specifying Deny or

Allow. The Edit Features dialog box also allows you to enable rules that restrict access by domain name. However, if you restrict by domain name, server performance is affected because it requires a DNS lookup for every request.

Authentication

Authentication helps you confirm the identity of clients who request access to your sites and applications. IIS 7.0 supports the following forms of authentication:

▶ **Anonymous:** Allows any user to access any public content without providing a username and password. By default, Anonymous authentication is enabled in IIS 7.0. Use Anonymous authentication when you want all clients who visit your site to be able to view its content.

▶ **ASP.NET Impersonation:** ASP.NET impersonation allows you to run ASP.NET applications under a context other than the default ASPNET account. Use impersonation with other IIS authentication methods or set up an arbitrary user account.

▶ **Basic Authentication:** Requires that users provide a valid username and password to gain access to content. Basic authentication transmits passwords across the network in clear text. You should use Basic authentication only when you know that the connection between the client and the server is secure.

▶ **Digest Authentication:** Uses a Windows domain controller to authenticate users who request access to content on your server. Consider using Digest authentication when you need improved security over Basic authentication. Any browser that does not support the HTTP 1.1 protocol cannot support Digest authentication.

▶ **Forms Authentication:** Uses client-side redirection to forward unauthenticated users to an HTML form where they can enter their credentials, which are usually a username and password. After the credentials are validated, users are redirected to the page they originally requested. Because Forms authentication sends the username and password to the web server as plain text, you should use Secure Sockets Layer (SSL) encryption for the logon page and for all other pages in your application.

▶ **Windows Authentication:** Uses NTLM or Kerberos protocols to authenticate clients. Windows authentication is best suited for an intranet environment. Windows authentication is not suited for use on the Internet because credentials are usually not encrypted.

▸ **AD Client Certificate Authentication:** Enables you to use Active Directory directory service features to map users to client certificates for authentication. Mapping users to client certificates lets you automatically authenticate users, without other authentication methods such as Basic, Digest, or Integrated Windows authentication.

EXAM ALERT

Be sure to know the different forms of authentication used within websites.

To configure authentication for a website, application, or virtual folder's authentication, click the site, application, or virtual folder and double-click Authentication. The default setting for Windows authentication is Negotiate. This setting means that the client can select the appropriate security support provider (see Figure 4.3).

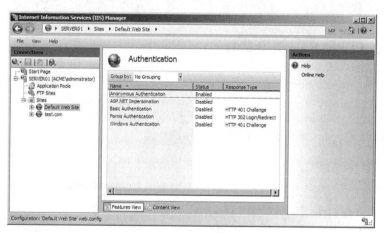

FIGURE 4.3   Authentication options in IIS Manager.

Secure Sockets Layer and Digital Certificates

Secure Sockets Layer (SSL) encryption protects data sent to and from a website. SSL uses a cryptographic system that uses two keys to encrypt data:

▸ A public key known to everyone.

▸ A private or secret key known only to the recipient of the message.

When using SSL with your browser, the browser will start with https instead of http.

To enable SSL, you must obtain and install a valid server certificate (*digital certificate*). You can acquire a server certificate from a *Certificate Authority (CA)*, also referred to as a Certification Authority, which can be an internal Windows domain CA or a trusted third-party public CA. You can also create a self-signed server certificate for troubleshooting, testing, or application development. Server certificates can be configured only at the web server level, but site bindings and SSL settings can be configured only at the site, application, or physical directory level. After obtaining the server certificate, you must install the certificate and bind the HTTPS protocol to your website.

EXAM ALERT

You need to know how to obtain a digital certificate from a CA and how to install it onto a website.

Obtaining a Digital Certificate

There are a number of ways to obtain a server certificate. You can generate a self-signed certificate, purchase a certificate from external third-party public CAs, or request a certificate from an internal domain CA. Of the three options, self-signed certificates are the least secure and should be used only for testing or troubleshooting applications that use HTTPS.

To request an Internet server certificate, follow these steps:

1. Open IIS Manager and click the server that you are managing.

2. In Features View, double-click Server Certificates.

3. In the Actions pane, click Create Certificate Request.

4. On the Distinguished Name Properties page of the Request Certificate Wizard, type the following information, and then click Next:

   ▶ In the Common Name text box, type a name for the certificate.

   ▶ In the Organization text box, type the name of the organization in which the certificate will be used.

   ▶ In the Organizational Unit text box, type the name of the organizational unit in the organization in which the certificate will be used.

   ▶ In the City/Locality text box, type the unabbreviated name of the city or locality where your organization or organizational unit is located.

▶ In the State/Province text box, type the unabbreviated name of the state or province where your organization or organizational unit is located.

▶ In the Country/Region text box, type the name of the country or region where your organization or organizational unit is located.

5. On the Cryptographic Service Provider Properties page, select either Microsoft RSA SChannel Cryptographic Provider or Microsoft DH SChannel Cryptographic Provider from the Cryptographic service provider drop-down list. By default, IIS 7.0 uses the Microsoft RSA SChannel Cryptographic Provider.

6. In the Bit Length drop-down list, select a bit length that can be used by the provider. By default, the RSA SChannel provider uses a bit length of 1024. The DH SChannel provider uses a bit length of 512. A longer bit length is more secure, but it can affect performance.

7. Click Next.

8. On the File Name page, type a filename in the Specify a File Name for the Certificate Request text box, or click Browse to locate a file, and then click Finish.

9. Send the certificate request to a public CA.

When you receive a response from a public CA to whom you sent a certificate request, you must complete the process by installing the server certificate on your web server. You can install the server certificate only on the computer from which you sent the certificate request.

Installing a Digital Certificate

To install an Internet certificate:

1. Open IIS Manager and navigate to the level you want to manage.

2. In Features View, double-click Server Certificates.

3. In the Actions pane, click Complete Certificate Request.

4. On the Complete Certificate Request page, in the File Name that Contains the Certification Authority's Response text box, type the path of the file that contains the response from the CA, or click Browse to search for the file.

5. Type a friendly name for the certificate in the Friendly Name text box, and then click OK.

From the SSL Settings page, you can define whether SSL is required and the level of encryption. Select Require SSL only to enable a 40–bit data encryption method that you can use to help secure transmissions between your server and clients. Also select Require 128 bit SSL to provide stronger encryption than the 40–bit version.

You can also define how client certificates are used. The options are

- **Ignore (default option):** Select this setting if you do not want to accept client certificates if they are provided. This option does not require clients to verify their identity before gaining access to your content. Therefore, this is the least secure of these settings.

- **Accept:** Select this setting if you want to accept client certificates (if they are provided), and to verify client identity before allowing the client to gain access to content.

- **Require:** Select this option to require that certificates verify client identity before allowing the client to gain access to content.

Importing and Exporting Digital Certificates

From time to time, you may need to import and export digital certificates. Certificates are distributed in different formats:

- **X509 format (.cer and .crt file extension for Windows):** A widely supported digital certificate that represents the individual certificate.

- **Cryptographic Message Syntax-PKCS #7 Format (.p7b file extension for Windows):** Used to export the complete chain of digital certificates.

- **Personal Information Exchange syntax–PKCS #12 Format (.pfx and .p12 file extensions for Windows):** Used for exporting the public/private key pair.

- **Certificate Signing Request (CSR) Syntax–PKCS #10 Format:** Used in generating signing requests to trusted certificate signing authorities.

For example, if you have multiple web servers that make up a farm, each web server should have the same digital certificates for the same websites on each server. You would then install a digital certificate on the first web server and then export it to a .pfx format so that it includes the public and private key pair. You then import the .pfx certificate into the other web servers.

To export a digital certificate, follow these steps:

1. Open IIS Manager and navigate to the level you want to manage.

2. In the Features View, double-click Server Certificates.

3. In the Actions pane, click Export.

4. In the Export dialog box, type a filename in the Export To box or click the Browse button to navigate to the name of a file in which to store the certificate for exporting.

5. Type a password in the Password box if you want to associate a password with the exported certificate. Retype the password in the Confirm Password box.

6. Click OK.

To import a certificate, follow these steps:

1. Open IIS Manager and navigate to the level you want to manage.

2. In the Features View, double-click Server Certificates.

3. In the Actions pane, click Import.

4. In the Import Certificate dialog box, type a filename in the Certificate File box or click the Browse button to navigate to the name of a file where the exported certificate is stored. Type a password in the Password box if the certificate was exported with a password.

5. Select Allow This Certificate to Be Exported if you want to be able to export the certificate, or clear Allow This Certificate to Be Exported if you want to allow additional exports of this certificate.

6. Click OK.

Client Certificate Mapping Authentication

When you want each Windows user account to map to a single client certificate, use one-to-one IIS certificate mapping. This mapping provides added protection for your server because the certificate sent by the client must be identical to the copy of the client certificate stored on the server. Of course, before you can map client certificates, you must enable Secure Sockets Layer (SSL) for your site.

When you want to verify that a client certificate contains specific information, such as issuer or subject, use IIS many-to-one certificate mapping. This mapping method uses wildcard matching rules to accept all the client certificates that fulfill the specific mapping criteria you define. Before you can map client certificates, you must enable SSL for your site. If you use IIS many-to-one certificate mapping, you cannot use Active Directory certificate mapping.

When you want to use Windows Active Directory to authenticate domain users who have client certificates, configure Active Directory certificate mapping. If you use Active Directory certificate mapping, you cannot use IIS certificate mapping. The basic steps in using Active Directory certificate mapping are:

1. Install and configure a domain controller.

2. Set up a CA for the domain.

3. Submit a user certificate request to the domain CA.

4. Configure SSL for your site, application, virtual or physical directory, or file (URL).

5. Map a certificate to a user account.

Active Directory certificate mapping cannot be used with a self-signed certificate. You must use either a domain certificate or an Internet certificate.

Machine Key

The Machine Key feature page is used to configure encryption and decryption keys used to help protect forms authentication cookie data and page-level view state data. The Machine Key enables you to specify the encryption (AES, MD5, SHA1, and Triple DES) and decryption method used and how those keys are generated.

Delegate Permissions

If you have multiple sites, you may need to allow other users to connect to and/or manage individual websites. Before allowing an IIS Manager user to connect to a site or an application, you must first add the IIS Manager user account at the server level in IIS Manager. IIS Manager user credentials consist of a username and password that are created in IIS Manager and are used exclusively for IIS Manager to access the IIS configuration files.

To add an IIS Manager user, follow these steps:

1. Open IIS Manager.

2. In the Connections pane, click the server node.

3. In Features View, double-click IIS Manager Users.

4. On the IIS Manager Users page, in the Actions pane, click Add User.

5. In the Add User dialog box, in the User Name box, type a username.

6. In the Password and Confirm password boxes, type a password.

7. Click OK.

NOTE

For IIS Manager users to connect to sites and applications for which you grant permission, you must configure the management service to accept connections from users who have IIS Manager credentials.

To allow an IIS Manager user to connect to a site or an application, follow these steps:

1. Open IIS Manager.

2. In the Connections pane, expand the Sites node and select the site for which you want to grant permission to an IIS Manager user. Or, expand the site and select the application for which you want to grant permission to an IIS Manager user.

3. In Features View, double-click IIS Manager Permissions.

4. On the IIS Manager Permissions page, in the Actions pane, click Allow User.

5. In the Allow User dialog box, select IIS Manager to select a user account that is valid within IIS Manager but that is not a Windows account. Then click Select to open the Users dialog box.

6. On the Users dialog box, select a user and then click OK.

7. Click OK to dismiss the Allow User dialog box.

To allow a Windows user or group to connect to a site or an application:

1. Open IIS Manager.

2. In the Connections pane, expand the Sites node and select the site for which you want to grant permission to a Windows user or group. Or, expand the site and select the application for which you want to grant permission to a Windows user or group.

3. In Features View, double-click IIS Manager Permissions.

4. On the IIS Manager Permissions page, in the Actions pane, click Allow User.

5. On the Allow User dialog box, select Windows to select a Windows user or group. Then click Select to open the Select User or Group dialog box.

6. Optionally, click Object Types to select the type of Windows objects for which you want to search. You can select the check box for Users, Groups, or both.

7. Optionally, click Locations if you want to search for users or groups on a domain to which the computer is joined. Otherwise, leave the value in the From This Location box as the computer name to search for a user or group on the local computer.

8. In the Enter Object Name to Select box, type the name of a user or group and then click Check Names.

9. Click OK to dismiss the Select User or Group dialog box, and then OK to dismiss the Allow User dialog box.

ASP.NET Code Access Security

Code Access Security within ASP.NET is used to incrementally limit a website's exposure to security attacks and provides an extra degree of application isolation. It enables you to constrain your web application by restricting the types of resources it can access and the types of operations it can perform.

By default, ASP.NET version 1.1 and version 2.0 web applications and web services run with Full trust. When an application runs with Full trust, code access security places no restrictions on the resources and operations it can access, and resource access is based solely on operating system security and Windows access control lists (ACL).

To protect your ASP.NET application, you can use code access security to restrict the resources the application can access and the privileged operations it can perform. You do this by configuring the `<trust>` element in either the machine-level `Web.config` file or the application's `Web.config` file and setting it to one of the predefined trust levels, as shown here:

```
Copy Code<trust level="Full¦High¦Medium¦Low¦Minimal" />
```

The `<trust>` element supports a number of predefined trust levels. Each level in succession provides a more restrictive environment (with fewer code access security permissions) in which to run your application.

▶ Full: No restrictions imposed by code access security.

▶ High: No unmanaged code. No enterprise services. It can access Microsoft SQL Server and other OLE DB data sources and send email by using SMTP servers. It does have full access to the file system and to sockets. It does not enable you to write to the event log, call unmanaged code, call serviced components, access ODBC, OleDb, or Oracle data sources.

▶ Medium: Permissions are limited to what the application can access within the directory structure of the application. No file access is permitted outside the application's virtual directory hierarchy. It can access SQL Server and send email by using SMTP servers. It has limited rights to certain common environment variables. To access web resources, you must explicitly add endpoint URLs—either in the originUrl attribute of the <trust> element or inside the policy file.

▶ Low: Intended to model the concept of a read-only application with no network connectivity. Read-only access for file I/O within the application's virtual directory structure.

▶ Minimal: Execute only. No ability to change the IPrincipal on a thread or on the HttpContext.

> **EXAM ALERT**
>
> You need to know how to configure the ASP.NET Code Access Levels.

Simple Mail Transfer Protocol (SMTP)

Simple Mail Transfer Protocol (SMTP) is the protocol for sending email messages from server to server. With IIS 7.0, you can configure SMTP with each web application. You can also load IIS 6.0 to create an SMTP server.

Enabling SMTP Within Web Applications

To send email from an ASP.NET application using the System.Net.Mail API, you must configure SMTP email. The IIS SMTP service is a simple component for forwarding email messages to an SMTP server for delivery. Configuring email services tells the System.Net.Mail API to which SMTP server the email generated by your application should be delivered. You can also configure your application to deliver email to a file location on disk where it can be retrieved for delivery later.

To configure SMTP email for a web application, follow these steps:

1. Open IIS Manager and navigate to the level on which you want to configure SMTP.

2. In Features View, double-click SMTP E-mail.

3. On the SMTP E-mail page, type the email address of the sender in the E-mail Address text box.

4. On the SMTP E-mail page, select one of the following delivery methods:

   ▶ **Deliver E-mail to SMTP Server**: To deliver email messages immediately. This requires an operational SMTP server for which the user has credentials.

   ▶ **Store E-mail in Pickup Directory**: To store emails in a file location on disk for later delivery by an application such as an ASP.NET application, or by a user, such as an administrator.

5. If Deliver email to SMTP server is selected, do the following:

   ▶ Type the unique name of your SMTP server in the SMTP Server text box or select the Use Localhost box to set the name to LocalHost. Setting the name to LocalHost means that ASP.NET will use an SMTP server on the local computer. Typically, this is the default SMTP virtual server.

   ▶ Enter a TCP port in the Port text box. Port 25 is the SMTP standard TCP port and is the default setting. More than one virtual server can use the same TCP port if all servers are configured to use different IP addresses.

   ▶ Under Authentication Settings, specify the authentication mode and credentials if your SMTP server requires these.

6. If Store E-mail in Pickup Directory is selected, type the batch email location in the Store Email in Pickup Directory text box.

7. Click Apply in the Actions pane.

Configuring SMTP Within IIS 6.0

When you enable SMTP by using IIS 6.0 and you send a message, the message is copied to the Pickup directory (c:\inetpub\mailroot\pickup). If a messages comes through the designated TCP port (the default TCP port is port 25), it is put in the Queue directory (c:\inetpub\mailroot\queue). If the recipients are local, the message is delivered.

If the recipients are not local, the message is processed for remote delivery. The SMTP service tries to connect to the receiving mail server. If the server is not ready, the message remains in the queue and delivery is tried again at designated intervals, up to a maximum number of attempts. These intervals are the retry settings.

After recipients are verified, the message is sent. After the receiving server acknowledges the transmission, SMTP delivery is finished. All messages for remote domains can be sent to a smart host, which can then send them to the recipients.

If you right-click the SMTP Virtual Server in the IIS 6.0 management console and select Properties, you open the SMTP Virtual Server Properties dialog box. Within the dialog box are six tabs to configure SMTP (see Figure 4.4).

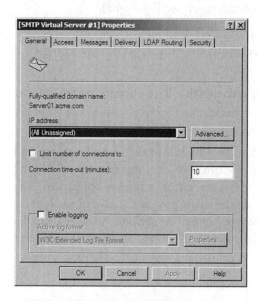

FIGURE 4.4 SMTP options (General tab) in IIS Manager.

The six tabs are

▶ **General:** Identifies the IP address that is used by the SMTP virtual server, configures multiple identities for the SMTP virtual server, sets the connection limit and time-out, and enables logging. By default, the SMTP virtual server can respond to connection requests for all IP addresses configured on the computer.

EXAM ALERT

If you have multiple websites that need to send email through SMTP and you want to use individual SMTP virtual servers for each website, you need to make sure that each SMTP virtual server has unique IP address/TCP port number combination.

▶ **Access:** Contains settings to require authentication and the use of Transport Layer Security (TLS) for all incoming connections. If you are not familiar with TLS, it is a type of SSL encryption for all protocols. You can also grant or deny both general and relay access to specific computers or networks.

▶ **Messages:** Configures message limits and determines how to manage undeliverable messages.

▶ **Delivery:** Contains settings that determine how the virtual server delivers messages, including the number of messages sent per connection, how the virtual server routes messages, and retry intervals and expiration time-out for attempts to resend messages (see Figure 4.5).

▶ **LDAP Routing:** Contains settings for Lightweight Directory Access Protocol (LDAP) that allow access to directories that comply with the X.500 directory structure.

▶ **Security:** Designates the user accounts that have operator permissions to configure the SMTP service.

SMTP within IIS 6.0 can use DNS to find an MX record and attempt to send an email message to the mail server. You can also select the Forward All Mail to Smart Host option to specify that messages sent to a remote domain are forwarded to a smart host. You designate the smart host in the Advanced Delivery dialog box (see Figure 4.6), which you access by clicking Advanced on the Delivery tab. You can specify the fully qualified domain name or IP address of the server through which you want to route messages for this remote domain.

NOTE

If you specify an IP address for the Smart Host, you need to surround the address with brackets ([ ]).

You can allow incoming mail to be relayed through your SMTP server. When a server allows email to be relayed through it, it can be used by spammers who want to send email through your server. All spam email will look as if it originated from your server. Therefore, by default, SMTP Server is configured to block computers from relaying unwanted mail to the remote domain. By selecting the Allow Incoming Mail to Be Relayed to This Domain check box, you override the relay restriction setting on the Access tab.

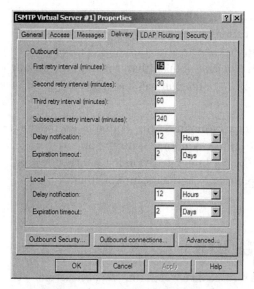

FIGURE 4.5 SMTP options (Delivery tab) in IIS Manager.

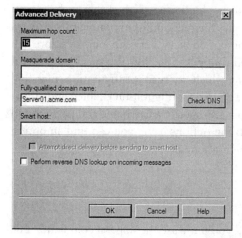

FIGURE 4.6 Advanced Delivery in the SMTP options in IIS Manager.

In addition to specifying which hosts can send email to your SMTP server, you can also specify authentication, which verifies the user's identity and grants access by using the configured authentication mechanism. By default, only anonymous access is enabled. The following options are available:

▶ **Allow Anonymous:** Select this option to allow anonymous access to this SMTP virtual server. No username or password is required.

▶ **Basic Authentication:** Select this option to enable Basic (clear-text) authentication. Basic authentication transmits the password in clear text. If you select Basic authentication, you can also configure the Requires TLS encryption option and the default domain that is used as the default domain for Basic authentication. The domain name is appended to the account name.

▶ **Integrated Windows Authentication:** Select this option to enable the client and the server to negotiate the Windows Security Support Provider Interface. Of course, using Integrated Windows Authentication requires a mail client that supports this authentication method.

Shared Configuration

If you have multiple web servers that make up a web farm, you have several web servers that must have the same web configuration. So if you make a change on one server, you want those changes to be duplicated to the other web servers. With IIS 7.0, Microsoft has included the Shared Configuration feature page to share IIS configuration files and encryption keys between one or more IIS servers. In addition to enabling shared configuration, you also specify a physical path (typically a shared folder) from which to read configuration files and encryption keys. All servers must have Shared Configuration enabled and pointing to the same physical path. You must also specify a username and password to protect access to these files. Lastly, in the Actions pane, you can find an option to apply changes and export the configuration.

IIS 7.0 Backup

To back up the IIS 7.0 configuration, you must use the appcmd command. The general syntax to perform backup and restores is

```
appcmd add backup <backupname>
appcmd restore backup <backupname>
appcmd list backup
appcmd backup /? (for help on commands)
```

You should also note that by default, IIS captures a config history when configuration changes are made. Therefore, you can restore from previous configurations stored in the %systemdrive%\inetpub\history folder.

File Transfer Protocol

File Transfer Protocol (FTP) is a TCP/IP protocol that enables a user to transfer files between local and remote host computers. You place your files in directories on your FTP server so that users can establish an FTP connection and transfer files with an FTP client or FTP-enabled web browser. When you load FTP, you are loading IIS 6.0 to host the FTP sites. Therefore, to manage the FTP sites, you need to open Internet Information Services 6.0 from the Administrative tools.

After FTP is loaded, there will already be a Default FTP site created with C:\inetpub\ftproot as the FTP working folder. By default, you can read from the FTP site but you need to enable Write if you wish for the FTP site to be used to upload files.

To create an FTP site, use the IIS 6.0 Manager to do the following:

1. In IIS Manager, expand the local computer, right-click the FTP Sites folder, point to New, and click FTP Site.

2. When the FTP Site Creation wizard starts, click Next.

3. In the Description box, type a description of your FTP site and then click Next.

4. Under Enter the IP Address to Use this FTP Site, type a new IP address, and leave the TCP port setting at 21.

5. Choose the user isolation mode you want to use and click Next. The available isolation modes are

   ▶ **Do Not Isolate Users:** This mode does not enable FTP user isolation and it works similarly to earlier versions of IIS.

   ▶ **Isolate Users:** This mode authenticates users against local or domain accounts before they can access the home directories that match their usernames. All user home directories are in a directory structure under a single FTP root directory where each user is placed and restricted to a home directory. Users are not permitted to navigate out of the home directory.

▶ **Isolate Users Using Active Directory:** This mode authenticates user credentials against a corresponding Active Directory container, rather than searching the entire Active Directory, which requires large amounts of processing time. Specific FTP server instances can be dedicated to each customer to ensure data integrity and isolation.

NOTE

The isolation mode cannot be changed after it has been set.

6. Specify the location of the home directory where the files will be stored on the hard drive and click Next.

7. Specify Read and/or Write permission. Click Next.

8. Click Finish.

To modify the properties of an FTP site, right-click the FTP site and select Properties (see Figure 4.7). Many FTP sites are configured to connect with an anonymous connection because FTP usernames and passwords are sent in clear text (unencrypted) unless you are going through a VPN or some other encrypted pathway. Therefore, if you select Allow Anonymous Connections under the Security Accounts tab and select Allow Only Anonymous Connections, the only usernames and passwords sent are the user account and password specified in the Security Accounts tab. The Home Folder tab enables you to change the Read and/or Write permissions for a folder as well as the location of the FTP folder.

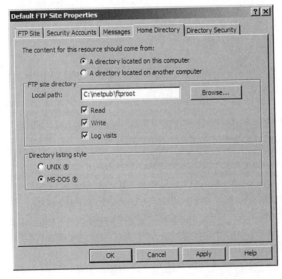

FIGURE 4.7 FTP Properties in IIS Manager.

Although you can use the IIS Manager to manage the FTP server, you can also use two command-prompt commands located in the systemroot\System32 folder:

- ▶ `iisftp.vbs`: Used to create and delete FTP sites, start and stop FTP sites, and list FTP sites.

- ▶ `iisftpdr.vbs`: Used to create, delete, and display virtual directories on FTP sites.

WMI Command-Line Tool

Windows Management Instrumentation (WMI) is a layer of software that runs as a service. It functions in much the same way a database does. A series of providers abstract and expose the operating system. These providers enable developers to reference a multitude of classes. The classes represent things such as your network configuration, running processes, installed services, hardware, and software. In many cases these providers expose data structures that resemble tables, making code that interacts with them simple and easy to write.

The WMI Command-line tool (WMIC) is a command-line interface for working with WMI. Using WMIC, you can manage multiple computers running different versions of Microsoft Windows. It can gather information on its hardware and services and it can be used to enable or disable services such as FTP.

Troubleshooting IIS Problems

Some problems with websites and applications can be easily identified and corrected. With others, you may need a little help in pinpointing the problem. This can be done with logging, tracing failed requests, and viewing worker processes.

Logging

IIS provides several tools for troubleshooting. First you need to enable logging. As soon as server logging is enabled, you can enable selective logging for any site on the server. You can also then view the log file to see which requests are failing and which requests are succeeding. By default, logging is enabled in IIS 7.0.

To enable or disable logging using the IIS Manager:

1. Open IIS Manager and navigate to the level you want to manage.

2. In Features View, double-click Logging.

3. On the Logging page, in the Actions pane, click Enable to enable logging or click Disable to disable logging.

To configure log file rollover options:

1. Open IIS Manager and navigate to the level you want to manage.

2. In Features View, double-click Logging.

3. On the Logging page, in the Log File Rollover section, select one of the following options:

   ▶ Schedule

   ▶ Maximum file size

   ▶ Do not create new log files

Failed Request Tracing

You can also configure tracing, which generates an error log when specific error conditions defined in the Failed Request Tracing Rules are met. The rules can be based on IIS status codes or on the length of time a process takes to run. When an error condition is detected, a detailed trace of events is written to an XML-based log so that you can troubleshoot the problem without having to reproduce it.

To enable tracing, follow these steps:

1. Open IIS Manager and navigate to the level you want to manage.

2. In the Connections pane, click Sites.

3. In Features View, select the site for which you want to enable trace logging.

4. In the Actions pane, under Configure, click Failed Request Tracing.

5. In the Edit Web Site Failed Request Tracing Settings dialog box, select Enable to enable logging for this site.

6. In the Directory text box, type the path where you want to store the log files or click Browse to find a location on the computer. The default is %SystemDrive%\inetpub\logs\FailedReqLogFiles.

7. In the Maximum Number of Trace Files text box, type the maximum number of trace log files that you want to keep, and then click OK.

To create a tracing rule for failed requests:

1. Open IIS Manager and navigate to the level you want to manage.

2. In Features View, double-click Failed Request Tracing Rules.

3. On the Failed Request Tracing Rules page, click Add in the Actions pane.

4. In the Specify Content to Trace area of the Add Failed Request Tracing Rule dialog box, select one of the following:

   ▶ **All Content (*):** When you want to track all files in a directory.

   ▶ **ASP.NET (*.aspx):** When you want to track all .aspx files in a directory.

   ▶ **ASP (*.asp):** When you want to track all .asp files in a directory.

   ▶ **Custom:** When you want to define a failure for a custom set of content, such as xyz.exe or *.jpg. This can contain, at most, one wildcard and must be local to the directory where the failed request definition is set.

5. Click Next.

6. In the Define Trace Conditions area of the Add Failed Request Tracing Rule dialog box, select one or more of the following conditions to trace:

   ▶ **Status Code(s):** Enter the status code(s) you want to trace. You can enter multiple status codes in this list by using commas to separate each code. You can also refine your status codes by using sub status codes, such as "404.2, 500."

   ▶ **Time Taken:** Enter the maximum time, in seconds, that a request should take.

   ▶ **Event Severity:** Select the severity level you want to trace from the Event Severity drop-down list. You can select Error, Critical Error, or Warning.

7. Click Next.

8. In the Select Trace Providers area of the Add Failed Request Tracing Rule dialog box, under Providers select one or more of the following trace providers:

   ▶ **ASP:** When you want to trace the start and completion of the execution of an ASP request.

   ▶ **ASP.NET:** When you want to see transitions into and out of managed code. This includes *.aspx requests.

▶ **ISAPI Extension:** When you want to trace the transition of a request into and out of an ISAPI extension process.

▶ **WWW Server:** When you want to trace requests through the IIS worker process.

9. In the Select Trace Providers area of the Add Failed Request Tracing Rule dialog box, under Verbosity select one or more of the following verbosity levels:

▶ **General:** Provides information that gives context for the request activity, for example, a GENERAL_REQUEST_START event that logs the URL and the verb for the request.

▶ **Critical Errors:** Provides information about actions that can cause a process to exit or that are about to cause a process to exit.

▶ **Errors:** Provides information about components that experience an error and cannot continue to process requests. These errors usually indicate a server-side problem.

▶ **Warnings:** Provides information about components that experience an error but can continue to process the request.

▶ **Information:** Provides general information about requests.

▶ **Verbose:** Provides detailed information about requests. This is the default selection.

10. If you selected the ASP.NET trace provider in step 8, in the Select Trace Providers area of the Add Failed Request Tracing Rule dialog box, under Areas, select one or more of the following functional areas for the provider to trace:

▶ **Infrastructure:** When you want to trace events that are primarily related to entering and leaving various parts of the ASP.NET infrastructure.

▶ **Module:** When you want to trace events that are logged as a request enters and leaves various HTTP pipeline modules.

▶ **Page:** When you want to generate trace events that correspond to the execution of specific ASP.NET page-related events, such as Page_Load, and so on.

▶ **AppServices:** When you want to trace events that are logged as part of the new application services functionality.

11. If you selected the WWW Server trace provider in step 8, in the Select Trace Providers area of the Add Failed Request Tracing Rule dialog box, under Areas, select one or more of the following functional areas for the provider to trace:

   ▶ **Authentication:** When you want to trace authentication attempts, for example, the name of the authenticated user, the authentication scheme (anonymous, basic, and so on), and the results of the authentication attempt (successful, failed, error, and so on).

   ▶ **Security:** When you want to generate trace events when requests are rejected by the IIS server for security-related reasons, such as if a client request was denied access to a resource.

   ▶ **Filter:** When you want to determine how long it takes an ISAPI filter to process requests.

   ▶ **StaticFile:** When you want to trace how long it takes requests for static files to be completed.

   ▶ **CGI:** When you want to generate trace events when a request is for a CGI file.

   ▶ **Compression:** When you want to generate trace events when a response is compressed.

   ▶ **Cache:** When you want to generate trace events for cache operations associated with the request.

   ▶ **RequestNotifications:** When you want to capture all request notifications, both on entrance and on exit.

   ▶ **Module:** When you want to trace events that are logged when a request enters and leaves various HTTP pipeline modules, or to capture trace events for managed modules.

12. Click Finish.

Viewing Worker Processes

In IIS 7.0, you can view performance information about worker processes in application pools. Additionally, you can view information about requests currently executing in a worker process. This information can help you determine where problems occur on your server, such as application hanging or memory leaking.

IIS 7.0 lists worker processes with associated application pool names, and provides the following information for each worker process:

- **Application Pool Name:** The name of the application pool. In the case of web gardens, the same application pool may be listed more than once in the grid to account for different worker processes running in the application pool.

- **Process ID:** The worker process identifier (ID) associated with the application pool.

- **State:** The state of the process, such as starting, running, or stopping.

- **CPU %:** The percentage of time that the worker process has used the CPU since last update. This corresponds to CPU Usage in Task Manager.

- **Private Bytes (KB):** The current size of memory committed to a worker process, which cannot be shared with other processes. This corresponds to Virtual Memory Size in Windows Task Manager.

- **Virtual Bytes (KB):** The current size of the virtual address space for a worker process. This does not correspond to anything in Windows Task Manager.

When you notice that a worker process is using many resources on your web server, or requests are taking a long time to process, you can view a list of current requests that are processing in a specific worker process. This information can help you determine where a problem occurs in a specific area of a site or application, such as a request for a particular file that causes high memory usage or high processor utilization.

The currently executing request information in IIS Manager returns the following information about requests in a worker process:

- **Site ID:** The site identifier (ID) for the specific request.

- **Url:** The requested Uniform Resource Locator (URL).

- **Verb:** The Hypertext Transfer Protocol (HTTP) verb used in the request.

- **Client IP:** The IP address of the client who made the request.

- **State:** The current pipeline module state in which the request is.

- **Module Name:** The current module where the request is.

- **Time Elapsed:** The period of time the request has been in process.

To view currently executing requests in a worker process, follow these steps:

1. Open IIS Manager.

2. In the Connections pane, select the server node in the tree.

3. In Features View, double-click Worker Processes.

4. Select a worker process from the grid.

5. Click View Current Requests in the Actions pane.

6. View the list of requests in the grid.

Exam Prep Questions

1. You have several Windows Server 2008 servers running IIS. You want to redirect users from website1 to website2. What command would you use?

   ○ **A.** `appcmd set config /section: Redirect/`
   `+[wildcard='' website1',destination=website2']`

   ○ **B.** `appcmd set config /section: Redirecthttp/`
   `+[wildcard=' website1 ' ,destination=website2 ']`

   ○ **C.** `appcmd set config /section:httpRedirect/`
   `+[wildcard='website2',destination='website1']`

   ○ **D.** `appcmd set config /section:http:Redirect/`
   `+[wildcard='website1',destination="website2']`

2. You have a website on your Windows Server 2008 computer. The website has static HTML pages, images, and other content. Which handler permissions should you use on the website that would prevent the web server from running any unauthorized scripts on your website?

   ○ **A.** Enable Read and Scripts.

   ○ **B.** Enable Read and Execute.

   ○ **C.** Enable Read and disable Scripts.

   ○ **D.** Enable Read and configure Custom.

3. You have a Windows Server 2008 computer with IIS 7.0. You want to configure URL authorization rules that prohibit users in the Temps role from accessing a website hosted on your server. What command should you use?

   ○ **A.** `appcmd set config /section:authorization /`
   `+"[accessType='Deny',roles='Temp']"`

   ○ **B.** `appcmd set config /section:authorization /`
   `+"[accessType='Deny',users="Temp']"`

   ○ **C.** `appcmd set config /section:authorization /`
   `+"[accessType='Deny',users='*']"`

   ○ **D.** `appcmd set config /section:authorization /`
   `+"[accessType='Deny',users='?']"`

4. You have a Windows Server 2008 computer with IIS. On this server, you have a web application that uses ASP.NET technology. You want to make sure that the web application cannot access files outside the application directory. What do you need to do?

  ○ **A.** Configure the trust level of code access to Low, Minimum, or Medium.

  ○ **B.** Configure the trust level of code to High or Full.

  ○ **C.** Disable the Write permission.

  ○ **D.** Disable the NTFS permissions on all other folders.

5. You have a Windows Server 2008 server running IIS on your domain. You plan to use certificate-based authentication and you want to ensure that each certificate sent by clients is identical to the respective copy of the client certificate stored on the web server. What should you do?

  ○ **A.** Use one-to-one IIS certificate mappings.

  ○ **B.** Use Active Directory certificate mappings.

  ○ **C.** Use many-to-one IIS certificate mapping.

  ○ **D.** Use Integrated Windows authentication.

6. You have a Windows Server 2008 computer with IIS. You have a new sales website that you would like to install. To make sure that all transactions are secure, you want to enable SSL. What should you do? (Choose two answers.)

  ○ **A.** Install a digital certificate on the IIS server.

  ○ **B.** Run the `Appcmd set config` command `"Sales"` `/section` `//sslFlags:Ssl` `/commit:APPHOST` command.

  ○ **C.** Enable Active Directory certificate mappings.

  ○ **D.** Create an HTTPS binding for the Sales website.

7. You have a Windows Server 2008 server with IIS and SMTP. You are hosting two websites, Acme.com and LooneyTunes.com, each with its own SMTP virtual server. You are having problems sending emails through SMTP for one of the two sites. What could be the problem?

  ○ **A.** The two SMTP virtual servers cannot have the same name.

  ○ **B.** The two SMTP virtual servers cannot have the same IP addresses.

  ○ **C.** The two SMTP virtual servers cannot use the same TCP port.

  ○ **D.** The two SMTP virtual servers cannot have the same domain name.

8. You decide to copy a website from one server to another server, using the `xcopy` command. What option creates the folder if the folder does not already exist?

   ○ **A.** /s

   ○ **B.** /e

   ○ **C.** /i

   ○ **D.** /x

9. You have a Windows Server 2008 computer with IIS. You plan to configure Internet Application Program Interface (SPI) and Common Gateway Interface (CGI) restrictions in IIS 7.0 to allow the ISAPI program ASP.DLL, which is stored in the %windir%\ system32\intetsrv folder path, to execute on the web server. What command would you use to do this?

   ○ **A.** `appcmd set config /section:isapiCgiRestriction /+"[path='%windir%\system32\inetsrv\asp.dll', description='Active Server Pages',allowed='True']"`

   ○ **B.** `appcmd set config /section:isapiCgiRestriction /+"[path='%windir%\ssytem32\inetsrv\asp.dll', description='Active Server Pages',allowed='False']"`

   ○ **C.** `appcmd set config /section:isapiCgiRestriction /- [path='%windir%\system32\inetsrv\asp.dll', description='Active Server Pages',allowed='True'] .allowed:False`

   ○ **D.** `appcmd set config /section:isapiCgiRestriction /- path='%windir%\system32\inetsrv\asp.dll', description='Active Server Pages',allowed='False'] .allowed:True`

10. What command would you use to enable HTTP logging on your Windows Server 2008 server with IIS?

   ○ **A.** `appcmd set config /section:logging /Log:True`

   ○ **B.** `appcmd set config /Log:True`

   ○ **C.** `appcmd set config /section:httpLogging /dontLog:True / selectiveLogging:Log`

   ○ **D.** `appcmd set config /section:httpLogging / dontLog:False /selectiveLogging:LogAll`

11. You have a Windows Server 2008 computer with IIS. You want to move the virtual directory's content to a new server. Which two parameters do you need to use with the appcmd command to point to the new location?

   ○ **A.** /vdir.name

   ○ **B.** /app.name

   ○ **C.** /path

   ○ **D.** /physicalPath

12. You have a Windows Server 2008 with IIS. IIS hosts two websites, one of which is a public site and one of which is an internal website. You need to configure SSL for both sites with the least cost incurred. What would you need to do?

   ○ **A.** Request two certificates from your internal CA.

   ○ **B.** Request one certificate from your internal CA and one from a third-party CA.

   ○ **C.** Request two certificates from a trusted third-party CA.

   ○ **D.** Request one certificate from a third-party CA.

13. You have a Windows Server 2008 computer with IIS. You want to create a new website. What parameters would you use to assign an ID of 3 when using the appcmd command?

   ○ **A.** /name:3

   ○ **B.** /id:3

   ○ **C.** /bindings:*:3

   ○ **D.** /idset=3

14. You have a Windows Server 2008 computer with IIS 7.0 in an Active Directory environment. You have a website with which you want a user to modify documents stored in the Documents virtual directory. But you want to make sure that that the user cannot add or delete documents in that directory. What permissions should you assign?

   ○ **A.** Read

   ○ **B.** Write

   ○ **C.** Modify

   ○ **D.** Read & Execute

15. You have a Windows Server 2008 with IIS. You want to enable emails to be sent through the web server. What do you need to do to enable email?

- ○ **A.** Install the SMTP server role in Server Manager.
- ○ **B.** Enable the SMTP service in Services.
- ○ **C.** Install the SMTP feature in Server Manager.
- ○ **D.** Add the SMTP protocol in Add/Remove programs.

16. You have a Windows Server 2008 with IIS. How do you back up the global server configuration?

- ○ **A.** Run the Windows Server Backup utility with the Full Server option and System State.
- ○ **B.** Run the Windows Server Backup utility with the Custom option.
- ○ **C.** Use the IIS Manager.
- ○ **D.** Use the `Appcmd.exe` command-line utility.

17. You have a Windows Server 2008 computer with IIS. You need to support a CGI application on one of your websites. What command would you use that would allow CGI applications to function?

- ○ **A.** `appcmd set config /section:handlers / accessPolicy:Script`
- ○ **B.** `appcmd set config /section:handlers / accessPolicy:Execute`
- ○ **C.** `appcmd set config /section:handlers / accessPolicy:NoRemoteScript`
- ○ **D.** `appcmd set config /section:handlers / accessPolicy:NoRemoteExecute`

18. You have a Windows Server 2008 computer with IIS. You want to make sure that the website's physical folders are not displayed. What command would you use?

- ○ **A.** `Appcmd set config /section:directoryBrowse / enabled:False`
- ○ **B.** `Appcmd set config /section:directoryBrowse / enabled:True /showFlags:None`
- ○ **C.** `Appcmd set config /section:defaultDocument / enabled:True`
- ○ **D.** `Appcmd set config /section:defaultDocument / enabled:False`

19. You have a Windows Server 2008 with IIS on an Active Directory domain. You want to configure it so that all users that access the website are authenticated with the Windows Server 2008 domain controllers. All websites (internal and external) are HTTP 1.1 protocol-based web applications. Which secure authentication method would you use?

    ○ **A.** Basic

    ○ **B.** Digest

    ○ **C.** Windows

    ○ **D.** Anonymous

20. You have a Windows Server 2008 computer with IIS. You have a manager who is leaving the company. Therefore, you need to remove the assistant's permissions to the site. Which two answers would complete this task?

    ○ **A.** In the Connections page, click the server node, and in Features View, double-click IIS Manager Users.

    ○ **B.** On the IIS Manager Permissions page, select the user, and in the Actions pane, click Deny User.

    ○ **C.** On the IIS Manager Connections page, select the user, and in the Actions pane, click Deny User.

    ○ **D.** On the IIS Manager Users page, select the user account, and in the Actions pane, click Disable.

21. You have a Windows Server 2008 computer with IIS that hosts several websites for various companies. You have a documents folder to which users need to connect on a new website that is located on another server that uses a shared folder. Although users can access the main site, they cannot access the content of the virtual directory on the other server. What do you need to do to give them access?

    ○ **A.** Right-click the virtual folder and select Enable.

    ○ **B.** Restart IIS so that the virtual folder can attach to the remote server.

    ○ **C.** Configure to connect as a specific user that has access to the shared folder in the properties of the virtual directory.

    ○ **D.** Give the Read permission to the virtual folder to a group of users who need access to the virtual folder.

22. You have a Windows Server 2008 computer running IIS. On the IIS server, you are running an FTP site. What command would you use to stop the FTP service?

    ○ **A.** `IISFtp.vbs`

    ○ **B.** `IISFtpdr.vbs`

    ○ **C.** `IISReset.vbs`

    ○ **D.** `IISWeb.vbs`

Answers to Exam Prep Questions

1. Answer D is correct. You need to use the `appcmd set config` command with the `http:Redirect` option to redirect website1 to website2. Answers A and B are incorrect because the section is called `httpRedirect`. Answer C is incorrect because website1 and website2 are out of place.

2. Answer C is correct. You need to have the Read permission to be able to access the website. You want to disable scripts because this would prevent unauthorized scripts from running. Answer A is incorrect because you do not want scripts to run. Answer B is incorrect because you don't need the Execute permission because you are not executing any executables on the website. Answer D is incorrect because there is no custom permission.

3. Answer A is correct. The `appcmd set config /section:authorization / +"[accessType='Deny',roles='Temp']"` command is the correct syntax to disable access to the Temp role. Answer B is incorrect because you want to deny the Temp role, not user Temp. Answer C is incorrect because it would deny all users, not just the Temp role. Answer D is incorrect because it would deny anonymous users.

4. Answer A is correct. By having Low, Minimum, or Medium ASP code access, you limit access to folders outside the application. Answer B is incorrect because if the application is set to High or Full code access, the application can access directories outside the application folder. Answer C is incorrect because the Write permission does not affect other folders outside the actual web folder. Answer D is incorrect because NTFS permissions are impractical because you would have to lock down every other folder on the server.

5. Answer A is correct. Using one-to-one IIS certification mappings ensures that each certificate sent by clients must be identical to the one stored on the web server. Answer B is incorrect because Active Directory mappings use Active Directory to authenticate domain users with client computers. It does not map clients to their respective copies of client certificates stored on the web server. Answer C is incorrect because this does not map clients to their respective copies on the web server. Answer D is incorrect because Integrated Windows authentication does not use digital certificates.

6. Answers A and D are correct. You need to have a digital certificate installed on the IIS server and that digital certificate must be bound to the Sales website. Answer B is incorrect because it would require SSL communication but does not enable it. Answer C is incorrect because this would allow access only to Active Directory users.

7. Answer B is correct. When you have multiple SMTP virtual servers, each server must have a unique IP address/TCP port number combination. Of course, the recommended port is TCP port 25. Answer A is incorrect because two SMTP virtual servers can have the same name. Answer C is incorrect because they can have the same TCP port (most likely TCP port 25), but different addresses. Answer D is incorrect because two SMTP virtual servers can have the same domain name.

8. Answer C is correct. The /i creates a new directory if Source is a directory or contains wildcards and Destination does not exist. Answer A is incorrect because /s is used to copy over subfolders and their files. Answer B is incorrect because /e copies over empty subdirectories. Answer D is incorrect because /x is used to copy the audit information.

9. Answer A is correct. The `appcmd set config /section:isapiCgiRestriction /` `+"[path='%windir%\system32\inetsrv\asp.dll',description='Active` `Server Pages',allowed='True']"` command allows an ISAPI program, named ASP.DLL, stored in '%windir%\system32\inetsrv folder path, to execute on the web server. Answer B is incorrect because it would prohibit the ASP.DLL program from executing on the web server. To allow the ASP.DLL program to execute on the web server, you must set the value of the allowed parameter to `'True'`. Answer C is incorrect because the command is set to prohibit the ASP.DLL program from executing on the web server. The scenario requires that you write a new restriction that allows the ASP.DLL program to execute. Answer D is incorrect because this command would change an existing ISAPI restriction setting that prohibits the ASP.DLL program from executing on the web server, and sets it to allow the ASP.DLL program to execute on the web server.

10. Answer D is correct. The correct syntax to enable logging is `appcmd set config` `/section:httpLogging /dontLog:False /selectiveLogging:LogAll`. Answer A is incorrect because the `/Log:True` should be `/dontLog:True`. Answer B is incorrect because `/Log:True` is an invalid option. Answer C is incorrect because this option would shut off logging.

11. Answers A and D are correct. When using the `appcmd set vdir` command, the `vdir.name` specifies the name of the virtual directory and the `/physicalpath` specifies the new location. Answer B is incorrect because the `appcmd set vidr` command does not support the appname parameter. Answer C is incorrect because the `path` parameter is used to specify the virtual path to the virtual directory.

12. Answer B is correct. You only need one digital certificate from a third-party Certificate Authority for your public website. You can use an internal certificate authority for your internal website, which would not cost anything to generate. Answer A is incorrect because the internal certificate would not be trusted for users accessing the public website from outside your organization. Answer C is incorrect because you don't need to spend money for a digital certificate for your internal website. Answer D is incorrect because you still need a digital certificate for your internal network.

13. Answer B is correct. To assign the ID, you would use the /id option. Answer A is incorrect because the /name option is used to assign the name of the website. Option C is incorrect because the /bindings option specifies the port that the website will use. Answer D is incorrect because the /idset option does not exist with the appcmd command.

14. Answer B is correct. The Write permission enables users to only modify documents but not add or delete documents in that directory. Answer A is incorrect because the Read permissions enable the user to only view contents and properties of the documents. Answer C is incorrect because it also allows the user to add or delete documents. Answer D is incorrect because it allows the user to run executable files and scripts but does not give the user permission to modify documents.

15. Answer C is correct. SMTP is a Windows feature that enables you to send emails. Answer A is incorrect because SMTP is not a server role. Answer B is incorrect because SMTP cannot be enabled in the Services console. Answer D is incorrect because SMTP cannot be added through the Control Panel's Add/Remove programs function.

16. Answer D is correct. To back up the IIS configuration, you need to use the `appcmd.exe` command. Answers A and B are incorrect because Windows Backup does not copy the individual IIS configuration. Answer C is incorrect because the IIS Manager cannot be used to back up the IIS configuration.

17. Answer B is correct. To allow CGI applications, you need to allow Execute permissions so that the website can run executables, including CGI applications. Answer A is incorrect because assigning script permissions runs only scripts but not executables. Answer C is incorrect because the `/accessPolicy:Script` option enables handlers that require script rights to run scripts in a virtual directory. Answer D is incorrect because the `/accessPolicy:NoRemoteExecute` option is used to prevent handlers from running executables, such as CGI scripts, when handlers receive a remote request.

18. Answer A is correct. To disable directory browsing, you must change the option to False. Answer B is incorrect because this would turn directory browsing on. Answers C and D are incorrect because these commands are used to configure the default document.

19. Answer B is correct. Digest authentication ensures that your users are using HTTP 1.1 protocol-based web browsers and are authenticated by the Windows Server 2008 domain controllers. Digest authentication ensures that all users, including internal and external network users, who attempt to connect to the web server are authenticated via a domain controller. Answer A is incorrect because the Basic authentication method prompts users to provide a valid username and password before it allows them to connect to the web server. In addition, passwords are transmitted unencrypted across the network, resulting in security-related issues unless you also enable SSL. Answer C is incorrect because you should not use Windows authentication. It is typically used in an intranet environment where you require the client to access the web server by using the NTLM or Kerberos protocols. This authentication method is not recommended for an Internet environment. Answer D is incorrect because Anonymous does not provide authentication.

20. Answers B and D are correct. You can deny user access or disable the user account using IIS Manager. Answer A is incorrect because you should not click the server node in the Connections page and double-click IIS Manager Users in Features View. This lists all the users in the IIS manager's group; it does not remove a user's permissions. Answer C is incorrect because you should not select the user account on the IIS Manager Connections page and in the Actions pane, click Deny User. This operation is performed on the IIS Manager Permissions page and not the IIS Manager Connections page.

21. Answer C is correct. Users need to attach to the virtual folder with an account that has access to the folder. Answer A is incorrect because there is no option to enable or disable a virtual folder. Answer B is incorrect because you don't need to restart IIS or a website to get a virtual folder to attach to a remote server. Answer D is incorrect because this is not a permissions problem.

22. Answer A is correct. The IISFtp.vbs command can be used stop the FTP service. Answer B is incorrect because IISFtpdr is used to create, delete, or query an FTP virtual directory or directory. Answer C is incorrect because the IISReset.vbs command is used to safely start, stop, enable, and disable the IIS services, not the FTP services. Answer D is incorrect because the IISWeb.vbs tool is used to stop, start, pause, delete, or query the web service, or to create a website, not the FTP server.

Need to Know More?

For more information about IIS 7.0, including IIS 7.0 Web Resources, IIS 7.0 Deployment Guide, and IIS 7.0 Operations Guide, visit the following website:

http://technet2.microsoft.com/windowsserver2008/en/library/4b40220c-ae1e-494e-902a-1b41057661fa1033.mspx?mfr=true

For more information on the appcmd.exe commands, visit the following website:

http://technet2.microsoft.com/WindowsServer2008/en/library/ec52c53b-6aff-4d76-995e-3d222588bf321033.mspx

For more information about using the xcopy command, visit the following website:

http://technet.microsoft.com/en-us/library/bb491035.aspx

For more information about the Windows Management Instrumentation Command-line (WMIC) tool, visit the following website:

http://technet2.microsoft.com/windowsserver/en/library/8bc3a9f5-cc8b-4ae1-b97d-60bdbb8670351033.mspx?mfr=true

CHAPTER FIVE

Microsoft Windows SharePoint Services

Terms you'll need to understand:

- ✓ Windows SharePoint Services (WSS)
- ✓ SharePoint Products and Technology Configuration Wizard
- ✓ SharePoint 3.0 Central Administration
- ✓ site collection
- ✓ subsites
- ✓ WSS search service
- ✓ alternate access mapping
- ✓ quota
- ✓ Psconfig.exe
- ✓ Stsadm.exe
- ✓ Recycle Bin
- ✓ document library
- ✓ alerts
- ✓ workflows
- ✓ tasks

Techniques/concepts you'll need to master:

- ✓ Install and configure Windows SharePoint Services (WSS) 3.0.
- ✓ Perform backups using Central Administration and Stsadm.exe for WSS 3.0.
- ✓ Enable and configure outgoing and incoming email in WSS 3.0.
- ✓ Configure permissions for users and groups within WSS 3.0.
- ✓ Create tasks and workflow for a document library within WSS 3.0.
- ✓ Create a quota template and apply it to a WSS 3.0 site.
- ✓ Create individual quotas within WSS 3.0.
- ✓ Use the psconfig.exe and Stsadm to manage and configure WSS 3.0.
- ✓ Manage documents within a WSS 3.0 document library.

Microsoft *Windows SharePoint Services (WSS)* turns a website hosted on Internet Information Services (IIS) server into a web portal that allows for

▶ Document Storage and Management

▶ Information Management and Communication

▶ Collaboration

The version of WSS included with Windows Server 2008 is 3.0, which was released on November 16, 2006 as part of the Microsoft Office 2007 suite. WSS 3.0 is built using .NET Framework 2.0 and .NET Framework 3.0 Windows Workflow Foundation to add workflow capabilities to the basic suite.

WSS provides a centralized repository for shared documents, as well as browser-based management and administration of them. You can create numerous document libraries, which are collections of files that can be shared for collaborative editing. You can configure who can access and view the documents and who can upload new documents or edit the current documents. You can also configure the document libraries to require an approver or approvers before a document is posted and seen by everyone else, or you can set up a document to go through multiple people who add parts to the document or who are responsible for editing the document (see Figure 5.1).

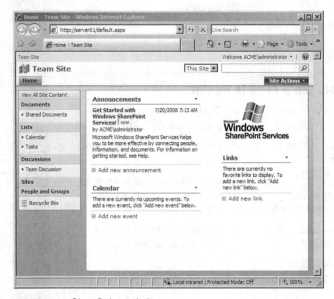

FIGURE 5.1 SharePoint website.

WSS is an essential component to Microsoft Office SharePoint Server (MOSS) 2007 and Microsoft Project Server 2007. MOSS adds more functionality to WSS by including better document management, enterprise search functionality, navigation features, RSS support, as well as features from Microsoft Content Management Server. The Enterprise edition of MOSS also includes features for business data analysis, such as Excel Services and the Business Data Catalog.

MOSS also provides integration with Microsoft Office applications, such as project management capabilities with Microsoft Project Server. Microsoft Project Server is a portal that interfaces with Microsoft Project to manage projects.

As a *document library*, WSS also enables you to keep track of multiple versions or revisions of a document. When a person first posts a document, it appears as version 1.0. When the document is updated and approved, it becomes version 2.0. Depending on the configuration of WSS, you may be able to access both versions.

WSS also includes a collection of web parts, which are web widgets that can be embedded into web pages to provide certain functionality. WSS already includes many web parts such as workspaces and dashboards, navigation tools, lists, *alert*s (including email alerts), shared calendars, contact lists, and discussion boards. In addition to the document collaboration, WSS offers workflow management for many of its parts and tools. This helps you create *task*s and lists that require input or approval from multiple people.

> **EXAM ALERT**
>
> The questions on the exam focus on installing, configuring, and managing WSS. The exam does not focus on using WSS.

Installing and Configuring WSS

To install WSS 3.0, the server needs to meet minimum hardware and software requirements. The WSS server must meet the following minimum hardware requirements:

- ▶ Dual-processor with processor clock speeds of 2.0 gigahertz (GHz) or higher.

- ▶ A minimum of 1 gigabyte (GB) of random access memory (RAM). Of course, for improved performance, use 2GB of RAM.

The WSS server must meet the following minimum software requirements:

▶ Microsoft Windows Server 2003 (with SP1) or 2008.

▶ NTFS file system.

▶ Microsoft IIS 6.0 or 7.0 in worker process isolation mode.

▶ Microsoft .NET Framework 3.0.

▶ ASP.NET 2.0.

▶ Microsoft SQL Server 2000 with SP4 or SQL Server 2005 for server farm installations. When installing WSS 3.0 on a single server that does not include a SQL server, Windows Internal Database Engine (included with Windows Server 2008) can be installed and used with WSS.

Planning SharePoint Services

You should do some planning before you actually install WSS 3.0 and start creating sites. First, you need to determine the web applications to be created, their purpose, and the paths to access these web applications. You can use specific paths to contain *site collection*s. When you create a web application, two paths are created by default:

▶ **Root path (/):** This path has an explicit inclusion that can contain one site collection. For example, if you want a Unified Resource Locator (URL) to appear as http://domainname/default.aspx, you would create the site collection at this root path.

▶ **Sites path (/sites):** This path has a wildcard inclusion that can contain many site collections. For example, when you use the /sites path, the URL for a site called Site1 would be http://server_name/sites/Site1/default.aspx.

You need to determine whether the WSS site can be used as an internal website (intranet), as an external website (Internet), or as an extranet website (used by internal and external users).

You also need to determine whether you are going to install WSS and the internal SQL server or are going to create a WSS on a server farm where you have a dedicated SQL server. For heavily used SharePoint services websites or large SharePoint services websites with many documents and many WSS sites, you should consider creating a server farm with a dedicated SQL server.

Installing SharePoint Services

To install Windows SharePoint Services (WSS 3.0) with SP1, you must first download it from the following website:

http://www.microsoft.com/downloads/details.aspx?familyid=EF93E453-75F1-45DF-8C6F-4565E8549C2A&displaylang=en

When you run the installation program, a wizard starts that gives you the option to install only on this server or install as part of a server farm, which requires you to connect SharePoint to a SQL Server database before you can create and use a Windows SharePoint Services site. If you specify only on this server, you also need to specify a Simple Mail Transfer Protocol (SMTP) server so that SharePoint can send emails out to the various users.

Upgrading SharePoint Services

You can upgrade between versions of the same product or technology (such as Windows SharePoint Services 2.0 to Windows SharePoint Services 3.0 or Microsoft Office SharePoint Portal Server 2003 Service Pack 2 to Microsoft Office SharePoint Server 2007), but you cannot attempt to run more than one version of more than one of these technologies together on the same hardware, such as both Windows SharePoint Services 3.0 and SharePoint Portal Server 2003.

Some of the SharePoint Products and Technologies can co-exist with each other (such as Office SharePoint Server 2007 and Microsoft Office Project Server 2007), or be upgraded across products or versions (such as from Windows SharePoint Services 3.0 to Office SharePoint Server 2007).

Before you run any upgrade process, you need to determine which upgrade approach to take. The upgrade paths include the following:

- **In-place upgrade:** Upgrades the content and configuration data in place, at one time. Although it is the easiest approach, which retains the original URLs, you have no ability to revert to the original site.

- **Gradual upgrade:** Installs the new version side by side with the previous version. The server administrator determines which site collections to upgrade and when to upgrade them.

- **Gradual upgrade for shared services:** Same as gradual upgrade, but enables you to upgrade parent and child portal sites individually.

- **Deploy a new farm and migrate data:** Requires the server administrator to install the new version on a separate farm or separate hardware, and then manually migrate the databases into the new environment.

SharePoint Products and Technology Configuration Wizard

The *SharePoint Products and Technologies Configuration Wizard* performs basic tasks that require minimal user input and that must be performed to start SharePoint Central Administration or tasks that cannot be performed anywhere else.

In addition to using the configuration wizard to perform the initial configuration, you can use the configuration wizard at any time to perform the following:

▸ Identify missing components.

▸ Validate your configuration.

▸ Identify, repair, or reset security and low-level configuration settings.

You must successfully complete the configuration wizard before the server deployment is finished and you can access SharePoint Central Administration to configure your site.

Deploying SharePoint Products and Technologies in a single server environment installs all the components and features on a single computer under default settings. The configuration wizard does not prompt you for any configuration settings or credentials. Instead, the configuration wizard uses default values to create the web application, core services, and standard security groups that are required to start Central Administration.

When you select the Advanced option in the Setup Wizard, the configuration wizard enables you to install into a server farm, use an existing database, deploy a new one, or connect to an existing server farm. You can create new databases or use existing databases. In your server farm one or more computers can be web servers, and another computer can provide database services through Microsoft SQL Server.

You can use Repair to overwrite changed or damaged files and Registry settings. For example, you can use Repair if you cannot start Central Administration in a farm that was working. This can happen if the IIS administration web application has been accidentally deleted. When you repair an installation, the files that were installed are verified, missing components are detected, and then the configuration is repaired.

SharePoint 3.0 Central Administration

After the configuration wizard completes, you must open *SharePoint 3.0 Central Administration* (found in Administrative Tools) to complete configuring WSS. When you first open the Central Administration, you see a list of Administrator Tasks on the Home tab, which include tasks that need to be completed for WSS to be fully functional. Some of these tasks include configuring incoming and outgoing email settings, adding anti-virus protection, and configuring the *WSS search service* (see Figure 5.2).

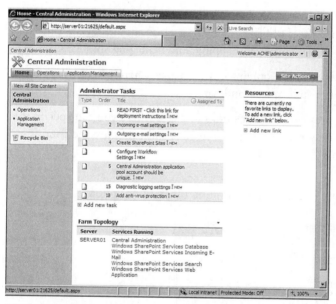

FIGURE 5.2   SharePoint Central Administration.

Operations Settings

The Operations tab enables you to manage your server or server farm, performing tasks such as changing the server farm topology, specifying which services are running on each server, and changing settings that affect multiple servers or applications. The Application Management tab contains links to pages that help you configure settings for applications and components that are installed on the server or server farm. The primary sections found on the Operations tab include:

▶ **Topology and Services:** Contains links to pages where you can administer services, farm topology, and email settings.

▶ **Security Configuration:** Contains links to pages where you can administer security settings, including antivirus and blocked file types for downloading and uploading.

▶ **Logging and Reporting:** Contains links to pages that help you understand the state of your servers.

▶ **Upgrade and Migration:** Contains links to pages where you can complete such tasks as upgrading sites and servers, enabling features, and migrating content.

▶ **Global Configuration:** Contains links to pages where you can administer settings that affect the farm globally, such as administering timer jobs, configuring alternative access mapping, and managing solutions.

▶ **Backup and Restore:** Contains links to pages where you can back up and restore both applications and data.

▶ **Data Configuration:** Contains links to pages where you can specify the default database server for SharePoint sites and configure the data retrieval service.

Figure 5.3 shows the Central Administration Operations option.

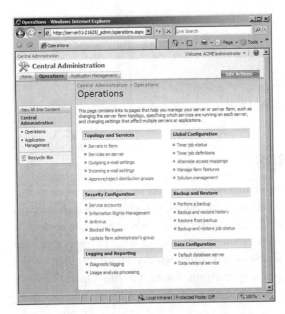

FIGURE 5.3 Operations options in SharePoint Central Administration.

After Setup finishes, your browser window opens to the home page of your new SharePoint site. Although you can start adding content to the site or you can start customizing the site, you should first perform some administrative tasks by using the SharePoint Central Administration website, including the following:

- ▶ **Configuring outgoing email settings:** You can configure outgoing email settings so that your SMTP server sends email alerts to site users and notifications to site administrators. You can configure both the From email address and the Reply email address that appear in outgoing alerts.

- ▶ **Configuring incoming email settings:** You can configure incoming email settings so that SharePoint sites accept and archive incoming email. You can also configure incoming email settings so that SharePoint sites can archive email discussions as they happen, save emailed documents, and show emailed meetings on site calendars. In addition, you can configure the SharePoint Directory Management Service to provide support for email distribution list creation and management.

- ▶ **Configuring diagnostic logging settings:** You can configure several diagnostic logging settings to help with troubleshooting. This includes enabling and configuring trace logs, event messages, user-mode error messages, and Customer Experience Improvement Program events.

- ▶ **Configuring antivirus protection settings:** You can configure several antivirus settings if you have an antivirus program that is designed for Windows SharePoint Services 3.0. Antivirus settings enable you to control whether documents are scanned on upload or download and whether users can download infected documents. You can also specify how long you want the antivirus program to run before it times out, and you can specify how many execution threads the antivirus program can use on the server.

- ▶ **Creating SharePoint sites:** When Setup finishes, you have a single web application that contains a single SharePoint site collection that hosts a SharePoint site. You can create more SharePoint site collections, sites, and web applications if your site design requires multiple sites or multiple web applications.

Outgoing Email Settings

Several features of SharePoint, including workflows and alerts/subscriptions, require emails to be sent to SharePoint users. Before SharePoint can be configured to send outgoing email, you must first install an SMTP server.

After an SMTP server is available, you need to do the following:

1. On the Operations page, click Outgoing E-mail Settings in the Topology and Services section.

2. On the Outgoing E-Mail Settings page, in the Mail Settings section, type the SMTP server name for outbound email in the Outbound SMTP server box.

3. In the From Address text box, type the From address as you want it to appear to email recipients.

4. In the Reply-to Address box, type the email address to which you want email recipients to reply.

5. In the Character Set menu, select the character set appropriate for your language.

6. Click OK.

> **EXAM ALERT**
>
> To use outgoing email, you need to install an SMTP server and you need to configure Outgoing E-mail Settings using SharePoint Central Administration.

Incoming Email Settings

If you need SharePoint to receive and store incoming messages in a list, you can configure sites, lists, and groups with their own email addresses. To use automatic mode to enable incoming email, you must install the IIS SMTP server.

If the incoming E-mail Settings are not in automatic mode, you need to specify a drop folder by following these procedures:

1. On the Operations page, in the Topology and Services section, click Incoming E-mail Settings.

2. If you want to enable sites on this server to receive email, select Yes in the Enable Incoming E-Mail section on the Incoming E-Mail Settings page.

3. Select either the Automatic or the Advanced settings mode. If you select Advanced, you can specify a drop folder rather than use an SMTP server.

4. If you want to connect to the SharePoint Directory Management Service, in the Directory Management Service section, select Yes. You can connect to the SharePoint Directory Management Service for SharePoint sites to manage email addresses in SharePoint lists.

5. In the Directory Management Service URL box, type the URL of the SharePoint Directory Management Service.

6. In the E-mail Server Display Address box, type the email server name (for example, mail.sharepoint.fabrikam.com).

7. Answer the following two questions by selecting Yes or No:

   ▶ Does the Directory Management Service manage distribution lists?

   ▶ Should distribution lists accept mail only from authenticated senders?

8. In the Incoming E-Mail Server Display Address section, type a display name for the email server in the E-mail Server Display Address box.

9. In the Safe E-Mail Servers section, select one of the following options:

   ▶ Accept Mail from All E-mail Servers

   ▶ Accept Mail from These Safe E-mail Servers. If you select this option, type the IP addresses (one per line) of the email servers that you want to specify as safe in the corresponding box.

10. In the E-mail Drop Folder section, in the E-mail Drop Folder box, type the name of the folder in which Microsoft Windows SharePoint Services polls for incoming email from the Windows SMTP Service. This option is available only if you selected Advanced mode.

11. Click OK.

Backup Settings

SharePoint sites can quickly become an essential component to an organization. Of course, you must make sure that you perform backups on a regular basis. To perform a backup of WSS, follow these steps:

1. Open Central Administration.

2. Click Operations on the top navigation bar.

3. In the Backup and Restore section of the Operations page, click Perform a Backup.

4. On the Select Component to Backup page, choose the components you want to back up, such as a Farm, a web application, or a content database. You can select any one component and all components under it.

5. When you have selected all the components you want to back up, click Continue to Backup Options. On the Start Backup page, in the Backup File Location section, enter the UNC path to the backup folder.

6. Click OK.

You can view the backup job status on the backup status page by clicking Refresh. The page also refreshes every 30 seconds automatically. Backup and recovery is a Timer service job, so it may take about a minute for the backup to start. If you receive any errors, you can find more information by looking in the spbackup.log file at the UNC path you specified above.

Antivirus Settings

To keep your network infrastructure secure, you need keep it free of viruses. Therefore, you must make sure that the document does not contain a virus when it is added to SharePoint. To enable virus protection within SharePoint, follow these steps:

1. On the Operations page, in the Security Configuration section, click Antivirus.

2. On the Antivirus page, in the Antivirus Settings section, select one or all of the following:

   ▶ Scan documents on upload

   ▶ Scan documents on download

   ▶ Allow users to download infected documents

   ▶ Attempt to clean infected documents

3. In the Antivirus Time Out section, in the Time Out Duration (in Seconds) box, type a value for how long to wait for the virus scanner before timing out.

4. In the Antivirus Threads section, in the Number of Threads box, type a value for the number of threads that the virus scanner can use.

Service Account Settings

When you configure the web applications and application pools, you need to specify under which service account the web application or application pool is to run. Follow these steps to change the service account:

1. On the Operations page, in the Security Configuration section, click Service accounts.

2. On the Service Accounts page, in the Credential Management section, under Select the Component to Update, select web application pool.

3. In the Web Service list, click a web service.

4. In the Application Pool list, click the application pool that you want associated with the web application.

5. Under Select an Account for This Component, select one of the following:

   ▸ **Predefined:** Select this option to use a predefined account, such as the Network Service account or the Local Service account.

   ▸ **Configurable:** Select this option to specify a different account.

6. Click OK.

Application Management Settings

The Application Management page contains links where you can create and administer web applications and site collections, and it contains links to pages where you can configure related settings. The main categories found in the Application Management page include:

▸ **SharePoint Web Application Management:** Contains links to pages where you can manage web applications, configure email settings at the web application level, and manage content databases.

▸ **SharePoint Site Management:** Contains links to pages where you can manage site collections and site use. It also includes options to create and delete site collections and to create and configure quotas.

▸ **External Service Connections:** Contains links to pages where you can administer connections to services that are external to web applications, including document conversion services.

▸ **Workflow Management:** Contains links to pages where you can manage workflow settings.

▸ **Office SharePoint Server Shared Services:** Contains links to pages where you can manage shared services at the farm level.

▸ **Application Security:** Contains links to pages where you can administer security at the web application level.

▸ **InfoPath Forms Services:** Contains links to pages where you can manage forms and Forms Services settings.

Figure 5.4 shows the Application Management options in SharePoint Central Administration.

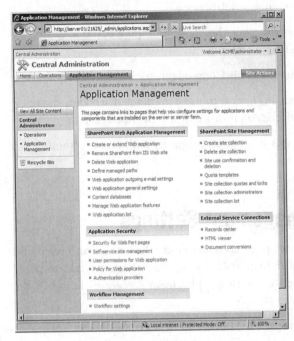

FIGURE 5.4 Application Management options in SharePoint Central Administration.

Creating a Web Application

After you have installed the general configuration steps, you are then ready to create a web application that will host a WSS site. To create a web application, click the Create or Extend Web Application link under the Application Management tab. The Create New Web Application dialog appears (see Figure 5.5). When you create a new web application, you can use an IIS website that is already created or you can create a new website that will host the web application. You also need to define security configuration, the application pool to use, the name of the database server and database name, and the name of the search server.

Creating a SharePoint Website

In SharePoint, you can create a single site collection that contains a single SharePoint site or you can create many site collections that include many sites under each site collection. To build a SharePoint site, you can create a site collection by either creating a top-level site or by adding *subsites* to an existing site collection. Subsites can be used to organize and separate web content to make it easier for users to locate information, or they can be used as security boundaries.

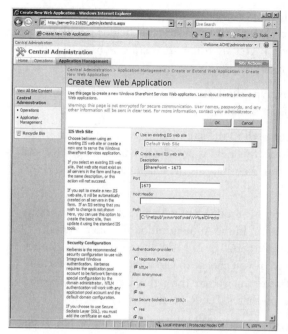

FIGURE 5.5 Create New Web Application options in SharePoint Central Administration.

Before you can create a site or a site collection, you must first create a web application. A web application comprises an IIS site with a unique application pool and can be assigned to an SSP (Shared Services Provider). You then create a site collection, which can then be accessed by the users.

To create a web application, follow these steps:

1. On the Central Administration home page, click Application Management.

2. On the Application Management page, in the SharePoint Web Application Management section, click Create or Extend Web Application.

3. On the Create or Extend Web Application page, in the Adding a SharePoint Web Application section, click Create a New Web Application.

4. To choose to use an existing website, select Use an Existing Web Site, and specify the website on which to install your new web application by selecting it from the drop-down menu. To choose to create a new website, select Create a New IIS Web Site, and type the name of the website in the Description box.

5. In the Port box, type the port number you want to use to access the web application. If you are creating a new website, this field is populated with a suggested port number. If you are using an existing website, this field is populated with the current port number.

6. In the Host Header box, type the URL you want to use to access the web application. This is an optional field.

7. In the Path box, type the path to the site directory on the server. If you are creating a new website, this field is populated with a suggested path. If you are using an existing website, this field is populated with the current path.

8. In the Security Configuration section, configure authentication and encryption for your web application. In the Authentication Provider section, choose either Negotiate (Kerberos) or NTLM. In the Allow Anonymous section, choose Yes or No. If you choose to allow anonymous access, this enables anonymous access to the website through the computer-specific anonymous access account (that is, IUSR_<computername>).

9. In the Use Secure Sockets Layer (SSL) section, select Yes or No. If you choose to enable SSL for the website, you must configure SSL by requesting and installing an SSL certificate.

10. In the Load Balanced URL section, type the URL for the domain name for all sites that users will access in this web application. This URL domain is used in all links shown on pages within the web application. By default, the box is populated with the current server name and port.

11. The Zone box is automatically set to Default for a new web application, and cannot be changed from this page.

12. In the Application Pool section, choose whether to use an existing application pool or create a new application pool for this web application. To use an existing application pool, select Use Existing Application Pool. Then select the application pool you want to use from the drop-down menu. To create a new application pool, select Create a New Application Pool and specify the name of the new application pool and the security account under which the application pool will run.

13. In the Reset Internet Information Services section, choose whether to allow Windows SharePoint Services to restart IIS on other farm servers.

14. Under Database Name and Authentication, choose the database server, database name, and authentication method for your new web application.

To create a site collection, click the Create Site Collection link under the Application Management tab. When you create a site collection, you can then specify a collaboration template or a meeting template.

The following are the available collaboration templates that allow team members to work together:

▶ **Team Site:** This template creates a site where teams can create, organize, and share information. It includes a Document Library and basic lists, such as Announcements, Calendar, Contacts, and Links.

▶ **Blank Site:** This template creates a website with a blank home page that can be customized with a web browser or a Windows SharePoint services–compatible web design program through the addition of interactive lists and other features.

▶ **Document Workspace:** This template creates a site where team members can work together on documents. It provides a document library for storing the primary document and supporting files, a Task list for assigning to-do items, and a Links list for resources related to the document.

▶ **Wiki Site:** This template creates a site where users can quickly and easily add, edit, and link web pages.

▶ **Blog:** This template creates a site where users can post information and allow others to comment on it.

The following are the available meeting templates that allow the more efficient running of meetings and posting the results of meetings:

▶ **Basic Meeting Workspace:** This template creates a site that provides all the basics to plan, organize, and track meetings. It contains the following lists: Objects, Attendees, Agenda, and Document Library.

▶ **Blank Meeting Workspace:** This template creates a blank Meeting Workspace site that can be customized based on the organization's requirements.

▶ **Decision Meeting Workspace:** This template provides a Meeting Workspace in which to review relevant documents and record decisions. It contains the following lists: Objectives, Attendees, Agenda, Document Library, Tasks, and Decisions.

▶ **Social Meeting Workspace:** This template creates a site that provides a planning tool for social occasions, featuring a discussion board and a picture library to post pictures of the event. It contains the following lists and web parts: Attendees, Directions, Image/Logo, Things To Bring, Discussions, and Picture Library.

▶ **Multipage Meeting Workspace:** This template creates a site that provides all the basics to plan, organize, and track your meeting with multiple pages. It contains the following lists: Objectives, Attendees, and Agenda, in addition to two blank pages for you to customize based on your requirements.

After a site collection is created, you can then create subsites by opening the Site Actions menu, selecting Create (see Figure 5.6) and selecting Sites and Workspaces. You would then specify the name of the subsite, the template to use, and whether user permissions flow down from the parent site or use unique permissions.

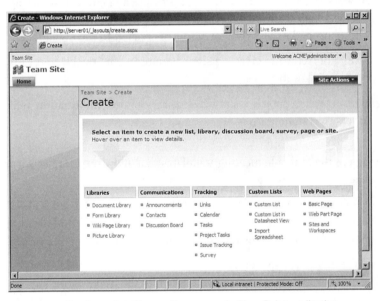

FIGURE 5.6　Creating a list, library, site, or page in SharePoint application.

You can also use the Create option to create document libraries (document, form, wiki page, or picture), announcements, contacts, discussion boards, links, calendar, tasks, project tasks, issue tracking, surveys, custom list, and basic web pages.

After you create your site collections, you should consider adding your administrators to the Site Collection Administrators. You do this by clicking open the Site Actions menu and selecting Site Settings (see Figure 5.7). Then click Site Collection Administrators in the Users and Permissions group and add your users.

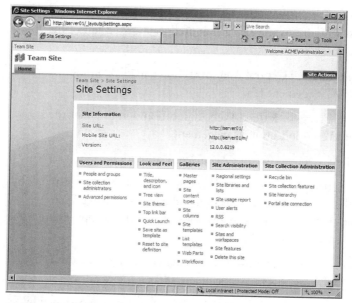

FIGURE 5.7 Site Settings in SharePoint.

After you create your sites, you should then consider starting the WSS Search Service. Although this service is not mandatory, it enables users to search and locate content in the site collections easily, and is therefore recommended. To start the WSS Search service, a username and password must be provided for the service account as well as for the account for accessing content. The Search databases and the indexing schedule to start the WSS Search services also need to be specified.

Accessing Mappings and Zones

The default URL is the URL that was specified on the Create Portal Site for ServerName page when the portal site was created. Typically, this URL is http://ServerName, where ServerName is the NetBIOS computer name. When you configure the Default Web Site in IIS to require SSL, you must modify the default URL for the portal site to use HTTPS and to include the internal FQDN of the SharePoint Portal Server deployment. Each web application can be associated with a collection of mappings between internal and external public URLs. Many internal URLs can be associated with a single public URL in multi-server farms (for example, when a load balancer routes requests to specific IP addresses to various servers in the load-balancing cluster).

Each web application supports five collections of mappings per URL; the five collections correspond to five zones (default, intranet, extranet, Internet, and custom). When the web application receives a request for an internal URL in a particular zone, links on the pages returned to the user have the public URL for that zone.

To properly create an *Alternate Access Mapping*, an IIS website needs to be extended with SharePoint, while also configured as an extension of the appropriate web application:

1. Open SharePoint 3.0 Central Administration and click on the Application Management tab.

2. Click on the Create or Extend Web Application option under the section SharePoint Web Application Management.

3. Click on the Extend an Existing Web Application option.

4. Select the web application to which you want to add the external link by selecting the drop-down No Selection and clicking Change Web Application. When the new window appears, select the appropriate web application by clicking on the name.

5. Create a new IIS website: Give it any name you would like; this is displayed in the IIS websites.

6. Specify any free port on the server. By default this is auto-assigned by the wizard.

7. Modify the host header with the new URL.

8. Specify the load balance URL. When you specify the load balance URL, you are modifying all links shown on the pages within the web application. By default, the load-balance URL is set to the current server name and port.

9. Specify the zone for the web application.

Of course for your server to respond to the new address, you must make sure it is accessible through any firewalls that you have and that the name is resolved to the correct address through DNS.

Creating Self-Service Sites

Microsoft Windows SharePoint Services allows members of the Administrator site group to create subsites off of their websites. These subsites can be fully functioning SharePoint sites, complete with a home page, document libraries, and so on, and they can even have their own unique permissions. Self-Service Site Creation is a feature enabled by administrators that allows users to create their own top-level websites. The user does not need administrator permissions on the server or virtual server, only permissions on the website where Self-Service Site Creation is hosted. The user simply enters some basic information and the new top-level website is created with the user as the owner and administrator. When you enable Self-Service Site Creation, you free yourself from having to create top-level websites on demand for your users—they can do it themselves.

To enable Self-Service Site Creation for a virtual server, follow these steps:

1. Open the Central Administration website.

2. On the top navigation bar, click Application Management.

3. On the Application Management page, in the Application Security section, click Self-Service Site Management.

4. On the Self-Service Site Management page, in the Web Application section, verify that the web application you want to change is selected. On the Select Web Application page, select the web application for which you want to enable self-service site creation.

5. On the Self-Service Site Management page, in the Enable Self-Service Site Creation section, select On. When you enable Self-Service Site Creation, an announcement is added to the Announcements list on the home page of the top-level website in the root site collection for the web application. The announcement provides a link to the site creation page (scsignup.aspx in the _layouts directory; for example, http://server_name/_layouts/scsignup.aspx).

6. To require users of self-service site creation to supply a secondary contact name for sites that they create when using the sign-up page, select the Require Secondary Contact check box.

7. Click OK.

To disable Self-Service Site Creation, go to the Configure Self-Service Site Creation page; next to Self-Service Site Creation, select Off, and then click OK.

Setting Quota Limits

If you are using WSS in a large environment, you need to keep control of your resources. When you set a *quota* limit for storage, you can set two values: a warning value and a maximum value. When a site passes the warning limit, an email message is sent to the site administrator and owner notifying them that their site is near to their storage quota. Email messages are sent daily until the storage level drops below the warning level. When a site meets the maximum limit, another email message is sent to the owner and administrator, and no new content can be added to the site. Note that before email messages can be sent, you must configure the email server settings and be running the Microsoft SharePoint Timer service.

The quota feature is disabled by default in Windows SharePoint Services. To specify quotas, you would typically create a quota template and apply the template to a server, server farm, virtual server, or site collection. You can also set quota values to a single site only.

Follow these steps to create a quota template:

1. Open SharePoint Central Administration.

2. Click the Application Management tab.

3. Under SharePoint Site Management, Click Quota templates.

4. You can choose to start the template from a new blank template or from a template that has already been selected.

5. On the Quota Templates page, specify the name of the quota template in the New Template Name text box.

6. In the Storage Limit Values section, select the Limit Site Storage to a Maximum of: ___ MB check box, and then type the amount of storage to allow at a maximum.

7. Select the Send Warning E-mail When Site Storage Reaches ___ MB check box, and then type the amount of storage to allow before sending a warning email message.

8. Click OK.

Follow these steps to apply quotas to a site:

1. Click Site Collection and Locks.

2. Select the Site Collection.

3. Under the Site Quota Information, select Individual Quota or a quota template for the current quota template.

4. If you selected Individual Quota, specify the quota settings.

5. Click OK.

EXAM ALERT

Be sure you know how to configure individual quotas and quotas using templates, including how to send email messages when quotas are being exceeded.

Using the `Psconfig.exe` Command-Line Tool

In SharePoint Products and Technologies, you can use the `psconfig.exe` command-line tool as an alternate interface to perform several operations that control how the SharePoint Products and Technologies are configured. You must be a member of the Administrators group on the local computer to perform these operations.

When you run `psconfig.exe` from the command line, you can specify commands to control how the tool runs. To run `psconfig.exe` from the command line, navigate to the C:\Program Files\Common Files\Microsoft Shared\ web server extensions\12\bin folder, and then type the commands by using the following syntax:

`Psconfig.exe -cmd <command> [optional parameters]`

To view Help, on the command line, type

`psconfig.exe -?`

To get Help about a specific command, type

`psconfig.exe -help <command name>`

The commands in `psconfig.exe` need to be run in a specific order to run successfully. If you use the SharePoint Products and Technologies Configuration Wizard to configure your installation, it calls the commands in the correct order for you. However, if you use the command line to run `psconfig.exe`, you need to be sure you are performing the tasks in the correct order. The `psconfig.exe` commands must be performed in the following order:

1. `configdb`

2. `helpcollections`

3. `secureresources`

4. `services`

5. `installfeatures`

6. `adminvs`

7. `evalprovision` (only for standalone installations)

8. `applicationcontent`

9. `upgrade`

When you install Windows SharePoint Services 3.0 on a single server, you run the setup program by using the Basic option. This option uses the Setup program's default parameters to install Windows SharePoint Services 3.0 and Windows Internal Database. Windows Internal Database uses SQL Server technology as a relational data store for Windows roles and features only, such as Windows SharePoint Services, Active Directory Rights Management Services, UDDI Services, Windows Server Update Services, and Windows System Resources Manager.

If you uninstall Windows SharePoint Services 3.0, and then later install Windows SharePoint Services 3.0 on the same computer, the Setup program could fail when creating the configuration database, causing the entire installation process to fail. You can prevent this failure by either deleting all the existing Windows SharePoint Services 3.0 databases on the computer or by creating a new configuration database. You can create a new configuration database by running the following command:

```
psconfig -cmd configdb -create -database <uniquename>
```

EXAM ALERT

If you need to re-create a configuration database, use the `psconfig -cmd configdb` command.

Using the `Stsadm` Command

SharePoint does include a `Stsadm.exe` command, which profiles command-line administration of Windows SharePoint Services servers and sites. `Stsadm` provides a method for performing the Windows SharePoint Services 3.0 administration tasks at the command line or by using batch files or scripts. `Stsadm` provides access to operations not available by using the Central Administration site, such as changing the administration port.

For 32-bit versions of Windows Server 2008, `Stsadm` is located at the following path:

%PROGRAMFILES%\common files\microsoft shared\web server extensions\12\bin

For x64-based versions of Windows Server 2008, `Stsadm` is located at the following path:

%drive%\program files (x86)\common files\microsoft shared\web server extensions\12\bin

You must be an administrator on the local computer to use `Stsadm`.

One of the best uses for `Stsadm` is backing up and restoring sites and webs. For small- to medium-sized installations, this functionality can be the cornerstone of a disaster recovery plan. The backup operation is self-explanatory and very easy to use. Simply tell `Stsadm` which site to back up and where to write the backup file, like this:

```
stsadm -o backup -url http://localhost -filename site.bak
```

This operation dumps the entire site collection to the file `site.bak`. It includes all site content, such as webs, document versions, lists, and users. It does not back up any site definitions or changes you've made at the file system level of your servers.

To export a website, use the following simple command:

```
stsadm -o export -url http://localhost/web -filename backup.dat
```

To import a website back to the server, use the following command:

```
stsadm -o import -url http://localhost/web2 -filename backup.dat
```

To create a new content database and add a database that needs to be upgraded, use the `Addcontentdb` option:

```
stsadm -o createcontentdb –dbname "SharePoint_Content 1" -webapp
➥"http://acme.com/portal" -maxsites 500 -warningsitecount 400
```

Managing WSS Sites

When you need to manage WSS sites, you can find most options in the Site Settings page. Some of these options include

- ▶ Manage users and groups
- ▶ Manage permissions
- ▶ Site look and feel
- ▶ Site galleries
- ▶ User alerts
- ▶ RSS
- ▶ Recycle Bin

Users, Groups, and Permissions

As a SharePoint Administrator, you have to control what users or groups of users can access your SharePoint sites. WSS uses Windows users and domain groups and Windows authentication mechanisms to manage and authenticate users. As a site owner, you can either add Windows user accounts directly to your site or add them to SharePoint groups to manage user accounts at the top-level website or subsite level.

Three SharePoint groups are provided by default. They include

▶ Owners, which has Full Control Permissions to a site.

▶ Members, which has Contribute Permissions to a site.

▶ Visitors, which has Read Permissions to a site.

You can also assign permissions directly to users. The main permissions that are available are shown in Table 5.1.

TABLE 5.1   Permission Levels and Descriptions

Permission Level	Description
Full Control	This permission level contains all permissions. Assigned to the *site name* Owners SharePoint group, by default. This permission level cannot be customized or deleted.
Design	Can create lists and document libraries, edit pages, and apply themes, borders, and style sheets in the website. Not assigned to any SharePoint group, by default.
Contribute	Can add, edit, and delete items in existing lists and document libraries. Assigned to the *site name* Members SharePoint group, by default.
Read	Read-only access to the website. Users and SharePoint groups with this permission level can view items and pages, open items, and documents. Assigned to the *site name* Visitors SharePoint group, by default.
Limited Access	The Limited Access permission level is designed to be combined with fine-grained permissions to give users access to a specific list, document library, item, or document, without giving them access to the entire site. However, to access a list or library, for example, a user must have permission to open the parent website and read shared data such as the theme and navigation bars of the website. The Limited Access permission level cannot be customized or deleted.

If you want to add a user to a SharePoint site, follow these steps:

1. Open the SharePoint site page.

2. Click the Site Actions located in the top-right corner and select Site Settings.

3. Under Users and Permissions, click People and Groups.

4. Click New.

5. Under Add Users, specify the Users/Groups and specify the SharePoint group to which they should be added or assign user permissions directly. You can also click the Add All Authenticated Users link to add the NT authority\authenticated users group if you want to add everyone from your domain to the SharePoint site.

6. Click OK.

If you want to give someone full permission over a WSS site, you can assign that user to the site collection administrators group:

1. Open the SharePoint site page.

2. Click the Site Actions located in the top-right corner and select Site Settings.

3. Under Users and Permissions, click Site Collection Administrators.

4. Specify the username in the Site Collection Administrators box. If you have more then one user or group that you want to add, separate them with a semicolon (;).

5. Click OK.

To modify the SharePoint user or group permissions, follow these steps:

1. Open the SharePoint site page.

2. Click the Site Actions located in the top-right corner and select Site Settings.

3. Under Users and Permissions, click the Advanced Permissions link.

4. Click the user or group that you want to modify.

5. Select or deselect the desired permissions.

6. Click OK.

Recycle Bin

When you delete a file from your hard drive, it is sent to the *Recycle Bin*. The same is true when deleting Site Collection items. When you delete an item from WSS, deleted items are sent to the WSS Recycle Bin. Items in the Recycle Bin remain there until you decide to permanently delete them from your website, or until the items are permanently deleted after a set number of days, which is based on a schedule defined in Central Administration.

When you delete an item from a website, the item is sent to the user's Recycle Bin. If you click Recycle Bin on the Quick Launch, you can see all the items that you've deleted from your site. You can either restore or delete the items from the Recycle Bin.

When you delete an item from the Recycle Bin, the item is sent to the Site Collection Recycle Bin, where it can be restored or deleted by an administrator. The Site Collection Recycle Bin gives the administrator of a site collection greater control over deleted items by providing you with a second-stage safety net before an item is permanently deleted from a site.

To view items in the Site Collection Recycle Bin, follow these steps:

1. On the top-level site, click the Site Actions menu, and then click Site Settings.

2. On the Site Settings page, in the Site Collection Administration section, click Recycle Bin.

3. On the Site Collection Recycle Bin page, in the Select a View section, click one of the following:

   ▶ To view items that the user has sent to the Recycle Bin, click End User Recycle Bin Items.

   ▶ To view items that the user has deleted from the Recycle Bin and has sent to the Site Collection Recycle Bin, click Deleted from End User Recycle Bin.

If you want to delete items from the Recycle Bin because it is considered sensitive or because you need to clear space from the SharePoint site, follow these steps:

1. On the top-level site, click the Site Actions menu, and then click Site Settings.

2. On the Site Settings page, in the Site Collection Administration section, click Recycle Bin.

3. On the Site Collection Recycle Bin page, in the Select a View section, do one of the following:

   ▶ To view items that the user has sent to the Recycle Bin, click End User Recycle Bin Items.

   ▶ To view items that the user has deleted from the Recycle Bin and sent to the Site Collection Recycle Bin, click Deleted from End User Recycle Bin.

4. Select the check box next to the items that you want to delete. To select all of the items at once, select the check box next to Type.

5. Click Delete Selection.

To restore items in the Recycle Bin, Select the check box next to the items that you want to restore. To select all the items at once, select the check box next to Type and click Restore Selection.

Document Library

A library is a location on a site where you can create, collect, update, and manage files with team members. Each library displays a list of files and key information about the files, which helps people use the files to work together.

Creating a Document Library

You can create and manage documents, spreadsheets, presentations, forms, and other types of files in a library. The Shared Documents library is created for you when Microsoft Windows SharePoint Services creates a new site. You can customize the library for your purposes, or you can create additional libraries (assuming you have the Manage List permission on the site where you want to create the library).

To create a document library, follow these steps:

1. Click View All Site Content, and then click Create on the All Site Content page. In most cases, you can use the Site Actions menu instead to complete this step.

2. Under Libraries, click the type of library that you want, such as Document Library. The type of library that you use depends on the kinds of files that you are sharing:

   ▶ **Document library:** Used to store many file types, including documents and spreadsheets.

> ▶ **Picture library:** Used to share a collection of digital pictures or graphics. Although pictures can be stored in other types of SharePoint libraries, picture libraries have several advantages, including the capability to view pictures in a slide show, download pictures to your computer, and edit pictures with graphics programs that are compatible with Windows SharePoint Services.

> ▶ **Wiki page library:** Used to create a collection of connected wiki pages. A wiki enables multiple people to gather routine information in a format that is easy to create and modify. You can add to your library wiki pages that contain pictures, tables, hyperlinks, and internal links.

> ▶ **Form library:** Used to manage a group of XML-based business forms.

3. In the Name box, type a name for the library. The library name is required. The name appears at the top of the library page, becomes part of the address for the library page, and appears in navigational elements that help users to find and open the library.

4. In the Description box, type a description of the purpose of the library. The description is optional. The description appears at the top of the library page, underneath the name of the library. If you plan to enable the library to receive content by email, you can add the email address of the library to its description, so that people can easily find it.

5. To add a link to this library on the Quick Launch, verify that Yes is selected in the Navigation section.

6. If an Incoming E-mail section appears, your administrator has enabled your site to receive content by email. If you want people to add files to the library by sending them as attachments to email messages, click Yes. Then, in the E-mail Address box, type the first part of the address that you want people to use for the library.

7. To create a version each time a file is checked into the library, in the Document Version History or Picture Version History section, click Yes. You can later choose whether you want to store both major and minor versions and how many versions of each you want to track.

8. Depending on the type of library you are creating, a Document Template section may be available, which lists the compatible programs that are available as the default for creating new files. If content types are enabled, the default template is specified through the content type. In the Document Template section, in the drop-down list, click the type of default file that you want to be used as a template for files that are created in the library.

9. Click Create.

After your library is created, you can further customize it by clicking Settings and then clicking the settings for the library that you want to customize, such as Document Library Settings.

Configuring Alerts

To notify you when a document is added or changed, you can configure an alert to be sent. To configure alerts, go to the document library and click the Actions menu and select Alert Me. You can then specify the name of the alert, to whom the alert is going to be sent, the type of alert (all changes, new items added, modified items, deleted items or web discussion updates), and how often the alerts will be sent. If you want to view your existing alerts on this site, click on the appropriate option at the top of the New Alert page (see Figure 5.8).

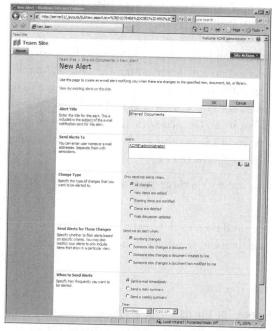

FIGURE 5.8 Creating a New Alert in SharePoint.

Workflows

Workflows are automated movements of documents or items through a specific sequence of actions or tasks that are related to a business process. You can think of them as a series of tasks that produce an outcome. Workflows can be used to consistently manage common business processes within an organization by enabling organizations to attach business logic to documents or items in a SharePoint list or library. Business logic is basically a set of instructions that specifies and controls actions that happen to a document or item.

A simple workflow may be when you post a document, you can specify that a manager has to approve the document before it is viewable on the SharePoint site. A more complex workflow maybe used to track the initialization of a server, which may including installing the operating system, installing patches, installing software, configuring monitoring of the server, provide training, and so forth. Whenever a task within the workflow is due to be completed by workflow participants, an email alert is sent notifying participants of the task. When the workflow participants complete their workflow tasks by approving or rejecting the document, the workflow ends. The workflow automatically takes the appropriate actions on the document, and it alerts the workflow owner about the outcome of the workflow.

Windows SharePoint Services 3.0 site includes a predefined three-state workflow. The three-state workflow supports business processes that require organizations to track the status of an issue or item through different phases. Specifically, the workflow tracks a list item through three different states involving two transitions. With each transition between states, the workflow assigns a task to a person and sends that person an email alert about the task. When this task is completed, the workflow updates the status of the item appropriately and progresses to the next state. The three-state workflow is designed to work with the Issue Tracking list template, but it can be used with any list that is set up to contain a Choice column with three or more values. The values in this choice column serve as the states that the workflow tracks.

To create an issue-tracking list for use with a three-state workflow, follow these steps:

1. Click View All Site Content, and then click Create on the All Site Content page. In most cases, you can use the Site Actions menu instead to complete this step.

2. Under Tracking, click Issue Tracking.

3. In the Name box, type a name for the list. The list name is required. The name appears at the top of the list page, becomes part of the web address for the list page, and appears in navigational elements that help users to find and open the list.

4. In the Description box, type a description of the purpose of the list. The description is optional.

5. To add a link to this list on the Quick Launch, click Yes in the Navigation section.

6. Click Create.

Troubleshooting WSS

To ensure that WSS servers and the site collections perform at their best, you will need to continually monitor the sites and RAM and disk space usage. You should also periodically view the event logs to assess the performance of the WSS servers.

You can use the Site Collection Usage Summary page to display information such as the amount of storage space used, the number of users added to the site collection, and the total number of hits for a site collection. To access the Site Collection Usage summary page, you need to enable Usage Analysis Processing and define storage quota.

To enable Usage Analysis Processing, follow these steps:

1. Open SharePoint Central Administration.

2. On the top navigation bar, click Operations.

3. On the Operations page, in the Logging and Reporting section, click Usage Analysis Processing.

4. On the Usage Analysis Processing page, in the Logging Settings section, select the Enable Logging check box.

5. In the Log File Location box, accept the default path for the log file, or type a new path.

6. In the Number of Log Files to Create box, type a value for the number of log files to keep per web application. When that number of log files is reached, no more files are created until some are deleted.

7. If you want to enable usage analysis processing on web server computers, in the Processing Settings section select the Enable Usage Analysis Processing check box. Specify what time each day to process usage analysis data by using the Start and End lists.

8. Click OK.

Usage data is processed for an entire site collection on one server at a time. The usage data is collected and stored per site. You can use the Usage Summary page to see the total number of hits for a site collection. Take these steps to view the usage summary report:

1. Navigate to the top-level website, and select Site Settings.

2. Select Go to Site Administration.

3. Under Site Collection Administration, select Usage Summary.

Exam Prep Questions

1. You have a Windows Server 2008 computer with SharePoint Services 3.0. You want to enable outgoing email so that users are notified when workflows and subscriptions are used. What do you need to do?

   - ○ **A.** Install and configure a DNS server.

   - ○ **B.** Install message queuing.

   - ○ **C.** Install and configure a SMTP server.

   - ○ **D.** Install the Application server role.

2. You have a Windows Server 2008 with SharePoint Services 3.0. You decide to uninstall the SharePoint Services 3.0 role from the server. When you try to reinstall SharePoint Services, your installation fails. What do you need to do to complete the installation process?

   - ○ **A.** Use `psconfig.exe cmd configdb <parameters>`

   - ○ **B.** Use `psconfig.exe cmd services <parameters>`

   - ○ **C.** Use `psconfig.exe cmd applicationcontent <parameters>`

   - ○ **D.** Use `psconfig.exe cmd installfeatures <parameters>`

3. You have a Windows Server 2003 computer with SharePoint Services 2.0 installed. You need to upgrade to a Windows Server 2008 platform with Windows Office SharePoint Server 2007. Which of the following upgrade paths can you choose? (Choose all that apply.)

   - ○ **A.** In-place upgrade

   - ○ **B.** Deploy a new farm and migrate content

   - ○ **C.** Gradual upgrade

   - ○ **D.** Scanning upgrade

4. You have a Windows Server 2008 computer with SharePoint Services 3.0 installed. How do you enable outgoing email? (Choose two answers.)

   - ○ **A.** Open Internet Information Services (IIS) 6.0 Manager and enable SMTP services on the same server as WSS.

   - ○ **B.** Open the SharePoint Central Administration website and click SMTP Role Administration.

   - ○ **C.** Open the SharePoint Central Administration website and click Operations. Then select Outgoing E-mail Settings.

   - ○ **D.** Open the SharePoint Central Administration website and click Application Management. Then select Outgoing E-mail Settings.

5. You have a Windows Server 2003 computer with SharePoint Services 3.0. You just purchased a new more powerful server for Windows Office SharePoint Server 2007. How should you migrate the SharePoint information over to the new server?

   ○ **A.** Back up the database on the first server. Install Windows Server 2008 and Windows SharePoint Server 2007 on the new server. Restore the database to the second server.

   ○ **B.** Install Windows Server 2008 and Windows SharePoint Server 2007 on the new server. Then perform a lock-and-load migration. Back up the database. Restore to the new server.

   ○ **C.** Perform an in-place upgrade on the new server. Specify the destination as the new server. Then install Windows SharePoint Server 2007.

   ○ **D.** Run the SharePoint migration utility and specify the destination as the new server. Then install Windows SharePoint Server 2007.

6. What command do you use to re-add a content database for SharePoint Services 3.0?

   ○ **A.** Use the `psconfig cmd installfeatures` command.

   ○ **B.** Run the `migrate.exe` command-line tool.

   ○ **C.** Use the `appcmd add backup <backupname>` command.

   ○ **D.** Run the `Stsadm.exe` command-line tool.

7. You have a Windows Server 2008 computer with Windows SharePoint Services 3.0. On WSS, you have several websites, including a staging WSS website. When you are testing new web parts, you want to make sure that the new web parts do not affect the production sites. What should you do?

   ○ **A.** Assign only non-administrative accounts to the test WSS sites.

   ○ **B.** Configure each web application to run in its own application pool.

   ○ **C.** Install a second instance of WSS.

   ○ **D.** Create a separate ISAPI filter for each of the WSS websites.

8. You have a Windows Server 2008 computer with Microsoft Windows SharePoint Services (WSS) 3.0. You create a document library for the managers in your company. You need to ensure that managers can only view and add content to the document library. Which permissions level should you provide for the managers?

   ○ **A.** Contributor

   ○ **B.** Members

   ○ **C.** Visitors

   ○ **D.** Owners

9. You have a Windows Server 2008 computer with WSS 3.0 on a single server. You need to restore your WSS website if the server fails. What do you need to do to minimize the time required to perform the restore?

   ○ **A.** Use Windows Backup to back up the System State and SharePoint folders.

   ○ **B.** Download Microsoft SQL Management Console from Microsoft.com, install it on the SharePoint computer, and back up all related databases.

   ○ **C.** Use IIS to perform a full backup of SharePoint.

   ○ **D.** Use the Central Administration site to back up the web application and the content database.

10. You have a Windows Server 2008 with WSS 3.0. A user reports that a document got deleted. She remembers accessing the document about six weeks ago. What do you need to do to recover the lost document?

   ○ **A.** Instruct the user to open the Windows Recycle Bin.

   ○ **B.** Instruct the user to open the Recycle Bin in SharePoint.

   ○ **C.** Open the site collection Recycle Bin and undelete the document.

   ○ **D.** Restore the document using the Central Administration backup and restore options.

11. You have a Windows Server 2008 computer with WSS 3.0. You want to move SharePoint from one server to another server. What is the best way to accomplish this?

   ○ **A.** Run the `Stsadm.exe` command to back up each SharePoint site on the first server and use the `Stsadm.exe` command to restore on the second server.

   ○ **B.** On the second server, use the `stsadmin.exe` command to migrate from the first server to the second server.

   ○ **C.** On the second server, use the `smigrate.exe` command to migrate from the first server to the second server.

   ○ **D.** Run the `smigrate.exe` command to back up each SharePoint site on the first server and use the `smigrate.exe` command to restore on the second server.

12. You have a Windows Server 2008 computer with WSS 3.0. A user is reporting that a document had recently disappeared. What should you do?

   ○ **A.** Instruct the user to open the Windows Recycle Bin.

   ○ **B.** Instruct the user to open the Recycle Bin in SharePoint.

   ○ **C.** Open the site collection Recycle Bin and undelete the document.

   ○ **D.** Restore the document using the Central Administration backup and restore options.

13. You have public reports that need to be reviewed by a senior manager and the legal department before they are published within the SharePoint services website so that all employees can view them. You create a task list named Review that includes tasks that must be completed before a document can be moved to the Released Document library. What do you need to do to make sure that the documents are not put into the Released Document library before they are reviewed by everyone needed?

   ○ **A.** Give the managers and legal department Full Control to the Released Document library.

   ○ **B.** Configure an alert notifying managers and lawyers when a new document is posted.

   ○ **C.** Configure the Review Document library to use the three-state workflow and the Review task list.

   ○ **D.** Do not use SharePoint. Instead send the documents to senior management. When the managers have reviewed a document, have them send the document to the legal department. When the legal department is done, you can then post the document in SharePoint.

14. You have a Windows Server 2008 computer with SharePoint. You had to increase the storage capacity for SharePoint several times over the last year because the SharePoint database is growing at a fast rate. You have also noticed that some old documents are not getting removed when necessary. What can you do to help alleviate this problem?

   ○ **A.** Notify users once a week to clean up old documents.

   ○ **B.** Schedule the SharePoint Cleanup utility to clean up old documents once a week.

   ○ **C.** Set a quota for each individual.

   ○ **D.** Create a quota template and apply it to each site. Configure the quota template to email messages when each site is near its storage quota.

Answers to Exam Prep Questions

1. Answer C is correct. You need to install SMTP so that it can deliver emails. Answer A is incorrect because DNS is used for name resolution. Answer B is incorrect because message queuing provides guaranteed message delivery, efficient routing, security, and priority-based messaging between applications. It is not used for emails. Answer D is incorrect because the Application server role provides a complete solution for hosting and managing high-performance distributed business applications built around Microsoft .NET Framework 3.0, COM+, Message Queuing, web services, and Distributed Transactions.

2. Answer A is correct. If you uninstall SharePoint using Basic setup, the configuration database still exists in the internal database. Therefore, you need to re-create a new configuration database, which is done with the psconfig.exe cmd configdb command. Answer B is incorrect because the services option is used to manage the SharePoint Products and Technologies services. Answer C is incorrect because the applicationcontent option is used to manage the shared application content. Answer D is incorrect because the installfeatures option is used to register the SharePoint Products and Technologies features placed on the file system of the server with the server farm.

3. Answers A, B, and C are correct. Four upgrades methods can be used, including the in-place upgrade, gradual upgrade, gradual upgrade with shared services, and deploy new farm and migrate content. Answer D is incorrect because there is no such thing as a scanning upgrade.

4. Answers A and C are correct. You must first enable SMTP on the computer and then you need to configure SharePoint to use SMTP. To configure SharePoint, you need to open the SharePoint Central Administration website, click Operations, and then click Outgoing E-mail Settings. Answer B is incorrect because the there is no SMTP Role link under the SharePoint Administration website. Answer D is incorrect because email is not configured under the Application Management page.

5. Answer A is correct. You need to back up the data first. Install Windows Server 2008 and Windows SharePoint Server 2007 on the new server. Then restore the database to the second server. Answer B is incorrect because there is no such thing as a lock-and-load migration. Answer C is incorrect because the in-place migration only upgrades SharePoint on the same server. It cannot be used to migrate to another server. Answer D is incorrect because there is no SharePoint migration utility to move to another server.

6. Answer D is correct. Use the stsadm command-line tool with the addcontentdb operation to re-add the content database. Answer A is incorrect because it is used to register the SharePoint Products and Technologies features placed on the file system of the server with the server farm. Answer B is incorrect because there is no utility in SharePoint called migrate.exe. Answer C is incorrect because appcmd add backup is for backing up IIS.

7. **Answer B is correct.** To make sure that one website does not affect another website, you must run the test SharePoint sites in their own application pools so that the websites run in their own memory pools. Answer A is incorrect because assigning accounts to each website does not affect the other websites. Answer C is incorrect because you cannot install a second instance of WSS on the same server. Answer D is incorrect because ISAPI filters enhance or limit a particular website. Therefore, ISAPI filters have no effect on what can or cannot affect the other website.

8. **Answer B is correct.** Members have the contribute permissions to the site, which allows them to view and add content to the document library. Answer A is incorrect because contributor is not a permission level; however, contribute is a permission. Answer C is incorrect because visitors would have read only permission and not contribute. Answer D is incorrect because owners would have additional permissions including creating lists and libraries.

9. **Answer D is correct.** To properly back up SharePoint so that you can do a quick restore, you would use Central Administration to back up the web application and content database. Answer A is incorrect because you cannot use Windows Backup to back up SharePoint and to perform a restore. Answer B is incorrect because you cannot download Microsoft SQL Management Console. Answer C is incorrect because you cannot use IIS to perform a backup of the SQL databases where most of the data is stored.

10. **Answer C is correct.** After a set number of days, items that have been deleted are moved into the collection Recycle Bin, which acts as a safety net. Instruct the user to recover the document from the Recycle Bin on her computer. Answer A is incorrect because items deleted in SharePoint are not moved into the Windows Recycle Bin. Answer B is incorrect because as the document was probably deleted a few weeks ago, it is not likely to be in the user's Recycle Bin. Answer D is incorrect because when you use the Central Administration, it is used to back up and restore the entire SharePoint site, not individual items within SharePoint.

11. **Answer A is correct.** You can use the `Stsadmin` to back up each site on server and use it to restore on the other server. Answer B is incorrect because the `stsadmin.exe` command does not have a migration feature. Answers C and D are incorrect because `smigrate.exe` was a utility in WSS 2.0, not 3.0.

12. **Answer B is correct.** When a document is deleted from SharePoint, it is moved into the document library's Recycle Bin. Answer A is incorrect because items deleted in SharePoint are not moved into the Windows Recycle Bin. Answer C is incorrect because the document was only recently deleted. Therefore, it should be in the document library's Recycle Bin. Answer D is incorrect because when you use the Central Administration, it is used to back up and restore the entire SharePoint site, not individual items within SharePoint.

13. **Answer C is correct.** If you set up a three-state review and task list, the document must be approved by the managers and legal department before being posted. Answer A is correct because giving Full Control would not ensure that the documents get reviewed.

Doing so would also give unnecessary permissions to the managers and legal department. Answer B is incorrect because documents would be posted for all to see without being reviewed. Answer D is the incorrect answer because it is more difficult to perform then using SharePoint to track the documents. In addition, someone could still post the documents without going through the necessary steps.

14. Answer D is correct. You need to create a quota template and assign it to each site. This automatically prompts users to perform cleanup when their quota is close to being exceeded. Answer A is incorrect because this is a complicated solution which may or may not give the desired results. Answer B is incorrect because there is no SharePoint Cleanup utility to clean up old documents once a week. Answer C is incorrect because configuring quotas for each individual is a complicated and lengthy process to accomplish the same thing as using a quota template and applying it to all users that use the site.

Need to Know More?

For more information about Windows SharePoint Services, including downloading WSS 3.0 and the evaluation guide and to access SharePoint Services 3.0 Help, visit the following website:

http://office.microsoft.com/en-us/sharepointtechnology/default.aspx

To access the SharePoint Services 3.0 Technical Library, including Getting Started, Planning and Architecture, Deployment, Operations, and Technical Reference, visit the following website:

http://technet.microsoft.com/en-us/windowsserver/sharepoint/default.aspx

For Windows Server 2008 Resource Center for SharePoint Products and Technologies, visit the following website:

http://technet.microsoft.com/en-us/windowsserver/sharepoint/bb735844.aspx

For more information about the `Stsadm.exe` command, visit the following websites:

http://technet.microsoft.com/en-us/library/cc261956.aspx

http://msdn2.microsoft.com/en-us/library/bb507233.aspx

For more information about the `psconfig.exe` command, visit the following website:

http://technet.microsoft.com/en-us/library/cc263093.aspx

CHAPTER SIX

Windows Media Server

Terms you'll need to understand:

- ✓ Streaming media
- ✓ Windows Media Services (WMS)
- ✓ Multiple bit rate (MBR) streaming
- ✓ Real-Time Streaming Protocol (RTSP)
- ✓ fast start
- ✓ advanced fast start
- ✓ fast cache
- ✓ fast recovery
- ✓ fast-forward
- ✓ fast-rewind
- ✓ on-demand streaming
- ✓ live content streaming
- ✓ publishing point
- ✓ announcement file
- ✓ playlist
- ✓ Digital Rights Management (DRM)
- ✓ license key
- ✓ license key seed
- ✓ key ID

Techniques/concepts you'll need to master:

- ✓ Install and configure Windows Media Services.
- ✓ Configure Digital Rights Management (DRM).

Streaming media is multimedia such as audio and/or video that is constantly sent to and received by the end-user from a provider. Because the information is sent as a continuous stream, the client browser or plug-in can start displaying the data before the entire file has been transmitted. As a result, you can listen to a radio station or watch a television program or newscast as it is being transmitted while keeping network traffic to a minimum. In addition, by using streaming technology, you can stream to hundreds or even thousands of machines at the same time. In addition, you can use several security options to control to whom the stream is broadcasted and who has permission to view the stream.

Windows Media Services (WMS) is a software component of Microsoft Windows Server 2008 that enables an administrator to generate streaming media (audio/video). WMS offers the capability to cache and record streams, enforce authentication and restrict access, and limit connections by various methods.

Streaming Media

There are two ways to run media files over the network. The traditional method is to download the file and save the file on a disk. You can then double-click the media file, and Windows Media player or a similar player plays the media file. Unfortunately, this method is time consuming because you have to download the entire file before you can play it. Many of these files can be quite large, consuming large amounts of disk space. In addition, this method does not use the network bandwidth efficiently, which can also affect the performance of other network applications.

The other method is to deliver it as a stream that is delivered from a Windows Media server and assigned to a *publishing point*. You can then access the media through an URL of the publishing point or by creating an announcement file. Different from downloading the media file, you can play the media much more quickly than you can with downloading. Different from downloaded files, streaming uses bandwidth more efficiently because it sends data over the network only at the speed that is necessary for the client to render it properly. It also uses a buffer where the data is temporarily stored. If you have higher network bandwidth, the buffer is smaller. When the buffer is filled up, you can start playing the file before it is completely downloaded. This also enables you to deliver live content.

To use the network efficiently, Windows Media Services has to use different technology than what is available to a traditional web server. This includes using

▸ Multiple bit rate (MBR) streaming

▸ Unicast versus multicast streams

▸ TCP versus UDP

▸ HTTP versus Real-Time Streaming Protocol (RTSP)

Multiple Bit Rate Streaming (MBR)

When you play media and do not have sufficient network bandwidth, your sound and/or video sounds choppy or pauses often, has poor resolution, produces images that are not sharp, or provides audio only. For content to stream smoothly, the bit rate of the content must be lower than the bandwidth of the network connection.

Some websites may enable you to choose at which bandwidth you want to play. Of course, if you have two choices in bandwidth, you would have to create two media files or streams made for the two different bandwidths. One technology developed for streaming media is *multiple bit rate (MBR) streaming*, which has the same content encoded in different bit rate data streams. Therefore, a client with a lower available bit rate can request a lower bit rate stream from the server so that a steady stream can be delivered.

To dynamically assign a bit rate, the Media Server offers intelligent streaming, in which the Windows Media server works with Windows Media Player to detect network conditions and adjust the properties of a stream automatically to maximize playback quality. With intelligent streaming, users receive a continuous flow of content tailored to their specific connection speeds. To take advantage of intelligent streaming, content must be encoded as a multiple-bit-rate stream, in which multiple bit rate streams are encoded into a single Windows Media stream.

TCP Versus UDP

The protocols that work on top of the IP protocol are TCP and UDP. The Transmission Control Protocol (TCP) is a reliable, connection-oriented delivery service that breaks data into manageable packets, wraps them with the information needed to route them to their destination, and reassembles the pieces at the receiving end of the communication link. It establishes a virtual connection between the two hosts or computers so that they can send messages back and forth for a period of time. A virtual connection appears to be always connected, but in reality it is made of many packets being sent back and forth independently. The TCP uses acknowledgements to verify that the data were received by the other host. If an acknowledgement is not sent, the data are re-sent.

Another transport layer protocol is the User Datagram Protocol (UDP). Unlike TCP, which uses acknowledgements to ensure data reliability, UDP does not. Therefore, UDP is considered unreliable, "best effort" delivery. Because it is considered unreliable, UDP is used for protocols that transmit small amounts of data at one time or for broadcast (packets sent to everyone). Being unreliable, however, does not mean that the packets are not delivered; rather, there is no guarantee or check to ensure that they get to their destination. Because no acknowledgements are used with UDP, UDP consumes less network traffic than TCP packets.

Unicast Versus Multicast

Another technology used in data delivery is unicast or multicast. A unicast stream is a one-to-one connection between the server and a client. If you have five people playing the same media stream, you will have five concurrent streams delivering five sets of data packets. If you have many people connecting to a media server, unicast streaming can consume a large amount of data bandwidth. One advantage of using unicast streaming is that you can start and stop the content for each client independently. Unicast streaming is the default method by which a Windows Media Server delivers content and is automatically enabled by the WMS Unicast Data Writer plug-in, which is enabled by default.

To use the network more efficiently, multicast streaming can be used. Multicast streaming creates a one-to-many connection between the server and multiple clients receiving the stream. If you have five people playing the same media stream, you will have one stream delivering one set of data packets to all five clients. Of course, for you to use multicast streaming, your network routers must be multicast-enabled, meaning that they can transmit class-D IP addresses. If your network routers are not multicast-enabled, you can still deliver content as a multicast stream over the local segment of your local area network. Lastly, all multicast content must have a specified time-to-live (TTL) value that limits the number of routers that the multicast can traverse before it expires.

> **NOTE**
>
> Multicast packets use only UDP.

Data Transfer Protocols

Because media sent over the network is broken down into data packets and sent to a host, you need to use a data transfer protocol to get the data packets delivered. The data transfer protocol determines the method for error checking, data compression, and end-of-file acknowledgements. The protocols used to stream Windows Media–based content are Hypertext Transfer Protocol (HTTP) and Real-Time Streaming Protocol (RTSP).

HTTP is the traditional protocol used on web servers using port 80 to view web pages. Because HTTP is designed to deliver packets, it can be used to stream content from an encoder to a WMS server and it can also be used to distribute media streams. One advantage of HTTP over RTSP is that HTTP supports Windows Media Player found in Windows XP and Windows Vista, as well as earlier versions of Windows Media Player. Last, because it is a well-established and commonly used protocol, it can also be used to distribute streams through a firewall. HTTP for the Media Server is disabled by default.

The *Real-Time Streaming Protocol (RTSP)* is a protocol designed to be used in streaming media systems. It enables a client to remotely control a streaming media server, issuing VCR/DVD-like commands such as play and pause, and allows time-based access to files on a server. RTSP delivers content to Windows Media Player 9 Series or later. RTSP, which is enabled by default, listens on port 554. RTSP using UDP is called RTSPU; RTSP using TCP is called RTSPT. See figure 6.1, which shows enabling the HTTP and RTSP during installation.

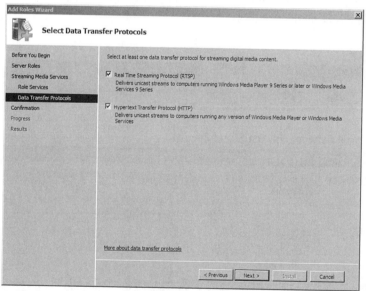

FIGURE 6.1   Enabling the data transfer protocol during Streaming Media Services installation.

EXAM ALERT

By default, RTSP uses port 554.

Windows Media Services manages the use of these protocols by using control protocol plug-ins. Windows Media Services includes the WMS RTSP Control Protocol plug-in and the WMS HTTP Control Protocol plug-in. The control protocol plug-in receives the incoming client request, determines what action is indicated by the request (for example, to start or stop streaming), translates the request into a command form, and then passes the command to the server. Control protocol plug-ins can also return notification information to clients if there is an error condition or a change of status.

Installing Windows Media Services

Before installing Windows Media Services, you must make sure that the network will support the new services. Therefore, you need to make sure you have sufficient bandwidth and that you have configured the firewalls to allow the appropriate traffic. Although unicast streaming is a common configuration, if you decide to use multicasting, you have to enable multicast routing.

If you choose to use unicast streaming over the Internet, you also need to open the ports on your firewall. Table 6.1 shows ports used for unicast streaming. In addition, by default, encoders use HTTP port 8080 to connect to a server that is running Windows Media Services.

> **EXAM ALERT**
>
> By default, encoders use HTTP port 8080 to connect to a server that is running Windows Media Services.

TABLE 6.1 Ports Used for Unicast Streaming

Ports	Description
In: UDP on port 5005	Receives re-send requests from clients streaming by using RTSPU.
Out: UDP between ports 1024-5000	Sends data (RTSPU) to Windows Media Player and other clients.
Out: TCP on port 80, 554	Sends data (HTTPS, RTSPT) to Windows Media Player and other clients.
In: TCP on port 80, 554	Accepts incoming HTTP connections (port 80) or RTSP connections (port 554) from Windows Media Player and other clients.

The system requirements for Windows Media Services are shown in Table 6.2. It is recommended that you use load balancing to prevent any one server from becoming overloaded and to provide fault tolerance.

TABLE 6.2   System Requirements for Windows Media Services

Component	Requirement	Recommendation
Processor	1GHz	3GHz or more multiple cores
Memory	512MB	4GB or RAM or higher
Network interface card	Ethernet card and TCP/IP	Dual Gigabit Ethernet cards with TCP/IP
Free hard disk space	50MB	500MB or more for content

Windows Media Services can be installed only on Windows Server 2008 Standard and Enterprise editions. In addition, Windows Media Services is not included with the Windows Server 2008 operating system. Instead, you need to install the Microsoft Update Standalone Package (MSU) file so that the Streaming Media Services role will appear. The MSU file can be downloaded from the following website:

http://www.microsoft.com/windows/windowsmedia/forpros/serve/prodinfo2008.aspx

Of course, you have to download the 32-bit or 64-bit file appropriate for your machine. After the file has been installed, you can then start Server Manager to enable the role on the Windows Server 2008 computer.

EXAM ALERT

You can install Windows Media Services only on Windows Server 2008 Standard and Enterprise editions.

Implementing Content Streaming

On-demand streaming is used to deliver streams at the request of the user. On-demand streaming has many advantages. First, users control playback, including start/stop, fast-forward, and rewind. And although two users may be looking at the same media, no two users are viewing the same content at the same time. Instead, two separate streams are created. On-demand streaming also supports multiple data sources that can be used for media content, including network location and the local hard drive.

EXAM ALERT

To perform on-demand streaming, you must use unicast.

WMS uses plug-ins for retrieving media from different sources. The data source plug-ins included with WMS are

▶ File Data Source

▶ Network Data Source

▶ HTTP Download Data Source

▶ Push Data Source

By default, WMS uses the Network Service account to access content. The Network Service account must have at least read permission to content that WMS retrieves.

EXAM ALERT

If you are using the Network Service account to access content, it must have at least read permission to the content.

Content Streaming Features

Windows Media Server has several features that enhance the media player experience:

▶ **Fast Start:** When you connect to a media server and begin downloading media, the media starts playing as soon as the buffer is filled without waiting for the entire media stream to be downloaded. *Fast Start* is available to Windows Media Player 9 and later.

▶ **Advanced Fast Start:** Similar to Fast Start, except Windows Media Player begins playing the stream before its buffer is full. *Advanced Fast Start* requires Media Player 10.

▶ **Fast Cache:** To prevent playback quality problems due to network issues, the stream is cached before it is needed. The stream is rendered in Windows Media Player at the specified data rate, but the client is able to receive a much larger portion of the content before rendering it. *Fast Cache* is available only for on-demand publishing points.

▶ **Fast Recovery:** Uses forward error correction (FEC) on a publishing point, which enables it to recover lost or damaged data packets without having to request that the Windows Media server resend the data. *Fast Recovery* also enables the client to reconnect to the server automatically and restart streaming.

▶ **Fast-forward/rewind:** Improved version of standard *fast-forward/rewind* that minimizes network utilization, minimizes disk activity, and improves playback quality by using multiple copies of content to avoid the problems that faster key frame delivery can cause. To enable advanced fast-forward/rewind, you must create a .tmi file that references the various content at various speeds.

Figure 6.2 shows some of the content streaming features available for a publishing point.

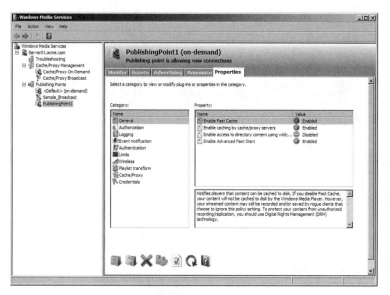

FIGURE 6.2   General properties for a Publishing Point.

Implementing On-Demand Publishing

To implement on-demand publishing, you create an on-demand publishing point and a broadcast publishing point. You must also enable the publishing point to accept new connections. Follow these steps to implement on-demand publishing:

1. Create a folder where you will store the media files.

2. Share the folder with the default share permissions.

3. Copy the content to the new shared folder.

4. Open the Windows Media Services console.

Figure 6.3 shows the Windows Media Services console.

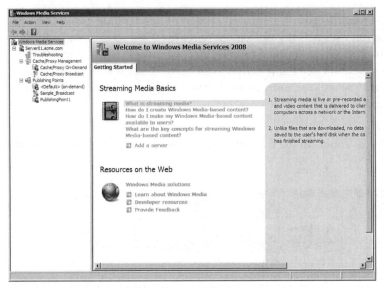

FIGURE 6.3 The Windows Media Services console.

5. Right-click Publishing Points and select Add Publishing Point (Wizard).

6. When the wizard begins, click Next.

7. Specify a name for the publishing point. Click Next.

8. Specify the content type (encoder, playlist, one file, or files in a directory). For on-demand publishing, select Files. Click Next (see Figure 6.4).

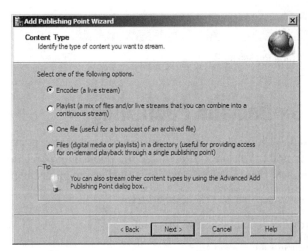

FIGURE 6.4 Specifying the content type.

9. Select On-Demand Publishing Point. Click Next.

10. Specified the location of the shared directory. The default folder is C:\WMPub\WMRoot.

11. Specify the Content Playback options such as Loop or Shuffle. Click Next (see Figure 6.5).

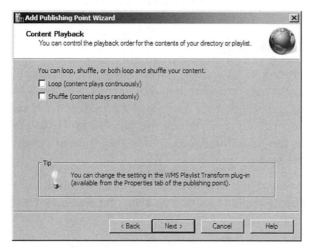

FIGURE 6.5 Specifying content playback.

12. If you desire logging, select the Yes, Enable Logging for the Publishing Point. Click Next.

13. When the publishing point summary appears, click Next.

14. When the wizard is complete, click Finish. At this point, you can also create an announcement file, wrapper playlist, or web page (see Figure 6.6).

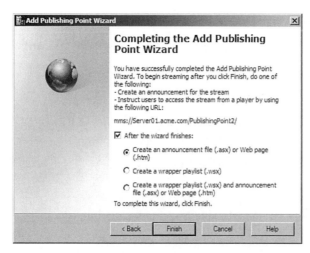

FIGURE 6.6 Completing the Add Publishing Point Wizard.

You can access content in the default on-demand publishing point at mms://servername/filename. You can access content in non-default, on-demand publishing points at mms://servername/publishingpointname/filename.

Live Content Streaming

Live content streaming uses broadcast publishing points to allow remote users to view live events. Live Content uses broadcast publishing points, which can be sent as unicast or multicast streams. Because they are being broadcast and are played as they are being broadcast, they cannot be paused, fast forwarded, or rewound. The live content can be archived, however, so that you can use the archive to play it back in the future.

To start a live content streaming, you must take a little bit of care in planning for the live content, including establishing a start and end time and having the equipment all set up.

An encoder converts digital media to a format that you can stream with the Windows Media Server. To select the format for encoding the media, you select a compression/decompression algorithm (codec). The most commonly used encoder for WMS is Windows Media Encoder. It is available for download from the Windows Media Encoder website (http://www.microsoft.com/windows/windowsmedia/forpros/encoder/default.mspx). To prepare the encoder, determine bit rate and frame rate. Use production techniques to limit bandwidth requirements.

To set up a broadcast publishing point, follow these steps:

1. Right-click Publishing Points and select Add Publishing Point (Wizard).

2. When the wizard begins, click Next.

3. Specify a name for the publishing point. Click Next.

4. Specify the content type (encoder, playlist, one file, or files in a directory). For live stream, select Encoder (live stream).

5. With the broadcast publishing point selected, click Next.

6. Specify the URL for the encoder.

7. If you desire logging, select Yes, Enable Logging for the Publishing Point. Click Next.

8. When the publishing point summary appears, click Next.

9. When the wizard is complete, click Finish.

Publishing Point Properties

After you create a publishing point, you can configure the properties of the publishing point by clicking the publishing point and clicking the Properties tab. Some of the options include the following:

▶ **General options:** Allows you to enable or disable fast cache, caching by the proxy server, and advanced fast start.

▶ **Authorization:** Enables you to control who can access the stream based on NTFS, IP address, or publishing points ACL.

▶ **Logging:** Allows you to enable or disable logging.

▶ **Authentication:** Specifies authentication based on anonymous, negotiate (Kerberos or NTLM), or Digest authentication.

▶ **Limits:** Specifies various limits, including number of players and bandwidth.

▶ **Wireless:** Enables or disables forward error correction.

▶ **Playlist transform:** Enables or disables you to control the order in which the contents of a directory or playlist play.

▶ **Cache/Proxy:** Specifies how long a cache or proxy server can access the cached content or stream split broadcast.

Figure 6.7 shows the properties of a publishing point.

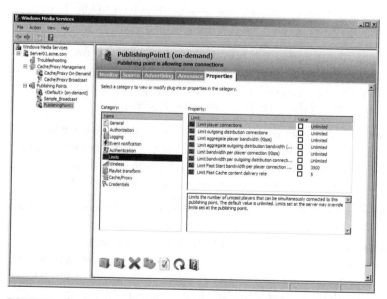

FIGURE 6.7 Configuring a Publishing Point in Windows Media Services.

Announcement Files

When implementing live content streaming, the easiest way to direct users to the live content stream is with an announcement file. An *announcement file* is an XML-based file that contains metadata about content and directs users to the content location. The announcement files have either the .asx (unicast) or .msc (multicast) file extension. After the announcement page is created, it can be distributed on a web page, by file share, or by email.

SMIL-Based Playlists

A *playlist* is an XML-based language standard that is being developed by the World Wide Web Consortium (W3C). The playlist enables web developers to send separate content streams to a client computer, where they will be displayed as a single stream. You can edit playlists with the Playlist Editor or any other Text or XML editor.

The Playlist Editor is a tool that provides a simple, graphical interface for creating playlists and specifying attributes for the item in the playlist. You can access the Playlist Editor from the Summary tab of the Publishing Points console tree or by clicking the View Playlist Editor button on the Source tab of a publishing point.

Advertisements for Publishing Points

For many content providers it is important to have advertisements or promotions in between content segments to generate revenue. Windows Media Services provides three methods to provide advertisements:

▶ **Wrapper advertisements**: Streaming advertisements that play before or after the user views the live content. The Wrapper advertisements are created in a playlist. The playlist is assigned to the publishing point on the Advertising tab in the Windows Media Services snap-in.

▶ **Interstitial advertisements**: Streaming advertisements that are inserted into a playlist with your content. You must use a playlist to make use of interstitial advertising. In the playlist editor, the element defines the streaming content that has the Role attribute set to Advertisement.

▶ **Banner advertisements**: Static or multimedia advertisements that appear on a play independent of the streaming content. You can implement these advertisements by associating an advertising banner Uniform Resource Locator (URL) with a banner metadata element in the announcement file. You can also implement these advertisements by using the bannerURL attribute with the clientData element in a playlist file.

Security in Windows Media Server

Anytime you place a Windows Media Server within your enterprise infrastructure, security is always a concern. To alleviate these concerns, configure the following security parameters:

▸ **IP address restriction**: A range of IP addresses that can either allow or deny access to the Windows Media Service or a specific publishing point based on the client computer's IP address (see Figure 6.8).

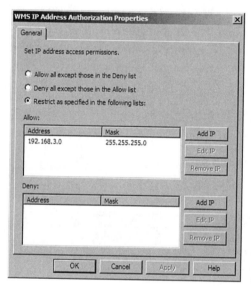

FIGURE 6.8 Restricting access by IP address.

▸ **User authentication**: You can use Windows NT LAN Manager (NTLM), Kerberos protocol, or Digest authentication to restrict client access. You can authorize users and give them specific permissions on the publishing point or on the stream content files stored on an NTFS partition.

▸ **Content expiration**: Using Windows Media Rights Manager, you can assign usage rules to content. You can ensure the security of downloadable media to local users, remote users, vendors, clients, and partners.

▸ **Digital Rights Management**: Assign usage rules to content, including enforcement of license usage rules provided by Windows Media Rights manager. You can also apply limits to the content, including the number of client connections on the server, the amount of bandwidth that can be consumed by streams for a specific publishing point, and the amount of bandwidth that can be consumed by a single client.

Troubleshooting Windows Media Services

Although the Windows Media Services is dependent on multiple services and a stable network connection that often goes through switches, routers and firewalls, you have to use a systematic approach when dealing with media service problems. Windows Media Server problems typically are related to configuration issues, limitation issues, or network connectivity problems.

To verify whether the server is functioning well, you can start by testing the publishing point and its stream to make sure that all configured protocols and configuration settings are working. If you are capturing content from an encoder, you also should test the server stream to ensure that the player is reproducing the encoded content properly.

To help test the streams from the server, you can

▶ Test a stream with the Stream Test Utility (see Figure 6.9).

▶ Test a stream captured from an encoder.

▶ Test a stream with Windows Media Player.

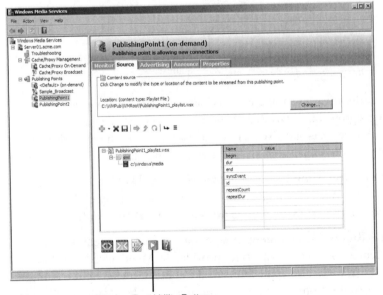

Stream Test Utility Button

FIGURE 6.9   The Stream Test Utility button tests the streams from your server.

To troubleshoot network connectivity problems, you need to use standard TCP troubleshooting tools such as ping and tracert and try to use Windows Media Player to access the media server. Using these tools in this order, you should verify the following to determine where the problem begins:

1. Locally (on server)

2. Local switch

3. Local subnet

4. Remote subnet

5. Outside the firewall

6. Over the Internet

Other troubleshooting tools are available:

- ► Client logging to track what is streamed from your server

- ► Network monitor to view and troubleshoot communication

- ► Forward error correction to recover from network errors

Digital Rights Management (DRM)

Combined with the authentication and authorization options, Windows Media Server also works with *Digital Rights Management (DRM)*, which makes it possible to control content usage for those situations in which WMS authentication and authorization cannot. To protect the files, DRM encrypts the file. To decrypt DRM encrypted files, the client software obtains a license, which defines the authorized uses of the content, including:

- ► **Subscription:** The initial license for content has an expiration date. After the subscription is renewed, a new license is issued with a new expiration date.

- ► **Rental:** The license for content has an expiration date and the license is not renewed.

- ► **File purchase:** The license does not have an expiration date but restricts usage.

- ► **Events:** A license is issued to decode a live event after a payment is received.

To establish a Windows Media DRM, follow these steps:

1. Use Windows Media Rights Manager to package the digital media file.

2. Distribute the media, using the Windows Media server or by distributing the file through a website, a CD, or email.

3. Establish a license server, using the Windows Media Rights Manager License Service.

4. Provide a *license key* to the consumer so he can unlock the file and play a packaged digital media file.

5. Play the digital media file with a player that supports the Windows Media DRM, such as Windows Media Player 10.

When a user acquires an encrypted digital media file from a website, the user needs to acquire a license that contains a key to unlock the file before the content can be played. Windows Media Rights Manager packages the digital media file. The packaged media file has been encrypted and locked with a key. This key is stored in an encrypted license, which is distributed separately. Other information is added to the media file, such as the URL where the license can be acquired. This packaged digital media file is saved in Windows Media Audio format (with a .wma file name extension) or Windows Media Video format (with a .wmv file name extension). The packaged file can be placed on a website for download, placed on a media server for streaming, distributed on a CD, or emailed to consumers.

To generate a key, a license key seed and a key ID are needed. The *license key seed* is a value that is known only to the content owner and license clearing house. The *key ID* is created by the content owner for each Windows Media file. This value is included in the packaged file.

When the license clearing house needs to issue a license for a packaged file, a key can be re-created by retrieving the key ID from the packaged file. The Windows Media License Service uses the license key seed (which the clearing house provides) and the key ID from the packaged file to create a key. The key is included in the license sent to the consumer's computer. Using the key included in the license, the player on the consumer's computer can open and play the protected file.

To play a packaged digital media file, the consumer must first acquire a license key to unlock the file. The process of acquiring a license begins automatically when the consumer attempts to acquire the protected content, acquires a pre-delivered license, or plays the file for the first time. Windows Media Rights Manager either sends the consumer to a registration page where information is requested or payment is required (nonsilent), or "silently" retrieves a license from a clearing house.

Exam Prep Questions

1. On which versions of Windows Server 2008 can you install the Windows Media Server? (Choose all that apply.)

   ○ **A.** Windows Server 20080 Web edition

   ○ **B.** Windows Server 2008 Standard edition

   ○ **C.** Windows Server 2008 Enterprise edition

   ○ **D.** Windows Server 2008 Datacenter

2. You have a Windows Server 2008 computer running Windows Media Server. Your network has been having some problems lately, in which users have been disconnected from the media server and then have to reconnect to the media server. In addition, users sometimes complain it takes videos a long time to start. What option can you use to help alleviate this problem? (Choose two answers.)

   ○ **A.** Enable Advanced Fast Start.

   ○ **B.** Install a proxy server between the media server and the clients.

   ○ **C.** Enable Fast Reconnect.

   ○ **D.** Fast Forward/Rewind.

3. You have a Windows Server 2008 Standard Edition computer. You want to install the Streaming Media Services role. However, when you open the Server Manager to install the Streaming Media Service role, there is no Streaming Media Services role available. What do you need to do?

   ○ **A.** You need to run the Windows Update and retrieve the latest updates.

   ○ **B.** You need to install the Microsoft Update Standalone Package (MSU) for the Streaming Media Services role.

   ○ **C.** You need to install Windows Media Player 11.

   ○ **D.** You need to load Windows Server 2008 Enterprise edition.

4. What is the default port used by RTSP?

   ○ **A.** 80

   ○ **B.** 443

   ○ **C.** 554

   ○ **D.** 1433

5. What is the easiest way to direct users to the live content stream?

   ○ **A.** Have the users log on to a nearby proxy server that is pointing to the Streaming Media Server.

   ○ **B.** Use an announcement file.

   ○ **C.** Send an automatic broadcast to the media players on each person's machine.

   ○ **D.** Have the users log on to the Streaming Media Server.

6. You have a Windows Server 2008 computer. You want to enable users to download digital media files. As they download them, they should be directed to a website to get the license key. What method should you use to deliver the licenses?

   ○ **A.** Silent

   ○ **B.** Nonsilent

   ○ **C.** Predelivered

   ○ **D.** Send a hyperlink and a key via email.

7. You have a Windows Server 2008 with Windows Media Services. You create a media package file. You need to send the media package file to another company. What do you need to send with the file so that they can decrypt and unlock the media content?

   ○ **A.** License key seed

   ○ **B.** Key

   ○ **C.** The proper codec

   ○ **D.** The interstitial advertisement

8. What version of Windows Media Player do you need to support Windows Media DRM?

   ○ **A.** Windows Media Player 6 or higher

   ○ **B.** Windows Media Player 9 or higher

   ○ **C.** Windows Media Player 10 or higher

   ○ **D.** Windows 6 or higher with the Media DRM Plug-in

Answers to Exam Prep Questions

1. Answers B and C are correct. You can install Windows Media Server only on Windows Server 2008 Standard and Enterprise edition. Answers A and D are incorrect because you cannot install the Windows Media Server on the Windows Server 2008 Web Edition and Datacenter edition.

2. Answers A and C are correct. You should enable Advanced Start and enable Fast Reconnect. Advanced Fast Start enables the users to start viewing the content sooner. Fast Reconnect minimizes the impact to each client during a temporary network outage by enabling the client to reconnect to the server automatically and restart streaming. Answer B is incorrect because although a proxy server helps cache web pages, it does not overcome network problems. Answer D is incorrect because Fast Forward and Rewind do not help with network problems or decrease the time it takes for a media file to start playing.

3. Answer B is correct. You need to install the MSU package for the Streaming Media Services role before it shows in the role list to install. Answer A is incorrect because updates would not add the Streaming Media Services role. Answer C is incorrect because having Windows Media Player 11 would not add the Streaming Media Services role. Answer D is incorrect because you can install Microsoft Update Standalone Package on Windows Server 2008 Standard and Enterprise edition.

4. Answer C is correct. RTSP uses port 554. Answers A and B are incorrect because port 80 is used by HTTP and 443 is used by secure HTTP (SSL). Answer D is incorrect because port 1433 is used to communicate with a SQL server.

5. Answer B is correct. You can create an announcement file, which is an XML-based file that contains metadata about content and directs users to the content location. After the announcement page is created, it can be distributed on a web page, by file share, or by email. Answers A and D are incorrect because logging on to a proxy server or a Streaming Media Server does not allow the users to play the media files. Answer C is incorrect because a broadcast can be sent out, but the user has to tune into the broadcast; it doesn't automatically start playing on an individual computer.

6. Answer B is correct. You need to use nonsilent delivery of the license, which redirects the users to a website. Answer A is incorrect because the silent delivery method does not require any interaction for end users to receive a license. Answer C is incorrect because the predelivered method sends the license before or at the same time as the content without prompting users for any information. Answer D is incorrect because sending a key before or at the same time as the content without prompting describes the predelivered method.

7. Answer B is correct because recipients need a key to decrypt the package. Answer A is incorrect because the license key seed and key ID is used to make up the key. Answer C is incorrect because the codec is used to compress and decompress a media file. Answer D is incorrect because interstitial advertisement is a streaming advertisement that is inserted into a playlist with your content.

8. Answer C is correct because you need Windows Media Player 10 or higher to support Windows Media DRM. Windows A and B are incorrect because you need version 10, not version 6 or 9. Answer D is incorrect because there is no such thing as the Media DRM plug-in.

Need to Know More?

For more information about Windows Media Services, visit the following websites:

http://www.microsoft.com/windows/windowsmedia/forpros/server/server.aspx

http://technet.microsoft.com/en-us/windowsmedia/default.aspx

For Windows Media Digital Rights Management (DRM) tutorials, visit the following website:

http://www.microsoft.com/windows/windowsmedia/forpros/drm/tutorial.aspx

CHAPTER SEVEN

High Availability

Terms you'll need to understand:

✓ five nines
✓ failover cluster
✓ failback
✓ load balance
✓ heartbeat
✓ convergence

Techniques/concepts you'll need to master:

✓ Identify hardware components that make a computer more fault-tolerant.
✓ Install and configure an active-passive failover cluster.
✓ Configure failback in an active-passive failover cluster.
✓ Configure network roles for an active-passive failover cluster to accommodate public and private networks.
✓ Install and configure a network load balancing (NLB) cluster.

Servers provide network services and applications. Most likely, some of these servers are critical to an organization. Therefore, any downtime could be staggering to a company. Such servers that require high availability usually aim at 99.999% (known as *five nines*) up-time, which means that they can be offline only 5.25 minutes per year. As a network administrator, you need to minimize any down time on these servers by making them fault tolerant against hardware failure, network failure, and power failure.

Hardware Redundancy

Because computers consist of electronic and mechanical devices, they do fail from time to time. Mechanical components tend to fail more often then electronic components. Therefore, drives and power supplies are considered high failure items. To reduce downtime, many servers use RAID to protect against drive failure and redundant power supplies to protect against faulty power supplies. In high-end servers, these types of drives and power supplies are hot-swappable so that they can be replaced without shutting down the system.

High-end servers also have additional features that make them more resistant to hardware failure and that enable monitoring of the server. For example, most high-end servers use a more expensive Error Correcting Code (ECC) memory. ECC memory is a type of memory that includes special circuitry for testing the accuracy of data as it passes in and out of memory. In addition, ECC memory corrects a single failed bit in a 64-bit memory block.

Some of the extra monitoring features include reading the temperature of processors, memory, and the chassis, the speed of the fans, and the voltages supplied by the power supplies and voltages at key points along the motherboard. You can then use special monitoring software that can automatically send messages to the network administrators so that you correct many of these problems before they take down the server.

Network connections can also cause major problems for a server. A single faulty cable can bring down a single server or bring down multiple servers if it is the primary link on a switch that links multiple servers. Also, if a switch fails, it brings down multiple servers. Therefore, you protect against cable and switch failures by teaming multiple network cards to act as one link. This provides additional bandwidth for the server and redundant network connections. If you have two switches that are trunked together, they also provide links to redundant switches.

Finally, all servers should be connected to an uninterruptable power supply (UPS) to protect against power fluctuations including power failure. To enhance the capabilities when connected to a UPS, you can connect a cable from the UPS to the server. When power fails, you can configure Windows to perform certain tasks, including shutting down gracefully and sending messages to network administrators so that they can respond. Of course, because UPSs are designed to provide power for a limited time, you may also consider backup generators.

Hot-Add and Hot-Replace Memory and Processors

Because processors and memory can fail just like any other electronic device, Windows Server 2008 Enterprise and Datacenter version added some new features to overcome these types of failures. First, Windows Server 2008 Enterprise allows you to hot-add memory. Windows Server 2008 Datacenter extends the capabilities of Windows Server 2008 Enterprise by enabling you to hot-add memory and hot-replace memory, and hot-add or hot-replace processors.

Hot-add of processors and memory enables you to quickly scale up these resources without having to restart the server. Hot-replace of processors and memory enables administrators to quickly recover from failed processors or memory by enabling replacement of the defective parts without having to stop and restart the server.

> **NOTE**
>
> For Windows Server 2008 to support hot-add and hot-replace memory and processors, the server hardware must also support hot-add and hot-replace memory and processors.

Failover Clustering

Of course, although you may be using servers with RAID, redundant power supplies, and redundant network cards, servers still can fail. Faulty memory, processors, motherboards, or other components can still bring down a server. In addition, operating system and application files on a server could also become corrupted or deleted. If a server cannot be down for even a minute, you need to consider installing redundant servers using a fail-over cluster or network load balancing.

A cluster is a set of independent computers that work together to increase the availability of services and applications. Each server that makes up the cluster is known as a node. Clustering is most commonly used for database applications such as Exchange Server or SQL server, file servers, print services, or network services such as DHCP servers.

If one of the nodes fails, the remaining nodes respond by distributing the load amongst themselves. 32-bit versions of Windows Server 2008 Enterprise or Windows Server 2008 Datacenter provide rapid, automatic failover with up to 8-node clusters, and up to 16-node clusters are possible with the 64-bit versions. Windows Server 2008 for Itanium-Based Systems supports up to eight nodes in a *failover cluster*.

The most common failover cluster is the active-passive cluster because one node is active, providing the network services and applications, and the other node is passive, waiting to become active. If the current active node goes down, the passive node becomes the new active node, taking over in providing the network services and applications.

Another failover cluster configuration is the active-active, wherein the cluster has multiple resources that are being shared amongst the cluster nodes, spreading the load. Some resources run on one node and other resources run on the other node. If one of the nodes fails, all the resources fail over to the remaining node.

Cluster nodes are kept aware of the status of other cluster nodes and services through the use of heartbeats. A *heartbeat* (sent no more than every 500ms) is sent through a dedicated network card, is used to keep track of the status of each node, and is also used to send updates on the cluster's configuration.

Typically, the network resources are assigned to a cluster, which can be enabled or disabled when the node is active or inactive. Some of the terms that you need to understand include

- **Cluster resource:** A network application service or hardware device (including network adapters and storage systems) that is defined and managed by the cluster service.

- **Cluster resource group:** Resources grouped together. When a cluster resource group fails and the cluster service cannot automatically restart it, the entire cluster resource group is placed in an offline status and failed over to another node.

- **Cluster virtual server:** A cluster resource group that has a network name and IP address assigned to it. Cluster virtual servers are then accessed by their NetBIOS name, DNS name, and IP address.

For example, if you have an active-passive cluster, you assign a different NetBIOS name, DNS name, and IP address to each of the two nodes so that each node can be addressed individually. You then define a cluster virtual server that represents the cluster as a whole, which receives a third NetBIOS name,

DNS name, and IP address. Other resources that are shared between the two nodes are defined as cluster resources and assigned to a cluster resource group. When a node is active, it has control of those cluster resources. When the server goes down, the heartbeat shows that the server is not accessible and the second node becomes active, taking over the cluster resources.

To keep track of the cluster configuration, the cluster uses a witness disk, known as a quorum disk, to hold the cluster configuration database. It defines the nodes participating in the cluster, the applications and services defined within the cluster resource group, and the status of each node and cluster resource. Because the quorum disk has to be shared by all the nodes, it is typically located on a shared storage device, either as a SAN or a shared SCSI array.

Failover Clustering System Requirements

To create a failover cluster, you need two severs, which are virtually identical to each other. They must follow these requirements:

Server Requirements

- ▶ Hardware must be compatible with Windows Server 2008.

- ▶ The servers should have identical components including identical processors of the same brand, model, and version (stepping).

- ▶ The servers must run the same Windows Server 2008 Enterprise or Windows Server 2008 Datacenter and the same hardware version, such as 32-bit or x64.

- ▶ The servers should have the same software updates and service packs.

Network Requirements

- ▶ You need to have at least two network adapters dedicated to network communications for each clustered server.

- ▶ The network adapter must be independent of the network adapter that is used for iSCSI.

- ▶ It is recommended for the best performance that you use Gigabit Ethernet or higher.

Storage Requirements

- ▶ You need to use identical mass-storage device controllers that are dedicated to the cluster storage with identical firmware versions.

- You should have either a network adapter or a host bus adapter that is dedicated to the cluster storage. If you are using iSCSI, you must have a network adapter dedicated to iSCSI.

- You need at least two separate logical unit numbers (LUN) that are configured at the hardware level. One volume is used for the quorum and the other volume contains the files that are being shared to users.

- In most cases, a LUN used for one set of cluster servers should be isolated from all other servers through LUN masking or zoning.

- You need to use basic disks, not dynamic disks, for clustering.

- It is recommended that you format all partitions with NTFS. The witness/quorum disk must be NTFS.

Infrastructure Requirements

- The servers in the cluster must use Domain Name System (DNS) for name resolution.

- All servers in the cluster must be in the same Active Directory domain and within the same organizational unit.

Installing the Failover Clustering Feature

Before you create a failover cluster, we strongly recommend that you validate your configuration—that is, that you run all tests in the Validate a Configuration Wizard. By running the tests, you can confirm that your hardware and settings are compatible with failover clustering.

The Failover Clustering feature is included in Windows Server 2008 Enterprise and Windows Server 2008 Datacenter. It is not included in Windows Server 2008 Standard or Windows Web Server 2008. To install Failover Clustering, use the Add Features command in the Initial Configuration Tasks or from Server Manager. Of course, you need to be a local administrator or equivalent.

Using the Cluster Validation Tests

If you have installed the Failover Clustering feature, you can use the Validate a Configuration Wizard that runs tests to confirm that your hardware and hardware settings are compatible with failover clustering. You can also use it to test your cluster after the cluster has been established.

The Validate a Configuration Wizard includes four types of tests:

▶ **System Configuration tests:** Validate that system software and configuration settings are compatible across servers. Tests include validating Active Directory Configuration to ensure that each tested server is in the same domain and organizational units, validating the same processor architecture, validating all signed drivers, and validating software updates and service pack levels.

▶ **Inventory tests:** Provide an inventory of the hardware, software, and settings (such as network settings) on the servers, and information about the storage.

▶ **Network tests:** Validate that your networks are set up correctly for clustering, including that there are at least two network adapters for each server and verifying that each network adapter has a different IP address. The test also validates that the computers can communicate on all network connections.

▶ **Storage tests:** Validate that the storage on which the failover cluster depends is behaving correctly and supports the required functions of the cluster, including that the computers can access the shared storage required for the quorum disk.

The report from the Validate a Configuration Wizard includes one of the following messages about each test:

▶ The tested item meets requirements for a failover cluster.

▶ The tested item might meet the requirements, but there is a warning about something that you should check.

▶ The test item does not meet requirements.

▶ The test could not be run (for example, if you are testing a single node by itself, certain tests do not run).

To validate the failover cluster configuration, follow these steps:

1. Open the failover cluster snap-in by opening Administrative Tools and selecting Failover Cluster Management (see Figure 7.1).

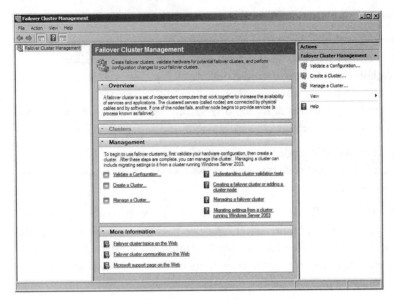

FIGURE 7.1 Failover Cluster Management console.

2. If the User Account Control dialog box appears, confirm that the action it displays is what you want, and then click Continue.

3. Confirm that Failover Cluster Management is selected and then, in the center pane under Management, click Validate a Configuration.

4. Follow the instructions in the wizard to specify the two servers and the tests, and then run the tests. To fully validate your configuration, run all tests before creating a cluster.

5. The Summary page appears after the tests run.

6. While still on the Summary page, click View Report and read the test results.

To view the results of the tests after you close the wizard, see C:\Windows\ Cluster\Reports\Validation Report date and time.html.

Creating the Cluster

After the hardware has been validated, the Failover Clustering feature has been added to the server and the network cards, and network cables and drives have been connected, you are then ready to create the cluster.

Take these steps to create a new failover cluster:

1. Open the Administrative Tools and click Failover Cluster Management.

2. If the User Account Control dialog box appears, confirm that the action it displays is what you want, and then click Continue.

3. In the Failover Cluster Management snap-in, confirm that Failover Cluster Management is selected and then, under Management, click Create a Cluster.

4. In the Select Servers page, type the name of the first node in the Enter Server Name field, and click Add. Repeat this step for each subsequent node. You can also use the Browse button to browse Active Directory for the computers you want to add. After all nodes have been added to the list of Selected Servers, click Next (see Figure 7.2).

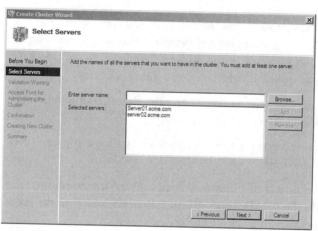

FIGURE 7.2   Specifying server nodes in a cluster.

5. On the Validation Warning page, if you wish to run validation tests on the current server, select Yes. If you don't, select No.

6. In the Cluster Name field, type the name for the failover cluster. This is the name that you use to connect to and administer the cluster (see Figure 7.3).

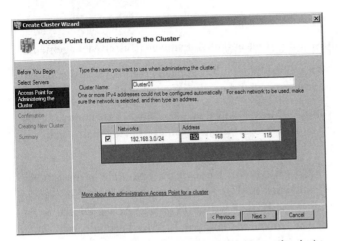

FIGURE 7.3 Specifying the cluster name and IP address of a cluster.

7. In the Networks field, ensure that the networks you want to use are selected. Clear the check boxes for any networks that you do not want to use for cluster administration. In the Address field for each selected network, type the appropriate IP addresses, and then click Next.

8. The Confirmation page appears. Verify that the cluster configuration is correct, and click Next to create the cluster.

9. After the cluster is successfully formed, the Summary page appears. Click Finish to close the wizard.

10. After the wizard runs and the Summary page appears, if you want to view a report (stored in the C:\Windows\Cluster\Reports folder) of the tasks that the wizard performed, click View Report.

Configuring the Cluster

Before the cluster provides any services, you must install and configure the services on the clustered servers. For example, if you are creating a file server cluster, you should use the Manage-Failover Cluster option in the Failover Cluster console to add file server roles. You can also use the manage Failover Cluster option to configure options such as the name of the clustered file server and the storage location used by the file server.

To configure a two-node file server failover cluster:

1. Under Administrative Tools, open the Failover Cluster snap-in.

2. If the User Account Control dialog box appears, confirm that the action it displays is what you want, and then click Continue.

3. In the console tree, if the cluster that you created is not displayed, right-click Failover Cluster Management, click Manage a Cluster, and then select the cluster you want to configure.

4. In the console tree, click the plus sign next to the cluster that you created to expand the items underneath it.

5. If the clustered servers are connected to a network that is not to be used for network communication in the cluster (for example, a network intended only for iSCSI), then under Networks, right-click that network, click Properties, and then click Do Not Allow the Cluster to Use This Network. Click OK.

6. Click Services and Applications. Under Actions (on the right), click Configure a Service or Application.

7. Review the text on the first page of the wizard, and then click Next.

8. Click the services that you want for high availability such as File Server, DHCP Server, and so on (see Figure 7.4).

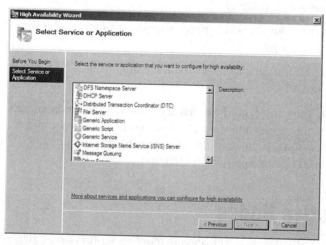

FIGURE 7.4 Using the High Availability Wizard to select services.

9. Follow the instructions in the wizard to specify the following details:

   ▸ A name for the clustered file server

   ▸ Any IP address information that is not automatically supplied by your DHCP settings—for example, a static IPv4 address for this clustered file server

   ▸ The storage volume or volumes that the clustered file server should use

10. After the wizard runs and the Summary page appears, to view a report of the tasks the wizard performed, click View Report.

11. To close the wizard, click Finish.

If you were making a high availability file server, you need to do the following:

1. In the console tree, make sure Services and Applications is expanded, and then select the clustered file server that you just created.

2. Under Actions, click Add a Shared Folder. The Provision a Shared Folder Wizard appears. This is the same wizard that you would use to provision a share on a nonclustered file server.

3. Follow the instructions in the wizard to specify the following settings for the shared folder:

   ▸ Path and name

   ▸ NTFS permissions (optional)

   ▸ Advanced settings for the SMB protocol (optional) such as user limits and offline settings

   ▸ Whether the NFS protocol will be used, for support of UNIX-based clients (optional)

4. After completing the wizard, confirm that the clustered file server comes online. If it does not, review the state of the networks and storage and correct any issues. Then right-click the new clustered file server and click Bring This Service or Application Online.

Changing Active Nodes

To perform a basic test of failover or to manually move to another node, right-click the clustered file server, click Move This Service or Application to Another Node, and click the available choice of node. When prompted, confirm your choice. You can observe the status changes in the center pane of the snap-in as the clustered file server instance is moved.

Cluster Network Role and Type

By default, the New Server Cluster Wizard sets up all cluster networks as mixed (public and private) networks. Optionally, you can change this so that the networks are set up as private networks (that is, for node-to-node communication only) or public networks (that is, for client access only).

To check the role that is configured for a cluster network, follow these steps:

1. Click Start, click Administrative Tools, and then click Failover Cluster Management. If the User Account Control dialog box appears, confirm that the action it displays is what you want, and then click Continue.

2. In the Failover Cluster Management snap-in, if the cluster you want to configure is not displayed, in the console tree, right-click Failover Cluster Management, click Manage a Cluster, and select or specify the cluster you want.

3. If the console tree is collapsed, expand the tree under the cluster that you want to configure, and then expand Networks.

4. Right-click the network for which you want to check settings, and then click Properties.

5. If you want to use this network for the cluster, make sure that Allow the Cluster to Use This Network is selected. If you select this option and you want the network to be used by clients (not just the nodes), make sure Allow Clients to Connect Through This Network is selected.

Verifying that an IP Address Resource Can Come Online

In a cluster, an IP Address resource is important because in most cases, other resources (such as a Network Name resource) depend on it. An IP Address resource can come online only if it is configured correctly, and is supported correctly by available networks and network configurations.

To check to see whether an IP Address Resource is online:

1. To open the failover cluster snap-in, click Start, click Administrative Tools, and then click Failover Cluster Management. If the User Account Control dialog box appears, confirm that the action it displays is what you want, and then click Continue.

2. In the Failover Cluster Management snap-in, if the cluster you want to manage is not displayed, in the console tree, right-click Failover Cluster Management, click Manage a Cluster, and then select or specify the cluster that you want.

3. If the console tree is collapsed, expand the tree under the cluster you want to manage, and then expand Services and Applications.

4. In the console tree, click a clustered service or application.

5. In the center pane, expand the Name listing for the clustered service or application that uses the IP Address resource that you want to verify. View the status of the IP Address resource.

6. If an IP Address resource is offline, bring it online by right-clicking the resource and then clicking Bring This Resource Online.

Cluster Resources

To customize the way your clustered service or application works, you can add a resource manually. Of course, it is always recommended to use the High Availability Wizard. To add a resource to a clustered service or application, follow these steps:

1. Ensure that the software or feature that is needed for the resource is installed on all nodes in the cluster.

2. If the cluster you want to configure is not displayed in the Failover Cluster Management snap-in, right-click Failover Cluster Management in the console tree, click Manage a Cluster, and select or specify the cluster you want.

3. If the console tree is collapsed, expand the tree under the cluster that you want to configure.

4. Expand Services and Applications, and then click the service or application to which you want to add a resource.

5. Under Actions (on the right), click Add a Resource.

6. Click the resource that you want to add, or click More Resources and then click the resource that you want to add. If a wizard appears for the resource you chose, provide the information requested by the wizard.

7. In the center pane, right-click the resource that you added and click Properties.

8. If the property sheet includes a Parameters tab, click the tab and then configure the parameters that the resource needs.

9. Click the Dependencies tab, and then configure the dependencies for the resource. Click OK.

10. In the console tree, select the service or application (not the individual resource), and then under Actions (on the right), click Show Dependency Report.

11. Review the dependencies between the resources. For many resources, you must configure the correct dependencies before the resource can be brought online. If you need to change the dependencies, close the dependency report and then repeat step 9.

12. Right-click the resource that you just added, and then click Bring This Resource Online.

Quorum Configuration

The quorum configuration in a failover cluster determines the number of failures that the cluster can sustain. If an additional failure occurs, the cluster must stop running. The relevant failures in this context are failures of nodes or, in some cases, failures of a witness disk (which contains a copy of the cluster configuration) or witness file share. It is essential that the cluster stop running if too many failures occur or if there is a problem with communication between the cluster nodes.

In most situations, use the quorum configuration that the cluster software identifies as appropriate for your cluster. Change the quorum configuration only if you have determined that the change is appropriate for your cluster. Of course, the full function of a cluster depends not just on quorum, but on the capacity of each node to support the services and applications that fail over to that node.

The quorum configuration choices are

▸ **Node Majority** (recommended for clusters with an odd number of nodes): Can sustain failures of half the nodes (rounding up) minus one. For example, a seven-node cluster can sustain three node failures.

▸ **Node and Disk Majority** (recommended for clusters with an even number of nodes): Can sustain failures of half the nodes (rounding up) if the witness disk remains online. For example, a six-node cluster in which the witness disk is online could sustain three node failures. Can sustain failures of half the nodes (rounding up) minus one if the witness disk goes offline or fails. For example, a six-node cluster with a failed witness disk could sustain two (3–1=2) node failures.

▸ **Node and File Share Majority** (recommended for clusters with special configurations): Works in a similar way to Node and Disk Majority, but instead of a witness disk, this cluster uses a witness file share.

▸ **No Majority: Disk Only** (not recommended): Can sustain failures of all nodes except one (if the disk is online). However, this configuration is not recommended because the disk might be a single point of failure.

Owners and Failback

When a particular application or service fails, you can configure how the cluster responds to the failover. For example, if the cluster fails to the backup node and the primary node comes back up, you can configure whether it fails back to the primary node or fails back during nonpeak hours. Because the cluster may take a couple of minutes to fail back, you would consider scheduling *failback* during nonpeak hours.

You can create a preferred owners list to control which nodes host clustered applications. Using preferred owners ensures that applications run on server nodes where they will perform the best and not interfere with other clustered applications.

In an Active/Passive cluster, you can specify one server to be preferred over another server because it seems to be more reliable or is faster. In an Active/Active cluster with two clustered file servers, one clustered file server has one cluster node as the preferred owner and the other clustered file server has the other node as a preferred owner. This spreads the load across the cluster nodes.

To modify failover settings for a clustered service or application, follow these steps:

1. If the cluster you want to configure is not displayed in the Failover Cluster Management snap-in, right-click Failover Cluster Management in the console tree, click Manage a Cluster, and select or specify the cluster you want.

2. If the console tree is collapsed, expand the tree under the cluster that you want to configure.

3. Expand Services and Applications.

4. Right-click the service or application for which you want to modify failover settings, and then click Properties.

5. On the General tab, specify which node should be the preferred owner for the service or application.

6. Select the Failover tab and select one of the following options:

   ▶ If you don't want to automatically fall back to the preferred node, you would select Prevent Failback.

   ▶ If you want automatic failback when the preferred owner comes back online, you can select Allow Failback and select Immediately.

   ▶ Because the failover may take a couple of minutes, you can schedule the automatic failback to occur after hours. This is configured by selecting Allow Failback, and selecting Failback Between and then setting the time interval.

7. To configure the number of times that the cluster service should attempt to restart or failover a service or application in a given time period, click the Failover tab and specify values under Failover.

Often, a clustered resource, such as a shared disk, can be owned by only one node at a time. Of course, that would be the active node. You can configure which nodes can own a clustered resource and which ones cannot. You can specify the possible owners of the resource by opening the properties of a clustered resource.

EXAM ALERT

If you have one node that cannot access a resource but the other nodes can (assuming they are the active node), you need to check to make sure that the node that is not accessing a resource is listed as a possible owner.

Troubleshooting Cluster Issues

If you have problems where a cluster cannot access a SAN, you should try the following:

1. Check physical connections.

2. Check the logs for each of the hardware components.

3. Run the Validate a Configuration Wizard to verify that the current cluster configuration is still supportable.

NOTE

When running the Validate a Configuration Wizard, be sure that the storage tests you select can be run on an online failover cluster. Several of the storage tests cannot be run without causing loss of service on the clustered disk.

To troubleshoot group and resource failures:

1. Use the Dependency Viewer in the Failover Cluster Management snap-in to identify dependent resources.

2. Check the Event Viewer and trace logs for errors from the dependent resources.

3. Determine whether the problem happens only on a specific node, or nodes, by trying to re-create the problem on different nodes.

Network Load Balancing

Windows Server 2008 also provides network load balancing (NLB) clustering, in which all incoming connection requests are distributed among the various members of the NLB cluster. In addition, using NLB to provide fault tolerance enables it to provide better performance because all members of the NLB cluster are servicing requests.

An NLB cluster uses a virtual IP address and a virtual media access control (MAC) address for network communication. All NLB nodes use the same virtual IP address and virtual MAC address. When an incoming packet is addressed to the virtual IP address and virtual MAC address, all NLB nodes receive it, but only the appropriate node responds.

In addition, all NLB nodes must have the same data to ensure that all nodes respond identically to requests. To ensure that this is the case, you can synchronize data between nodes or store the data in a common location. The option you select depends on the type of application the NLB cluster is hosting.

EXAM ALERT

For NLB to operate properly, all NLB members must be on the same subnet.

Because any server in a network load balancing cluster can respond to a client request, the application files and data on all servers must be exactly the same. Traditional NLB clustering is used to connect to any server in the cluster, such as web and FTP servers. To accomplish this with web servers, you would install and configure identical websites on each NLB member and use a separate back-end server (such as a SQL server or SQL failover cluster) that stores and provides data to the front-end servers. This way, when a user makes a change such as to their user account or to place an order, it is written to the SQL server. When the same user connects to the NLB cluster (although the connection may be to a different member within the NLB cluster), the user can still access the same data because it is centrally stored with the SQL server or cluster. You can also use NLB clusters as firewall, proxy, and virtual private network (VPN) services. With Windows Server 2008, NLB can also integrate with terminal services to create a terminal service farm so that users can reconnect back to their existing sessions.

> **EXAM ALERT**
>
> Network Load Balancing clusters are often used to act as front-end servers where content does not change and failover clusters provide a back-end server that hosts the changing data.

> **EXAM ALERT**
>
> Windows Server 2008 NLB clusters can contain as many as 32 nodes.

> **NOTE**
>
> You cannot use both types of clustering—fail-over clusters and network load balancing clusters—on the same servers. In earlier versions of Windows Server, you could perform NLB by using IPv4 only. With Windows Server 2008, you can configure NLB by using IPv6.

NLB Options

As mentioned earlier, a virtual MAC address and IP address are assigned to the NLB cluster. Requests made to a network load balancing cluster send inbound traffic to every host in the cluster by one of two methods:

▶ **Unicast:** NLB overwrites the original MAC address of the cluster network adapters with the unicast MAC address that is assigned to all the cluster nodes. Therefore, all cluster nodes share an identical unicast MAC address.

▶ **Multicast:** Each cluster node retains the original MAC address of the cluster network adapter. The cluster network adapter is then assigned an additional multicast MAC address, which all the nodes in the cluster share. Inbound client requests can then be sent to all cluster nodes through the multicast MAC address.

Because unicast packets overwrite the MAC, causing the nodes not to be able to communicate among themselves, if you have one network card, you need to use multicast. If you have more than one network card, you can assign one to host the NLB cluster member and the other network card to communicate with the other members of the NLB cluster.

Similar to the failover cluster, the NLB clusters exchange heartbeat messages to maintain consistent data about the cluster's membership. By default, when a host fails to send heartbeat messages for five seconds or more, the other nodes see that host as failed. The remaining hosts in the cluster converge by doing the following:

▶ Establishing which hosts are still active members of the cluster.

▶ Electing the host with the highest priority as the new default host.

▶ Ensuring that all new client requests are handled by the surviving hosts.

When the failed host begins to send heartbeat messages again, it rejoins the cluster during the *convergence*. After all cluster hosts agree on the current cluster membership, the client load is redistributed to the remaining hosts and the convergence completes. Convergence generally takes only a few seconds, so interruption in client service by the cluster is minimal.

Each cluster node is identified by a unique host priority number ranging from 1 to 32. During the cluster convergence, the remaining cluster node with the lowest numeric host priority triggers the end of convergence and becomes the default host. No two cluster nodes can have the same host priority assignment.

Installing and Configuring NLB

To install and configure NLB, you must use an account that is listed in the Administrators group on each host. You would open Server Manager or use the Initial Configuration Tasks window and use the Add Features Wizard to install NLB (see Figure 7.5).

After NLB is installed, you can configure an NLB cluster by using the NLB Manager. To open NLB Manager, click Start, click Administrative Tools, and then click Network Load Balancing Manager. You can also open Network Load Balancing Manager by typing **nlbmgr** at a command prompt.

To configure the NLB cluster, you must configure three types of the parameters:

▶ Host parameters, which are specific to each host in a NLB cluster.

▶ Cluster parameters, which apply to an NLB cluster as a whole.

▶ Port rules, which control how the cluster functions. If you specify which ports are allowed through the NLB, all other traffic is blocked. By default, a port rule equally balances all TCP/IP traffic across all servers.

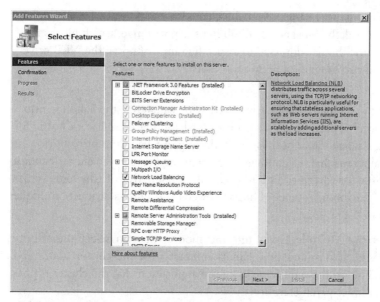

FIGURE 7.5 Installing Network Load Balancing.

EXAM ALERT

If you need to specify specific ports, you need to delete the port rule and create a new port rule.

When you define the port rules, you also specify the filtering mode. By configuring filtering, you can specify whether only one node or multiple nodes within the NLB cluster are allowed to respond to multiple requests from the same client during a single session (connection).

The following are the available filtering modes:

▶ **Multiple hosts:** Specifies that multiple hosts in the cluster will handle network traffic for the associated port rule. Multiple hosts filtering provides scaled performance and fault tolerance by distributing the network load among multiple hosts. You can specify that the load be equally distributed among the hosts or that each host is to handle a specified load weight.

▶ **Single hosts:** Specifies that network traffic for the associated port rule be handled by a single host in the cluster according to the specified handling priority. Single hosts filtering provides port-specific fault tolerance for handling network traffic.

▶ **Disable this port range:** Specifies that all network traffic for the associated port rule be blocked. By disabling the port range, which blocks network traffic that is addressed to a specific range of ports, the NLB driver filters all corresponding network packets.

If you select the Single Hosts filtering mode, you can define the handling priority, which specifies the local host's priority for handling the network traffic for the associated port rule. The host with the highest handling priority (lowest numerical value) for this rule among the current members of the cluster handles all of the traffic for this rule. The allowed values range from 1 (the highest priority), to the maximum number of hosts allowed (32). This value must be unique for all hosts in the cluster.

If you select the Multiple Hosts filtering mode, you also select the affinity options. Affinity determines how clients interact with the cluster nodes and varies depending on the requirements of the application that the cluster is providing. The affinity parameters are:

▶ **None:** Specifies that multiple connections from the same client IP address can be handled by different cluster hosts; in other words, there is no client affinity. This option results in increased speed, but is suitable only for providing static content to clients such as static websites and FTP downloads.

▶ **Single hosts:** All traffic that meets the port rule criteria is sent to a specific cluster node. The Single Host filter might be used in a website that has only one SSL server; thus the port rule for TCP port 443 would specify that all traffic on this port must be directed to that one node.

▶ **Network:** Specifies that NLB direct multiple requests from the same TCP/IP class C address range to the same cluster host. This option ensures that all clients, who use multiple proxy servers to access the cluster, have their TCP connections directed to the same cluster host.

EXAM ALERT

Enabling Single or Network affinity ensures that only one cluster host handles all connections that are part of the same client session. This is important if the server application that is running on the cluster host maintains a session state (such as server cookies) between connections.

To create a new NLB cluster, follow these steps:

1. Open the Administrative Tools and open the Network Load Balancing Manager.

2. Right-click Network Load Balancing Clusters, and then click New Cluster.

3. To connect to the host that is to be a part of the new cluster, in the Host text box, type the name of the host, and then click Connect.

4. Select the interface that you want to use with the cluster, and then click Next. (The interface hosts the virtual IP address and receives the client traffic to *load balance*.)

5. In Host Parameters, select a value in Priority (Unique Host Identifier). This parameter specifies a unique ID for each host. The host with the lowest numerical priority among the current members of the cluster handles all the cluster's network traffic that is not covered by a port rule.

6. You can override these priorities or provide load balancing for specific ranges of ports by specifying rules on the Port Rules tab of the Network Load Balancing Properties dialog box.

7. In Host Parameters, you can also add dedicated IP addresses, if necessary.

8. Click Next.

9. In Cluster IP Addresses, click Add and type the cluster IP address that is shared by every host in the cluster. NLB adds this IP address to the TCP/IP stack on the selected interface of all hosts that are chosen to be part of the cluster.

> **NOTE**
>
> NLB does not support Dynamic Host Configuration Protocol (DHCP). NLB disables DHCP on each interface that it configures, so the IP addresses must be static.

10. Click Next to continue.

11. In Cluster Parameters, select the appropriate values in the IP Address and Subnet Mask section. (For IPv6 addresses, a subnet mask value is not needed.) Then Type the full Internet name that users should use to access this NLB cluster.

12. In Cluster operation mode, click Unicast to specify that a unicast media access control (MAC) address should be used for cluster operations. In unicast mode, the cluster's MAC address is assigned to the computer's network adapter, and the built-in MAC address of the network adapter is not used. We recommend that you accept the unicast default settings.

13. Click Next to continue.

14. In Port Rules, click Edit to modify the default port rules, if needed.

15. To add more hosts to the cluster, right-click the new cluster, and then click Add Host to Cluster. Configure the host parameters (including host priority, dedicated IP addresses, and load weight) for the additional hosts by following the same instructions that you used to configure the initial host. Because you are adding hosts to an already configured cluster, all the cluster-wide parameters remain the same.

To add a host to the NLB cluster, follow these steps:

1. To open Network Load Balancing Manager, click Start, click Administrative Tools, and then click Network Load Balancing Manager. You can also open Network Load Balancing Manager by typing **nlbmgr** at a command prompt.

2. Right-click the cluster where you want to add the host and choose Add Host to Cluster. If NLB Manager does not list the cluster, connect to the cluster.

3. Type the host's name and click Connect. The network adapters that are available on the host are listed at the bottom of the dialog box.

4. Click the network adapter that you want to use for Network Load Balancing and then click Next. The IP address configured on this network adapter is the dedicated IP address for this host.

5. Configure the remaining host parameters as appropriate, and then click Finish.

Stopping or Starting Handling Network Load Balancing Cluster Traffic

To stop or start handling NLB cluster traffic by using the Windows interface, follow these steps:

1. Under Administrative Tools, open the NLB Manager (see Figure 7.6).

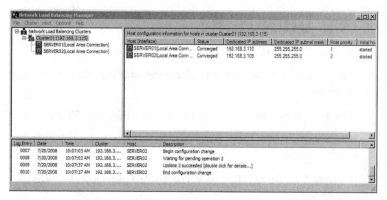

FIGURE 7.6 Using the Network Load Balancing Manager.

2. If NLB Manager does not list the cluster, connect to the cluster.

3. If you want to stop cluster operations on all cluster hosts, right-click the cluster, point to Control Hosts, and then click Stop. If you want to stop the cluster service on only a particular host, right-click the host, point to Control Host, and then click Stop.

4. If you want to start cluster operations on all cluster hosts, right-click the cluster, point to Control Hosts, and then click Start. If you want to start the cluster service on only a particular host, right-click the host, point to Control Host, and then click Start.

Exam Prep Questions

1. What does the phrase "five nines" mean?

   ○ **A.** "Five nines" means that the server must be up for at least 99,999 minutes per year.

   ○ **B.** "Five nines" means that servers cannot ever have 99.999% CPU utilization.

   ○ **C.** "Five nines" means that the servers must be up for at least 99.999% of the time.

   ○ **D.** "Five nines" means that all servers must have a minimum of five 90GB hard drives.

2. You want to configure a two-node failover cluster using two Windows Server 2008 computers to be used as a file server. What is the minimum number of volumes required?

   ○ **A.** 1

   ○ **B.** 2

   ○ **C.** 3

   ○ **D.** 4

3. If a cluster fails over, you want to manually fail back the cluster. What do you need to do to configure this?

   ○ **A.** On the Failback tab on the cluster group properties, select Prevent Failback.

   ○ **B.** On the Recovery tab on the cluster group properties, deselect Failback Between.

   ○ **C.** On the Failback tab on the cluster group properties, select Manual Failback

   ○ **D.** On the Recovery tab on the cluster group properties, deselect Automatic Failback.

4. You have a failover cluster using Windows Server 2008 computers. Each server has two network cards. The first network card is for the cluster network and the second network card is for the public network. Although the heartbeat is functioning properly, clients cannot connect to the cluster. What is the problem?

   ○ **A.** Ensure that the first network card has the Allow Clients to Connect Through This Network option selected.

   ○ **B.** Ensure that the first network card has the Allow the Cluster to Use This Network option selected.

○   **C.** Ensure that the second network card has the Allow Clients to Connect Through This Network option selected.

○   **D.** Ensure that the second network card has the Allow the Cluster to Use This Network option selected.

5. How are cluster nodes aware that a node has failed?

○   **A.** They use special management packets over the cluster network.

○   **B.** They use heartbeats.

○   **C.** They use a ping every five seconds.

○   **D.** They do a WMI call every five seconds.

6. How many nodes does Windows Server 2008 Standard edition support for a failover cluster?

○   **A.** 8

○   **B.** 16

○   **C.** 32

○   **D.** It does not support failover clusters.

7. How many nodes does Windows Server 2008 Enterprise Edition support for a failover cluster?

○   **A.** 8

○   **B.** 16

○   **C.** 32

○   **D.** It does not support failover clusters.

8. How many nodes does Windows Server 2008 Enterprise Edition support for an NLB cluster?

○   **A.** 8

○   **B.** 16

○   **C.** 32

○   **D.** It does not support NLB clusters.

9. When a host in an NLB cluster fails, the missing node is detected because no heartbeat is received from the failed node. When the remaining nodes see that a node is no longer available, the cluster redistributes the work amongst the remaining nodes. What is this called?

   ○ **A.** Hot-swapping system

   ○ **B.** Convergence

   ○ **C.** Virtual distribution

   ○ **D.** Virtual scalability

10. You need to deploy a two-tier system. The front-end tier will be a web server and the back-end tier will be a SQL Server. Fault tolerance is important while maintaining a high level of performance. What should you do?

   ○ **A.** The front end and the back end should be failover clusters.

   ○ **B.** The front end should be a failover cluster and the back end should be an NLB cluster.

   ○ **C.** The front end should be an NLB cluster and the back end should be a failover cluster.

   ○ **D.** The front end and back end should be NLB clusters.

11. You have a failover cluster with three nodes that supports all your printers by providing print services. When testing your cluster, you fail over to each node and test the printing. It works fine on the first two nodes but fails when you try the third node. What should you do?

   ○ **A.** Configure failback to the first server.

   ○ **B.** Configure the third node as the preferred owner for the print services.

   ○ **C.** Remove the first node as the preferred owner for the print services.

   ○ **D.** Make sure that the third node is configured as a possible owner of the print services.

12. You decide to create a failover cluster to provide services for your SQL server. However, when you start the High Availability Wizard to create the SQL service group, the wizard generates an error, indicating that no disks are available when you are supposed to select the storage. What should you do?

   ○ **A.** Create a new volume on an existing hard disk on one of the nodes.

   ○ **B.** Add an additional shared disk to the cluster and create a new volume on the disk.

   ○ **C.** Add a new hard drive on one of the nodes and create a new volume on the disk.

   ○ **D.** Convert the disk to a dynamic disk so that it can be recognized by the cluster.

Answers to Exam Prep Questions

1. Answer C is correct. Five nines means that the system should be up for 99.999% of the time, which means it can be offline for only 5.25 minutes per year. Answers A, B, and D are incorrect because they do not define "five nines."

2. Answer B is correct. You need at least two volumes for a two-node file server cluster. One drive is the quorum drive and the second one is for the file storage. Answers A, C, and D are incorrect because you need at least two volumes, not 1, 3, or 4.

3. Answer A is correct. You would open the cluster group properties and select Prevent Failback on the Failback tab. Answers B and D are incorrect because you cannot configure failback options in the Recovery tab. Answer C is incorrect because there is no Manual Failback option.

4. Answer C is correct because you need to ensure that Allow Clients to Connect Through This Network is selected so that clients can also access the cluster through the public network. Answer A is incorrect because the clients access through the public network, not the cluster network. Answer B is incorrect because the first network card is not for public use; it is used for the cluster, which is working fine. Answer D is incorrect because the second network card is for public use and it is not being used for the cluster.

5. Answer B is correct. To see the status of the cluster nodes, the nodes use heartbeats sent through a dedicated network card, no more than every 500ms. Answers A, C, and D are incorrect because they use heartbeats, not special management packets, ping packets, or WMI calls.

6. Answer D is correct. Windows Server 2008 Standard Edition does not support failover clusters. You must use Windows Server 2008 Enterprise or Datacenter editions to support failover clusters. Answers A, B, and C are incorrect because Windows Server 2008 does not support failover clusters.

7. Answer B is correct. The Windows Server 2008 Enterprise Edition and Data Center Edition support 16 nodes. Answers A, C, and D are incorrect because the 64-bit versions of Windows Server 2008 Enterprise Edition supports 16 nodes.

8. Answer C is correct. The Windows Server 2008 Enterprise Edition and Data Center Edition support 32 nodes. Answers A, B, and D are incorrect because Windows Server 2008 Enterprise Edition supports 32 nodes.

9. Answer B is correct. Convergence is when the work is redistributed among the cluster's other members and the network topology of those hosts remain stable. Answer A is incorrect because although this can be described as a hot-swappable system, it is called convergence. Answers C and D are incorrect because virtual distribution and virtual scalability are made-up terms that don't exist.

10. Answer C is correct. The front end should be an NLB cluster. The two web servers will work together to service requests providing high performance. If one server fails, the other one will continue to work, including absorbing the workload of the failed server. The data will be retrieved from the SQL server, so you need to create a failover cluster because you need to make sure that the SQL records are being retrieved by only one server at a time. If the active node fails, the passive node takes over. Answer A is incorrect because the front end should be an NLB, not a failover cluster. Answer B is incorrect because the front end should be an NLB cluster and the back end should be a failover cluster. Answer D is incorrect because the back end should be a failover cluster.

11. Answer D is correct. Although the first two nodes work fine, the failure could be explained if the third node is not a possible owner of the services. Therefore, if the cluster fails over to the third node, it cannot start the print services because the third node is not a possible owner. Answer A is incorrect because although failback can be configured, this configuration would not get the third node to operate properly. Answers B and C are incorrect because changing the preferred owner does not fix the problem because the third node is not a possible owner.

12. Answer B is correct. You need to add a centralized shared disk that is usable by both cluster nodes and create a volume on it. Then when you rerun the wizard, the disk will show. Answers A and C are incorrect because adding or preparing a volume on one of the nodes does not allow it to be seen by the other nodes. It has to be a shared disk to function on the cluster. Answer D is incorrect because the cluster does not care if it is a basic disk or dynamic disk, as long as it is a shared disk.

Need to Know More?

For more information about Windows Server 2008 availability and scalability, including step-by-step guides in configuring NLB, two-node file server failover clusters, and two-node print server failover clusters and the NLB deployment guide, visit the following site:

http://technet2.microsoft.com/windowsserver2008/en/library/13c0a922-6097-4f34-ac64-18820094128b1033.mspx?mfr=true

To view the Failover Cluster Frequently Asked Questions, please visit the following website:

http://www.microsoft.com/windowsserver2008/en/us/clustering-faq.aspx

CHAPTER EIGHT

Terminal Services

Terms you'll need to understand:

- ✓ Terminal Services
- ✓ Remote Desktop
- ✓ Remote Desktop Connection (RDC)
- ✓ Terminal Services Web Access (TS Web Access)
- ✓ Terminal Service Gateway (TS Gateway)
- ✓ Session Directory
- ✓ TS Licensing
- ✓ Terminal Server Client Access License (TS CAL)
- ✓ Terminal Services License Server
- ✓ RemoteApp
- ✓ Network Policy Server (NPS)
- ✓ Connection Authorization Policy (CAP)
- ✓ Resource Authorization Policy (RAP)
- ✓ Terminal Services Session Broker (TS Session Broker)
- ✓ user profile
- ✓ Terminal Services Easy Print
- ✓ Windows System Resource Manager (WSRM)

Techniques/concepts you'll need to master:

- ✓ Enable and configure Remote Desktop on a Windows Server 2008 computer.
- ✓ Enable and configure Terminal Services Web Access.
- ✓ Enable and configure Terminal Services Gateway.
- ✓ Install and configure Terminal Services Load Balancing.
- ✓ Configure and monitor Terminal Services resources.
- ✓ Configure Terminal Services Licensing.
- ✓ Use and configure Remote Desktop Connections (RDC).
- ✓ Configure Terminal Services server options.

Terminal Services in Windows Server 2008 is a powerful centralized application platform. With Terminal Services, you can remotely connect to a computer as if you were sitting at that computer. Using *Remote Desktop*, which is available in Windows XP and Windows Vista, you can access the remote computer's desktop in Windows, which can be expanded to full screen. It enables you to input with your own mouse and keyboard and see everything as you were viewing the system through a local monitor. You can run any program that is available on the remote system and easily access local and remote resources such as drives, printer, clipboard, and computer sound. Similar to terminal emulation (telnet), all client application execution, data processing, and data storage occur on the server that you are accessing. The advantage of using Terminal Services is to remotely configure and manage the computer and for multiple users to access centrally managed applications and resources and reduce hardware costs. Because only screen, keyboard, and mouse information is exchanged between the client and server, it is an ideal solution for the remote dial-up network or for using a shared application on a single server that many people need to access from distant locations (across the Internet or via dial-up).

Windows Server 2008 also supports the following additional functionalities in Terminal Services:

▶ **TS RemoteApp:** Enables users to access remote applications on their local PCs. Although the application looks as if it is running from your local machine in its own normal application window, in reality, it is still being hosted by the remote application.

▶ *TS Web Access:* An interface that makes the Terminal Services Remote Programs available to users from a web browser. It is a customizable web part, which can also be integrated in an Office SharePoint site.

▶ *TS Gateway:* Provides access to Terminal Server sessions by encapsulating the RDP protocol in the HTTPS protocol. The session is secure and you need to keep only firewall port 443 open to make a connection. You can control access through this gateway for each user or for each workstation.

▶ *Session Directory:* A feature that enables users to easily and automatically reconnect to a disconnected session in a load-balanced Terminal Server farm. The session directory contains a list of sessions indexed by username and server name. By using the Terminal Services Session Directory, users can reconnect to the same Terminal Server from which they got disconnected and users can resume working in that session. Users can also reconnect to the session from a different client computer. The Session Directory server must be a highly available network server that is not a Terminal Server.

Remote Desktop

When you enable Remote Desktop, your Windows Server 2008 computer acts as a Terminal Server that allows up to two remote connections (three if you count the console connection, which is connected as if you were logged directly on to the computer). By default, Remote Desktop uses port 3389.

To enable Remote Desktop:

1. Right-click Computer and select Properties.

2. Click Remote Settings.

3. Select Allow Connections from Computers Running Any Version of Remote Desktop (Less Secure) or Allow Connections Only from Computers Running Remote Desktop with Network Level Authentication (more secure).

4. Click OK.

You can also go straight to the Remote Settings tab by selecting Enable Remote Desktop from the Initial Configuration Tasks window.

The Remote Desktop local user group on a Terminal Server is used to give users and groups permission to remotely connect to a Terminal Server. Members of the local Administrators group can connect even if they are not listed.

After Remote Desktop has been enabled, you can add users and groups to the Remote Desktop Users group by following these steps:

1. Start the System tool by clicking the Start button, selecting Run, and typing **control system**. Then click OK.

2. Under Tasks, click Remote Settings.

3. In the System Properties dialog box, click Select Users on the Remote tab. Then add the users or groups you need to connect to the Terminal Server.

Remote Desktop for Server Core

Although you can use the MMC to remotely connect to Windows Server 2008 Server Core computers, you need to do some things from the command prompt on the Server Core computers. To remotely connect to these computers, you must first enable Remote Desktop by executing the following command:

```
cscript scregedit.wsf /ar 0
```

To disable Remote Desktop, use the following command:

```
cscript scregedit.wsf / ar 1
```

To view your current Remote Desktop settings, type the following command:

```
cscript scregedit.wsf /ar /v
```

If you have a Windows XP computer running an older Remote Desktop connection, you need to disable the enhanced security by running the following command:

```
cscript scregedit.wsf /cs 0
```

Remote Desktop Connection

To connect to a Terminal Server or a computer that has Remote Desktop enabled, you use the *Remote Desktop Connection (RDC)* program, assuming that you have network connectivity to the computer and you have the permissions to connect to it. You can also start the Remote Desktop by executing the mstsc.exe program.

When you start RDC, you specify an IP address or host name that is resolved to the computer's IP address. To configure RDC including display settings, local resources (sound, printer, clipboard and keyboard), and server authentication, click on the Options button on the initial Remote Desktop Connections box. From the General tab, you can also save the current connection settings (in the form of an rdp file (*.rdp) so that you can easily open a remote connection with the configured settings in the future just by double-clicking the rdp file.

In addition to interfacing with your monitor, keyboard, and mouse, RDC supports the following:

- ▶ **Audio Redirection:** Enables users to run an audio program on the remote desktop and have the sound redirected to the local computer.

- ▶ **File System Redirection:** Enables users to use their local files on a remote desktop within the terminal session.

- **Printer Redirection:** Enables users to use their local printer within the terminal session as they would with a locally or network shared printer.

- **Port Redirection:** Enables applications running within the terminal session to access local serial and parallel ports directly.

- **Clipboard Sharing:** Enables clipboards to be shared between the remote computer and the local computer.

- **Increased Security:** Users can set 128-bit encryption by using the RC4 encryption algorithm and Transport Layer Security (TLS).

Windows Server 2008 includes RDP 6.1 and Windows Vista includes RDP 6.0. Although Windows XP has RDP 5.1 and Windows Server 2003 has RDP 5.2, you can upgrade Windows Server 2003 with Service Pack 1 and Windows XP with Service Pack 2 to RDP 6.0 by using Windows Update or by downloading it from the Microsoft Download website. RDP 6.0 has the following improvements over older versions of RDP:

- **Server authentication:** Verifies that you are connecting to the correct remote computer or server.

- **Resource redirection:** Portable Devices can be redirected, specifically media players, based on the Media Transfer Protocol (MTP), and digital cameras, based on the Picture Transfer Protocol (PTP).

- **Single Sign-On (SSO):** An authentication method that enables a user with a domain account to log on once, using a password or smart card, and then gain access to remote servers without being asked for credentials again. SSO is controlled with group policies. For SSO to function, the client computer and Terminal Server must be joined to the same domain. In addition, Single Sign-On for remote connections functions only on Windows Vista-based computers that are attempting to access Windows Server 2008-based Terminal Servers.

- **Visual enhancements:** Enhancements include 32-bit color, font smoothing (ClearType), higher resolution desktops, support for additional display resolution ratios to support the newer widescreen monitors, and spanning multiple monitors horizontally that have the same resolution to form a single desktop. The total resolution across all monitors cannot exceed 4096×2048.

- **Single Application:** Users can access a single application instead of the entire desktop.

▶ **Increased Security:** Users can configure front-end Internet Information Services over an HTTPS connection by using the TS Gateway feature.

▶ **Windows Aero Features:** Users can use the Windows Aero features, including translucent windows, taskbar buttons with thumbnail-sized window previews, and a view of your open Windows in a three-dimensional stack on your desktop that was introduced with Windows Server 2008.

Using the `mstsc` Command:

As mentioned before, the Remote Desktop Connections can be started from the command prompt with the mstsc command. The syntax for the `mstsc` command is

```
mstsc [<connection file>] [/v:<server[:port]>] [/console]
➥[/f[ullscreen]] [/w:<width>] [/h:<height>] [/public] ¦
➥[/span] [/edit "connection file"] [/migrate] [/?]
```

▶ `/v:<server[:port]>` specifies the remote computer to which you want to connect as well as an optional port value (port 3389 is the default; it can be changed on all versions of Windows).

▶ `/console` enables you to connect to the console session of older versions of Windows. This setting does not work with Windows Vista or Windows Server 2008.

▶ `/f` starts Remote Desktop Connection in full-screen mode.

▶ `/w:<width>` specifies the width of the Remote Desktop Connection window.

▶ `/h:<height>` specifies the height of the Remote Desktop window.

▶ `/public` runs Remote Desktop Connection in public mode. In public mode, the RDP client does not cache any data to the local system. Use public mode, for example, when connecting to a business server from a system in a conference center.

EXAM ALERT

Be sure you understand the syntax of the `mstsc` command, including the `/console` mode, `/span` option, and `/w` and `/h` options.

The Remote Desktop Protocol File

When you use the Remote Desktop Protocol (RDP) to connect to a remote computer, the Default.rdp file is created on the client computer. By default, the Default.rdp file is created in your My Documents folder.

You can save the RDC configuration by saving the connection settings in the Remote Desktop Connection program by clicking the options button and selecting the General tab.

Because the .rdp files are text files, they can be edited with any text editor, such as Notepad. For example, you can configure the width and height of the terminal session by editing the following two lines:

```
desktopwidth:i:<value>
desktopheight:i:<value>
```

where *<value>* is the resolution, such as 1680 or 1050.

To enable monitor spanning through an .rdp file, you need to open the .rdp file with a text editor and change the value of the Span:i setting to 1. To disable monitor spanning, you need to change the value of the Span:i setting to 0.

For more information about the .rdp files, visit the following website:

http://technet2.microsoft.com/windowsserver2008/en/library/fc0b405b-07ef-4767-8716-198d7f0949011033.mspx?mfr=true

Using Group Policies with RDC

Depending on your available bandwidth, bandwidth-intensive actions such as large print jobs can have an adverse affect on display and input of the RDC session. The default bandwidth ratio is 70:30. Display and input data are allocated 70% of the bandwidth, and all other traffic, such as clipboard, file transfers, or print jobs, is allocated 30% of the bandwidth.

You can adjust the display data prioritization settings by making changes to the Registry of the Terminal Server. You can change the value of the following entries under the HKEY_LOCAL_MACHINE\SYSTEM\CurrentControlSet\Services\TermDD subkey:

▶ FlowControlDisable: If FlowControDisable is set to 1, display data prioritization is disabled and all requests are handled on a first-in-first-out basis. The default value for FlowControlDisable is 0.

▶ `FlowControlDisplayBandwidth`: You can set the relative bandwidth priority for display (and input data) by setting the `FlowControlDisplayBandwidth` value. The default value is `70`; the maximum value allowed is `255`.

▶ `FlowControlChannelBandwidth`: You can set the relative bandwidth priority for other virtual channels (such as clipboard, file transfers, or print jobs) by setting the `FlowControlChannelBandwidth` value. The default value is `30`; the maximum value allowed is `255`. The bandwidth ratio for display data prioritization is based on the values of `FlowControlDisplayBandwidth` and `FlowControlChannelBandwidth`. For example, if `FlowControlDisplayBandwidth` is set to `150` and `FlowControlChannelBandwidth` is set to `50`, the ratio is 150:50, so display and input data are allocated 75% of the bandwidth.

▶ `FlowControlChargePostCompression`: The `FlowControlChargePostCompression` value determines whether flow control calculates the bandwidth allocation based on precompression or postcompression bytes. The default value is `0`, which means that the calculation is made on precompression bytes.

If these entries do not appear, you can add them. To do this, right-click `TermDD`, point to New, and then click DWORD (32-bit) Value. If you make any changes to the Registry values, you need to restart the Terminal Server for the changes to take effect.

Remote Desktops Snap-In

Another tool worth mentioning is the Remote Desktops snap-in. As an administrator, there will be times when you will need to use Terminal Services to remotely administer several computers at the same time. The Remote Desktops snap-in is ideal for administrators who are remotely administering multiple servers by creating multiple Remote Desktop connections with one utility. To allow the easy switching between Terminal Servers, a navigable tree display provides easy switching between connections. Different from Remote Desktop Connections, the Remote Desktops snap-in connects you to the console session of the computer you specify in the connection (see Figure 8.1).

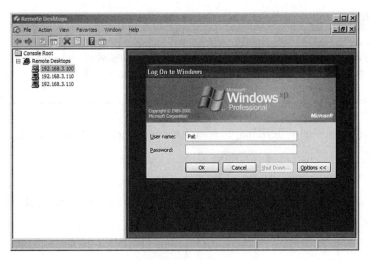

FIGURE 8.1 The Remote Desktops snap-in.

Licensing

The number of users that can access a Terminal Server is based on the number of applications running in a session, resources consumed by each application, and user activity patterns. Because 64-bit Windows removes the kernel virtual address space limitations, 64-bit Windows supports many more users than 32-bit Windows. Also, more resources are needed for the same workload set. On a 64-bit system, you need about 1.3 to 1.7 times the memory that was needed on a 32-bit system.

If you need to have more than two users connect to a computer at once, you need to install the Terminal Services role. You also need to manage your licenses.

License Management System

A license management system known as *TS Licensing* is available with Windows Server 2008 as a role, which can be used to manage TS licenses for Windows Server 2003 and Windows Server 2008 Terminal Servers. You can choose between Terminal Services client access licenses (TS CAL) for devices and users. TS Licensing is used only with Terminal Services and not with Remote Desktop.

NOTE

A Terminal Server running Windows Server 2008 cannot communicate with a license server running Windows Server 2003. However, it is possible for a Terminal Server running Windows Server 2003 to communicate with a license server running Windows Server 2008.

The features and benefits of Terminal Service Licensing include the following:

▶ Centralized administration for Terminal Services Client Access Licenses and the corresponding tokens.

▶ License accountability, tracking, and reporting for each device and each user.

▶ Simple support for various communication channels and purchase programs.

▶ Minimal impact on network and servers.

The license server can be installed on any server, and not just the domain controllers. One license server can serve many Terminal Servers simultaneously. Therefore, if you have a large company, you should place the license server on a separate server so that it can support multiple Terminal Servers. Small companies place the Terminal Services Licensing server on the Terminal Server.

NOTE

Only 20% of a specific version of a CAL can be revoked at a time.

To use Terminal Services Licensing, there must be at least one Terminal Server with the following primary components:

▶ **Microsoft Clearinghouse:** A facility that Microsoft maintains to activate license servers, to issue Client Access Licenses to license servers, to recover CALs, and to reactivate license servers.

▶ *Terminal Services License Server:* A computer on which the Terminal Services License is installed. A license server stores all TS CAL tokens that have been installed for a group of Terminal Servers and tracks the license tokens that have been issued. A license server can serve many Terminal Servers and must connect to an activated license server. In most large deployments, the license server is deployed on a separate server, though it can be found on the Terminal Server.

▶ **Terminal Servers:** A Terminal Server provides clients access to Windows-based applications that run entirely on the server, and supports multiple client sessions on the server.

▶ **CALs:** You must purchase and install the appropriate number of CALs for each user or each device that connects to the Terminal Server. CALs are available on a user-based or device-based licensing. You can decide on the appropriate licensing mode for your organization.

By using the Terminal Server License Server Activation Wizard, you can activate a license server to certify the server, and to enable the server to issue temporary licenses. You must activate the server within 120 days (see Figure 8.2).

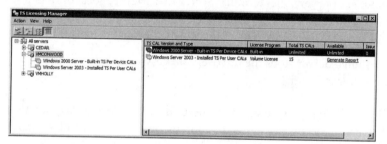

FIGURE 8.2 The Terminal Services Licensing Manager.

You can activate a license server by using one of the following connection methods:

▶ **Web:** You can use the web method to activate a license server when the device running the Terminal Services Licensing management tool does not have Internet connectivity, but you have connectivity through a web browser from another computer.

▶ **Telephone:** You can use the telephone method to talk to a Microsoft customer service representative to complete the activation or license installation transactions.

▶ **Internet:** You can use the Internet method when you have Internet connectivity from the device running the Terminal Services Licensing management tool.

License Server Discovery and User-Based License Tracking

The process of a Terminal Server automatically locating a license server is called license server discovery. The license server discovery process includes the following steps:

1. The Terminal Server first checks the local Registry for information about the license server.

2. The Terminal Server tries discovery through Active Directory by using Lightweight Data Access Protocol (LDAP) instead of RPC.

3. For domain discovery, the Terminal Server first tries the local or on-site domain controllers. If the Terminal Server fails to locate the on-site domain controllers, it tries contacting off-site domain controllers.

4. The Terminal Server stops the discovery process as soon as the first license server is found.

When a Terminal Server receives a request for a user-based license, the Terminal Server queries Active Directory for the associated user object and checks whether the object has a license to present. If not, the Terminal Server requests a license from a license server. The license queries Active Directory and then updates the user account information in Active Directory with information about the license issuance. To update the user account information in Active Directory, the license server must be a member of the Terminal Server License Server group in Active Directory.

Migrating Licenses

If you have the licenses on one server and you want to migrate them to another server, you need to go though the process of migration. To move licenses from one computer to another, you would call Microsoft Clearinghouse and obtain the keypacks that go with the new server ID. Each activated license server is unique and is identified with a certificate provided during activation. Therefore, it is not sufficient to move the licensing database from one computer to another to complete the migration process. You must also reinstall licenses on the new computer.

Troubleshooting License Issues

A Terminal Server must be able to contact (discover) a Terminal Services License server to request *Terminal Services Client Access Licenses* (*TS CAL*) for users or computing devices that are connecting to the Terminal Server. In addition, the Terminal Services Licensing server needs to be properly configured to provide licenses. If a Terminal Server cannot access a license server to get a license, an Event ID 1069, TS CAL Availability, would appear in the Event Viewer.

If a Terminal Server is incapable of issuing licenses to the clients, you need to check the following:

▶ Check to see whether the licensing mode has not been set on the license servers.

▶ Check to see whether the licensing mode matches between the license servers and the Terminal Server.

▶ Check to see whether the Terminal Servers can connect to the license server.

Configuring and Managing Terminal Services

The most common utility used to configure Terminal Services is the Terminal Services Configuration console (see Figure 8.3). Using the Terminal Services Configuration console, you can configure settings for new connections, modify the settings of existing connections, and delete connections. You can configure settings on a per-connection basis, or for the server as a whole.

To make most changes, right-click RDP-Tcp and select Properties. From here, you can see eight tabs (see Figure 8.4):

▶ **General:** Used to configure the security layer, encryption, and network-level authentication requirements.

▶ **Logon Settings:** Used to configure automatic logon.

▶ **Sessions:** Used to specify how long a session remains active and how long a session remains disconnected.

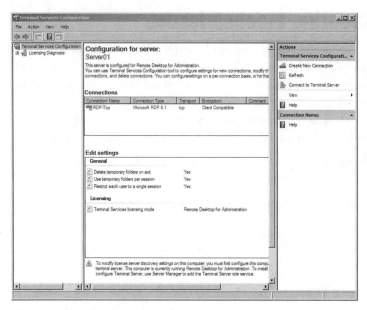

FIGURE 8.3   Terminal Services Configuration settings.

▶ **Environment:** Used to specify what programs automatically start during login.

▶ **Remote Control:** Used to specify whether a session can be taken over by another user's session.

▶ **Client Settings:** Used to specify the maximum color depth and used to disable device (drive, printer, LTP, COM, clipboard, audio, and plug-and-play) redirection.

▶ **Network Adapter:** Used to specify the maximum number of connections.

▶ **Security:** Specify the security used for terminal sessions.

By default, a Terminal Server is configured to restrict users to a single session. If you restrict users to a single session on the Terminal Server, you can minimize the number of remote sessions that are created on the Terminal Server, which in turn increases performance by conserving system resources.

To restrict each user to a single session setting on the Terminal Server, follow these steps:

1. Open Terminal Services Configuration by clicking Start, pointing to Administrative Tools, pointing to Terminal Services, and then clicking Terminal Services Configuration.

2. Under General, double-click Restrict Each User to a Single Session.

3. On the General tab of the Properties dialog box, select the setting for Restrict Each User to a Single Session that is most appropriate for your environment, and then click OK.

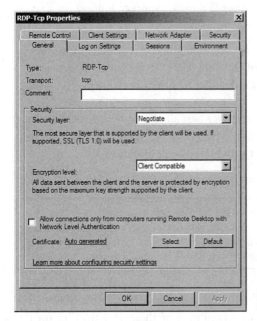

FIGURE 8.4 Terminal Services Configuration RDP-Tcp Properties tabs.

If the Terminal Server is configured to restrict users to a single session and the user disconnects from the Terminal Server while the session is still running, the user automatically reconnects to that session the next time the user connects to the Terminal Server.

NOTE

You can also restrict users to a single session on the Terminal Server by enabling the Restrict Terminal Services Users to a Single Remote Session Group Policy setting, located at Computer Configuration\Administrative Templates\Windows Components\ Terminal Services\Terminal Server\Connections.

By default, Terminal Services create a separate temporary folder, located under the Temp folder under the user's profile folder (named with the sessionid) on the Terminal Server for each active session that a user maintains on the Terminal Server. To free up disk space, the temporary folder is deleted when the user logs off from a session.

To configure temporary folders on the Terminal Server, follow these steps:

1. Open Terminal Services Configuration by clicking Start, pointing to Administrative Tools, pointing to Terminal Services, and then clicking Terminal Services Configuration.

2. Under General, double-click either Delete Temporary Folders on Exit or Use Temporary Folders per Session.

3. On the General tab of the Properties dialog box, make the appropriate selection for your environment for the Delete Temporary Folders on Exit and the Use Temporary Folders per Session check boxes.

If you clear the Use Temporary Folders per Session check box, a user's temporary files for all sessions on the Terminal Server are stored in a common Temp folder under the user's profile folder on the Terminal Server.

> **NOTE**
>
> You can also configure temporary folders on the Terminal Server by using the Do Not Delete Temp Folder upon Exit and the Do Not Use Temporary Folders per Session Group Policy settings, located at Computer Configuration\Administrative Templates\ Windows Components\Terminal Services\Terminal Server\Temporary folders.

If you have a Terminal Server used by many users and those users like to save files to the My Documents folders or Desktops of their user profiles on the Terminal Server, you can quickly run out of disk space on the Terminal Server. You can avoid this by enabling disk quotas on the volume where the profiles are stored and limit how many megabytes of files a user can store.

If you plan to take the server down for maintenance, you may want to prevent users from logging on to the Terminal Server. Therefore, you can specify that users cannot connect to a Terminal Server. To configure the user logon mode on the Terminal Server, follow these steps:

1. Open Terminal Services Configuration by clicking Start, pointing to Administrative Tools, pointing to Terminal Services, and then clicking Terminal Services Configuration.

2. Under General, double-click User Logon mode.

3. On the General tab of the Properties dialog box, select the user logon mode setting that is most appropriate for your environment, and then click OK.

The available user logon modes are

▶ Allow All Connections (default)

▶ Allow Reconnections, but Prevent New Logons

▶ Allow Reconnections, but Prevent New Logons Until the Server Is Restarted

After a user logs on to a terminal session, you can manage the session by using the Terminal Services Manager console. For example, when you open the console, you right-click any session and disconnect, reset the session, or force the user to log off. In addition, you can use the Terminal Services Manager console to view the sessions and the processes run by each session (see Figure 8.5).

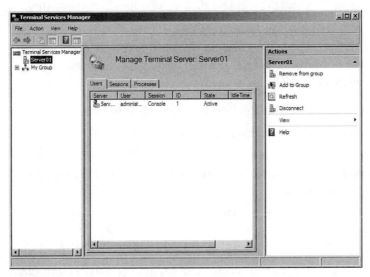

FIGURE 8.5 Terminal Services Manager sessions.

You can also use the Terminal Session Manager to connect the local Terminal Server or any other computer running Terminal Services or Remote Desktop. To specify another computer, you just right-click Terminal Session Manager and select Connect to Computer.

NOTE

If all sessions are being used, you can still connect to the Terminal Server or computer running Remote Desktop by connecting in console mode.

Using Terminal Services Command-Line Tools

Terminal Services offer several Terminal Services command-line tools. The list of available commands can be found at http://go.microsoft.com/fwlink/?LinkId=89674.

The `logoff` command can be used to log off a user from a session on a Terminal Server and delete the session from the server:

```
logoff [<SessionName> ¦ <SessionID>] [/server:<ServerName>] [/v]
```

- ► `<SessionName>`: Specifies the name of the session.

- ► `<SessionID>`: Specifies the numeric ID that identifies the session to the server.

- ► `/server:<ServerName>`: Specifies the Terminal Server that contains the session whose user you want to log off. If unspecified, the server on which you are currently active is used.

- ► `/v`: Displays information about the actions being performed.

- ► `/?`: Displays help at the command prompt.

The Change logon command enables or disables logons from client sessions, or displays current logon status:

```
change logon {/query ¦ /enable ¦ /disable ¦ /drain ¦ /drainuntilrestart}
```

- ► `/query`: Displays the current logon status, whether enabled or disabled.

- ► `/enable`: Enables logons from client sessions, but not from the console.

- ► `/disable`: Disables subsequent logons from client sessions, but not from the console. Does not affect currently logged on users.

- ► `/drain`: Disables logons from new client sessions, but allows reconnections to existing sessions.

- ► `/drainuntilrestart`: Disables logons from new client sessions until the computer is restarted, but allows reconnections to existing sessions.

- ► `/?`: Displays help at the command prompt.

Logons are re-enabled when you restart the system.

The command to change the install mode for the Terminal Server is change user (chgusr):

```
change user {/execute | /install | /query}
chguser   {/execute | /install | /query}
```

- ► /execute: Enables .ini file mapping to the home directory. This is the default setting.

- ► /install: Disables .ini file mapping to the home directory. All .ini files are read and written to the system directory. You must disable .ini file mapping when installing applications on a Terminal Server.

- ► /query: Displays the current setting for .ini file mapping.

- ► /?: Displays help at the command prompt.

The change user command and chguser commands are interchangeable.

You would use the chguser /install command before installing an application so that it can create an .ini files for the application in the system directory. These files are used as the source when user-specific .ini files are created. After installing the application, use change user /execute to revert to standard .ini file mapping. The first time that you run the application, it searches the home directory for its .ini files. If the .ini files are not found in the home directory, but are found in the system directory, Terminal Services copies the .ini files to the home directory, ensuring that each user has a unique copy of the application .ini files. Any new .ini files are created in the home directory. Each user should have a unique copy of the .ini files for an application. This prevents instances where different users might have incompatible application configurations (for example, different default directories or screen resolutions).

Single Sign-On

When you use Single Sign-On in Terminal Services, you are using credentials of the currently logged on user to log on to a remote computer. If you use the same username and password when you log on to your local computer and connect to a Terminal Server, enabling Single Sign-On enables you to do it seamlessly, without having to type in your password again.

To enable Single Sign-On, using domain or local group policy, follow these steps:

1. Enable the Computer Configuration\Administrative Templates\ System\Credentials Delegation\Allow Delegating Default Credentials.

2. Click on the Show button to get to the server list and add TERMSRV/<Your server name> to the server list.

You can add one or more server names. Using one wildcard (*) in a name is allowed. For example, to enable Single Sign-On to all servers in MyDomain.com, you can type **TERMSRV/*.MyDomain.com**. When the Concatenate OS Defaults with Input Above check box is selected, your servers are added to the list of servers enabled by the OS by default. For Single Sign-On this default list is empty, so the check box has no effect.)

If you have Single Sign-On enabled but want to use different credentials, you need to start RDC:

1. Click Options.

2. Select the Always Ask for Credentials check box.

You will be asked for credentials next time you connect.

TS Remote Applications

A new role added to Windows Server 2008 is RemoteApp, which allows users to access remote applications on their local PCs. Although the application looks as if it is running from your local machine in its own normal application window, in reality, it is still being hosted by the remote application. A user can minimize, maximize, and resize the program window, and can easily start multiple programs at the same time. If a user is running more than one RemoteApp program on the same Terminal Server, the RemoteApp programs share the same Terminal Services session.

Users can run RemoteApp programs by

▶ Double-clicking a Remote Desktop Protocol (.rdp) file that has been created and distributed by their administrator.

▶ Double-clicking a program icon on the desktop or Start menu that has been created and distributed by an administrator with a Windows Installer (.msi) package.

▶ Double-clicking a file whose extension is associated with a RemoteApp program. (This can be configured by an administrator with a Windows Installer package.)

▶ Accessing a link to the RemoteApp program on a website by using TS Web Access.

The .rdp files and Windows Installer packages contain the settings needed to run RemoteApp programs. After opening the RemoteApp program on a local computer, the user can interact with the program that is running on the Terminal Server as if it were running locally.

To add a program to the RemoteApp Program list, follow these steps:

1. Start the TS RemoteApp Manager by clicking Start, selecting Administrative Tools, selecting Terminal Services, and selecting TS RemoteApp Manager.

2. In the Actions pane, click Add RemoteApp Programs.

3. On the Welcome to the RemoteApp Wizard page, click Next.

4. On the Choose Programs to Add to the RemoteApps Program list page, select the check box next to each program that you want to add to the list of RemoteApp programs. You can select multiple programs. The list is generated from All Users Start menu. If the program is not listed, click Browse to specify the location of the program's executable file.

5. To configure the properties for a RemoteApp program, click the program name and then click Properties. You can configure the program name and path to the program executable file if the program is available through TS Web Access and determine whether command-line arguments are allowed, not allowed, or whether to use command-line arguments that you specify.

6. When you are finished configuring program properties, click OK, Next.

7. On the Review Settings page, review the settings and then click Finish.

Figure 8.6 shows the TS RemoteApp Manager console.

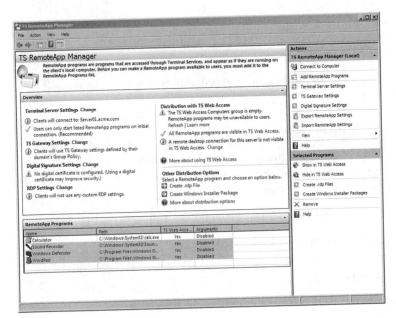

FIGURE 8.6 TS RemoteApp Manager programs.

To access RemoteApp programs that are deployed as .rdp files or as Windows Installer packages, the client computer must be running Remote Desktop Connection (RDC) 6.0 or RDC 6.1. A supported version of the RDC client is included with Windows Vista and Windows Server 2008. The RDC version 6.0 software is available for use on Windows XP with SP2 and Windows Server 2003 with SP1. You can download the installer package from article 925876 in the Microsoft Knowledge Base (http://go.microsoft.com/fwlink/?LinkId=79373).

> **EXAM ALERT**
>
> To use a RemoteApp program, you need to have RDC 6.0 or better.

TS Web Access

TS Web Access is a role service that lets you make TS RemoteApp programs available to users from a web browser. With TS Web Access, users can visit a website to access a list of available RemoteApp programs. When they start a RemoteApp program, a Terminal Services session is started on the Windows Server 2008-based Terminal Server that hosts the RemoteApp program.

With TS Web Access, a user can visit a website, view a list of RemoteApp programs, and then just click a program icon to start the program. When you install Terminal Services Web Access, you can use the default web page to deploy the TS RemoteApp program over the web or you can integrate it within Windows SharePoint Services. If IIS is not installed, IIS will automatically be installed.

You install TS Web Access as a role along with IIS 7.0. Whereas the TS Web Access server is used to access RemoteApps on a Terminal Server, the TS Web Access server does not have to be a Terminal Server. For users to use TS Web Access, client computers must be running RDC 6.1. RDC 6.1 is included with Windows Server 2008, Windows Vista with SP1, and Windows XP with Service Pack 3.

To enable simple-mode deployment of web access for RemoteApp programs, follow these steps:

1. Install the Terminal Server, install the user applications on the Terminal Server, and verify remote connection settings.

2. Add the applications to the list of RemoteApp programs enabled for TS Web Access, and configure global deployment settings. Open the TS RemoteApp Manager to add each of the applications to the RemoteApps list. After they are added, use the TS RemoteApp Manager to configure global deployment settings, such as Terminal Server settings and digital signature requirements.

3. Install TS Web Access.

4. Populate the TS Web Access Computers security group. Note: This step is required if the TS Web Access server and the RemoteApp Terminal Server are separate machines.

5. Populate the TS Web Access RemoteApp list from the single Terminal Server.

To administer the website, you must connect to the TS Web Access website by using either the local Administrator account or an account that is a member of the TS Web Access Administrators group on the TS Web Access server. On the TS Web Access server, click Start, point to Administrative Tools, point to Terminal Services, and then click TS Web Access Administration.

By default, TS Web Access populates the list of Remote Programs from Active Directory. However, by using a Simple Publishing configuration, you can configure the Terminal Services Remote Programs to populate its list of Remote Programs from a single Terminal Server. When you specify a single Terminal Server as the data source, the Web Access web part is populated by all Remote Programs that are configured for web access on that server's Allow list. To access the website, type the URL of the TS Web Access website into a web browser. By default, the TS Web Access website is http://server_name/ts (see Figure 8.7).

If you are using a computer that is used by more than one person, you should clear the check box in the lower-left corner that reads I Am Using a Private Computer That Complies with My Organization's Security Policy. In public mode, you are not provided with the option to save your credentials.

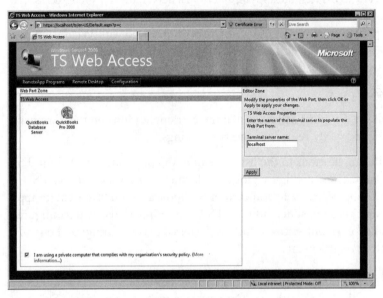

FIGURE 8.7   TS Web Access options.

TS Gateway

TS Gateway allows authorized remote users to connect to a Terminal Server, a Terminal Server running the RemoteApp program, or a computer running Remote Desktop on an internal corporate or private network, from any Internet-connected device. TS Gateway creates a tunnel (Remote Desktop Protocol [RDP] over HTTPS [port 443]) to establish a secure, encrypted connection between remote users on the Internet and the internal network resources on which their productivity applications run without configuring a Virtual Private Network (VPN) connection. Because it is based on SSL, TS Gateway will function even if the user and Terminal Server are separated by a network address translation (NAT) traversal-based router.

Installing TS Gateway

To function correctly, TS Gateway requires several role services and features to be installed and running, including

- ▶ Remote procedure call (RPC) over HTTP Proxy

- ▶ Internet Information Services 7.0, running web services

- ▶ Network Policy and Access Services

To install and configure TS Gateway, follow these steps:

1. Install the TS Gateway role service.

2. Configure the IIS settings for the TS Gateway server.

3. Obtain an externally trusted digital SSL certificate for the TS Gateway server.

4. Configure a certificate for the TS Gateway server.

5. Create a CAP for the TS Gateway server.

6. Create a RAP and resource group for the TS Gateway server.

Connection Authorization and Resource Authorization Policies

You manage TS Gateway by using the TS Gateway Management snap-in console. To specify who can connect to Terminal Services and Terminal Server resources, you need to define *Connection Authorization Policies (CAP)*. The CAPs are stored on a *Network Policy Server (NPS)*, a Microsoft implementation of a Remote Authentication Dial-In User Service (RADIUS) server. Using CAPs, you can require that users, user groups, or computer groups meet specific conditions to access a TS Gateway server. In each CAP, specific conditions can be specified, such as requiring a user to use a smart card to connect through TS Gateway. Users are granted access to a TS Gateway server only if they meet or exceed the conditions specified in the CAP that contains their group name.

To create a CAP for TS Gateway, use the Authorization Policies wizard or use TS Gateway Manager to manually configure authorization policies. To manually create the CAP:

1. Open TS Gateway Manager.

2. In the console tree, select the node that represents your TS Gateway server.

3. Expand the Policies node and click the Connection Authorization Policies folder.

4. Right-click the Connection Authorization Policies folder, click the Create New Policy option, and then click the Custom option.

5. Type a name for the policy on the General tab and ensure that the Enable This Policy check box is selected.

6. Configure the Requirements tab to specify the requirements that users must meet to connect to the TS Gateway server.

7. The new TS CAP then appears in the TS Gateway Manager results pane (see Figure 8.8).

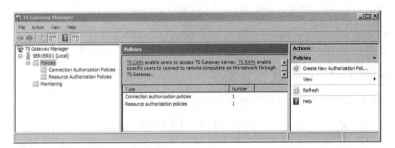

FIGURE 8.8 TS Gateway Manager policies.

After you define CAPs, you must create resource groups and *Resource Authorization Policies* (*RAP*), which enable you to specify the internal network resources to which remote users can connect through a TS Gateway server. When you create a TS RAP, you can create a computer group (a list of computers on the internal network to which you want the remote users to connect) and associate it with the TS RAP (see Figure 8.9).

EXAM ALERT

CAPs specify who can access a TS Gateway server and RAPs specify the groups of remote computers that users can access. Remote users connecting to an internal network through a TS Gateway server are granted access to computers on the network if they meet the conditions specified in at least one TS CAP and one TS RAP.

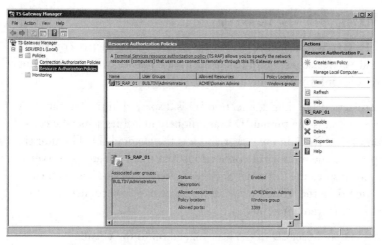

FIGURE 8.9   Resource Authorization Policies (RAP) in TS Gateway Manager.

To create a TS RAP for TS Gateway with the Authorization Policies Wizard, follow these steps:

1. Open TS Gateway Manager.

2. In the console tree, select the node that represents your TS Gateway server.

3. Expand the Policies node and click the Resource Authorization Policies folder to create a TS RAP.

4. Right-click the Resource Authorization Policies folder, click the Create New Policy option, and then click the Custom option.

5. Type a name for the policy on the General tab in the Description box.

6. On the User Groups tab, add the user groups to which this TS RAP applies. Click Add and specify the user groups in the Select Groups dialog box, and then click OK.

7. On the Computer Group tab, specify the computer group to which users can connect through TS Gateway. You can specify an existing Windows group, an existing TS Gateway–managed computer group, or a new TS Gateway-managed computer group. You could also allow users open access to network resources.

The new TS RAP appears in the TS Gateway Manager results pane.

Monitoring TS Gateway

You can use TS Gateway Manager to view information about active connections from Terminal Services clients to internal corporate network resources through TS Gateway. This information includes:

▶ The connection ID. The connection ID is displayed in the format <a:b>, where *a* is the tunnel ID that uniquely identifies a specific connection to the TS Gateway server and *b* is the channel ID. The tunnel ID represents the number of connections that the TS Gateway server has received since the Terminal Services Gateway service has been running. Each time the TS Gateway server receives a new connection, the tunnel ID is incremented by 1.

▶ The domain and user ID of the user logged on to the client.

▶ The full name of the user logged on to the client.

▶ The date and time when the connection was initiated.

▶ The length of time the connection was active.

▶ The length of time that the connection is idle, if applicable.

▶ The name of the internal network computer to which the client is connected.

▶ The IP address of the client. If your network configuration includes proxy servers, the IP address that appears in the Client IP Address column (in the Monitoring details pane) might reflect the IP address of the proxy server, rather than the IP address of the Terminal Services client.

▶ The port on the internal network computer to which the client is connected.

You can also specify the types of events that you want to monitor, such as unsuccessful or successful connection attempts to internal network computers through a TS Gateway server. When these events occur, you can monitor the corresponding events by using Windows Event Viewer. TS Gateway events are stored in Event Viewer under Application and Services Logs\Microsoft\ Windows\Terminal Services-Gateway\.

Group Policy Settings for TS Gateway

You can use Group Policy and Active Directory Domain Services to centralize and simplify the administration of TS Gateway policy settings. The following three Group Policy settings are available for TS Gateway server:

▶ **Set the TS Gateway Server Authentication Method:** Enables you to specify the authentication method that Terminal Services clients must use when connecting to internal network resources through a TS Gateway server.

▶ **Enable Connections Through TS Gateway:** Enables you to specify that, when Terminal Services clients cannot connect directly to an internal network resource, they will attempt to connect to the internal network resource through the TS Gateway server that is specified in the Set the TS Gateway Server Address Policy setting.

▶ **Set the TS Gateway Server Address:** Enables you to specify the TS Gateway server that Terminal Services clients use when they cannot connect directly to an internal network resource.

Load Balancing Terminal Servers

Windows Server 2008 offers load balancing, in which Terminal Server distributes sessions across multiple servers for improved performance. The multiple Terminal Servers working together as one are known as a farm.

Configuring Network Load Balancing with Terminal Servers

Using Network Load Balancing (NLB) with Terminal Services offers increased availability, scalability, and load-balancing performance. You can use NLB with a Terminal Server farm to scale the performance of a single Terminal Server by distributing sessions across multiple servers.

To configure NLB, you need the following:

▶ Two or more Terminal Servers logically grouped into a Terminal Server farm.

▶ A Session Directory server.

▶ In each Terminal Server, at least one network adapter for load balancing.

▶ Only TCP/IP used on the adapter for which NLB is enabled. Do not add any other protocols (for example, IPX) to this adapter.

▶ All hosts in the NLB cluster must reside on the same subnet.

▶ All Terminal Servers in the Terminal Server farm should be joined to the same domain.

You would then do the following:

1. Install the TS Session Broker service on a Windows Server 2008 that is not a member of the farm.

2. Configure the Terminal Servers in the farm to join a farm in TS Session Broker, and to participate in TS Session Broker Load Balancing.

3. Configure DNS round robin entries for Terminal Servers in the farm.

4. Add the Terminal Servers in the farm to the Session Directory Computers local group on the TS Session Broker server.

5. Set up a Terminal Server farm with TS Session Broker.

6. Install NLB.

7. Create an NLB cluster.

Some of the considerations for load-balancing Terminal Servers are:

▶ Consider splitting network traffic between two network adapters: one for Terminal Services connections and the other for access to other network resources and infrastructure. This allows for network access to the server in case the adapter bound to the cluster becomes unavailable.

▶ Place all load-balanced Terminal Servers into an Organizational Unit (OU) and apply Group Policy settings to that OU for easier administration.

▶ Configure home directories and other user data storage in such a way that the users can easily access their data no matter to which server they are logged in.

TS Session Broker

TS Session Broker is a role service in Windows Server 2008 that enables a user to reconnect to an existing session in a load-balanced Terminal Server farm. Windows Server 2008 includes the TS Session Broker Load Balancing feature, which enables you to distribute the session load between servers in a load-balanced Terminal Server farm.

When a user, using Remote Desktop Connection version 5.2 or later, connects to the Terminal Server farm, the initial connection is distributed by a preliminary load-balancing mechanism such as Domain Name System (DNS) round robin. After a user authenticates, the Terminal Server that accepted the initial connection queries the TS Session Broker server to determine where to redirect the user. New user sessions are redirected to the Terminal Server with the fewest sessions. The TS Session Broker stores the session state information that includes session IDs and their associated usernames, as well as the name of the server where each session resides. A user who disconnects while a session is running is automatically connected to the same connection upon return.

Configuring TS Session Broker

There are four steps to creating your own Load Balanced Terminal Server farm:

1. Install the TS Session Broker role service on a server using Server Manager.

2. Add all the Terminal Servers to the Session Directory Computers local group on the computer with the Terminal Server Session Broker role.

3. Join the Terminal Servers to the Session Broker and make them participate in the Load Balancing.

4. Add DNS entries for all Terminal Servers in the same farm.

When you add the Terminal Server to the Session Directory Computers local group, you allow the computer to join the Session Broker. To join the Terminal Server to the Session Broker, you could open the Terminal Service Configuration tool (tsconfig.msc) on each Terminal Server, open the properties of the Terminal Server and specify the Session Broker and the relative weight of the Terminal Server. If the Terminal Server has a higher relative weight, it is assigned a larger load than other Terminal Servers with a lesser weight.

Another way you can assign the Terminal Server to a session broker is to use group policies:

▶ **Join TS Session Broker:** Specifies whether the Terminal Server should join a farm in TS Session Broker. If this policy setting is enabled, the Terminal Server joins the farm that is specified in the TS Session Broker Farm Name policy setting on the TS Session Broker server that is specified in the TS Session Broker Name policy setting. If you disable this policy setting, you cannot join the Terminal Server to the TS Session Broker by using other tools.

▶ **TS Session Broker Farm Name:** Specifies the farm name.

▸ **Use IP Address Redirection:** Set this policy to Yes if you want to be able to connect to disconnected sessions. This policy allows for session reconnection by using the IP address of the Terminal Server. You should disable this policy setting only if your network load-balancing solution supports the use of TS Session Broker routing tokens (usually supported by hardware load balancing such as Cisco) because when you disable this policy, the IP address of the Terminal Server is not sent to the client but the IP address is embedded in a token instead.

▸ **TS Session Broker Name:** Specify the computer name (FQDN) of the Server running the Session Broker.

▸ **TS Session Broker Load Balancing:** Configures whether or not the Terminal Servers should participate in Load Balancing. Enabling this setting does not interfere with users connecting to their disconnected sessions.

Terminal Server Profiles

A *user profile* describes the configuration for a specific user, including the user's environment and preference settings. Unless you carefully plan and manage user profiles in a Terminal Server environment, user profiles can consume large amounts of disk space and can cause slow logons when a user connects to a Terminal Server.

You should assign a separate profile for Terminal Services sessions because many of the common options that are stored in profiles, such as screen savers and animated menu affects, are not desirable when using Terminal Services. Therefore, you can specify a Terminal Services–specific profile path and home folder for a user connecting to a Terminal Server. You can manually configure these settings on the Terminal Services Profile tab on the Properties sheet of a user account in the Local Users and Groups snap-in or the Active Directory Users and Computers snap-in.

You can also use the following Group Policy settings to configure these settings:

Computer Configuration\Administrative Templates\Windows
Components\Terminal Services\Terminal Server\Profiles

Terminal Services Printing

Terminal Services printing has been enhanced in Windows Server 2008 by the addition of the *Terminal Services Easy Print* printer driver and a Group Policy setting that enables you to redirect only the default client printer. Terminal Services provides printer redirection, which routes printing jobs from a server to a printer that is attached to a client computer or to a shared printer that is available to the client computer.

On a Terminal Server, you can use the Terminal Services Easy Print printer driver to simplify printer configuration. The Terminal Services Easy Print driver is useful if a Terminal Server does not have a printer driver installed that matches the printer driver on a client computer. By default, the Terminal Server first tries to use the Terminal Services Easy Print driver. If the client computer does not support this driver, the server looks for a matching printer driver on the server. You can either install a matching printer driver on the Terminal Server, or you can create a custom printer mapping file.

To use Terminal Services Easy Print, the client computer must have the following components installed:

- Remote Desktop Connection (RDC) 6.1.

- Microsoft .NET Framework 3.0 with Service Pack 1. The version of Microsoft .NET Framework that is included with Windows Server 2008 and Windows Vista with Service Pack 1 supports Terminal Services Easy Print.

EXAM ALERT

You need to have RDC 6.1 and .NET Framework 3.0 with SP1 or higher to use Easy Print.

You can use Group Policies (Computer Configuration\Administrative Templates\Windows Components\Terminal Services\Terminal Server\Printer Redirection) to change the default printer driver behavior. By using this policy setting, you can configure the Terminal Server to do any of the following:

- Use the Terminal Services Easy Print driver first. If that fails, look for a matching printer driver (fallback printer). (This is the behavior if you enable or enable but do not configure the policy setting.)

▶ Look for a matching printer driver first. If that fails, use the Terminal Services Easy Print driver. (This is the behavior if you disable the policy setting.)

▶ Other printer redirection policy settings that are available in this node of Local Group Policy Editor include:

    ▶ Do not allow client printer redirection.

    ▶ Do not set the default client printer to be the default printer in a session.

    ▶ Redirect only the default client printer.

Managing Terminal Services by Using Windows System Resource Manager

Windows System Resource Manager (WSRM) is included in Windows Server 2008, but it is not installed by default. You can use the WSRM tool to allocate CPU and memory resources to application, services, and processes. By using WSRM, you can reduce the chance of applications, services, or processes affecting the system's overall performance. WSRM can be used on a single computer or to manage users on a computer with Terminal Services.

Creating Resource Allocation Policies

After you determine what you want to monitor and limit, you need to create a resource allocation policy. Such a policy consists of one or more resource allocations, which, as they are used in WSRM, consist of a process-matching criterion (the mechanism WSRM uses to match running processes to a resource allocation policy) and one or more of the following criteria:

▶ **Process-matching criteria:** Enable you to select services or applications to be managed by resource allocation policy rules. You can choose by filename or command, or you can specify users or groups.

▶ **Resource allocation policies:** Allocate processor and memory resources to processes that are specified by the process-matching criteria that you create.

▶ **Exclusion lists:** Exclude applications, services, users, or groups from management by Windows System Resource Manager.

▶ **Scheduling:** Uses a calendar interface to control one-time events or recurring changes to resource allocation. Different resource allocation policies can be active at different times of day, on different days of the week, or according to other scheduling paradigms.

▶ **Conditional policy application:** Automatically switches resource allocation policies in response to certain system events (such as installing new memory or additional processors, starting or stopping a node, or changing the availability of a resource group in a cluster).

Of the resource allocation policies, two are specifically designed for computers running Terminal Services. The two Terminal Services–specific resource allocation policies are

▶ Equal_Per_User: Ensures that each user connecting to the Windows Server 2008 Application server using Terminal Services has an equal share of the CPU resources on the computer. This policy prevents a user with two active sessions from using more resources than a user with a single session.

▶ Equal_Per_Session: Ensures that each user connecting to the Windows Server 2008 Application server using Terminal Services has an equal share of the CPU resources on the computer. When the Equal_per_session resource allocation policy is implemented, resources are allocated on an equal basis for each session connected to the Windows Server 2008.

To implement the Equal_Per_Session resource allocation policy, follow these steps:

1. Open the Windows System Resource Manager snap-in.

2. In the console tree, expand the Resource Allocation Policies node.

3. Right-click Equal_Per_Session, and then click Set as Managing Policy.

4. If a dialog box appears informing you that the calendar will be disabled, click OK.

Running Managing State or Profiling State

When you run a resource allocation policy, you run it in either a managing state or a profiling state. In the managing state, WSRM manages the system, allocates the resources according to the resource allocation policy currently in effect, and collects data on the running processes. In the profiling state, the allocations defined in the resource allocation policy do not take effect, but the process-matching criteria runs and the accounting data is collected. With this accounting data, administrators can study the effect of the policy on the system, without the policy being in effect.

> **NOTE**
>
> You can have only one resource allocation policy running at a time. You cannot have a managing policy and a profiling policy running at the same time.

Importing and Exporting Criteria and Resource Allocation Policies

If you need to use the same WSRM criteria, resource allocation policies, calendar events, and schedules to multiple computers, you can create a shared folder for which you can import and export these settings.

1. Open Windows System Resource Manager.

2. Right-click Windows System Resource Manager.

3. Click either Import WSRM information or Export WSRM information.

4. Do one of the following:

   ▶ To import, in the Location box, type the path to the appropriate XML files. Or, click Browse and go to the directory where the files are located. Click OK.

   ▶ To export, in the Location box, type the path to the directory where you want to save the process-matching criteria, resource-allocation policies, calendar events, and schedules. Or click Browse and go to the directory where you want to save the files. Click OK.

Exam Prep Questions

1. You have a server running Windows Server 2008. You have a program that does not use the Microsoft Windows Installer packages for installation and it does make changes to the user Registry during installation. You need to make sure that this application supports multiple sessions. What do you need to do?

○ **A.** Install the application using RDC in console mode.

○ **B.** Run the `chgusr /execute` command and install the application. Then run the `chguser /install` command.

○ **C.** Run the `chgusr /install` command and install the application. When the program is installed, run the `chgusr /execute` command.

○ **D.** Install the application for each user that will be using the program.

2. You have two servers (server1 and server2) that need to be configured for load balancing. What do you need to do for these two servers to load balance?

○ **A.** You need to add server1 and server2 to a Session Broker Computer.

○ **B.** You need to open the server1 Remote Desktop console and add server2 to the partner list. You then need to open the server2 Remote Desktop console and add server1 to the partner list.

○ **C.** You need to configure a remote desktop to require secure RDC communications to the two Terminal Servers.

○ **D.** You need to configure an NPS listing both servers.

3. You have a Windows Server 2008 computer that is running Terminal Services. You have a printer on the network that supports only PostScript. You must make sure that all users can print to this printer if they do not have PostScript drivers. What do you need to do to make sure that Terminal Services automatically provides generic printer support for this printer?

○ **A.** Add the PostScript driver to the server.

○ **B.** Create a GPO that automatically installs PostScript drivers to all computers.

○ **C.** Create a GPO that specifies a Terminal Server fallback printer driver behavior policy to PostScript if a printer is not found. Apply the policy to the server.

○ **D.** Create a GPO that specifies a Terminal Server fallback printer driver behavior policy to PostScript if a printer is not found. Apply the policy to all client computers.

4. You have a Windows Server 2008 computer with the Terminal Services role installed. The Terminal Server user profiles are stored in a folder named TSProfiles on the server. You monitor Server01 and observe that you are almost out of disk space on the volume where the TSProfiles are stored. You discover that users are storing data in their profiles instead of their home folders. You need to limit the amount of data that is stored in each user's profile to a maximum of 100MB. What should you do?

   ○ **A.** Create a GPO and apply it to Server01. Configure the Default Quota Limit to 100MB in the Default Quota Limit and Warning Level policy.

   ○ **B.** Create a new group policy object that applies to all users of Terminal Services. Configure the Folder Redirection settings to redirect the My Documents folders to where their roaming profiles are stored.

   ○ **C.** Activate disk quotas for the volume that hosts the TSProfiles folder. Configure the quota for the volume that hosts TSProfiles to deny space to users who exceed 100MB of data.

   ○ **D.** Configure the Profile Path attribute in the properties of each user account in the Active Directory directory service to store the Terminal Server profiles to the server where their roaming profiles are stored.

5. You have a Windows Server 2008 computer running as a Terminal Server. You need to make sure that each user gets an equal share of the CPU resources on the computer. What should you do?

   ○ **A.** Create an equal_per_session resource allocation policy.

   ○ **B.** Enable processor equalization in the Terminal Server Configuration console.

   ○ **C.** Set the maximum size of the paging file based on the number of users.

   ○ **D.** Create the maximum_processing_group resource allocation policy.

6. You have a Windows Server 2008 computer running Terminal Services. You installed applications on the Terminal Server. You want users on your network to access installed applications on their local PCs. What must you do first?

   ○ **A.** Install and configure the TS Web Access feature on the Terminal Server.

   ○ **B.** Create .rdp files for each application and distribute them to internal network users.

   ○ **C.** Create .msi files for each application and distribute them to internal network users.

   ○ **D.** Add all applications to the RemoteApps list on the Terminal Server.

7. What are the two methods used to disable logons to a Terminal Server? (Choose two answers.)

   ○ **A.** Execute the `chglogon /disable` command.

   ○ **B.** Execute the `chgusr /disable` command.

   ○ **C.** In Terminal Services Configuration, deselect Allow All Connections.

   ○ **D.** Disable the workstation service.

8. You have a Windows Server 2008 computer with Terminal Services. When a user who is using RDC 6.0 accesses a remote application, the application displays at a lower resolution than the monitor settings the user is using. What should you do to resolve the problem?

   ○ **A.** Change the display resolution on the server to match the remote app.

   ○ **B.** Modify the `.rdp` file.

   ○ **C.** Install the Desktop Experience feature on the server.

   ○ **D.** Make sure the computer has RDC 6.1 and .NET Framework 3.0 with SP1.

9. You have a Windows Server 2008 computer with Terminal Services and remote applications. You want to add a Terminal Services program icon to the desktops and Start menu. What should you do?

   ○ **A.** Create an `.rdp` file.

   ○ **B.** Configure a TS Web Access.

   ○ **C.** Add applications to the RemoteApps list.

   ○ **D.** Create a Windows Installer Package (`.msi`).

10. You have a Windows Server 2008 computer with Terminal Services. You want to implement a solution that you use the same login as your current Windows login. What should you enable?

   ○ **A.** Terminal Services Web Access (TS Web Access)

   ○ **B.** Terminal Services RemoteApp (TS RemoteApp)

   ○ **C.** Single Sign-On

   ○ **D.** Terminal Services Gateway (TS Gateway)

11. You have a Windows Server 2008 running Terminal Services. You want to access a terminal session spanned across multiple monitors. What should you do?

   ○ **A.** Ensure that the total screen resolution across all monitors is equal to less than 4096×4096 and that the monitors are placed horizontally.

   ○ **B.** Ensure that the total screen resolution across all monitors is equal to less than 4096×4096 and that the monitors are placed vertically.

   ○ **C.** Ensure that the screen resolution is configured identically on all monitors and that the monitors are placed horizontally.

   ○ **D.** Ensure that the screen resolution is configured identically on all monitors and that the monitors are placed vertically.

12. What do you need to use the Terminal Services Easy Print driver in Windows Server 2008? (Choose all that apply.)

   ○ **A.** Remote Desktop Connection (RDC) 6.0

   ○ **B.** Remote Desktop Connection (RDC) 6.1

   ○ **C.** .NET Framework 2.0 with SP1

   ○ **D.** .NET Framework 3.0 with SP1

13. You have a Windows Server 2008 computer running Terminal Services. You need to configure the Terminal Server to securely allow external users to connect to resources on the corporate network. What do you need to do?

   ○ **A.** Use Terminal Services Web Access (TS Web Access).

   ○ **B.** Use Terminal Services RemoteApp (TS RemoteApp).

   ○ **C.** Configure Single Sign-On.

   ○ **D.** Use Terminal Services Gateway (TS Gateway).

14. You have a Windows Server 2008 computer with Terminal Services. What do you use to restrict user access to the Terminal Services Gateway server?

   ○ **A.** Create a TS RAP.

   ○ **B.** Create a TS CAP.

   ○ **C.** Create both a TS CAP and a TS RAP.

   ○ **D.** Add users to the Remote Desktop Users group.

15. You have Windows Server 2008 with Terminal Services. You have a user using Windows XP with Service Pack 1 who is trying to access the Terminal Server. However, the user cannot use 32-bit color when accessing programs on the Terminal Server. What is the problem?

- ○ **A.** You need to upgrade Windows XP SP1 to SP2.

- ○ **B.** You need to install RDC 6.1.

- ○ **C.** You need to install RDC 6.0.

- ○ **D.** You need to Upgrade Windows XP SP1 to SP2 and install Remote Desktop Connection 6.0.

16. You have a Windows Server 2008 computer with Terminal Services. You install a Terminal Services Gateway. What do you use to specify which users can connect to specific Terminal Servers? (Choose two answers.)

- ○ **A.** Create a TS RAP.

- ○ **B.** Create a TS CAP.

- ○ **C.** Associate a group with the computers to the TS RAP.

- ○ **D.** Associate a group with the computers to the TS CAP.

17. You have a Windows Server 2008 computer with Terminal Services. You want to ensure that a user's session remains active for 90 minutes after he gets disconnected from a Terminal Server. What can you to do achieve this goal with the least amount of effort?

- ○ **A.** Configure the End a Disconnected Session list on the Sessions tab in the RDP-Tcp Properties dialog box in the Terminal Services Configuration module.

- ○ **B.** Configure the End a Disconnected Session list on the Sessions tab in the users' Properties dialog boxes in Active Directory.

- ○ **C.** Configure the Active Session Limit list on the Sessions tab in the RDP-Tcp Properties dialog box in the Terminal Services Configuration module.

- ○ **D.** Configure the Active Session Limit list on the Sessions tab in the users' Properties dialog box in Active Directory.

Answers to Exam Prep Questions

1. Answer C is correct. When you execute the `chguser /install` command, it forces the application to create `.ini` files in the system directory rather than in the user's folders. When a user runs the program for the first time, the program finds the `.ini` files in the system folder and copies them to their individual user folders. The `chguser /execute` command reverts back to the standard `.ini` file mapping. Answer A is incorrect because console mode does not help when you have multiple users using the application on the computer. Answer B is incorrect because you need to execute the `chgusr /install` command first before the installation. Answer D is incorrect because installing for each user is a lot of work and still does not work for new users.

2. Answer A is correct. The Terminal Services Session Broker enables a user to reconnect to an existing session in a load-balanced Terminal Server farm. In addition, the Session Broker distributes the session load between servers in a load-balanced Terminal Server farm. Answer B is incorrect because there is no Remote Desktop console and no partner list. Answer C is incorrect because requiring enhanced security for RDC does not help in load balancing. Answer D is incorrect because the Network Policy Server (NPS) is used to centralize the storage, management, and validation of Terminal Services access.

3. Answer C is correct. To make sure that Terminal Services automatically provides generic printer support for a printer, configure a group policy on the server. Answer A is incorrect because adding a PostScript driver would not apply to every client computer. Answer B is incorrect because installing a PostScript driver does not necessarily point the terminal session to the printer using the driver. Answer D is incorrect because you configure the group policy at the server, not the clients.

4. Answer C is correct. You need to enable disk quotas on the host with the profiles to make sure you don't run out of disk space. Of course, you need to do this only on the volume where the TSProfiles are stored. Answer A is incorrect because you want the disk quota to apply only to the volume where the Profiles are. Answer B is incorrect because Folder Redirection helps only with My Documents. It does not help with other folders in a person's profile such the Desktop folder. Answer D is incorrect because you don't want one user to see data files of other users.

5. Answer A is correct. You need to use the Equal_per_session Resource Allocation Policy so that resources are allocated on an equal basis for each session connected to the Windows Server 2008. Answer B is incorrect because there is no option in the processor equalization in the Terminal Server Configuration console. Answer C is incorrect because the size of the paging file does not limit or specify the share of the CPU resources on a computer. Answer D is incorrect because there is no `maximum_processing_group` resource allocation policy.

6. Answer D is correct. You need to add all applications to the RemoteApps list. When using a Terminal Server to grant users access to applications, must first open the TS RemoteApp Manager in the Server Manager console and add the applications to the RemoteApps list. Answer A is incorrect because before you can use TS Web Access, you must first add the applications to the RemoteApps list. In addition, if you add applications to the RemoteApps list, you can still access the remote applications using other methods. Answer B is incorrect because although the .rdp file gives you access to a remote application, you must first add each application to the RemoteApps list. Answer C is incorrect because you must first add the application to the RemoteApps list.

7. Answers A and C are correct. To disable logon to a Terminal Server, you would execute the chglogon /disable command or deselect the Allow All Connections option in the Terminal Services Configuration. Answer B is incorrect because the chgusr command is used to change the install mode. In addition, the chgusr command does not include the disable option. Answer D is incorrect because disabling the workstation service stops access to file shares and other network services on other computers.

8. Answer B is correct. By modifying the .rdp file, you can modify or specify the width and height of the RDC session. Answer A is incorrect because the problem is not the server resolution but the settings with the client RDC. Answer C is incorrect because installing the Desktop Experience feature on the server does not fix the support resolution. Answer D is incorrect because RDC 6.0 already supports the higher resolutions.

9. Answer D is correct. The Windows Installer Package creates links in the Start menu and desktop. You would then use group policies to distribute the MSI package. Answer A is incorrect because you still need to distribute the .rdp file and you cannot do that with group policies. Answer B is incorrect because enabling TS Web Access does not add shortcuts to the Start menu or desktop. Answer C is incorrect because adding applications to the RemoteApps list does not add shortcuts to the Start menu or desktop.

10. Answer C is correct. Using only one logon is Single Sign-On. Answers A and B are incorrect because both Web Access and RemoteApp are used to access programs on a terminal session locally on a PC. Answer D is incorrect because the TS Gateway is used to secure terminal sessions over the Internet.

11. Answer C is correct. To span a terminal session across multiple monitors, you must ensure that the screen resolution is configured identically on all monitors and that all monitors are placed horizontally. Answers A and B are incorrect because the maximum total resolution is 4096×2048. Answer D is incorrect because the monitors must be placed horizontally.

12. Answers B and D are correct. To use Easy Print, you must have Remote Desktop Connection (RDC) 6.1 and Microsoft .NET Framework 3.0 SP1 on client computers. Answers A and C are incorrect because RDC 6.0 and .NET Framework 2.0 with SP1 do not support Easy Print.

13. Answer D is correct. TS Gateway is used to securely connect to a Terminal Server externally such as the Internet. Answers A and B are incorrect because TS Web Access and TS RemoteApp are used to remotely run an application on a local PC. Answer C is incorrect because Single Sign-On is used to use the same Windows logon to access terminal sessions.

14. Answer B is correct. The Connection Authorization Policy is used to limit access to the TS Gateway. Answer A is incorrect because TS RAPs, short for Resource Authorization Policies, are used to specify which internal network resources can be accessed by remote users through a TS Gateway server. Answer C is incorrect because you don't need to create a RAP. Answer D is incorrect because the Remote Desktop Users group is used to allow access to a specific Terminal Server.

15. Answer D is correct. You need Windows XP with SP2 and RDC 6.0 to use 32-bit color. Answer A is incorrect because you also need RDC 6.0 or higher. Answers B and C are incorrect because you need to upgrade to SP2 to install RDC 6.0 and 6.1.

16. Answers A and C are correct. You need to create a TS Resource Authorization Policy (TS RAP) and associate a group with the computers to the TS RAP. Answers B and D are incorrect because a CAP specifies who can access the TS Gateway server.

17. Answer A is correct. The End a Disconnected Session setting keeps sessions active for the time specified. Answer B is incorrect because it would take more effort to configure each user that accesses the Terminal Server. Answers C and D are incorrect because the Active Session Limit specifies the maximum time an active session stays active before the session is terminated.

Need to Know More?

For more information about Terminal Services in Windows Server 2008, including Step-by-Step Guides and troubleshooting articles, visit the following website:

http://technet2.microsoft.com/windowsserver2008/en/servermanager/terminalservices.mspx

To configure Terminal Services Licensing, visit the following website:

http://technet2.microsoft.com/windowsserver2008/en/library/4b4dd54a-46df-4b18-813f-2424cbc865031033.mspx?mfr=true

For more information about configuring RemoteApp and Web Access, visit the following website:

http://technet2.microsoft.com/windowsserver2008/en/library/61d24255-dad1-4fd2-b4a3-a91a22973def1033.mspx?mfr=true

To enable TS Gateway Server, visit the following website:

http://technet2.microsoft.com/windowsserver2008/en/library/722f3aa8-2f22-462f-bcc6-72ad31713ddd1033.mspx?mfr=true

To install TS Session Broker and Network Load Balancing with Terminal Services, visit the following websites:

http://technet2.microsoft.com/windowsserver2008/en/library/f9fe9c74-77f5-4bba-a6b9-433d823bbfbd1033.mspx?mfr=true

http://technet2.microsoft.com/windowsserver2008/en/library/6e3fc3a6-ef42-41cf-afed-602a60f562001033.mspx?mfr=true

CHAPTER NINE

Virtual Machines

Terms you'll need to understand:

✓ Hyper-V

✓ enlightened operating system

✓ hypervisor

✓ virtual machine configuration (.vmc) file

✓ virtual hard disk (.vhd) files

✓ virtual machine

✓ Hyper-V Manager

✓ virtual network

✓ snapshot

✓ save state

✓ differencing disk

✓ quick migration

✓ System Center Virtual Machine Manager 2007 (SCVMM)

✓ integration components

Techniques/concepts you'll need to master:

✓ Install Hyper-V on a Windows Server 2008 computer.

✓ Create a virtual computer.

✓ Install an operating system on a virtual computer.

✓ Add and configure virtual hard drives, networks, and network cards to a Hyper-V virtual server.

✓ Create a snapshot of a virtual server.

✓ Use Quick Migration to migrate a virtual machine to another hosting server.

Over the last few years, virtualization has become a popular. *Virtual machine* technology enables multiple operating systems to run concurrently on a single machine. This allows for a separation of services while keeping cost to a minimum. In addition, you can easily and quickly create Windows test environments in a safe, self-contained environment. Of course, for a virtual machine to handle such a load, it has to have sufficient processing and memory resources.

Hyper-V Overview

Previously, Microsoft offered Virtual Server and Virtual PC. A replacement for Virtual Server is *Hyper-V*, which was designed to work on the Windows Server 2008 operating system.

Hyper-V Features

Hyper-V is a key feature of Windows Server 2008—even if it wasn't initially shipped with Windows Server 2008 (it shipped several months after Windows Server 2008 was released). It's both a standalone product and part of special "with Hyper-V" editions of Windows Server 2008.

The features of Hyper-V include:

- **New and Improved Architecture:** Includes new 64-bit micro-kernelized *hypervisor* architecture, which enables Hyper-V to provide a broad array of device support methods and improved performance and security.

- **Broad OS Support:** Includes broad support for simultaneously running different types of operating systems, including 32-bit and 64-bit systems across different server platforms, such as Windows, Linux, and others.

- **Symmetric Multiprocessors (SMP) Support:** Can support up to four multiple processors in a virtual machine environment, enabling you to take full advantage of multi-threaded applications in a virtual machine.

- **Network Load Balancing (NLB):** Includes new virtual switch capabilities. This means virtual machines can be configured easily to run with Windows NLB Service to balance load across virtual machines on different servers.

- **New Hardware Sharing Architecture:** Includes a new virtual service provider/virtual service client (VSP/VSC) architecture, which provides improved access and utilization of core resources, such as disk, networking, and video.

▶ *Quick Migration*: Enables you to rapidly migrate a running virtual machine from one physical host system to another with minimal downtime.

▶ **Virtual Machine Snapshot:** Enables you to take *snapshots* of a running virtual machine so you can easily revert to a previous state, and improve the overall backup and recoverability solution.

▶ **Scalability:** With the support of multiple processors/multiple cores and large amounts of RAM, you can increase the number of virtual processors (up to four virtual processors to each guest machine) and the amount of RAM for each virtual machine, allowing you to scale the server as needed. In addition, the virtualization environment supports a large number of virtual machines with a given host and continue to leverage quick migration for scalability across multiple hosts.

▶ **Extensible:** Standards-based Windows Management Instrumentation (WMI) interfaces and APIs in Hyper-V enable independent software vendors and developers to quickly build custom tools, utilities, and enhancements for the virtualization platform.

For more information about the features of Hyper-V, visit the following website:

http://www.microsoft.com/windowsserver2008/en/us/virtualization-consolidation.aspx

Supported Client Operating Systems

Hyper-V can host two categories of operating systems:

▶ *Enlightened operating systems*: Operating systems that work directly with Hyper-V and enjoy performance benefits with respect to device access and management benefits. Enlightened operating systems include Windows Server 2008 (32-bit and 64-bit), Windows Server 2003 (32-bit and 64-bit), and SUSE enterprise Linux Server 10 with Service Pack 1. Others will be added as time goes on.

▶ **Unenlightened operating systems:** Operating systems that do not work directly with Hyper-V. They include other Linux distributions, older versions of Windows Server, and other x86 operating systems.

Windows Server 2008 is fully enlightened, which means it takes advantage of all possible enlightenments, which are the methods for modifying an operating system's kernel to make it consume fewer resources in a virtual environment.

Other operating systems have varying degrees of support.

Hyper-V Architecture

Hyper-V is based on hypervisor, a virtual machine monitor which provides a virtualization platform that allows multiple operating systems to run on a host computer at the same time. To keep each virtual server secure and reliable, each virtual server is placed in its own partition. A partition is a logical unit of isolation, in which operating systems execute.

A hypervisor instance has to have at least one root partition running Windows Server 2008. The virtualization stack runs in the root partition and has direct access to the hardware devices. The root partition then creates the child partitions, which host the guests OSs.

A virtualized partition does not have access to the physical processor, nor does it handle its real interrupts. Instead, they have a virtual view of the processor and run in Guest Virtual Address, which, depending on the configuration of the hypervisor, may or may not be the entire virtual address space. The hypervisor handles the interrupts to the processor and redirects them to the respective partition, using a logical Synthetic Interrupt Controller (SynIC). Hyper-V can hardware-accelerate the address translation between various Guest Virtual Address spaces by using an IOMMU (I/O Memory Management Unit), which operates independently of the memory management hardware used by the CPU.

In addition to child partitions not having direct access to the physical processor, child partitions do not have direct access to hardware resources. Instead, they have a virtual view of the resources. Any request to the virtual devices is redirected via the VMBus to the devices in the parent partition, which manage the requests. The VMBus is a logical channel that enables inter-partition communication. The response is also redirected via the VMBus. Of course, the entire process is transparent to the guest OS.

Virtual Devices can also take advantage of a Windows Server Virtualization feature, named Enlightened I/O, for storage, networking, and graphics subsystems. Enlightened I/O is a specialized virtualization-aware implementation of high-level communication protocols such as SCSI to take advantage of VMBus directly, bypassing any device emulation layer. This makes the communication more efficient but requires the guest OS to support Enlightened I/O.

Each virtual machine runs on a separate thread in Hyper-V virtual server. This means that on a multiprocessor physical computer, more processors are available for use by the virtual machines. Each virtual machine uses a maximum of one processor; however, it may share the processor it is using with other virtual machines, depending on the number of processors on the physical computer and the number of running virtual machines.

Each virtual machine requires enough memory to run the operating system and applications, plus approximately 32MB required for the emulated video RAM and code cache. You specify an amount of memory for the virtual machine when you create the virtual machine. The amount you specify represents the maximum amount of memory that the virtual machine can consume. You can modify this memory allocation only when the virtual machine is turned off. The virtual machine consumes memory only when it is running or paused. A virtual machine does not start if there is not sufficient memory available when you try to start it. If the virtual machine does not start, an error is logged to the Virtual Server event log.

Virtual Server File Structure

By default, Hyper-V stores all the files that make up a virtual machine in one folder with the same name as the virtual server for simple management and portability. Renaming a virtual machine does not rename the virtual machine folder. By default, these folders are located in the Shared Virtual Machines folder, which is located in Documents and Settings\All Users\Documents\Shared Virtual Machines.

EXAM ALERT

Be sure you know the default storage location for virtual folders.

Each virtual machine uses the following files:

▶ A *virtual machine configuration (.vmc) file* in XML format that contains the virtual machine configuration information, including all settings for the virtual machine.

▶ One or more *virtual hard disk (.vhd) files* to store the guest operating system, applications, and data for the virtual machine. So if you create a 12GB partition for the virtual machine's hard drive, the virtual hard disk file is 12GB.

> **NOTE**
>
> Because the contents of the virtual server are stored in a file on the hard drive, the virtual server uses the disk extensively. Therefore, you need to make sure that your disk system can handle the demands of multiple virtual servers.

In addition, a virtual machine may use the following file:

▶ A saved-state (.vsv) file, if the machine has been placed into a saved state.

Installing Hyper-V

To install Hyper-V, you need the following:

▶ An x64 version of Windows Server 2008.

▶ 64-bit processors and a BIOS that support hardware-assisted virtualization (Intel VT or AMD-V) technology.

▶ Hardware Data Execution Prevention (DEP), which Intel describes as eXecuted Disable (XD) and AMD describes as No eXecute (NS). It is a technology used in CPUs to segregate areas of memory for use by either storage of processor instructions or for storage of data.

> **EXAM ALERT**
>
> Be sure to know the hardware and software requirements for Hyper-V.

Of course, before you install the Hyper-V role, you should first use Windows Update and update your Windows Server 2008 computer.

To add the Hyper-V role to your system, follow these steps:

1. Click Start, and then click Server Manager.

2. In the Roles Summary area of the Server Manager main window, click Add Roles.

3. On the Select Server Roles page, click Hyper-V.

4. On the Create Virtual Networks page, click one or more network adapters if you want to make their network connection available to virtual machines.

5. On the Confirm Installation Selections page, click Install.

6. The computer must be restarted to complete the installation. Click Close to finish the wizard, and then click Yes to restart the computer.

7. After you restart the computer, log on with the same account you used to install the role. After the Resume Configuration Wizard completes the installation, click Close to finish the wizard.

If Hyper-V does not appear as an available role, you have a standard version of Windows Server 2008 that does not include Hyper-V. Therefore, you have to download it from Microsoft.

Managing Virtual Servers

Windows Server 2008 Hyper-V, after it is installed, can be managed via MMC, similar to other roles in Windows Server 2008. To start the virtualization Management MMC console, click Start, Administrative Tools, *Hyper-V Manager*. With this console, you can manage either the local system or connect to other servers and manage them (see Figure 9.1).

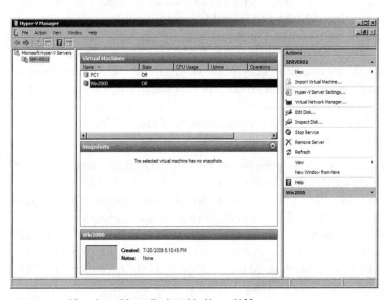

FIGURE 9.1   Virtual machines displayed in Hyper-V Manager.

Using Vmconnect.exe to Connect to a Virtual Machine

Besides using the Hyper-V Manager console, you connect to a virtual machine directly by using the vmconnect.exe located in the Hyper-V directory under Program Files. Launching this program displays a dialog that enables you to specify the Hyper-V server and virtual machine to connect to. You can also specify the Hyper-V server and virtual machine as command-line parameters so that you can make shortcuts or scripts to quickly connect to a VM:

```
"C:\Program Files\Hyper-V\vmconnect.exe" "name_of_host computer"
➥"name_of_virtual_machine"
```

You can also connect to a virtual machine using its GUID, which is useful if you have multiple virtual machines with the same name, by running

```
"C:\Program Files\Hyper-V\vmconnect.exe" localhost -G {GUID}
```

System Center Virtual Machine Manager

In addition to the Hyper-V Manager, you can also use the *System Center Virtual Machine Manager 2007 (SCVMM)*. SCVMM provides management of physical and virtual machines, consolidation of underutilized physical servers, and rapid provisioning of new virtual machines. Virtual Machine Manager provides physical-to-virtual (P2V) conversion. In addition, by using the Volume Shadow Copy Service (VSS), it creates a virtual machine faster and without having to interrupt the source physical server. The SCVMM that is being released at the same time as Hyper-V supports the management of Hyper-V hosts and guests, as well as Citrix XenServer and VMware ESX v3 hosts.

Microsoft will also be releasing the Server Virtualization Management Pack that plugs into Microsoft System Center Operations Manager (SCOM) to provide enterprise-wide monitoring of Microsoft virtual environments. The management pack monitors the health and availability of virtual machines deployed on hosts running Microsoft Virtual Server and Hyper-V and the health and availability of the hosts. The management pack also monitors the components of System Center Virtual Machine Manager 2007 (VMM), including the VMM server, database server, hosts, library servers, and self-service portals, and provides reporting for VMM.

Creating Virtual Machines

After you have installed Hyper-V, you can create a virtual machine and set up an operating system on the virtual machine. Of course, a little planning goes a long way. You need to consider such things as how much memory you want to allocate to the virtual machine, how much disk space you want to assign the virtual machine, and how you will install the operating system (physical media or ISO images) for each virtual machine.

To create and set up a virtual machine:

1. Open Hyper-V Manager from the Administrative Tools.

2. From the Action pane, click New, Virtual Machine.

3. From the New Virtual Machine Wizard, click Next.

4. On the Specify Name and Location page, specify what you want to name the virtual machine and where you want to store it.

5. On the Memory page, specify enough memory to run the guest operating system you want to use on the virtual machine.

6. On the Networking page, connect the network adapter to an existing *virtual network* if you want to establish network connectivity at this point.

> **NOTE**
>
> If you want to use a remote image server to install an operating system on your test virtual machine, select the external network.

7. On the Connect Virtual Hard Disk page, specify a name, location, and size to create a virtual hard disk so you can install an operating system on it.

8. On the Installation Options page, choose the method you want to use to install the operating system:

   ▶ Install an operating system from a boot CD/DVD-ROM. You can use either physical media or an image file (.iso file).

   ▶ Install an operating system from a boot floppy disk.

   ▶ Install an operating system from a network-based installation server. To use this option, you must configure the virtual machine with a network adapter connected to the same network as the image server.

9. Click Finish.

Now that you told the virtual server how you are going to install the operating system, you are ready to perform the operating system installation:

1. From the Virtual Machines section of the results pane, right-click the name of the virtual machine you just created and click Connect. The Virtual Machine Connection tool opens.

2. From the Action menu in the Virtual Machine Connection window, click Start.

3. Proceed through the installation.

After the operating system is set up, you need to load *integration components*, which are sets of drivers and services that help each Virtual Machine to have a more consistent state and perform better by enabling the guest to use synthetic devices. Some integrative components that come with Hyper-V are VMBUS (transport for Synthetic devices), Time Sync (used to keep VM clocks in sync with the root partition, sometimes called the host), Video Driver, Network Driver, Storage Driver. These components can be identified in the Device Manager because they start with Virtual or VMBus in the device name. To install the integration components, open the Action menu of Virtual Machine Connection and click Insert Integration Services Setup Disk. If Autorun does not start the installation automatically, you can start it manually by executing the `%windir%\support\amd64\setup.exe` command (see Figure 9.2).

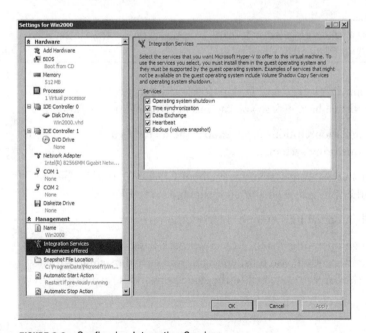

FIGURE 9.2 Configuring Integration Services.

EXAM ALERT

If you do not install Integration Services, some Windows built-in drivers will perform worse in Hyper-V compared to Virtual Server 2005. Therefore, it is important that after you install the Guest OS, you install the Integration Services.

When you are at the point where you need to provide input, move the cursor over virtual machine window. After the mouse pointer changes to a small dot, click anywhere in the virtual machine window. This action "captures" the mouse so that keyboard and mouse input is sent to the virtual machine. To return the input to the physical computer, press Ctrl+Alt+Left arrow and then move the mouse pointer outside the virtual machine window.

After the machine is installed and configured, the operating system is installed, and the integration services have been installed, you are ready to configure and manage the operating system. For Windows Server 2008, you can configure the IP configuration, enable Remote Desktop, and load the appropriate roles and functions and so forth. You can then log on to the virtual server remotely or use remote administration tools.

Managing Virtual Machines

Now that the virtual machine is created, you are ready to manage and customize the virtual hardware. To view or modify the virtual hardware that is configured for the virtual machine, right-click the name of the virtual machine you just created from the Virtual Machines pane and click Settings. From the Settings window, click the name of the hardware to view or change it.

Dynamically Expanded and Fixed Virtual Hard Disks

When you create a virtual hard drive, you can define the virtual hard disks as either of two things:

> ▶ **Fixed-size virtual hard disks:** Take up the full amount of disk space when created, even if there is no data using parts of the hard disk. The advantage of a fixed-size virtual hard disk is that if you have to defragment your drive, the large .vhd file will already be continuous, assuming that it was continuous when it was created. However, you have to shut down your virtual machine for a long period of time if you wish to defragment the .vhd files.

▶ **Dynamically expanding hard disks:** Expand as they need space, up to their full space. The advantage of a dynamically expanding hard disk is that it uses very little space when it is created. Any sectors that don't have content are not stored in the .vhd file; instead the .vhd file knows those sectors are not being used.

Unfortunately for dynamically expanded hard disks, after sectors are used, even if the files are deleted, the space is still used on the host unless you compress the .vhd files. To compress a .vhd:

1. Open the Hyper-V Management console.

2. Open the Actions menu and select Edit Disk.

3. Select the source .vhd by clicking the Browse button.

4. Click the Compact button.

5. Click the Finish button.

Snapshots

Hyper-V includes creating a snapshot of a virtual machine, which is a point-in-time image of a virtual machine that you can return. It is typically used during testing changes or when new applications are being loaded to a virtual server. If the changes or new application cause problems, you can revert back to the snapshot before the changes or new application were installed.

Snapshots (up to 10 levels) can be taken whether the virtual machine is running or stopped. If the virtual machine is running when the snapshot is taken, no downtime is involved to create the snapshot (see Figure 9.3).

Creating and deleting snapshots does not affect the running state of the virtual machine, meaning that taking a snapshot does not change the virtual machine hardware, applications, or the currently running processes. The snapshot files consist of the following:

▶ A copy of the VM configuration .xml file

▶ Any *save state* files

▶ A *differencing disk* (.avhd) that is the new working disk for all writes that are the children of the working disk prior to the snapshot

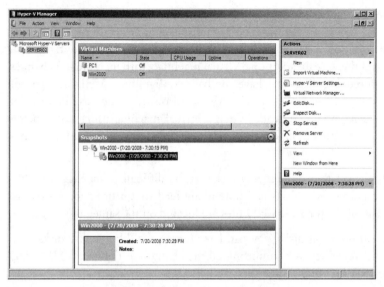

FIGURE 9.3 Created snapshots are shown in the middle pane.

If you create snapshots one right after another and never apply a previous snapshot, you produce a tree with one branch.

Snapshots can be created in the Hyper-V Manager (by selecting a virtual machine and selecting Snapshot from the Action menu or panel) and in the Virtual Machine Connection window (by clicking Snapshot in the toolbar or by opening the Action menu and selecting Snapshot). When you create a snapshot, a dialog box appears that enables you to enter a custom name for the snapshot. If you want, you can dismiss this dialog and have the snapshot use an auto-generated name. This auto-generated name consists of the name of the virtual machine, followed by the date and time when the snapshot was taken.

Differencing Disk

A differencing disk is a special type of dynamic disk that stores changes to virtual machine state in a file separate from the base .vhd file. Differencing disks are defined in the context of a parent-child relationship. In this relationship, each child differencing disk has one and only one parent disk, but a parent disk (which remains read-only) may be associated with multiple child differencing disks. When you create fixed and dynamically expanded hard disks, you specify a size or copy the contents of an available physical disk. For a differencing disk, you specify the location of the disk you want to use as the parent virtual hard disk.

You can use differencing disks to run several similar virtual machines while saving disk space. They can also be used in multiple complex configurations sharing a large common base. You have to build the common base configuration only once, and then create additional virtual machines with incremental changes by using differencing disks that have the base configuration VHD as a parent disk. This way you can have several VMs based on the same base image, but without the disk space overhead. When a virtual machine using differencing disks issues a write operation, the new data is written only to the child differencing disk.

The drawbacks are that differencing disks can be difficult to manage. In addition, large hierarchies of disks can potentially lead to performance problems, especially if all of the physical VHD files are located on the same disks or arrays.

After using differencing disks, you can later merge the differencing disks with their parent disk, either by committing all the changes to the base VHD or by creating a new VHD file.

Save States

In addition to snapshots, you also have the option to Save States. At any time, an administrator can select a guest session and choose Action, Save State. This Save State function is similar to the Hibernate mode on a desktop client system. It saves the image into a file with the option of bringing the saved state image file back to the state in which the image was prior to being saved.

Managing Virtual Networks and Network Cards

Virtual networks consist of one or more virtual machines configured to access local or external network resources. The virtual network is configured to use a network adapter in the physical computer.

If a network adapter in the physical computer is selected, then any virtual machines attached to the virtual network can access the networks to which that physical adapter is connected. If the virtual network is configured not to use a network adapter, then any virtual machine attached to the virtual network becomes part of the internal virtual machine network. An internal virtual machine network consists of all virtual machines attached to a virtual network that is configured to use no network adapter. Each internal virtual machine network is completely isolated from all other internal virtual machine networks.

> **NOTE**
>
> If you connect a virtual network to a physical network adapter that uses static settings, such as a static IP address, and IPv6 is not disabled, the new connection overwrites the static settings. Network connectivity is lost until you reapply the static settings to the physical network adapter.

Hyper-V enables you to create three network types:

- ▶ **External:** Binds to the physical network adapter so that the virtual machines can access a physical network, including a DHCP server, file and print servers, and the Internet.

- ▶ **Internal:** Connects all the virtual machines with the local host physical computer.

- ▶ **Private:** Connects virtual machines running on the local physical computer to each other. It does not allow connection to the host physical computer.

Figure 9.4 shows the Virtual Network Manager.

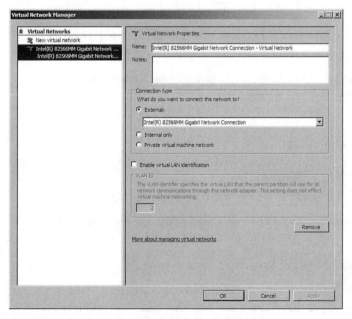

FIGURE 9.4 Configuring the network configuration type.

To add a virtual network:

1. Open Hyper-V Manager.

2. From the Actions menu, click Virtual Network Manager.

3. Under Create Virtual Network, select the type of network you want to create.

4. Click Add. The New Virtual Network page appears.

5. Type a name for the new network. Review the other properties and modify them if necessary.

6. Click OK to save the virtual network and close Virtual Network Manager, or click Apply to save the virtual network and continue using Virtual Network Manager.

To modify a virtual network:

1. Open Hyper-V Manager.

2. From the Actions menu, click Virtual Network Manager.

3. Under Virtual Networks, click the name of the network you want to modify.

4. Under Virtual Network Properties, edit the appropriate properties to modify the virtual network.

5. Click OK to save the changes and close Virtual Network Manager, or click Apply to save the changes and continue using Virtual Network Manager.

To remove a virtual network:

1. Open Hyper-V Manager.

2. From the Actions menu, click Virtual Network Manager.

3. Under Virtual Networks, click the name of the network you want to remove.

4. Under Virtual Network Properties, click Remove.

5. Click OK to save the changes and close Virtual Network Manager, or click Apply to save the changes and continue using Virtual Network Manager.

When creating virtual networks, keep the following in mind:

► You cannot connect a virtual network to a wireless network adapter. As a result, you cannot provide wireless networking capabilities to virtual machines.

► Only one virtual network can be attached to a specific physical network adapter at a time; you cannot attach multiple virtual networks to the same physical network adapter.

You can configure networking for virtual machines by adding, removing, and modifying their network adapters as necessary. Each network adapter can be connected to one of the virtual networks available on the server running Hyper-V.

To add a network adapter, follow these steps:

1. Open Hyper-V Manager. Click Start, point to Administrative Tools, and then click Hyper-V Manager.

2. In the Results pane, under Virtual Machines, select the virtual machine that you want to configure.

3. In the Action pane, under the virtual machine name, click Settings.

4. In the Navigation pane, click Add Hardware.

5. On the Add Hardware page, choose a network adapter or a legacy network adapter.

6. Click Add. The Network Adapter or Legacy Network Adapter page appears.

7. Under Network, select the virtual network to which you want to connect.

8. If you want to configure a static MAC address or virtual LAN identifier, specify the numbers you want to use.

9. Click OK.

NOTE

A network adapter requires a virtual machine driver to work. On all supported operating systems, install integration services in the guest operating system to install the virtual machine driver. The only exception about virtual machine network adapter drivers is if you use a legacy network adapter, which emulates a physical network adapter, multiport DEC 21140 10/100TX 100MB. A legacy network adapter also supports network-based installations because it includes the capability to boot to the Pre-Execution Environment (PXE boot). However, the legacy network adapter is not supported in the 64-bit edition of Windows Server 2003.

Virtual LAN Identification

A virtual LAN, commonly known as a VLAN, is a group of hosts with a common set of requirements that communicate as if they were attached to the same wire, regardless of their physical location. A VLAN has the same attributes as a physical LAN, but it allows for end stations to be grouped together even if they are not located on the same LAN segment. You can reconfigure the network through software rather than physically relocate devices.

The Hyper-V role of Windows Server 2008 can specify a Virtual LAN (VLAN) identification tag for the virtual machine network connection and for the parent partition network connection. To enable VLAN tagging for a parent partition, click to select the Enable Virtual LAN Identification check box to enable VLAN tagging and to specify an ID. Then to specify an ID, open the Virtual Network Manager page and open the Virtual Network Properties.

To enable VLAN tagging for a virtual machine, access the properties of the virtual machine, and then select the virtual network adapter. Click to select the Enable Virtual LAN Identification check box to enable VLAN tagging and to specify an ID that you want the virtual machine connection to use. A virtual machine may have multiple network adapters, and all these adapters may use either the same or different VLAN IDs. Therefore, you must perform this action on each network adapter.

Using High-Availability Features

If you have Windows Server 2008 Enterprise or Data Center, Hyper-V includes support for host-to-host connectivity and enables you to cluster all virtual machines running on a host through Windows Clustering (up to 16 nodes).

Hyper-V also supports Quick Migration, which enables you to rapidly migrate a running virtual machine across Hyper-V hosts with minimal downtime. Therefore, if you have several Windows Server 2008 servers with Hyper-V, you can migrate virtual machines from one Windows Server 2008 computer to another if the server fails or starts exhibiting some kind of problem.

EXAM ALERT

Quick Migration requires a cluster.

For a planned migration, quick migration saves the state of a running guest virtual machine (memory of original server to disk/shared storage), moves the storage connectivity from one physical server to another, and then restores the guest virtual machine onto the second server (disk/shared storage to memory on the new server). In the case of unplanned downtime, you would not be able to save the state of your workload; instead, the images written to the disk would be failed over from the shared storage automatically.

Managing Server Core and Hyper-V

Because Server Core is an operating system with minimum requirements, it is ideal to host Hyper-V. To enable the Windows Server 2008 Hyper-V role on a Server Core installation of Windows Server 2008, you should run the `Start /w ocsetup Microsoft-Hyper-V` command and restart the server when prompted. To manage Hyper-V, you can remotely connect to the server from an existing Hyper-V Manager Microsoft Management Console (MMC) snap-in on a different system by selecting the Connect to Server option.

Exam Prep Questions

1. You have a Windows Server 2008 computer running Hyper-V. You have the computer hosting several Windows Server 2008 hosts. You have a database application that is automatically shutting down. What should you do to troubleshoot this problem?

   ○ **A.** View the Event Viewer logs on the host server running Hyper-V.

   ○ **B.** View the Event Viewer logs on the virtual machine running the database.

   ○ **C.** Start the Resource Manager on the host server running Hyper-V.

   ○ **D.** View the Resource Manager on the virtual machine running the database.

2. You have a Server Core installation of Windows Server 2008. How do you install the Hyper-V role?

   ○ **A.** Run the `Start /w ocsetup Microsoft-Hyper-V` command on Server2.

   ○ **B.** Run the `Servermanager.exe -install Microsoft-Hyper-V` command on Server2.

   ○ **C.** Using Server Manager, run the Add Roles Wizard to add the Hyper-V role.

   ○ **D.** Run the `Servermanagercmd.exe -allSubFeatures Microsoft-Hyper-V` command on Server2.

3. Which of the following is NOT an enlightened operating system?

   ○ **A.** Windows Server 2003 (x32) Standard Edition

   ○ **B.** Windows Server 2008 (x32) Standard Edition

   ○ **C.** Windows Server 2008 (x64) Enterprise Edition

   ○ **D.** SUSE Enterprise Linux Server 10 with Service Pack 1

   ○ **E.** Windows 98

4. Which of the following describes hypervisor?

   ○ **A.** An administrative template used to create virtual machines.

   ○ **B.** An administrative console for managing the virtual machines of Hyper-V.

   ○ **C.** A virtual machine monitor that provides a logical unit of isolation in which the operating system executes.

   ○ **D.** The name of the root virtual machine created in Hyper-V.

5. The XML configuration file for a virtual machine in Hyper-V is what?

   ○ **A.** .vmc file

   ○ **B.** .vsv file

   ○ **C.** .vhd file

   ○ **D.** .bak file

6. Which of the following is NOT a requirement to load the Hyper-V?

   ○ **A.** A 64-bit version of Windows Server 2008

   ○ **B.** Processor DEP

   ○ **C.** IIS

   ○ **D.** Processor hardware–assisted virtualization

7. You have a Windows Server 2008 server with Hyper-V. You just created a virtual machine and installed Windows Server 2003. However, you notice that the machine is running extremely slowly. Doing further investigation, you notice that some of the devices have not been identified in Device Manager. What is the problem?

   ○ **A.** You need to patch Windows Server 2008 with the newest patch.

   ○ **B.** You need to patch Windows Server 2003 with the newest patch.

   ○ **C.** You need to enable turbo mode for the virtual server when running Windows operating systems.

   ○ **D.** You need to install Integration Services.

8. You have a Windows Server 2008 server with Hyper-V. On the computer, you have three virtual machines, each running Windows Server 2003 servers. On one of the servers, you want to install some patches. If the patches cause some problem, you want an easy way to roll back the patches. What should you do?

   ○ **A.** Create a snapshot before you install the patches.

   ○ **B.** Enable Transaction Logging so that you can undo the changes.

   ○ **C.** Make sure to create an undo disk before you install the patches.

   ○ **D.** Freeze the machine and make a copy of it. Then start the machine back up and apply the patches.

Answers to Exam Prep Questions

1. Answer B is correct. An application failing on a virtual machine is no different than an application failing on a physical server. Therefore, you open the event viewer on the virtual machine to troubleshoot the problem. Answer A is incorrect because the application that failed does not write to the Event Viewer on the host running Hyper-V. It writes to the local virtual machine. Answers C and D are incorrect because the Event Viewer would give you insight on why an application failed. The Resource Manager tells you whether the machine is running low on resources such as memory.

2. Answer A is correct. You should run the `Start /w ocsetup Microsoft-Hyper-V` command at a command prompt. Answers B and D are incorrect because the `Servermanager.exe` and `Servermanagercmd.exe` commands do not install Hyper-V on a Server Core installation. Answer C is incorrect because the Server Manager is not available on a Server Core computer.

3. Answer E is correct. Windows 98 is not an enlightened operating system that knows how to work directly with Hyper-V. Answers A, B, C, and D are incorrect because Windows Server 2003, Windows Server 2008, and SUSE Enterprise Linux Server 10 with SP1 are enlightened operating systems, which know how work directly with Hyper-V.

4. Answer C is correct. Hyper-V is based on hypervisor, a virtual machine monitor that provides a virtualization platform that allows multiple operating systems to run on a host computer at the same time. To keep each virtual server secure and reliable, each virtual server is placed in its own partition. A partition is a logical unit of isolation, in which operating systems execute. Answers A, B, and D do not describe hypervisor. The administrative templates do not have any special names. The administrative console is called Hyper-V Manager. Lastly, the root virtual machine does not have any special name.

5. Answer A is correct. The configuration files used for virtual machines are files that have the `.vmc` filename extension. Answer B is wrong because the `.vsv` file is a saved-state file. Answer C is incorrect because the `.vhd` file is the file that has the drive content for the virtual machine. Answer D is incorrect because `.bak` is a generic backup file.

6. Answer C is correct. IIS is not needed for Hyper-V. Answer A is incorrect because a 64-bit version of Windows Server 2008 is needed. Answers B and D are incorrect because to install Hyper-V, you also need Processor DEP and processor hardware–assisted virtualization.

7. Answer D is correct. You need to install Integration Services to install some of the virtual drivers need for the operating system to run at its best. Answers A and B are incorrect. Although keeping both operating systems patched is important, it does not fix the problem with the virtual drivers. Answer C is incorrect because there is no turbo mode for virtual servers in Hyper-V.

8. Answer A is correct. You need to create a snapshot before you install the patches. If there is a problem with the patches, you can reload the snapshot, which would make the virtual machine go back to its state at the time of the snapshot. Answer B is incorrect because Hyper-V does not using transaction logging. Answer C is incorrect because undo disks exist in earlier versions of Microsoft Virtual Servers, not in Hyper-V. Answer D is not correct because you would not freeze the machine to make a copy of it. A snapshot can be run without stopping the machine.

Need to Know More?

To see more information about the virtualization solutions provided by Microsoft, visit the following websites:

http://www.microsoft.com/windowsserver2008/en/us/virtualization-consolidation.aspx

http://technet.microsoft.com/en-us/virtualization/default.aspx

To see the Step-by-Step Guide to Getting Started with Hyper-V, the Server Manager Scenarios Step-by-Step Guide, and the Hyper-V release notes, visit the following website:

http://technet2.microsoft.com/windowsserver2008/en/servermanager/virtualization.mspx

For more information about Quick Migration with Hyper-V, access the following white paper:

http://download.microsoft.com/download/3/B/5/3B51A025-7522-4686-AA16-8AE2E536034D/Quick%20Migration%20with%20Hyper-V.doc

CHAPTER TEN

Practice Exam 1

1. What utility do you use to add roles in Windows Server 2008?

   ○ **A.** Computer Management console

   ○ **B.** Server Management console

   ○ **C.** Add/Remove Programs in the Control Panel

   ○ **D.** Add/Remove Roles in the Control Panel

2. You are an administrator of a company that has 30 Windows Server 2008 computers. You want to be able to remotely administer them from your Windows Vista computer at your desk. What should you load?

   ○ **A.** Terminal Services on your Windows Vista computer

   ○ **B.** Microsoft Remote Server Administration Tools (RSAT) on your Windows Vista computer.

   ○ **C.** Server Core on your Windows Vista computer.

   ○ **D.** SCVMM on your Windows Vista computer.

3. How would you log off of a Windows Server 2008 Server Core computer?

   ○ **A.** Use the shutdown /s command.

   ○ **B.** Use the shutdown /l command.

   ○ **C.** Use the log /off command.

   ○ **D.** Click Log Off at the bottom of the screen.

4. How would you change the time on a Windows Server 2008 Server Core computer?

   ○ **A.** Open the Control Panel and double-click the Date/Time applet.

   ○ **B.** Execute the timedate command.

   ○ **C.** Execute the datetime command.

   ○ **D.** Execute the control timedate.cpl command.

5. What command would you use to prepare a system so that it can be cloned to other computers?

 ○ **A.** sysprep

 ○ **B.** wim /export

 ○ **C.** wsdsutil

 ○ **D.** sys

6. What port does Key Management Services use by default?

 ○ **A.** 60

 ○ **B.** 443

 ○ **C.** 1433

 ○ **D.** 1688

7. What would you use to change a master boot record disk into a GUID partition table disk?

 ○ **A.** Use the convert /GUID command.

 ○ **B.** Use the diskpart command.

 ○ **C.** Right-click the disk in the Disk Management console and select GUID.

 ○ **D.** Right-click the disk in the Server Management console and select GUID.

8. What is the largest RAID 5 volume that you can create with the following disks?

Disk 1	50GB
Disk 2	50GB
Disk 3	20GB
Disk 4	60GB
Disk 5	30GB

 ○ **A.** 80GB

 ○ **B.** 100GB

 ○ **C.** 120GB

 ○ **D.** 210GB

9. What would you use to connect to an iSCSi volume on a SAN to a Windows Server 2008 computer?

  ○ **A.** Use an iSCSI Initiator.

  ○ **B.** Load an iSCSI driver.

  ○ **C.** Use the Add Hardware Wizard in the Control Panel.

  ○ **D.** Use the Disk Management console.

10. You have a Windows Server 2008 with Windows Deployment Services (WDS). You have a Windows Vista image that you stored on the WDS server and you need to install it on a computer that does not support Preboot Execution Environment (PXE). What do you need to do to install the image on the PC?

  ○ **A.** Capture a new image for computers that do not support Preboot Execution Environment.

  ○ **B.** Create a disk that contains PXE drivers.

  ○ **C.** Use a Discover image to boot the computer and discover the WDS server.

  ○ **D.** Boot the disk with a DOS-bootable disk and install the image with the SIM command.

11. You have a Windows Server 2008 computer with Key Management Services (KMS). You need to deploy eight new servers on your domain. You install two servers. Unfortunately, the two servers do not activate. What do you need to do to activate the new servers?

  ○ **A.** Complete the installation of the remaining servers.

  ○ **B.** Open the firewall so that Windows Management Instrumentation (WMI) exceptions can communicate through the firewall.

  ○ **C.** Install Volume Activation Management Tool (VAMT) on the KMS server and configure Multiple Activation Management Key (MAK) Proxy Activation.

  ○ **D.** Install Volume Activation Management Tool (VAMT) on the KMS server and configure Multiple Activation Key (MAK) Independent Activation.

12. You have a Windows Server 2008 computer that has the DNS role and has Key Management Service (KMS) installed and activated. When you try to activate some new computers with Windows Vista, you discover that the SRV record for KMS is not on the DNS server. What should you do?

  ○ **A.** Configure the DNS zone to accept nonsecure updates.

  ○ **B.** Run the `slmgr.vbs /ato` command.

  ○ **C.** On the Windows Server 2008 computer, execute the `net stop netlogon` command and then execute the `net start netlogon` command.

  ○ **D.** Reinstall the KMS with a domain administrator account.

13. You have two Windows Server 2008 computers with Hyper-V. While you are logged onto Server1, you want to manage the virtualization settings of Server2. What should you do?

    ○ **A.** Open the Virtualization Management Console on Server1. Right-click Server1 and select new. Then click Virtual Machine. Specify Server2.

    ○ **B.** Open the Virtualization Management Console on Server1. Right-click Virtualization Services and then click Connect to Server2.

    ○ **C.** From the command prompt, run the `vmconnect.exe server2` command.

    ○ **D.** From the command prompt, run the `mmc vmconnect.msc server2` command.

14. You have a Windows Server 2008 computer with Hyper-V. You have several virtual machines on the server. You want to update an application on the virtual machine. What can you do so that you roll the virtual machine back to its original state if you have problems with the updates?

    ○ **A.** Enable the Remote Differential Compression feature.

    ○ **B.** Create a snapshot using the Virtualization Management Console.

    ○ **C.** Shut down the server and save the state of the virtual machine.

    ○ **D.** Back up the virtual machine.

15. You have a Windows Server 2008 computer with Hyper-V. You need to merge a differencing disk and a parent disk. What should you do?

    ○ **A.** Edit the parent disk.

    ○ **B.** Edit the differencing disk.

    ○ **C.** Inspect the parent disk.

    ○ **D.** Inspect the differencing disk.

16. You have a Windows Server 2008 computer with Hyper-V. You create a new virtual machine. You need the virtual machine to communicate with the Windows Server 2008 host computer but not be able to communicate with the other servers. What should you do first?

    ○ **A.** Install the Microsoft Loopback Adapter.

    ○ **B.** Create a new virtual network switch.

    ○ **C.** Open the firewall and disable communications except to the IP address of the host server.

    ○ **D.** Disable the network connection on the virtual machine.

17. You have two Windows Server 2008 computers configured as a SQL failover cluster. You install a third computer onto the cluster. You find out that the cluster does not failover on the third node. What should you do?

- ○ **A.** Remove the SQL resource from the group.

- ○ **B.** Add the SQL resource to the third node.

- ○ **C.** Configure the third node as a possible owner for the SQL resource.

- ○ **D.** Configure the third node as the preferred owner for the SQL resource.

18. You just installed a new two-node Network Load Balancing cluster that is intended to provide high availability and load balancing for your company's website. You want the network load balancing cluster to support only TCP port 80. What do you need to do?

- ○ **A.** Open the Network Load Balancing Clusters console. Create a new Allow rule for TCP port 80.

- ○ **B.** Open the Network Load Balancing Clusters console. Delete the default port rules. Create a new Allow rule for TCP port 80.

- ○ **C.** Open the Network Load Balancing Clusters console. Run the Port Wizard to reset the port rules to port 80.

- ○ **D.** Open the Network Load Balancing Clusters console and change the default port rule to a disabled port range rule, except port 80.

19. You have a Windows Server 2008 computer with three hard drives. Windows runs off the first drive. The other two disks have not been prepared. What should you do to make a redundant drive system to hold your data files? (Choose two answers.)

- ○ **A.** Initialize the second and third disks as basic disks.

- ○ **B.** Initialize the second and third disks to dynamic disks.

- ○ **C.** Create a striped volume across disks 2 and 3.

- ○ **D.** Create a new mirrored volume, using disks 2 and 3.

- ○ **E.** Create a new spanned volume using all three disks.

20. You have an iSCSI SAN. You want to make the data communication between the servers and iSCSI SAN as secure as possible. What should you do?

- ○ **A.** Create a Group Policy applied to the servers that enforce IPSec on the servers.

- ○ **B.** Implement IPSec security in the iSCSI Initiator properties. Then set up inbound and outbound rules by using the Windows firewall.

- ○ **C.** Implement mutual MS-CHAPv2 authentication in the iSCSI Initiator properties. Then set up inbound and outbound rules by using Windows Firewall.

- ○ **D.** Install an IPSec digital certificate on the servers.

21. You have a Windows Server 2008 computer with the Terminal Services server role. You have an application that you want to deploy on this server that does not use Microsoft Windows Installer packages for installation. In addition, it makes changes to the current user Registry during installation. What should you do so that the application can support multiple user sessions?

- ○ **A.** Run the RDC in console mode and install the application.

- ○ **B.** Run the change user /execute command on the server and install the application.

- ○ **C.** Run the change user /install command on the server and install the application.

- ○ **D.** Run the change logon /disable command on the server and install the application. Then run the change logon /enable command.

22. You have a Windows Server 2008 computer with the Terminal Services server role installed. You want to deploy a new application from the Terminal Services Web Access web page. What should you do?

- ○ **A.** Be sure that all Windows XP computers have SP2 or greater and remote Desktop Client 6.1.

- ○ **B.** Create a Microsoft Windows Installer package and distribute the Windows Installer package to the users.

- ○ **C.** Install and publish the application with the Terminal Services Gateway role on the server.

- ○ **D.** Use a group policy to publish the application to each individual computer.

23. You have a Windows Server 2008 computer with the Terminal Services Gateway role server. You need to have your users connect through the gateway to several servers in your office. You create a security group called Remote1 for those users who need to connect to the servers. What do you need to do next?

- ○ **A.** Add the Remote1 group to the remote desktop users group on each server.

- ○ **B.** Create a client authorization policy and add the Remote1 security group.

- ○ **C.** Create a resource authorization policy and add the Remote1 security group to the policy.

- ○ **D.** Create a group policy and apply it to all the servers to which the users need to connect. The group policy should specify connections to the servers.

24. You have a Windows Server 2008 computer with the Terminal Service server role installed. You have a published application on the Terminal Server. You install a Terminal Services Gateway role on another Windows Server 2008 computer because you need the published application to be available on the intranet and the Internet. What do you need to do next?

    ◯ **A.** Configure a default domain policy to enable the Enable Connection Through the TS Gateway settings and configure the Set TS Gateway server address group policy and configure the IP address of the TS Gateway.

    ◯ **B.** Configure Server Authentication on the Remote Desktop Connection client to Always Connect, even if the server authentication fails for all users.

    ◯ **C.** Enable the Set TS Gateway server authentication method Group Policy to the Ask for Credentials, Use NTLM Protocol settings. Then link the GPO to the domain.

    ◯ **D.** Install the Terminal Services Gateway role on the Terminal Server with the published application and link the two Terminal Services together.

25. You have a Windows Server 2008 computer with the Terminal Services Gateway role service installed. You need to specify which security group is allowed access to the TS Gateway server. What should you do?

    ◯ **A.** Add the security group to the Remote Desktop Users group.

    ◯ **B.** Add the security group to the TS Web Access Computers group.

    ◯ **C.** Create and configure a Resource Authorization Policy.

    ◯ **D.** Create and configure a Connection Authorization Policy.

26. You have a Windows Server 2008 computer with the Terminal Services server role installed. You need to ensure that a single user does not consume the processor utilization. What should you do?

    ◯ **A.** Use Windows System Resource Manager to create a resource allocation policy that limits each user to 30% of the total processor. Then set the policy as the profiling policy.

    ◯ **B.** Use Windows System Resource Manager to create a resource-allocation policy that limits each user to 30% of the total processor. Then set the policy as the managing policy.

    ◯ **C.** Use Windows System Resource Manager to create a resource-allocation policy that limits each user to 30% of the total processor. Then restart the Terminal Server.

    ◯ **D.** Use Windows System Resource Manager to create a resource allocation policy that limits each user to 30% of the total processor. Then apply the policy to a group in which the users are.

27. You have Windows Server 2008 with Terminal Services. You have a user using Windows XP with Service Pack 1 who is trying to access the Terminal Server. However, the user cannot use 32-bit color when accessing programs on the Terminal Server. What is the problem?

- ○ **A.** You need to upgrade Windows XP SP1 to SP2.
- ○ **B.** You need to install RDC 6.1.
- ○ **C.** You need to install RDC 6.0.
- ○ **D.** You need to Upgrade Windows XP SP1 to SP2 and install Remote Desktop Connection 6.0.

28. You have a Windows Server 2008 computer with Terminal Services server role. Each Terminal Services account is configured to allow session takeover without permission. You need to take over a session for John Smith (account name is JSmith) with a session ID of 1243. What command would do this?

- ○ **A.** `Chgusr 1243 /disable`, and then `Tscon 1243`
- ○ **B.** `Takeown /U JSmith 1243`, and then `Tscon 1243`
- ○ **C.** `Tsdiscon 1243`, and then `Chgport /U JSmith 1243`
- ○ **D.** `Tsdiscon 1243`, and then `Tscon 1243`

29. You have a Windows Server 2008 computer with the Terminal Services server role. You need to configure the server to end any sessions that are inactive for more than one hour. What should you do?

- ○ **A.** From Terminal Services Manager, create a new group.
- ○ **B.** From Terminal Services Manager, delete the inactive sessions.
- ○ **C.** From Terminal Services Configuration, modify the RDP-Tcp settings.
- ○ **D.** From Terminal Services Configuration, modify the User Logon Mode setting.

30. You have a Windows Server 2008 computer with IIS installed. You create a website called acme.com. You have a folder called WebApp. You need to enable the WebApp as an application. What should you do?

- ○ **A.** Run the `appcmd add` command at the command prompt.
- ○ **B.** Run the `appcmd add vdir` command at the command prompt.
- ○ **C.** Select the website from IIS Manager console and select Add Application.
- ○ **D.** Select the website from IIS Manager console and select Add Virtual Directory.

31. You have a Windows Server 2008 computer with IIS. You have the Acme website hosted on the IIS server. You need to configure the server to automatically release memory for a website. What should you do so that it will not affect other websites?

○ **A.** Edit the bindings for the website.

○ **B.** Create a new application pool and associate the website to the application pool.

○ **C.** Create a new virtual directory and modify the physical path credentials on the virtual directory.

○ **D.** From the Application Pool Defaults, modify the Recycling options.

32. You have a Windows Server 2008 computer with IIS. You need to create a virtual directory that points to the c:\appdata folder in the acme.com website. Which command should you execute?

○ **A.** `appcmd add app /app.name:acmeapp /`
`path:/hr /physicalPath:c:\appdata`

○ **B.** `appcmd add site /name:acmeapp /physicalPath:c:\`
`appdata`

○ **C.** `appcmd add vdir /app.name:acmeapp /path: /acmeapp /`
`physicalPath:c:\appdata`

○ **D.** `appcmd set vdir /vdir.name:acme /path: /acmeapp /`
`physicalPath:c:appdata`

33. You have a Windows Server 2008 computer with IIS. You want to host multiple websites with a single IP address and port 80. What do you need to configure on IIS to accommodate the multiple websites?

○ **A.** Configure a unique port for each website.

○ **B.** Configure a unique IP address for each website.

○ **C.** Configure a unique host header for each website.

○ **D.** Edit the Hosts file on the server to add all the website names associated with the network address.

34. You have a Windows Server 2008 computer with IIS. You have a website and need to make sure that the cookies sent from the website aren't encrypted on each user's computer. What should you configure to accomplish this?

- ○ **A.** EFS
- ○ **B.** Machine key
- ○ **C.** 802.11
- ○ **D.** Personal digital certificate

35. You have a Windows Server 2008 computer with IIS. You have a group of users that you do not want to be able to access a particular internal website. What can you use that would accomplish this without preventing other users from accessing the website?

- ○ **A.** Authentication
- ○ **B.** Authorization rules
- ○ **C.** IIS Manager Permissions
- ○ **D.** SSL Settings

36. You have Windows Server 2008 computer with the FTP role service installed. You need to have users upload to the FTP site. What do you need to do to accomplish this? (Choose two answers.)

- ○ **A.** Run the `appcmd unlock config` command on the server that runs Windows Server 2008.
- ○ **B.** Configure the NTFS permissions on the FTP destination folder so that it has Modify permissions.
- ○ **C.** Configure Write permissions on the FTP destination folder.
- ○ **D.** Make sure that the Compress attribute is off for the FTP destination folder.

37. You have a Windows Server 2008 computer with IIS and the SMTP Server feature. You need to configure the SMTP server to forward the mail to your ISP. What should you do?

- ○ **A.** Configure the Smart Host setting to use the local host.
- ○ **B.** Configure the Smart Host setting to use the mail server of the ISP.
- ○ **C.** Configure the SMTP delivery setting to Attempt Direct Delivery Before Sending to Smart Host.
- ○ **D.** Add an SMTP record in DNS to point to the ISP SMTP server.

38. You have a Windows Server 2008 computer with IIS. You have two websites using the same IP address. How can you get the first website to respond to acme.com and the second website to respond to looneytunes.edu?

- ○ **A.** Configure a PTR record in DNS that has a record for each website.

- ○ **B.** Configure each website with a host header.

- ○ **C.** Assign a different MAC address to each website.

- ○ **D.** Run the `appcmd add site` command to add a virtual directory to the first website that points to the second website.

39. You have a Windows Server 2008 computer with IIS. You notice unusually high traffic for a website. What can you do to determine the source of the traffic?

- ○ **A.** Enable Execute Permissions on the website.

- ○ **B.** Run the `netstat -a` command.

- ○ **C.** Open the Event Viewer Security logs and filter the traffic by source.

- ○ **D.** Enable website logging in the IIS Server Manager and filter the logs for the source IP address.

40. You have a website that you host for the Acme Company. You want to configure SSL for the http://owa.acme.com/exchange website. The Server is called Server1.acme.com. When you order the digital certificate, what name should you use so that users will not get security warnings when they connect to the URL?

- ○ **A.** owa.acme.com

- ○ **B.** Exchange

- ○ **C.** Server1

- ○ **D.** Server1.acme.com

- ○ **E.** Acme Company

41. You have a Windows Server 2008 computer with IIS. You have a website that runs an ASP.NET 3.0 web application, which must run under a security context that is separate from any other ASP.NET application on the web server. You create a local user account and grant account rights and permissions to run the ASP.NET web application. How do you configure authentication for the new website?

- ○ **A.** Configure the ASP.NET Impersonation setting to Enable and edit the ASP.NET Impersonate setting by specifying the new local user account.

- ○ **B.** Open the local security policy and add the local user account to the ASP.NET Impersonation user right.

- ○ **C.** Configure the ASP.NET Authentication setting to Enabled.

- ○ **D.** Add the ASP.NET account to the local administrators group.

42. You have a Windows Server 2008 computer with IIS. You need to configure a website to use SSL only while encrypting all authentication traffic. What should you do? (Choose three answers.)

○ **A.** Configure the website to require SSL.

○ **B.** Install a digital certificate on the website.

○ **C.** Configure the Digest Authentication setting to Enabled for the website.

○ **D.** Configure the Basic Authentication setting to Enabled and the Anonymous Authentication setting to Disabled for the website.

43. You have a Windows Server 2008 computer with the Streaming Media Services role installed. You need the users who are using Windows Vista and Windows Media Player 11 to be able to pause and rewind the media player. What should you do?

○ **A.** Configure the publishing point as an on-demand publishing point.

○ **B.** Configure the publishing point as a live-streaming publishing point.

○ **C.** Configure the server to use only Real-Time Streaming Protocol (RTSP).

○ **D.** Configure the server to use only Hypertext Transfer Protocol (HTTP).

○ **E.** Enable Fast Cache.

44. You have a Windows Server 2008 computer with the Windows Media Services server role installed with the license clearance house. You publish an audio file on your server. Later, you decide that you want the audio file to be used for only 3 days. What should you do?

○ **A.** Modify the key ID.

○ **B.** Modify the license key seed.

○ **C.** Modify the license.

○ **D.** Create a new package.

45. You have a Windows Server 2008 computer with the Windows Media Services server role installed. You plan to publish an audio file to the Internet by using the Media Server. What do you need to do to create a license for the audio file?

○ **A.** Publish the audio file to a new website.

○ **B.** Publish the audio file to the Windows Media Services server.

○ **C.** Package the audio file as a Windows Installer application.

○ **D.** Package the audio file by using Windows Media Rights Manager.

46. You have a Windows Server 2008 computer with Windows SharePoint Services (WSS). You are trying to configure WSS in a new server farm. However, when you run the Configuration Wizard, you get an error message saying that WSS failed to connect to the database server or the database name does not exist. What should you do?

   ○ **A.** Install the Windows Internal Database.

   ○ **B.** Install a Microsoft SQL Server 2005 server.

   ○ **C.** Be sure that the server has a host record for the SQL server.

   ○ **D.** Install the Active Directory Lightweight Directory Services role.

47. You have a Windows Server 2003 server with Microsoft SQL Server 2005 with SP2 and WSS 2.0. You are going to migrate the configuration and content from WSS 2.0 to WSS 3.0 to a new Windows Server 2008 server. What should you do?

   ○ **A.** Back up the SharePoint configuration and content from the Windows Server 2003 server. Install WSS 3.0 on the Windows Server 2008 computer and restore the configuration and content to the Windows Server 2008 computer.

   ○ **B.** Upgrade the old computer to Windows Server 2008. Then back up the SharePoint configuration and content from the old server. Install WSS 3.0 on the new server and restore the backup to the new server.

   ○ **C.** Back up the SQL Server 2005 configuration and the WSS 2.0 databases from the old server. Install SQL Server 2005 on the new server. Restore the SQL Server 2005 backup to the new server.

   ○ **D.** Back up the WSS 2.0 configuration and content from the old server. Install WSS 2.0 on the new computer. Restore the backup to the new computer. Perform an in-place upgrade of WSS 2.0 to WSS 3.0.

48. You have a Windows Server 2008 computer with Windows SharePoint Services (WSS). You have a managers group that you need to allow to view items, open items, and view versions, but not be able to change the content. What permissions should you assign?

   ○ **A.** Read

   ○ **B.** Design

   ○ **C.** Contribute

   ○ **D.** Full Control

49. You have a Windows Server 2008 computer with the Windows SharePoint Services (WSS) role installed. You need to configure WSS to support SMTP. What should you do?

- ○ **A.** Bind the SharePoint website to port 25.

- ○ **B.** Install the SMTP Server feature by using the Server Manager console.

- ○ **C.** Install the Application Server role by using the Server Manager console.

- ○ **D.** Install the IIS server role.

50. You have two Windows Server 2008 computers. The first one is a web server with several websites. The second server includes the SMTP feature. You configure the website to use the SMTP service on the second server. What do you need to do to ensure that the email messages from the first server are forwarded through the second server?

- ○ **A.** Make sure you have an MX record on the internal DNS server pointing to the first server.

- ○ **B.** Make sure you have an MX record on the internal DNS server pointing to the second server.

- ○ **C.** Create a new application pool with the same name on both servers and associate it with the new websites.

- ○ **D.** Configure the SMTP service on the second server to accept anonymous connections and to relay email messages.

CHAPTER ELEVEN

Answers to Practice Exam 1

Answers at a Glance

1. B	18. B	35. B
2. B	19. B, D	36. B, C
3. B	20. B	37. B
4. D	21. C	38. B
5. A	22. A	39. D
6. D	23. B	40. A
7. B	24. A	41. A
8. B	25. D	42. A, B, D
9. A	26. B	43. A
10. C	27. D	44. C
11. A	28. D	45. D
12. C	29. C	46. B
13. B	30. C	47. D
14. B	31. B	48. A
15. B	32. C	49. B
16. B	33. C	50. D
17. C	34. B	

Answers with Explanations

1. Answer B is correct. You use the Server Management console to add and remove programs. Answer A is correct because the Computer Management console does not have the capability to add or remove roles in Windows Server 2008. Answer C is incorrect because the Add/Remove Programs utility cannot be used to remove roles. Answer D is incorrect because there is no Add/Remove Roles option in the Control Panel.

2. Answer B is correct. Microsoft Remote Server Administration Tools can access all the normal roles found on the remote computers such as DHCP, DNS, and Active Directory so that you can manage them from your own computer. Answer A is incorrect because you cannot load Terminal Services on your Windows Vista computer and they would not help you remotely administer the other computers. Answer C is incorrect because Server Core cannot be loaded on your Windows Vista computer and it would not help you remotely administer the other computers. Answer D is incorrect because SCVMM is used to administer virtual servers only.

3. Answer B is correct. You can use either the `logoff` command or the `shutdown /l` command. Answer A is incorrect because the `shutdown /s` command shuts down the server. Answer C is incorrect because there is no `log /off` command available. Answer D is incorrect because you do not have any buttons available within the Server Core.

4. Answer D is correct. To open the date and time applet, you would execute the `control timedate.cpl` command. Answer A is incorrect because the Control Panel is not available in the Server Core. Answers B and C are incorrect because there is neither a `timedate` nor a `datetime` command.

5. Answer A is correct. The `sysprep` command removes the security ID and other unique information and prepares the system to be cloned. Answer B is incorrect because the `wim /export` command is used to export a WIM file to another WIM file. Answer C is incorrect because the `wsdsutil` is used to manage the Windows Deployment Server (WDS). Answer D is incorrect because the `sys` command is a DOS command used to make a disk bootable.

6. Answer D is correct. Port 1688 is used by default by the Key Management Services. Answer A is incorrect because 60 is a DHCP scope option you use to configure KMS. Answer B is incorrect because port 443 is used by SSL. Answer C is incorrect because port 1433 is used by the SQL server.

7. Answer B is correct. The `diskpart` command is a powerful disk management utility that can be used to convert the disk from MBR to a GUID partition table disk. Answer A is incorrect because the `convert` command with the `/fs:ntfs` option is used to convert a FAT or FAT32 volume to an NTFS volume. Answers C and D are incorrect because you cannot convert a MBR to a GUID partition table disk using the Disk Management console or the Server Management console.

8. Answer B is correct. A RAID 5 volume needs a minimum of three disks. Of the disks used in the RAID 5 volume, one of the disks will be used for parity/failure. Therefore, if you use three drives at 50GB each, you have 100GB of usable disk space. Answer A is incorrect because if you use all five drives at 20GB each, you have 80GB available. Answers C and D are incorrect because you do not have enough free disk space to create 120 or 210 RAID 5 volumes.

9. Answer A is correct. You need to load and configure iSCSI Initiator, software that communicates with the SAN and connects to the iSCSI volume. Answer B is incorrect because the initiator acts as a driver and a connector. Therefore, a driver does not have to be added to Windows Server 2008. Answer C is incorrect because the Add Hardware Wizard will not find a remote iSCSI volume. Answer D is incorrect because you have to use the iSCSI initiator before the volume will be recognized in the Disk Management console.

10. Answer C is correct. If your system does not support PXE, you need to boot the computer with a Discover image, which will find the WDS server. Answer A is incorrect because the problem is that you need to connect to a WDS server. The WDS server already has images to use. Answer B is incorrect because you do not create a disk that contains the PXE drivers. You use a Discover image instead. Answer D is incorrect because you would not use a DOS bootable disk; you would use the Discover image instead.

11. Answer A is correct. You need at least five servers to use KMS. So when you install the remaining servers, you will then have enough servers to use KMS. Answer B is incorrect because it is not a firewall problem that is not allowing activation; you do not have enough servers using KMS. Answers C and D are incorrect because you don't have to use MAK. You can still use VAMT if you have at least five servers.

12. Answer C is correct. If you install KMS, you may need to wait longer for the DNS SRV records to be created or you need to run the `net stop netlogon` and `net start netlogon` commands. Answer A is incorrect because the DNS zone does not need to accept non-secure updates. Answer B is incorrect because the `slmgr.vbs /ato` command is used to activate Windows over the Internet. Answer D is incorrect because you do not need to reinstall the KMS to generate the DNS records.

13. Answer B is correct. The Virtual Management Console, like most MMC consoles, can be connected to multiple servers. Answer A is incorrect because you don't want to create a new virtual server. Instead, you want to connect to a Windows Server 2008 computer with Hyper-V. Answer C is incorrect because the `vmconnect.exe` command is used to connect to a VM, not to edit settings. Answer D is incorrect because `vmconnect.msc` does not exist.

14. Answer B is correct. If you want to test an application or configuration change, you can create a snaptshot, which enables you to roll back if something goes wrong. Answer A is incorrect because there is no Remote Differential Compression feature with Hyper-V. Answer C is incorrect because saving the state of the virtual machine is meant for you to quickly roll back to a base build. Answer D is incorrect because although you could back up the virtual machine, it is much easier to create a snapshot. Therefore, Answer B is a better answer than D, which makes it the correct answer.

15. Answer B is correct. When you edit the differencing disk, you can merge them with the parent disk. Answer A is incorrect because changing the parent disk does not affect the differencing disk. Answers C and D are incorrect because inspecting does not merge the differencing disk and the parent disk.

16. Answer B is correct. Within the Hyper-V virtual environment, you can create a new virtual network switch that will be used only to communicate between the virtual machine and the host computer. Answer A is incorrect because the Microsoft Loopback Adapter is used to test a connection to itself (loopback). Answer C is incorrect because using the firewall is a very clumsy way to limit access and you would have to reapply every time you create another virtual server. Answer D is incorrect because if you disable the network connection on the virtual machine, the virtual machine cannot connect with the host machine.

17. Answer C is correct. You need to make sure all nodes are configured as possible owners for the SQL resource. Answer A is incorrect because removing the SQL resource from the group does not make it available to the cluster. Answer B is incorrect because the SQL resource is tied to the group, not to an individual node. Answer D is incorrect because the preferred owner does not work if it cannot be a possible owner.

18. Answer B is correct. You need to start the Network Load Balancing Clusters console. Then delete the default port rules and create a new Allow rule for TCP port 80. Answer A is incorrect because you need to delete the default port rule. Answer C is incorrect because there is no Port Wizard to reset the port rules to port 80. Answer D is incorrect because you need to delete the port rule first and create a new one.

19. Answers B and D are correct. Mirrored volume is a redundant disk system (RAID 1). To create a RAID 1 volume using Windows, the volumes must be dynamic. Answer A is incorrect because basic disks do not support RAID. Answers C and E are incorrect because a striped volume and a spanned volume are not redundant.

20. Answer B is correct. Out of all of these options, IPSec is the most secure way to encrypt data communications between the servers and the SAN. This is accomplished through the use of IPSec security in the iSCSI Initiator properties. Answer A is incorrect because this would require all communications to and from the server to be encrypted, not just the traffic between the SAN and the servers. Answer C is incorrect because MS-CHAPv2 is only for authentication and would not encrypt the data being sent back and forth. Answer D is incorrect because although a digital certificate can be used to encrypt traffic, just installing a digital certificate does not actually encrypt the traffic.

21. Answer C is correct. You must first run the `change user /install` command so that the Terminal Server will convert to installation mode. Answer A is incorrect because installing the application in console mode does not overcome the problem of writing to the Registry settings of the user. Answer B is incorrect because you need to change to the install mode, not the execute mode. Answer D is incorrect because the `change logon /disable` command only disables further logons. It would not help you install the application for multiple users.

22. Answer A is correct. To use a Remote App in Terminal Services, you need to have Windows XP SP2 and RDC 6.1. Answer B is incorrect because the application on the Terminal Server can be accessed through the website, an RDP program, or a Windows Installer package. Answer C is incorrect because the gateway is used to access a Terminal Server through a firewall/proxy server. Answer D is incorrect because publishing an application with group policies would be used to install a program, not access it through the web interface.

23. Answer B is correct. To allow access through the Terminal Services Gateway, you need to create a client authorization policy (CAP). Answer A is incorrect because adding users or groups to the local remote desktop users group does not get you through the TS Gateway server. Answer C is incorrect because resource authorization policies (RAP) are used to give you access to resources after you connect through the TS Gateway server. Answer D is incorrect because a group policy that gives access to a server does not allow you to connect through the TS Gateway.

24. Answer A is correct. If you decided to use group policies to configure the gateway connection, you would specify Enable the Connection Through the Gateway and the address to use if users cannot connect directly to the Terminal Server on the intranet. Answer B is incorrect because if you always connect even if the server authentication fails for all users, you would have a serious security problem. Answer C is incorrect because the problem is not asking for credentials. Instead, you need to get users pointed to the gateway. Answer D is incorrect because the gateway allows external users to connect to internal resources through a tunnel. You do not need to install a second gateway on the internal resources.

25. Answer D is correct. To specify who can access a TS Gateway server, you need to create a Connection Authorization Policy (CAP). Answer A is incorrect because the Remote Desktop Users group specifies who can access a Terminal Server. Answer B is incorrect because although TS Web Access does not need to be installed on a Terminal Server, if the TS Web Access server and the Terminal Server that hosts the RemoteApp programs are separate servers, the computer account of the TS Web Access server must be added to the TS Web Access Computers security group on the Terminal Server to enable the web part to display applications from that Terminal Server. Answer C is incorrect because the Resource Authorization Policies (RAP) specify the groups of remote computers that users can access.

26. Answer B is correct. You need to create a policy with Windows System Resource Manager (WSRM) and set the policy as the managing policy. Answer A is incorrect because the policy needs to be set as the managing policy, not the profiling policy. Answer C is incorrect because you need to set the policy as the managing policy. Restarting the Terminal Server does nothing. Answer D is incorrect because you apply the policy by making it the managing policy.

27. Answer D is correct. You need Windows XP with SP2 and RDC 6.0 to use 32-bit color. Answer A is incorrect because you also need RDC 6.0 or higher. Answers B and C are incorrect because you need to upgrade to SP2 to install RDC 6.0 and 6.1.

28. Answer D is correct. You must first disconnect the user from the session with the `tsdiscon` command and then connect to the session with the `tscon` command. Answer A is incorrect because the `chgusr` command is used to change the user mode (install mode/execute mode). Answer B is incorrect because the there is no `takeown` command. Answer C is incorrect because the `chgport` command does not take over a user's session.

29. Answer C is correct. You must use the Terminal Services Configuration console to modify when a session is automatically ended. Answers A and B are incorrect because the Terminal Services Manager does not automatically end any session. Answer D is incorrect because you have to modify the RDP-Tcp settings, not the user logon mode settings.

30. Answer C is correct. You just have to select the website and click Add Application. Answer A is incorrect because the `appcmd add` command is used to create websites. Answer B is incorrect because the `appcmd add vdir` command is used to create the virtual directory. Answer D is incorrect because creating a virtual directory does not create an application.

31. Answer B is correct. You need to create an application pool, which has its own memory resources, and assign the website to that application pool. Answer A is incorrect because binding enables you to specify the address and port to which the website responds. Answer C is incorrect because a virtual directory with physical path credentials still fills in the same memory space that was configured before. Answer D is incorrect because the recycling options are used only to recycle memory back after its job has been completed.

32. Answer C is correct. You need to use the `appcmd add vdir` command to create a virtual directory. You must specify the app.name, the path within the website, and the physical path of the folder to which it points on the hard drive. Answers A and B are incorrect because the `appcmd add app` and `appcmd add site` commands do not create a virtual directory. Answer D is incorrect because the `appcmd set vdir` does not add a virtual directory. The command must be `appcmd add vdir`.

33. Answer C is correct. You have to configure a unique host header for each website so that you can specify to what name each website responds. Answer A is incorrect because it was specified to use only port 80. Answer B is incorrect because you are supposed to use a single IP address. Answer D is incorrect because the host file is for name resolution, which only works for the server. It does not specify how each website will respond by name.

34. Answer B is correct. You need to use a machine key that would encrypt the key for a user's key. Answer A is incorrect because Encrypted File System (EFS) is used to encrypt files within a file system, not cookies being sent over the network. Answer C is incorrect because 802.11 is used for authentication in wireless systems. Answer D is incorrect because personal digital certificates are typically used to encrypt SSL traffic between two points, not specifically cookies.

35. Answer B is correct. Authorization specifies what a user can access. Therefore, you would need to configure an authorization rule to prevent particular users from accessing a website. Answer A is incorrect because authentication is used to prove who a user is. Answer C is incorrect because IIS Manager Permissions specify who can manage a particular website. Answer D is incorrect because SSL Settings are used to encrypt website traffic.

36. Answers B and C are correct. You need to make sure that FTP is configured to allow writing to the FTP site and you have to make sure that users also have NTFS permissions for the folder. Answer A is incorrect because the `appcmd unlock config` command would not unlock an FTP site. Answer D is incorrect because the Compress attribute has no effect on whether a user can write to a folder or not.

37. Answer B is correct. You need to configure the Smart Host settings to direct email to the ISP mail server. Answer A is incorrect because the Smart Host needs to go to the ISP email server, not to itself. Answer C is incorrect because a direct delivery attempts to bypass the ISP mail server. Answer D is incorrect because the MX record, not the SMTP record, is used to direct email on the Internet. It is not used to redirect email sent from a web server.

38. Answer B is correct. You need to configure host headers so that each website knows which name to respond to. Answer A is incorrect because the PTR records are used for reverse lookup (IP address to name). Answer C is incorrect because only one MAC address can be assigned to a network interface. Answer D is incorrect because having a virtual directory point to another website does not help a website respond to a particular name.

39. Answer D is correct. You need to enable logging so that you can see who is accessing the website. Answer A is incorrect because Execute Permissions is used to run applications on the web server, not to show you who is using the website. Answer B is incorrect because the `netstat` command is used to display protocol statistics and current TCP/IP network connections. The `-a` displays all connections and listening ports, but not where traffic is originating. Answer C is incorrect because the security logs do not display information on traffic received for a website.

40. Answer A is correct. The website is owa.acme.com. Therefore the digital certificate must be made for owa.acme.com. Answer B is incorrect because the Exchange is a folder on the owa.acme.com, not the name of the website itself. You need a digital certificate for the website. Answers C and D are incorrect because server1 and server1.acme.com are internal names for the server. Answer E is incorrect because Acme Company is the name of the company, not the website.

41. Answer A is correct. You need to enable ASP.NET Impersonal and which account to impersonate, using IIS Manager. Answer B is incorrect because there is no ASP.NET Impersonation user right. Answer C is incorrect because there is no ASP.NET Authentication setting. Answer D is incorrect because assigning the ASP.NET account to the local administrator group does not allow the website to run under the new local user account.

42. Answers A, B, and D are correct. You must first install a digital certificate on the website. Then to make sure users can connect to a website using SSL, you must configure the site to require SSL. You then must disable anonymous authentication so that the user must authenticate to access the website and configure basic authentication. Because you are required to use SSL, basic authentication traffic will be encrypted. Answer C is incorrect because you don't need Digest authentication because all traffic, including authentication traffic, is encrypted.

43. Answer A is correct. For you to allow users to pause and rewind, you must use on-demand publishing. Answer B is incorrect because live-streaming publishing point does not allow pause and rewind. Answers C and D are incorrect because the RRSP and HTTP protocols are used to deliver the media streams and have no effect on the pause and rewind of the media player. Answer E is incorrect because fast cache is used with on-demand publishing points to prevent playback quality problems.

44. Answer C is correct. You need to modify the license within the license clearance house to limit how long a file can be played. Answers A and B are incorrect, because the key ID and license key seed are used to make a key. Answer D is incorrect because the new package does not have to be created; just modify the license key to specify how long an audio file can be played.

45. Answer D is correct. You must package the audio file by using the Windows Media Rights Manager so that a key is bound with the audio file. Answers A, B, and C are incorrect because publishing the audio file to a website, to a Windows Media Services server, or as a Windows Installer application is not protected or limited with the license.

46. Answer B is correct. Because you are creating a farm, you must connect to a Microsoft SQL Server 2005 server. Answer A is incorrect because the farm requires a Microsoft SQL Server 2005 server. Answer C is incorrect because you are most likely to use DNS to get name resolution for the SQL Server. Answer D is incorrect because using the Active Directory Lightweight Directory Services role would not help find a SQL server.

47. Answer D is correct. You must put WSS 2.0 onto the new server with the configuration and content installed. You can then perform an upgrade. Answers A, B, and C are incorrect because none of these solutions actually upgrade the WSS 2.0 content to WSS 3.0.

48. Answer A is correct. You have to assign the read permission limit for the users to view the content. Answers B, C, and D are incorrect because the design and contribute permissions would give additional permissions to change the site or content.

49. Answer B is correct. To send email out from the server, you need to install the SMTP server role. Answer A is incorrect because binding the SharePoint website to port 25 would cause the website to respond to port 25 instead of port 80. Answer C is incorrect because the Application Server role would not allow email to flow. Answer D is incorrect because IIS is already installed if SharePoint is installed.

50. Answer D is correct. You must configure the second server to accept the email from the first server. Answers A and B are incorrect because the MX records specify where to deliver email to a domain. Answer C is incorrect because application pools are used to restrict websites to a memory area.

CHAPTER TWELVE

Practice Exam 2

1. You have several departments within your company. Within each department, you want to make sure that the IT teams that support the individual departments cannot access the images in other departments. What should you do?

   ○ **A.** Create a global group in Active Directory for each department and place the IT personnel and computers in the appropriate global group.

   ○ **B.** Create an organizational unit (OU) for each department and place the computers in the appropriate OU.

   ○ **C.** Place each regional office into a separate image group on the WDS server. Grant each administrator permissions to his or her regional office's image group.

   ○ **D.** Assign each user to a global group in Active Directory for each department and place the IT personnel in the appropriate global group. Then assign the appropriate NTFS permissions to the image files.

2. You have a Windows Server 2008 computer with Microsoft Hyper-V. You need to create five similar virtual servers that run Windows Server 2008. Unfortunately, you don't have a lot of disk space available. What can you do to reduce the amount of space required for these five virtual machines?

   ○ **A.** Create a virtual server. Then create five servers that have a differencing virtual hard disk attached.

   ○ **B.** Create one server and create five separate snapshots.

   ○ **C.** Create each virtual server and then compact the VHD files.

   ○ **D.** Compress the folder where the VHD files are stored.

3. You have a Windows Server 2008 computer with Hyper-V. You have a 40GB fixed-size virtual hard disk on one of your virtual servers that is using only approximately 5GB of disk space. You want to regain the unused disk space. What can you do?

   ○ **A.** Convert the disk to a differencing disk.

   ○ **B.** Convert the disk to a dynamically expanded VHD.

   ○ **C.** Convert the disk to a dynamically expanded VHD file and compact the disk.

   ○ **D.** Run Defrag on the hard drive that hosts the VHD files.

4. You have a Windows Server 2008 computer with Hyper-V. You want to make sure that each virtual machine is configured to shut down properly if you shut down the hosting server. What should you do?

   ○ **A.** Create a shutdown script on each virtual machine.

   ○ **B.** Install Integration Services on each virtual machine.

   ○ **C.** Create a batch file with the shutdown command for each virtual machine.

   ○ **D.** Enable the Shut Down the Guest Operating System option in the Automatic Stop Action properties on each virtual machine.

5. You have a Windows Server 2008 computer with Hyper-V, which has several virtual machines. How do you configure the virtual machines so that they can communicate only with each other and with no other machines on the network?

   ○ **A.** Select the Not Connected option for each virtual machine.

   ○ **B.** Enable the Enable Virtual LAN Identification option for each virtual machine and set the Connection to Host for the network interface card.

   ○ **C.** Enable firewalls on each virtual machine with rules that block all traffic to other servers.

   ○ **D.** Configure the firewall on the virtual switch.

6. You have a Windows Server 2008 computer with Hyper-V. You realize that on a new virtual machine that you created, you cannot connect to access network resources from the virtual machine. What do you need to do to ensure that the virtual host can connect to the physical network?

   ○ **A.** Download the newest network drivers from the Microsoft's update website.

   ○ **B.** Be sure to add the virtual machine to the virtual network representing all the virtual machines.

   ○ **C.** Be sure to enable the network card.

   ○ **D.** On the virtual machine, install Windows Server virtualization Guest Integration Components.

7. You have two computers configured as a Network Load Balancing cluster for your company's website. Currently, all HTTP traffic is evenly distributed between the two servers. You need to add support for HTTPS, but you want the second web server to be the only one to handle the HTTPS traffic. What can you do?

- ○ **A.** In the second server properties, add a new port rule for TCP 443.

- ○ **B.** In the cluster properties, add a new port rule for TCP 443 that has the Filter Mode option set to Multiple Hosts. Then for the second server properties, change the Handling Priority option to the value of 1.

- ○ **C.** In the cluster properties, add a new port rule for TCP 443 that has a Filtering Mode option set to Single Host. Then for the second server properties, change the Handling Priority option to the value of 1.

- ○ **D.** In the cluster properties, create a new port rule for port TCP 443 that has a Filtering Mode option set to Multiple Hosts and the Affinity option set to the value of Single.

8. You have a Windows Server 2008 computer with four 120GB disks. The first disk is the system boot disk. You want to create a large disk out of the remaining disks so that you can have redundancy with the largest volume possible. What should you do?

- ○ **A.** Add another disk. Create a striped volume.

- ○ **B.** Create a new striped volume from the remaining disks.

- ○ **C.** Create a new mirrored volume from the remaining disks.

- ○ **D.** Create a RAID-5 volume from the remaining disks.

9. You have a Windows Server 2008 computer with the Terminal Services role installed. You deploy a new application on the server that creates and uses data files with an .x12 filename extension. You need to ensure that users can launch the remote application from their computers by double-clicking a file that has the .x12 extension. What should you do?

- ○ **A.** Configure the Remote Desktop Connection Client on the users' computers to point to the server.

- ○ **B.** Configure the application as a published application by using a Remote Desktop Program file.

- ○ **C.** Configure the application as a published application by using a Windows Installer package file.

- ○ **D.** Configure the application as a published application by using a Terminal Server Web Access website.

10. You have a Windows Server 2008 computer with Terminal Services connected to your Active Directory domain. You have several applications that are published as a remote application. You want to ensure that no users are allowed to copy and paste information to a local computer during a Terminal Services session. What can you do to accomplish this?

- ○ **A.** Enable the Use Temporary Folders Per Session option.
- ○ **B.** Change the Security Encryption Level to FIPS Compliant.
- ○ **C.** Deselect the Clipboard option in the RDP settings for the published application.
- ○ **D.** Disable the Drive option in the RDP-Tcp Client Setting properties for the server.

11. You have a Windows Server 2008 computer with the Terminal Services role and the TS Web Access role. You decide to install the TS Gateway on the same server. You create a Terminal Services connection authorization policy. However, users still cannot connect to the Terminal Server. What should you do?

- ○ **A.** Configure Network Access Protection (NAP) on the server.
- ○ **B.** Configure the Terminal Services Resource Authorization Policy (RAP) on the server.
- ○ **C.** Be sure to add the users to the Remote Desktop group on the server.
- ○ **D.** Create a Terminal Services Group Policy object (GPO). Enable the Set Path for TS Roaming Profiles setting on the GPO. Create an organization unit (OU) named TSUsers. Link the GPO to the TSUsers OU.

12. You have two Terminal Services configured as a load balancing Terminal Server farm. In addition, you have a third server that has the Terminal Service Gateway (TS Gateway) installed. What do you need to do for the users to connect to the load balancing Terminal Server farm?

- ○ **A.** Install a Terminal Services Session Broker service on a fourth computer. Then create a group policy that specifies the name of the TS Session broker computer to the load balancing Terminal Server farm. Apply the GPO to the two load balancing Terminal Servers.
- ○ **B.** Install a Terminal Services Session Broker service on a fourth computer. Then create a group policy that specifies the name of the TS Session broker computer to the load balancing Terminal Server farm. Apply the GPO to the gateway.
- ○ **C.** Install a Terminal Services Session Broker service on a fourth computer. Specify the address of the two load balancing Terminal Servers.
- ○ **D.** Install a Terminal Services Session Broker service on a fourth computer. Specify the address of the two load balancing Terminal Servers in the host file.

13. You have four Windows Server 2008 computers, each with Terminal Services role installed. You have a Terminal Server Session Broker role installed onto a fifth computer. Although you need load balancing for the four Terminal Servers, you must ensure that the first server is the preferred server for the Terminal Services sessions. Which tool should you use?

- ○ **A.** Group Policy Manager

- ○ **B.** Terminal Services Configuration

- ○ **C.** Terminal Services Manager

- ○ **D.** TS Gateway Manager

14. If you have a Windows Server 2008 computer with the TS Gateway role, how can you find out whether a user has ever connected through the gateway?

- ○ **A.** View the events in the Monitoring folder from the TS Gateway Manager console.

- ○ **B.** View the Event Viewer Security log.

- ○ **C.** View the Event Viewer Application log.

- ○ **D.** View the Event Viewer Terminal Services-Gateway log.

15. You have a Windows Server 2008 computer. You detect an application using half of the available memory on a server. You want to terminate the application. What should you do?

- ○ **A.** Create a resource allocation policy in which the Maximum Working Set Limit option is set to half the available memory on the server. Set the new policy as a profiling policy.

- ○ **B.** Create a resource allocation policy in which the Maximum Working Set Limit option is set to half the available memory on the server. Set the new policy as a managing policy.

- ○ **C.** Create a resource allocation policy in which the Maximum Committed Memory option is set to half the available memory on the server. Set the new policy as a profiling policy.

- ○ **D.** Create a resource allocation policy in which the Maximum Committed Memory option is set to half the available memory on the server. Set the new policy as a managing policy.

16. You have 15 computers running Windows Server 2008 with the Terminal Services role and the Microsoft Windows System Resource Manager (WSRM) feature installed. You create and configure a resource-allocation policy that has the required custom settings on the first Terminal Server. You need to configure the WSRM settings on all the servers to match the WSRM settings on the first Terminal Server. What should you do?

- ○ **A.** Use the Windows Backup tool to back up only the System State data on the first Terminal Server. Use the Windows Backup tool to restore the System State data on each server.

- ○ **B.** Use the WSRM console on the first Terminal Server to export the WSRM information to a shared folder. Use the WSRM console to import the WSRM information from the shared folder.

- ○ **C.** Use the regedit tool to export the HKLM\SYSTEM\CurrentControlSet\ Services\WSRM Registry key on the first Terminal Server to a shared folder. On each server, delete this Registry key and use the regedit tool to import the Registry key from the shared folder.

- ○ **D.** Copy the C:\Windows\System32\WSRM folder from the first Terminal Server to the other Terminal Servers.

17. You have a Windows Server 2008 computer with the Terminal Server role installed and configured as a member server. You have a standalone (not part of the domain) Windows Server 2008 computer configured as the licensing computer. You try to enable the Terminal Services Per User Client Access License mode in the Terminal Services Licensing mode, but you cannot. What should you do to fix this problem?

- ○ **A.** Join the licensing computer to the domain.

- ○ **B.** Add the Terminal Server to the workgroup.

- ○ **C.** Create a Group Policy Object (GPO) that configures the Terminal Server to use the licensing server for licensing.

- ○ **D.** Reinstall the Terminal Server licensing role on the licensing computer.

18. You have a Windows Server 2008 computer with IIS. You need to configure a website called acme.com and a web application called AcmeApp on the web server so that it has a physical path of F:\AcmeApp instead of the D:\AcmeApp. What command should you use?

- ○ **A.** appcmd add app /site.name:acme.com /path:/AcmeApp / physicalPath:d:\AcmeApp

- ○ **B.** appcmd add app /site.name:acme.com /path:/AcmeApp / physicalPath:f:\AcmeApp

- ○ **C.** appcmd set app /site.name:acme.com /path:/AcmeApp / physicalPath:d:\AcmeApp

- ○ **D.** appcmd set app /site.name:acme.com /path:/AcmeApp / physicalPath:f:\AcmeApp

19. You have a Windows Server 2008 computer with IIS installed. After you make changes to a web application, you get reports that users are getting the 503 Service Unavailable message when they try to connect to the application. What command should you run to get things working again?

○ **A.** `appcmd set config`

○ **B.** `appcmd stop apppool`

○ **C.** `appcmd start apppool`

○ **D.** `appcmd set apppool`

20. You have a Windows Server 2008 computer with IIS. You have a web application that uses a custom application pool, which is set to recycle every 1,440 minutes. The web application does not support multiple worker processes. What do you need to do to make sure that users can access the web application after the application pool is recycled?

○ **A.** Set the Pause When in Use Recycling option to True.

○ **B.** Set the Process Orphaning Enabled option to True.

○ **C.** Set the Disable Recycling for Configuration Changes option to True.

○ **D.** Set the Disable Overlapped Recycling option to True.

21. You have a Windows Server 2008 computer with IIS. You have a Microsoft Exchange server that you use as a mail server that connects to the Internet. The internal firewall prevents all computers except the Exchange server from sending email over TCP port 25 (SMTP). What two things do you need to do for your website to send email through the Exchange server?

○ **A.** Configure the Exchange server as a relay agent for the web server.

○ **B.** On the internal DNS server, create an MX record for the Exchange server.

○ **C.** On the internal DNS server, create an MX record for the web server.

○ **D.** On the web server, configure the SMTP email feature for the website to forward email to the Exchange server.

22. You have multiple Windows Server 2008 computers with IIS combined together to form a farm. You need to allow changes to the web server configuration made to one server to be made to all servers in the farm with the least effort. What should you do?

○ **A.** On all servers, configure the Shared Configuration settings.

○ **B.** On one server, configure the Shared Configuration setting.

○ **C.** On one server, create a scheduled task that copies the Inetpub folder to the other servers.

○ **D.** Create a group policy that enables web sync.

23. You have a Windows Server 2008 computer with IIS. You want a team manager to administer the website. Which feature should you configure?

- ○ **A.** .NET Framework permissions
- ○ **B.** NTFS permissions
- ○ **C.** Authentication
- ○ **D.** IIS Manager permissions

24. You have a Windows Server 2008 computer with IIS. You need your company website to use SSL. What two actions do you need to perform to accomplish this?

- ○ **A.** Obtain and import a server certificate by using the IIS Manager console.
- ○ **B.** Select the Generate Key option in the Machine Key dialog box for the default website.
- ○ **C.** Add bindings for the HTTPS protocol to the default website by using the IIS Manager console.
- ○ **D.** Install the Digest Authentication component for the web server role by using the Server Manager console.

25. You have a Windows Server 2008 computer with IIS. You create an internal self-signed digital certificate and apply it to the website. However, users now get a warning message when they connect to the website using SSL. What are the two ways in which you can get rid of this warning?

- ○ **A.** Add the website to the list of Trusted Sites zone on all computers in the domain.
- ○ **B.** Open the Certificates console on the web server and export the self-signed certificate to a `.cer` file. Then install the `.cer` file on all computers in the domain.
- ○ **C.** Create a DNS Host (A) Record for the web server and reissue the self-signed certificate.
- ○ **D.** Replace the self-signed digital certificate with a trusted third-party digital certificate.

26. You have two Windows Server 2008 computers with IIS configured as a network load balancing cluster. You need to install a digital certificate on the company website hosted by the cluster. You create a digital certificate request and install the digital certificate on the first server. What do you need to do to ensure that the second server can use SSL too?

- ○ **A.** Open the IIS Manager console on the second server and create a self-signed certificate.

○ **B.** Open the IIS Manager console on the first server and export the SSL certificate to a `.pfx` file. Then Import the `.pfx` file to the second server.

○ **C.** Open the Certificates console on the first server. Export the SSL certificate to a `.cer` file. Import the `.cer` file to the second server.

○ **D.** Request a new SSL certificate from the public CA. Use the name of the second server as the Common Name in the request. Install the new certificate on the second server.

27. You have a Windows Server 2008 computer with IIS. You want to encrypt all authentication traffic sent to the intranet website while requiring users to use their Active Directory credentials. What should you do?

○ **A.** Disable Anonymous authentication and enable Digest Authentication and Windows Authentication.

○ **B.** Disable Anonymous and Basic Authentication and enable Digest Authentication and Windows Authentication.

○ **C.** Enable Basic Authentication and disable Digest authentication.

○ **D.** Enable Basic Authentication and Windows authentication.

28. You have a Windows Server 2008 computer with IIS. You have a company website that uses SSL. However, you just discovered that the authentication is set to Basic authentication. How can you overcome the problem that Basic authentication is sent as clear text (unencrypted)?

○ **A.** Be sure that the website is configured as Requiring SSL.

○ **B.** Change the Basic authentication to Digest authentication.

○ **C.** Disable Basic authentication.

○ **D.** Install a second digital certificate for the authentication traffic.

29. You have a Windows Server 2008 computer with the Windows Media Services server role installed. You need to distribute a video that can play while the computer is not connected to the Internet, but you want to prevent the video from unauthorized use and illegal distribution. What should you do?

○ **A.** From Windows Media Services, publish the video as streaming content.

○ **B.** From Windows Media Services, advertise the video. Publish the video as on-demand content.

○ **C.** From Windows Media Digital Rights Manager, package the video and then advertise the video on the corporate website.

○ **D.** From Windows Media Digital Rights Manager, create a package and a license for the video file. Burn the packaged video to a DVD.

30. You have a Windows Server 2008 computer with Windows SharePoint Services (WSS). You want to install a second Windows Server 2008 computer with SharePoint to make a farm out of the two servers. What do you need to do?

- ○ **A.** Configure the server as a failover cluster.

- ○ **B.** Install SharePoint on both servers with the same administrative account.

- ○ **C.** Uninstall and reinstall WSS on the first server and select the server farm mode during the installation.

- ○ **D.** Set the Microsoft .NET Framework Trust Level to Low on both SSP1 and SSP2.

31. You have a Windows Server 2008 computer with Windows SharePoint Services installed. What do you need so that users can create distribution lists from the SharePoint site?

- ○ **A.** Set the outgoing mail character set to 1200 (Unicode).

- ○ **B.** Enable the SharePoint Directory Management Service.

- ○ **C.** Configure the site to accept messages from authenticated users only.

- ○ **D.** Configure the site to use the default Rights Management server in Active Directory Domain Services.

32. What command would you use to manually activate a KMS client over the Internet?

- ○ **A.** `cscript \windows\system32\slmgr.vbs /ato`

- ○ **B.** `Slmgr.vbs /ipk <New_KMS_Key>`

- ○ **C.** `slui 4`

- ○ **D.** `Activate Now`

33. You have two Windows Server 2008 computers that are configured as a two-node failover cluster. Of the two nodes, you prefer the first server to be the primary node. If the cluster fails over to the second node, you want the cluster not to switch back during normal business hours (7:00 a.m. to 6:00 p.m.). What do you need to do?

- ○ **A.** Set the Period option to 8 hours in the Failover properties.

- ○ **B.** Set the Allow Failback option to allow failback between 18 and 7 hours in the Failover properties.

- ○ **C.** Enable the Prevent Failback option in the Failover properties.

- ○ **D.** Enable the If Resource Fails, Attempt Restart on Current Node policy for all APP1 resources. Set the Maximum restarts for specified period to 0.

34. You have a Windows Server 2008 computer with Windows SharePoint Services (WSS). You configure the server to accept incoming email. You create a document library. What do you need to do to ensure that users can send email to the document library?

   ○ **A.** Modify the RSS setting for the document library.

   ○ **B.** Modify the permissions for the document library.

   ○ **C.** Modify the incoming email settings for the document library.

   ○ **D.** Enable anonymous authentication for the web application.

35. You have several Terminal Servers arranged as a Terminal Server farm. You also have another server configured as the Terminal Services Gateway and another server as the Terminal Services Session Broker. The load balancing used by the servers is provided by a third-party hardware solution. Therefore, you need to make sure that all Terminal Servers work properly with the farm. What do you need to configure?

   ○ **A.** A GPO that enables the Use IP Address Redirection policy setting in the Session Directory section of the Terminal Server Group Policy template.

   ○ **B.** A GPO that disables the Use IP Address Redirection policy setting in the TS Session Broker section of the Terminal Server Group Policy template.

   ○ **C.** A GPO that enables the Use TS Session Broker Load Balancing policy setting in the Session Directory section of the Terminal Server Group Policy template.

   ○ **D.** A GPO that disables the Use TS Session Broker Load Balancing policy setting in the Session Directory section of the Terminal Server Group Policy template.

36. You have a Windows Server 2008 computer with TS Remote Apps installed. The Terminal Servers security layer is set to Negotiate. You need to ensure that the Windows Vista users can access the remote applications without being prompted for credentials. What should you do?

   ○ **A.** On the server, modify the Password Policy settings in the local Group Policy.

   ○ **B.** On the server, modify the Credential Delegation settings in the local Group Policy.

   ○ **C.** On all client computers, modify the Password Policy settings in the local Group Policy.

   ○ **D.** On all client computers, modify the Credential Delegation settings in the local Group Policy.

37. You have a Windows Server 2008 computer with Terminal Services. Clients that connect to the Terminal Server are all running Windows Vista with Service Pack 1. You need to ensure that all users are able to run Windows Media Player 11 during a Terminal Services session. What should you do?

- ○ **A.** Install the Desktop Experience feature on the Terminal Server.
- ○ **B.** Install the Windows Media Server on the Terminal Server.
- ○ **C.** Install the Windows Media codec on the Terminal Server.
- ○ **D.** Install the Windows Media compatibility pack on the server.

38. You have a Windows Server 2008 computer with Terminal Services installed. You need to prevent new sessions on the Terminal Server without affecting current user sessions. Which command should you run?

- ○ **A.** `Change logon /disable`
- ○ **B.** `Change user /execute disable`
- ○ **C.** `Tskill /server:<servername>/A`
- ○ **D.** `Taskkill /S <servername> /fi "MODULES eq TermSrv"`

39. You have a Windows Server 2008 computer with FTP. You want to make sure that the FTP server is unavailable after restarting the computer. What should you do?

- ○ **A.** Run the `iisreset` command on the FTPSrv1 server.
- ○ **B.** Run the `net stop msftpsvc` command on the FTP server.
- ○ **C.** Run the `WMIC /NODE:<Name of Node> SERVICE WHERE caption="FTP Publishing Service" CALL ChangeStartMode "Disabled"` command on the FTP server.
- ○ **D.** Configure the FTP services to run under a nonadministrative account.

40. You have a Windows Server 2008 computer with IIS 7.0 in an Active Directory environment. You have a website with which you want a user to modify documents stored in the Documents virtual directory. You also want the user to be able to add or delete documents in that directory. What permissions should you assign?

- ○ **A.** Read
- ○ **B.** Write
- ○ **C.** Modify
- ○ **D.** Read & execute

41. You have a website on your Windows Server 2008 computer. The website has static HTML pages, images, and other content. Which handler permissions should you use on the website that would prevent the web server from running scripts but not executables?

- ○ **A.** Enable Read and Scripts.

- ○ **B.** Enable Read and Execute.

- ○ **C.** Enable Read and disable Scripts.

- ○ **D.** Enable Read and configure Custom.

42. You have a Windows Server 2008 computer with IIS. On this server, you have a web application that uses ASP.NET technology. You want to make sure that the web application can access a SQL server using ODBC. What do you need to do?

- ○ **A.** Configure the trust level of code access to Low, Minimum, or Medium.

- ○ **B.** Configure the trust level of code to High or Full.

- ○ **C.** Configure NFTS full permissions to the c:\inetpub folder to the asp.net account.

- ○ **D.** Configure NTFS full permissions to the c:\inetpub folder to the account under which IIS is running.

43. You have a Windows Server 2008 Server Core computer. You need to change the time of the computer. What do you need to do?

- ○ **A.** Execute the `control timedate.cpl` command.

- ○ **B.** Execute the `control intl.cpl` command.

- ○ **C.** Execute the `cscript int.wsf` command.

- ○ **D.** Execute the `cscript control.cpl` command.

44. You have installed several Windows Server 2008 Server Core computers. What should you do to enable the Remote Desktop for Administration mode to accept connections on a computer running a Server Core installation of Windows Server 2008?

- ○ **A.** Open the system properties and enable remote desktop connections.

- ○ **B.** Run the `cscript scregedit.wsf /cs 0` command.

- ○ **C.** Run `cscript scregedit.wsf /AU 4` command.

- ○ **D.** Run the `cscript scregedit.wsf /AU 1` command.

45. What is the default port used for KMS?

○ **A.** 80

○ **B.** 443

○ **C.** 1688

○ **D.** 4343

○ **E.** 6523

46. You have just created a reference computer running Windows Vista. You want to deploy this reference computer to new computers using WDS. What should you do next?

○ **A.** Run the `WDSUTIL` `/add-image` `/imagefile:image` `/imagetype:boot` command.

○ **B.** Run the `sysprep` `/OOBE` `/Generalize` `/Reboot` command.

○ **C.** Run the `riprep` `/pnp` `/Reboot` command.

○ **D.** Run the `imagex` `/capture C:\` `image.wim` command.

47. What type of DNS record is the record that points out the location of the KMS server?

○ **A.** PTR

○ **B.** MX

○ **C.** SVR

○ **D.** SOA

48. What command do you use to re-add a content database for SharePoint Services 3.0?

○ **A.** Use the `psconfig cmd installfeatures` command.

○ **B.** Run the `migrate.exe` command-line tool.

○ **C.** Use the `appcmd add backup <backupname>` command.

○ **D.** Run the `stsadm.exe` command-line tool.

49. You have a Windows Server 2008 computer with WSS 3.0. A user is reporting that a document has disappeared and the last time she remembers accessing it was about six weeks ago. What should you do?

    ◯ **A.** Instruct the user to open the Windows Recycle Bin.

    ◯ **B.** Instruct the user to open the Recycle Bin in SharePoint.

    ◯ **C.** Open the site collection Recycle Bin and undelete the document.

    ◯ **D.** Restore the document, using the Central Administration backup and restore options.

50. What files make up the disks used in a Hyper-V virtual machine?

    ◯ **A.** `.vmc` file

    ◯ **B.** `.vsv` file

    ◯ **C.** `.vhd` file

    ◯ **D.** `.bak` file

51. You have a Windows Server 2008 computer with three hard drives. What type of RAID can you implement to provide fault tolerance?

    ◯ **A.** RAID 0

    ◯ **B.** RAID 1

    ◯ **C.** RAID 5

    ◯ **D.** RAID 1 and 5

13

Answers to Practice Exam 2

Answers at a Glance

1. C	18. D	35. B
2. A	19. C	36. D
3. C	20. D	37. A
4. D	21. A, D	38. A
5. B	22. A	39. C
6. D	23. D	40. C
7. C	24. A, C	41. A
8. D	25. B, D	42. B
9. C	26. B	43. A
10. C	27. B	44. B
11. B	28. A	45. C
12. A	29. D	46. B
13. B	30. C	47. C
14. D	31. B	48. D
15. D	32. A	49. C
16. B	33. B	50. C
17. A	34. C	51. D

Answers with Explanations

1. Answer C is correct. You need to create image groups to hold each department's image files. Then assign permissions to the image groups. Answer A is incorrect because assigning users into global groups does not control which images those users can access. Answer B is incorrect because assigning users into organizational units does not control which images those users can access. Answer D is incorrect because accessing image files through WDS is controlled by assigning permissions to the image groups using WDS, not through NTFS permissions.

2. Answer A is correct. If you create a virtual server and use differencing virtual hard disks, you can minimize disk usage. Answer B is incorrect because having only one server with five separate snapshots means that you still have only one virtual server. Answer C is incorrect because compacting the disks still uses much more space then using differencing virtual hard disks. Answer D is incorrect because compressing a folder where the VHD files are stored does not recover much disk space and is likely to decrease disk performance.

3. Answer C is correct. When you convert a dynamically expanded VHD file and you want to recover disk space that has been consumed, you need to compact the disk. Answer A is incorrect because a differencing disk uses less space only when it is used with one parent VHD file with several differencing disks to differentiate multiple virtual machines. Answer B is incorrect because you also need to compact the disk. Answer D is incorrect because defragging the host hard drive does not reduce disk space.

4. Answer D is correct. You need to enable the Shut Down the Guest Operating System option in the Automatic Stop Action properties on each virtual machine. Answer A is incorrect because shutdown scripts execute only when you properly shut down the operating system in the guest virtual machine. Answer B is incorrect because Integration Services are used to provide a smoother interface and necessary drivers for the VM environment, which has nothing to automatically shut down the hosting server. Answer C is incorrect because batch files would not be executed automatically during a host server shutdown.

5. Answer B is correct. You need to enable the Virtual LAN Identification option for each virtual machine so that the virtual machines and the virtual host server are the only ones that can communicate. Answer A is not correct because the virtual machine cannot communicate with any other server including other virtual machines if you do not connect the

network interface. Answer C is incorrect because the firewall would have to be reconfigured for each machine added, which is too much work. Answer D is incorrect because there is no firewall on the virtual switch.

6. Answer D is correct. Be sure to install the Integration Components so that the virtual host will have the necessary virtual drivers needed to operate properly. Answer A is not correct because you cannot connect to the Microsoft update site because you do not have network connection. Answer B is incorrect because you do not need to be connected to the virtual network to start communication. Answer C is incorrect because the network card is already enabled.

7. Answer C is correct. You need to first create a port rule for TCP 443 that is configured as Single Host. Then configure the second server with the Handling Priority option to the value of 1 so that it will be the first server serving the SSL requests. Answer A is incorrect because you add a port rule for the entire cluster, not an individual computer. Answer B is incorrect because you need to set the Filter Mode option to a single host because you want only one server servicing the SSL requests. Answer D is incorrect because you need to set the filtering option to a single host.

8. Answer D is correct. Of the remaining three hard drives, you can create a RAID-5 volume that is fault tolerant. Answers A and B are incorrect because a striped volume is not fault tolerant. Answer C is incorrect because a RAID-5 volume has more available disk space than a mirrored volume (which would use only two of the free disks).

9. Answer C is correct. If you install the application as a published application, the published application registers the .x12 filename extension so that the computer knows to run the published application when an .x12 file is opened. Answer A is incorrect because pointing a user's computer to a remote server does not register the filename extension. Answer B is incorrect because you do not use a remote desktop program file to publish applications. Answer D is incorrect because using a Terminal Server Web Access website to open a program does not register the .x12 filename.

10. Answer C is correct. For each application that is run through Terminal Server, be sure to deselect the clipboard so that it is not available to users when they run it. Answer A is incorrect because using temporary folders does not prevent cutting, copying, and pasting. Answer B is incorrect because changing the Security Encryption Level to FIPS compliant will not prevent cutting, copying, and pasting. Answer D is incorrect because disabling the Drive option in the RDP-Tcp client settings does not prevent cutting, copying, and pasting.

11. Answer B is correct. After you create a connection authorization policy (CAP) to allow connection to a gateway server, you then create a resource authorization policy (RAP) to specify what resources you can access through the gateway. Answer A is incorrect because NAP controls network access to a computer host based on the host's system health, not its connection to a Terminal Server. Answer C is incorrect because when you use a gateway, you need to create a CAP and RAP, not add users to the Remote Desktop group. Answer D is incorrect because roaming profiles do not help in connecting to the Terminal Services on the server.

12. Answer A is correct. You need to have a TS Session Broker with a group policy to identify the two load balancing Terminal Servers. Answer B is incorrect because you need to apply the GPO to the two load balancing Terminal Servers. Answer C is incorrect because the GPO points to the load balancing Terminal Server computers. Answer D is incorrect because the host file is used for name resolution.

13. Answer B is correct. You would use the Terminal Services Configuration tool to configure the relative weight of a Terminal Server within a farm. Answers A, C, and D are wrong because you cannot use these to configure the relative weight.

14. Answer D is correct. Connections are logged in the Event Viewer Terminal Services-Gateway log. Answers B and C are incorrect because the connections are not logged into the Event Viewer Security and Application logs, and answer A is incorrect because they are not written in the Monitor folder.

15. Answer D is correct. To limit memory utilization, you need to create a resource allocation policy, which needs to be set as a managing policy. Answers A and B are incorrect because you need to configure as the committed memory (or memory being used), not the available memory. Answer C is incorrect because profiling policy only monitors and records the memory usage, but does not stop the application.

16. Answer B is correct. To copy the WSRM settings, you need to import and export the settings using the WSRM console to a shared folder. Answer A is incorrect because you cannot copy the system state from the system to another to duplicate the WSRM settings from one computer to another. Answers C and D are incorrect because you cannot copy the Registry settings or the WSRM folder from one system to another to duplicate the WSRM settings.

17. Answer A is correct. The licensing computer needs to be a member of the domain to hand out per-user client licenses. Answer B is incorrect because the problem is with the licensing computer, not the Terminal Server. Answer C is incorrect because you do not have to create a group policy to point to the licensing server. Answer D is incorrect because you don't have to reinstall the Terminal Server licensing role. You just need to add it to the domain.

18. Answer D is correct. The correct command would be the `appcmd set app` command with a physical path set to `F:\AcmeApp`. Answers A and C are incorrect because they are pointing to the old path located on the D drive. Answer B is incorrect because you need to use the `appcmd set app` command instead of the `appcmd add app` command.

19. Answer C is correct. You need to start the application pool with the `appcmd start apppool` command. Answers A, B, and D are incorrect because none of these will start the application pool.

20. Answer D is correct. If you want to keep users from not being disconnected after an application pool is recycled, be sure to disable the overlapped recycling option. Answers A, B, and C are incorrect because the only way to let users continue working uninterrupted is to disable overlapped recycling.

21. Answers A and D are correct. You need to configure the Exchange server to relay emails from the web server to the Internet. You also need to configure the web server to forward the emails to the Exchange server. Answers B and C are incorrect because MX records are used to determine where to deliver email from a domain. Because the Exchange server is already delivering email, it clearly has the appropriate MX records in place.

22. Answer A is correct. You need to configure the Shared Configuration settings on all servers so that the servers will maintain synchronization. Answer B is incorrect because you must apply the settings to all servers. Answer C is incorrect because a scheduled task would be difficult to implement because you would have to duplicate the tasks on all computers. In addition, you could not keep track of which server has the most up-to-date changes. Answer D is incorrect because there is no group policy that enables web sync and there is no web sync.

23. Answer D is correct. You need to configure IIS Manager permissions so that you configure which user can make changes and what those changes are. Answer A is incorrect because the .NET Framework permissions are used by the application, not the user. Answer B is incorrect because the websites and applications are managed by IIS Manager, not the file system. Answer C is incorrect because authentication is used to identify users who want to use the website, not to manage them.

24. Answers A and C are correct. You must first install a digital certificate for the website and make sure that the website is bound to the HTTPS protocol. The default port for SSL is 443. Answer B is incorrect because the machine key is used to encrypt cookie traffic, not for SSL. Answer D is incorrect because authentication is used to identify users, and would not encrypt all traffic being sent to and from the website.

25. Answers B and D are correct. You could add the digital certificate to all users so that it would be trusted by that computer or you can add a trusted digital certificate to the website. Answer A is incorrect because the Trusted Sites zones do not affect the trusting of digital certificates. Answer C is incorrect because a DNS record is used for name resolution. It does not help in trusting the digital certificate.

26. Answer B is correct. You need to place the same digital certificate on both servers. Therefore, you need to export the digital certificate from the first sever and import it into the second server. Answer A is incorrect because the self-signed certificate would not be trusted. Answer C is incorrect because you need to use a .pfx file to import and export because it contains both the private and public keys necessary for proper encryption and decryption. Answer D is incorrect because you need to have the same digital certificate installed on both servers.

27. Answer B is correct. You need to disable anonymous and basic authentication. Anonymous does not require authentication and Basic authentication is sent in clear text. You need to enable Digest authentication and Windows authentication to make sure all authentication traffic is encrypted and that they are using Windows authentication. Answer A is incorrect because you also need to disable Basic authentication, which is not encrypted. Answers C and D are incorrect because you need to disable Anonymous authentication and require both Digest authentication and Windows authentication.

28. Answer A is correct. If the website is using SSL, all traffic including authentication is encrypted. You just need to make sure that the website is configured to require SSL so that HTTP cannot be used, only HTTPS. Answer B is a possible solution but some applications require Basic authentication only. In addition, the SSL would be a strong security solution. Answer C is incorrect because Basic authentication may be necessary for some applications, and if the website requires SSL, authentication traffic is being encrypted. Answer D is incorrect because you need only one digital certificate on the website to encrypt the traffic. Adding a second digital certificate would not enable you to encrypt the authentication traffic.

29. Answer D is correct. You need to use the Windows Media Digital Rights Manager to create a package and license and burn the package to a DVD. Answers A and B are incorrect because they require Internet access. Answer C is incorrect because you also need a license to go with the package.

30. Answer C is correct. Because the first server was configured as a stand-alone server, you need to uninstall it and reinstall it in server farm mode. Answer A is incorrect because a failover cluster has only one server running at a time. Answer B is incorrect because the installation using the same administrative account does not help install the two servers into a farm. Answer D is incorrect because the Microsoft .NET Framework Trust level does not help install the two servers into a farm.

31. Answer B is correct. For users to create distribution lists with a SharePoint site, you need to enable SharePoint Directory Management Service. Answer A is incorrect because setting the outgoing mail character would not help make distribution lists. Answer C is incorrect because configuring a site to accept messages from authentication users would allow the site to receive email, not create distribution lists. Answer D is incorrect because the Rights Management server in Active Directory Domain Services would not assist in creating distribution lists.

32. Answer A is correct. You need to run the `cscript \windows\ system32\slmgr.vbs /ato` command. Answer B incorrect because the `slmgr.vbs /ipk` command is what you use to assign a KMS key to a computer. Answer C is incorrect because the `slui 4` command is used to activate Windows over the phone. Answer D is incorrect because there is no `Activate Now` command.

33. Answer B is correct. To prevent automatic failback during normal business hours, you need to allow failback between 18 and 7 hours in the Failover properties. Answer A is incorrect you need to specify the time range, not the number of hours. Answer C is incorrect because failback would prevent the cluster from switching back to the primary mode automatically. Answer D is incorrect because that action would not execute or schedule a failover; it would just try to restart the resource immediately.

34. Answer C is correct. If the server can receive email, you then need to modify the incoming email settings for the document library to receive emails. Answer A is incorrect because RSS is used to get automatic notifications and announcements when a website is changed. Answer B is incorrect because for a document library to receive email, it has to be configured as such. Permissions would not help it receive emails. Answer D is incorrect because configuring authentication would not help a document library receive email.

35. Answer B is correct. Because you are using a third-party hardware load-balancing solution, you most likely need to disable IP Address Redirection, so that it uses Token Redirection instead. Answer A is incorrect because the IP Address Redirection is the default for Microsoft load balancing, but the hardware load balancing usually uses token redirection. Answer C is incorrect because you don't necessarily need to use the TS as a GPO. Answer D is incorrect because if you disable load balancing, load balancing would not be available to the Terminal Server and would not help communicate with the hardware load balancing.

36. Answer D is correct. Because the security layer is set to Negotiate, you need to modify the credentials delegation settings in the local group policy. The Credential Delegation policy allows saved credentials to be used for remote connections. Answers A and C are incorrect because the Password Policy specifies how often a password has to be changed and how complex or long it has to be. Answer B is incorrect because you need to configure the Credential Delegation on the local computers, not the server.

37. Answer A is correct. The Desktop Experience on the server includes a photo gallery, Windows Sidebar, Windows Calendar, Mail, and the Windows Media Player. Answer B is incorrect because the Media server provides media services, not a media player. Answer C is incorrect because you need a media player, not the codec. Answer D is incorrect because there is no such thing as a Windows Media compatibility pack.

38. Answer A is correct. You just need to disable logon with the `change logon /disable` command. Answer B would not prevent future logons. Answer C is incorrect because the `tskill` command is used to kill terminal sessions, and Answer D is incorrect because the `taskkill` is used to kill tasks on a server.

39. Answer C is correct. You would use the Windows Management Instrumentation Command-line (WMIC) to prevent FTP from being loaded. Answer A is incorrect because the `iisreset` command would restart IIS. Answer B would only stop the `msftpsvc`, but would not prevent it from starting automatically. Answer D is incorrect because specifying under which account the FTP service runs has no effect if it starts automatically or not during boot up.

40. Answer C is correct. The Modify permission enables you to write to documents and add and delete documents. Answer A is incorrect because the Read permissions enable the user to only view contents and properties of the documents. Answer B is incorrect because the user would not be able to add or delete documents. Answer D is incorrect because it would allow the user to run executable files and scripts but would not give the user permission to modify documents.

41. Answer A is correct. You need to have the Read permission to read the web pages and the scripts permission to run the scripts. Answer B is incorrect because although the Execute permission enables you to run scripts, it also enables you to run executables. Answer C is incorrect because you need to have the Script permission to run scripts. Answer D is incorrect because there is no Custom permission.

42. Answer B is correct. By having High or Full ASP code access, an application can use ODBC to connect to a SQL server. Answer A is incorrect because you need at least High code access to access the SQL server. Answers C and D are incorrect because NTFS permissions would not affect accessing a SQL server.

43. Answer A is correct. To change the time you have to run the `control timedate.cpl` command from the command prompt. Answer B is incorrect because the `control.intl.cpl` command would change the international settings of a computer running a Server Core, not the date and time. Answer C is incorrect because the `int.wsf` is a made-up command for the cscript to run. Answer D is incorrect because you don't use `cscript` to open the control panel, which is not available in Server Core.

44. Answer B is correct. The `cscript scregedit.wsf /cs 0` command is used to enable the Remote Desktop for Administration mode to accept connections on a computer running a Server Core installation of Windows Server 2008. Answer A is incorrect because you cannot open the control panel in a Server Core installation. Answer C is incorrect because the `cscript scregedit.wsf /UA 4` command is used to enable automatic updates. Answer D is incorrect because the `cscript scregedit.wsf /AU 1` command disables automatic updates on Server Core installation computers.

45. Answer C is correct. The default port for KMS is 1688. Therefore, Answers, A, B, D, and E are wrong because they do not list port 1688.

46. Answer B is correct. You need to use the `sysprep` command to assign a new security ID and other unique computer information. The Answer A is incorrect because the `WDSUTIL` command is used to add a boot image called `image`. Answer C is incorrect because the `riprep` command is used to capture the Windows 2000 Professional and Windows XP Professional images from a reference computer to a Remote Installation Services (RIS) server. Answer D is incorrect because the `imagex` command is used to capture an image. But you need to first run the `sysprep` command before you create an image because it needs to pull the unique information such as the security ID first.

47. Answer C is correct. The SVR, short for service records, would specify the location of certain services, including the KMS server. Answer A is incorrect because the PTR record is used for reverse lookup. Answer B is incorrect because the MX record is used to locate the mail server for a domain. Answer D is incorrect because the SOA, short for Start of Authority, is used to specify who is in charge of a DNS domain.

48. Answer D is correct. Use the `stdadm` command-line tool with the `add-contentdb` operation to re-add the content database. Answer A is incorrect because it is used to register the SharePoint Products and Technologies features placed on the file system of the server with the server farm. Answer B is incorrect because there is no utility in SharePoint called `migrate.exe`. Answer C is incorrect because the `appcmd add backup` command is for backing up IIS.

49. Answer C is correct. Because the document was not recently deleted, you can look in the site collection Recycle Bin to undelete the document. Answer A is incorrect because items deleted in SharePoint are not moved into the Windows Recycle Bin. Answer B is incorrect because the document was not recently deleted. So if it was deleted, it would have already been moved from the user's Recycle Bin to the site collection Recycle Bin. Answer D is incorrect because when you use the Central Administration, it is used to back up and restore the entire SharePoint site, not individual items within SharePoint.

50. Answer C is correct. The .vhd file is the file that has the drive content for a virtual machine. Answer A is incorrect because the configuration files used for virtual machines are files that have the .vmc filename extension. Answer B is wrong because the .vsv file is a saved-state file. Answer D is incorrect because .bak is a generic backup file.

51. Answer D is correct. RAID 1, disk mirroring, uses two disks to provide fault tolerance. RAID 5 uses at least three disks to provide fault tolerance. Answer A is incorrect because RAID 0, disk striping, does enhance performance, but does not provide fault tolerance. Answers B and C would be correct, but answer D is a better answer because you can choose only one answer.

What's on the CD-ROM

The CD-ROM features an innovative practice test engine powered by MeasureUp, giving you yet another effective tool to assess your readiness for the exam.

Multiple Test Modes

MeasureUp practice tests can be used in Study, Certification, or Custom Mode.

Study Mode

Tests administered in Study Mode enable you to request the correct answer(s) and explanation to each question during the test. These tests are not timed. You can modify the testing environment during the test by selecting the Options button.

You can also specify the objectives or missed questions you want to include in your test, the timer length, and other test properties. You can also modify the testing environment during the test by selecting the Options button.

In Study Mode, you receive automatic feedback on all correct and incorrect answers. The detailed answer explanations are a superb learning tool in their own right.

Certification Mode

Tests administered in Certification Mode closely simulate the actual testing environment you will encounter when taking a licensure exam and are timed. These tests do not allow you to request the answer(s) and/or explanation to each question until after the exam.

Custom Mode

Custom Mode enables you to specify your preferred testing environment. Use this mode to specify the categories you want to include in your test, timer length, number of questions, and other test properties. You can modify the testing environment during the test by selecting the Options button.

Attention to Exam Objectives

MeasureUp practice tests are designed to appropriately balance the questions over each technical area covered by a specific exam. All concepts from the actual exam are covered thoroughly to ensure that you're prepared for the exam.

Installing the CD

System Requirements:

- Windows 95, 98, ME, NT4, 2000, XP, or Vista

- 7MB disk space for testing engine

- An average of 1MB disk space for each individual test

- Control Panel Regional Settings must be set to English (United States)

- PC only

To install the CD-ROM, follow these instructions:

1. Close all applications before beginning this installation.

2. Insert the CD into your CD-ROM drive. If the setup starts automatically, go to step 6. If the setup does not start automatically, continue with step 3.

3. From the Start menu, select Run.

4. Click Browse to locate the MeasureUp CD. In the Browse dialog box, from the Look In drop-down list, select the CD-ROM drive.

5. In the Browse dialog box, double-click on `Setup.exe`. In the Run dialog box, click OK to begin the installation.

6. On the Welcome screen, click MeasureUp Practice Questions to begin installation.

7. Follow the Certification Prep Wizard by clicking Next.

8. To agree to the Software License Agreement, click Yes.

9. On the Choose Destination Location screen, click Next to install the software to C:\Program Files\Certification Preparation. If you cannot locate MeasureUp Practice Tests on the Start menu, see the section titled "Creating a Shortcut to the MeasureUp Practice Tests," later in this appendix.

10. On the Setup Type screen, select Typical Setup. Click Next to continue.

11. In the Select Program Folder screen, you can name the program folder where your tests will be located. To select the default, simply click Next and the installation continues.

12. After the installation is complete, verify that Yes, I Want to Restart My Computer Now is selected. If you select No, I Will Restart My Computer Later, you cannot use the program until you restart your computer.

13. Click Finish.

14. After restarting your computer, choose Start, Programs, Certification Preparation, Certification Preparation, MeasureUp Practice Tests.

15. On the MeasureUp Welcome Screen, click Create User Profile.

16. In the User Profile dialog box, complete the mandatory fields and click Create Profile.

17. Select the practice test you want to access and click Start Test.

Creating a Shortcut to the MeasureUp Practice Tests

To create a shortcut to the MeasureUp Practice Tests, follow these steps.

1. Right-click on your desktop.

2. From the shortcut menu, select New, Shortcut.

3. Browse to C:\Program Files\MeasureUp Practice Tests and select the MeasureUpCertification.exe or Localware.exe file.

4. Click OK.

5. Click Next.

6. Rename the shortcut MeasureUp.

7. Click Finish.

After you complete step 7, use the MeasureUp shortcut on your desktop to access the MeasureUp products you ordered.

Technical Support

If you encounter problems with the MeasureUp test engine on the CD-ROM, please contact MeasureUp at (800) 649-1687 or email support@measureup.com. Support hours of operation are 7:30 a.m. to 4:30 p.m. EST. In addition, you can find Frequently Asked Questions (FAQ) in the Support area at www.measureup.com. If you would like to purchase additional MeasureUp products, call (678) 356-5050 or (800) 649-1687, or visit www.measureup.com.

Glossary

A

Active Server Pages (ASP)
Microsoft's server-side script engine that generates dynamic web pages.

active/passive cluster A set of redundant servers that form a cluster. In an active/passive cluster, one node is actively performing the work and the other is waiting to take over the workload if the active node fails.

administrative tools Contains tools for system administrators and advanced users.

advanced fast start Similar to Fast Start except Windows Media Player begins playing the stream before its buffer is full.

alert A notification sent when a document is added or changed.

alternate access mapping
Additional names that are mapped to a SharePoint website.

announcement files An XML-based file that contains metadata about content and directs users to the content location.

anonymous authentication
Authentication that allows any user to access any public content without providing a username and password.

appcmd command A command interface used to configure and manage IIS 7.0 in Windows Server 2008.

application pool Defines a set of resources (worker process or a set of worker processes) used by a website or application that sets boundaries for the applications contained and prevents applications from one application pool from affecting applications running in other application pools.

ASP.NET Microsoft web application framework used to build dynamic websites, web applications, and XML web services.

authentication The process of identifying an individual, usually based on a username and password.

authorization The process of granting or denying access to a network resource.

B

basic authentication Authentication that requires that users provide a valid username and password to gain access to content. Basic authentication transmits passwords across the network in clear text.

basic disks A physical disk with primary and extended partitions.

binding The defining of a website name and port that listens for HTTP requests.

boot images Part of the Windows Deployment Services (WDS), images that you boot a client computer into before installing the operating system image. The boot image presents a boot menu that contains the images that users can install onto their computers.

C

capture images Boot images that launch the Windows Deployment Services Capture Utility instead of Setup. When you boot a reference computer (that has been prepared with Sysprep) into a capture image, a wizard creates an install image of the reference computer and saves it as a `.wim` file. You can also create media (such as a CD, DVD, or USB drive) that contains a capture image, and then boot a computer from the media.

Certificate Authority (CA) Trusted third-party organization or company that issues digital certificates used to create digital signatures and public-private key pairs. The role of the CA in this process is to guarantee that the individual granted the unique certificate is, in fact, who he or she claims to be.

clear text Data that is not encrypted.

Clearinghouse A facility that is used to activate license servers, to issue Client Access Licenses to license servers, to recover CALs, and to reactivate license servers.

client access license (CAL) A kind of software license, distributed by Microsoft, to allow clients to connect to its server software programs.

cluster A set of independent computers that work together to increase the availability of services and applications.

codec Short for compression/decompression, a software component that compresses and decompresses a media stream.

Common Gateway Interface (CGI) A standard protocol for interfacing external executable application software with IIS.

Computer Management Console Manages local or remote computers by using a single, consolidated desktop tool.

connection authorization policy (CAP) A policy that defines which users, user groups, or computer groups can access a TS Gateway server.

Control Panel A graphical tool used to configure the Windows environment and hardware devices.

convergence A process where cluster nodes all agree on the current cluster membership and the distribution of the workload among the active nodes.

D

Data Collector Set (DCS) A feature in Windows Reliability and Performance Monitor that groups data collectors into reusable elements. After a Data Collector Set is defined, you can schedule the collection of data using the DCS or see it in real time.

default document A directory's home page or an index page containing a site document directory listing. When a URL is entered into a browser that does not specify a filename, the default document is generated automatically by the server or is designated by the administrator.

differencing disk A special type of dynamic disk that stores changes to virtual machine state in a file separate from the base .vhd. Differencing disks are defined in the context of a parent-child relationship. In this relationship, each child differencing disk has one and only one parent disk, but a parent disk (which remains read-only) may be associated with multiple child differencing disks.

digest authentication Authentication that uses a Windows domain controller to authenticate users who request access to content on your server.

digital certificate An attachment to an electronic message used for security purposes. The most common use of a digital certificate is to verify that a user sending a message is who he or she claims to be, and to provide the receiver with the means to encode a reply.

Digital Rights Management (DRM)
Provides the capability to control content usage for those situations in which WMS authentication and authorization cannot.

discover images   Boot images that force Setup.exe to launch in Windows Deployment Services mode and then discover a Windows Deployment Services server. These images are typically used to deploy images to computers that are not PXE enabled or that are on networks that do not allow PXE.

disk management console   A graphical user utility used to manage, partition, and format disks in Windows Server 2008.

diskpart.exe command   A command-driven utility used to manage and partition disks in Windows Server 2008.

document library   A library that stores documents with a SharePoint website.

dynamic disks   A physical disk configuration that does not use partitions or logical drives, and the Master Boot Record (MBR) is not used. Instead, the basic partition table is modified and any partition table entries from the MBR are added as part of the Logical Disk Manager (LDR) database that stores dynamic disk information at the end of each dynamic disk. Dynamic disks can be divided into as many as 2,000 separate volumes, but you should limit the number of volumes to 32 for each dynamic disk to avoid slow boot time performance.

E

Easy Print   See *Terminal Services Easy Print*.

encoder   Software that converts digital media to a format that you can stream with the Windows Media Server.

encryption   The translation of data into a secret code. Encryption is the most effective way to achieve data security. To read an encrypted file, you must have access to a secret key or password that enables you to decrypt it. Unencrypted data is called plain text; encrypted data is referred to as cipher text.

enlightened operating system
Operating systems that work directly with Hyper-V and enjoy performance benefits with respect to device access and management benefits.

Extensible Markup Language (XML)
A specification developed by the W3C designed especially for web documents. It enables designers to create their own customized tags, enabling the definition, transmission, validation, and interpretation of data between applications and between organizations.

F

fabric   A network topology where devices are connected to each other through one or more high-efficiency data paths.

failback   The action of a cluster node that resumes the function and workload when it is brought back online.

failover cluster   A set of redundant servers that form a cluster. When one server fails, another one takes over its function and workload.

fast cache   Caching of a stream before it is needed to prevent playback quality problems due to network issues. The stream is rendered in Windows Media Player at the specified data rate, but the client is able to receive a much larger portion of the content before rendering it.

fast recovery   Technology that uses forward error correction (FEC) on a publishing point, which enables it to recover lost or damaged data packets without having to request that the Windows Media server resend the data. It also enables the client to reconnect to the server automatically and restart streaming.

fast start   Technnology that enables you to connect to a media server and begin downloading media. The media starts playing as soon as the buffer is filled without waiting for the entire media stream to be downloaded.

fast-forward/rewind   Improved version of standard fast-forward/rewind that minimizes network utilization, minimizes disk activity, and improves playback quality by using multiple copies of content to avoid the problems that faster key frame delivery can cause.

fibre channel   A gigabit-speed network technology primarily used for storage networking.

File Transfer Protocol (FTP)   The protocol for exchanging files over the Internet.

five nines   (99.999%) Up-time for a server or service, which means that it can only be offline 5.25 minutes per year.

forms authentication   Uses client-side redirection to forward unauthenticated users to an HTML form where they can enter their credentials, which are usually a username and password. After the credentials are validated, users are redirected to the originally requested page. Because forms authentication sends the username and password to the web server as plain text, you should use Secure Sockets Layer (SSL) encryption for the logon page and for all other pages in your application.

G-H

Global Unique Identifier (GUID) partition table (GPT) A partitioning style that supports disks in cluster storage. GPT disks support volume sizes up to 18 exabytes (EB) and can store up to 128 partitions on each disk.

heartbeat A special packet that is sent through a dedicated network card used to keep track of the status of each node. It is also used to send updates in the configuration of the cluster.

host bus adapter (HBA) An I/O adapter that sits between the host computer's bus and the Fibre Channel loop and manages the transfer of information between the two channels. To minimize the impact on host processor performance, the host bus adapter performs many low-level interface functions automatically or with minimal processor involvement.

HyperText Markup Language (HTML) The authoring language used to create documents on the World Wide Web.

Hypertext Transfer Protocol (HTTP) The underlying protocol used by the World Wide Web. HTTP defines how messages are formatted and transmitted, and what actions web servers and browsers should take in response to various commands.

Hyper-V Microsoft's technology that comes with Windows Server 2008 and that enables multiple operating systems to run concurrently on a single machine.

Hyper-V Manager The console to manage virtual machines.

Hypervisor A virtual machine monitor, which provides a virtualization platform that allows multiple operating systems to run on a host computer at the same time. To keep each virtual server secure and reliable, each virtual server is placed in its own partition, a logical unit of isolation, in which operating systems execute.

I

IDE Drives Fast, low-cost drives. IDE is short for Integrated Drive Electronics. IDE drives are the most popular consumer drives.

IIS Manager A console used to manage IIS.

Initial Configuration Tasks A console that first appears when a server is started for the first time and that performs many security-related tasks, such as setting the Administrator password, changing the name of the Administrator account, running Windows Updates, and configuring the Windows Firewall.

install images Part of the Windows Deployment Services (WDS), operating system images that you deploy to the client computer.

integration components A set of drivers and services that help each Virtual Machine to have a more consistent state and perform better by enabling the guest to use synthetic devices.

Internet Group Membership Protocol (IGMP) A protocol defined in RFC 1112 as the standard for IP multicasting in the Internet. It's used to establish host memberships in particular multicast groups on a single network. The mechanisms of the protocol allow a host to inform its local router, using Host Membership Reports, that it wants to receive messages addressed to a specific multicast group.

Internet Information Services (IIS) The built-in web server to Windows servers that enables you to share information with users on the Internet, an intranet, or an extranet.

Internet Server Application Programming Interface (ISAPI) filters Programs that you can add to IIS to enhance web server behavior.

iSCSI A protocol that enables clients to send SCSI commands over a TCP/IP network using TCP port 3260. Because it uses Ethernet switches and cabling, typically Gigabit Ethernet or Fibre, it can connect a SAN to multiple servers and provide long-distance connections.

iSCSI initiator The software that allows a host or device to connect to an iSCSI disk system or Storage Area Network (SAN).

K-L

key ID A stringe used to create a license key. It is created by the content owner for each Windows Media file that needs to be protected.

Key Management Service (KMS) A service used to establish a local activation enablement service that is hosted locally in the customer's environment.

license key A key used to protect a packaged digital media file.

license key seed A value that is known only to the content owner and license clearing house as part of the license key. The license key is used to protect a packaged digital.

live content streaming A broadcast publishing point that enables remote users to view live events (streaming media).

load balance A cluster that distributes the workload among multiple servers.

logical unit number (LUN) A unique identifier used on a SCSI bus or within a SAN to distinguish the device or volume.

M

MAK Proxy Activation   Client activation for computers that do not have Internet access.

Master Boot Record (MBR)
Traditional disk partitioning style. MBR disks support volume sizes up to two terabytes (TB) and allow up to four primary partitions per disk. Alternatively, MBR disks support three primary partitions, one extended partition, and an unlimited number of logical drive letters.

Microsoft Manager Console (MMC)
A fully customizable administrative console used as a common interface for most administrative tasks.

Microsoft Office SharePoint Server (MOSS) portal   A paid component that is built on top of WSS and adds more functionality to it, including better document management, enterprise search functionality, navigation features, RSS support, and enhanced workflow.

Microsoft Remote Server Administration Tools (RSAT)   A tool that enables administrators to remotely manage roles and features in Windows Server 2008 from a computer that is running Windows Vista with Service Pack 1 (SP1).

mirrored volumes   A volume stored on two separate physical disks, which has the data "mirrored" (written) onto both disks simultaneously and redundantly. This configuration is also referred to as RAID-1. If one of the

disks in the mirrored configuration fails, the system functions normally (unless the second disk fails) until the failed disk is replaced and then the volume can be mirrored again.

mount points   A volume or partition that is grafted into a folder on another drive. The mounting is handled transparently to the user and applications.

multicast   A method to transmit a single message to a select group of recipients.

Multiple Activation Key (MAK)   A one-time activation service with Microsoft's hosted activation services. Each MAK has a predetermined number of allowed activations, dependent upon the volume license agreement that the customer has. Each MAK activation with Microsoft's hosted activation service counts toward the predetermined activation limit. MAK activations can be reclaimed.

multiple bit rate (MBR) streaming
Technology developed for streaming media that has the same content encoded at different bit rates.

N

.NET Framework   A software component that is a part of modern Microsoft Windows operating systems and that provides a large body of pre-coded solutions to common program requirements. It also manages the execution of programs written specifically for the framework, much as Windows APIs provide an interface for programmers to give a program the same Microsoft Windows look and feel.

network load balance (NLB)   See *load balance.*

Network Policy Server (NPS)   A Microsoft implementation of a Remote Authentication Dial-In User Service (RADIUS) server used to authenticate remote connections to a server or network.

network-attached storage (NAS)   A file-level computer data storage device that is connected to a computer network to provide shared drives or folders.

node   A single server that makes up a cluster.

O-P

on-demand publishing   A publishing point used to deliver streaming media when the user asks for it.

partition   (1) A logical volume defined on a physical or virtual disk. Each partition functions as if it were a separate disk drive. (2) A term used in Microsoft's Hyper-V as a logical unit of isolation, in which operating systems execute.

playlists   An XML-based language standard that enables web developers to send separate content streams to a client computer, where they will be displayed as a single stream.

pre-boot execution environment (PXE)   Pronounced pixie, one of the components of Intel's WfM specification that allows a workstation to boot from a server on a network before the operating system boots on the local hard drive.

Prestage Client Computers   A method for creating computer accounts with Active Directory in advance of installing the computers and then joining them to the domain, using Remote Installation Service (RIS) or Windows Deployment Service (WDS) to install Windows.

Product Activation   The process that verifies that a software program's product key has not been used on more computers than intended by the software license.

Psconfig.exe   The command prompt interface to the SharePoint Products and Technology Configuration Wizard.

publishing point   A location where a media stream is pushed.

Q-R

quick migration   Enables you to rapidly migrate a running virtual machine across Hyper-V hosts with minimal downtime.

quota   A tool used to limit how space is used by a user within a SharePoint site.

RAID-5 volumes   A fault-tolerant volume that uses a minimum of three physical disks, limited to a maximum of 32 physical disks. Data is written across all but one drive. The last drive is used as a parity check to provide redundancy on the other drives.

Real-Time Streaming Protocol (RTSP) A protocol designed to be used in streaming media systems.

Recycle Bin   A temporary holding place to store deleted objects within a SharePoint site.

Redundant Arrays of Inexpensive Disks (RAID)   A category of disk drives that employ two or more drives in combination for fault tolerance and performance. RAID disk drives are used frequently on servers.

Remote Desktop   Software on a Windows Server 2008 computer that enables the server to act as a Terminal Server. Remote Desktop allows up to two remote connections (three if you count the console connection, which is the connection as if you were logged directly on the computer). By default, Remote Desktop uses port 3389.

Remote Desktop Connection (RDC) Software used to connect to a Terminal Server or a computer that has Remote Desktop enabled.

Remote Desktop snap-in   An administrative tool that is ideal for administrators who are remotely administering multiple servers by creating multiple Remote Desktop connections with one utility. The snap-in uses a navigable tree display to provide easy switching between connections. Different from Remote Desktop Connections, the Remote Desktop snap-in connects you to the console session of the computer you specify in the connection.

RemoteApp   Enables users to access remote applications on their local PC. Although the application looks as if it is running from your local machine in its own normal application window, in reality, it is still being hosted by the remote application.

resource authorization policy (RAP) Enables you to specify the internal network resources to which remote users can connect through a TS Gateway server.

S

save state file   A file with the saved content at a certain point in time.

SCSI Drives   SCSI, pronounced "skuzzy," is short for small computer system interface, a high-performance drive typically found in servers or high-powered workstations.

Secure Socket Layer (SSL)   A protocol used to transmit private documents via the Internet. SSL uses a cryptographic system that uses two keys to encrypt data—a public key known to everyone and a private or secret key known only to the recipient of the message. By convention,

URLs that require an SSL connection start with https: instead of http:.

Security Identifier (SID) A hexadecimal string that uniquely identifies the computer, users, and printers.

Server Core A minimal environment with no Windows Explorer shell for running specific server roles and no Start button.

Server Management Console A single, consolidated tool that simplifies the task of managing and securing server roles.

server roles Functions of the server.

Session Directory A feature that enables users to easily and automatically reconnect to a disconnected session in a load-balanced Terminal Server farm.

SharePoint 3.0 Central Administration The main tool used to configure SharePoint websites.

SharePoint Products and Technology Configuration Wizard A tool that performs basic tasks that require minimal user input to configure SharePoint services, which must be performed to start SharePoint Central Administration.

Simple Mail Transfer Protocol (SMTP) A protocol for sending email messages between servers.

simple volumes Disk space on a single physical disk. It can consist of a single area on a disk or multiple areas on the same disk that are linked together.

Single Sign-on (SSO) An authentication method that enables a user with a domain account to log on once, using a password or smart card, and then gain access to remote servers without being asked for credentials again.

site collection A collection of SharePoint websites.

snapshot A point-in-time image of a virtual machine to which you can return. It is typically used when testing changes or when new applications are being loaded to a virtual server. If the changes or new application causes problems, you can revert back to the snapshot before the changes or new application were installed.

spanned volumes Disk space from more than one physical disk. You can add more space to a spanned volume by extending it at any time.

storage area network (SAN) An architecture that attaches remote computer storage devices (such as disk arrays, tape libraries, and optical jukeboxes) to servers in such a way that, to the operating system, the devices appear as locally attached.

Storage Explorer An application available in Windows Server 2008 that allows you to view and manage the Fibre Channel and iSCSI fabrics that are available in your storage area network (SAN).

Storage Manager Windows Server 2008 feature that can be used to create and manage logical unit numbers (LUN) on both Fibre Channel and iSCSI disk storage subsystems that support Virtual Disk Service (VDS).

streaming media Multimedia such as audio and/or video that is constantly sent to and received by the end-user from a provider.

striped volume A disk volume that is made up of two or more physical disks. Data in a striped volume is allocated alternately and evenly (in stripes) to the disks contained within the striped volume. Striped volumes can substantially improve the speed of access to the data on disk. Striped volumes are often referred to as RAID-0; this configuration tends to enhance performance, but it is not fault tolerant.

stsadm.exe command A command used to administer SharePoint Services servers and sites.

subsite A website located within another website.

System Center Virtual Machine Manager 2007 (SCVMM) A console that provides management of physical and virtual machines, consolidation of underutilized physical servers, and rapid provisioning of new virtual machines.

System Preparation Tool (Sysprep) A tool that removes the security identifiers and all other user-specific or computer-specific information

from the computer before you run the disk cloning software to make the cloned disk image.

T

task A job that is assigned to a member within a SharePoint site and that includes the date and priority of the task and its status and progress.

Terminal Server client access license (TS CAL) A kind of software license, distributed by Microsoft, to allow clients to connect to a Terminal Server.

Terminal Service Gateway (TS Gateway) Software that provides access to Terminal Server sessions by encapsulating the RDP protocol in the HTTPS protocol. The session is secure and you need to keep only firewall port 443 open to make a connection. You can control access through this gateway for each user or for each workstation.

Terminal Services A powerful centralized application platform. With Terminal Services, you can remotely connect to a computer as if you were sitting at that computer.

Terminal Services Easy Print A tool used to simplify printer configuration in Terminal Services. The Terminal Services Easy Print driver is useful if a Terminal Server does not have a printer driver installed that matches the printer driver on a client computer.

Terminal Services License Server A server that keeps track of Terminal Server licenses as part of a Terminal Service Licensing system.

Terminal Services Session Broker (TS Session Broker) A role service in Windows Server 2008 that enables a user to reconnect to an existing session in a load-balanced Terminal Server farm.

Terminal Services Web Access (TS Web Access) An interface that makes the Terminal Services remote programs available to users from a web browser. It is a customizable web part, which can also be integrated in an Office SharePoint site.

TS Licensing A license management system available with Windows Server 2008 as a role, which can be used to manage TS licenses for Windows Server 2003 and Windows Server 2008 Terminal Servers.

U

unicast A one-to-one connection between the server and a client.

uninterruptable power supplies (UPS) Devices used to protect against power fluctuations, including power failure.

user profile A collection of folders and data that stores the user's current desktop environment and application settings.

V

virtual directory A directory name, used in a website that corresponds to a physical directory on the server.

Virtual Disk Specification (VDS) Provides a mechanism for remote configuration of disks, partitions, volumes, and iSCSI initiators on a server. Through the VDS protocol, a client can change the configuration of disks into partitions, partitions into volumes, and volumes into file systems.

virtual hard disk (.vhd) files A file that stores the guest operating system, applications, and data for the virtual machine.

virtual machine (VM) A software implementation of a machine (computer) that executes programs like a real machine.

virtual machine configuration (.vmc) file A file in XML format that contains the virtual machine configuration information, including all settings for the virtual machine.

virtual network One or more virtual machines configured to access local or external network resources. The virtual network is configured to use a network adapter in the physical computer.

volume A fixed amount of storage on a disk or tape. It is possible for a single disk to contain more than one volume or for a volume to span more than one disk.

Volume Activation Management Tool (VAMT) A tool used to automate and centrally manage the Microsoft Windows volume activation process for Windows Vista and Windows Server 2008 machines.

W

web application A grouping of content defined either at the root level of a website or in a separate folder under the website's root directory. It defines specific properties such as the application pool in which the application runs. Each site must have at least one application named as the root application, or default application.

web part A modular unit of information that has a single purpose and that forms the basic building block of a Web Part Page. A Web Part is actually composed of two basic files, often requires additional resource files, and its property values are stored in database tables.

web widget A portable chunk of code that can be installed and executed within any separate HTML-based web page by an end user without requiring additional compilation. They are derived from the idea of code reuse.

Windows authentication Authentication that uses NTLM or Kerberos protocols to authenticate clients. Windows authentication is best suited for an intranet environment. Windows authentication is

not suited for use on the Internet because credentials are usually not encrypted.

Windows Deployment Services (WDS) The successor to Remote Installation Services (RIS), which is used to deploy Windows Vista and Windows Server 2008.

Windows features Software programs that are not directly part of a role or that can support or augment the functionality of one or more roles, or enhance the functionality of the entire server.

Windows Imaging Format (WIM) file File-based imaging format that Windows Server 2008 uses for rapid installation on a new computer.

Windows Media Services (WMS) Software component of Microsoft Windows Server 2008 that allows an administrator to generate streaming media (audio/video).

Windows Preinstallation Environment (Windows PE or WinPE) Lightweight version of Windows XP, Windows Server 2003, or Windows Vista that is booted from a network disk, a CD, or a USB flash drive. Windows PE can be used to deploy workstations and servers, restore Windows back to manufacturing specifications, and as a tool to fix and troubleshoot a wide variety of problems.

Windows Reliability and Performance Monitor A Microsoft Management Console snap-in that provides tools for analyzing system performance.

Windows SharePoint Services (WSS)
A website hosted on an Internet Information Services (IIS) server into a web portal that allows for document storage and management, information management, and communication and collaboration.

Windows System Image Manager (Windows SIM) The tool used to create unattended Windows Setup answer files with a program that uses a GUI interface.

Windows System Resource Manager (WSRM) A tool used to allocate CPU and memory resources to applications, services, and processes.

workflow Automated movements of documents or items through a specific sequence of actions or tasks that are related to a business process.

WSS search service A service that allows users to search and locate content in the site collections easily.

X

xcopy command A command-driven tool used to copy files and folders from one place to another.

XML See *Extensible Markup Language (XML)*.

A

I

U

FREE Online Edition

Your purchase of **MCTS 70-643 Exam Cram: Windows Server 2008 Applications Infrastructure, Configuring** includes access to a free online edition for 120 days through the Safari Books Online subscription service. Nearly every Exam Cram book is available online through Safari Books Online, along with over 5,000 other technical books and videos from publishers such as Addison-Wesley Professional, Cisco Press, IBM Press, O'Reilly, Prentice Hall, Que, and Sams.

SAFARI BOOKS ONLINE allows you to search for a specific answer, cut and paste code, download chapters, and stay current with emerging technologies.

Activate your FREE Online Edition at www.informit.com/safarifree

> **STEP 1:** Enter the coupon code: VBKK-UKYJ-UIB5-BCJ3-MBH2.

> **STEP 2:** New Safari users, complete the brief registration form. Safari subscribers, just login.

If you have difficulty registering on Safari or accessing the online edition, please e-mail customer-service@safaribooksonline.com

   Cisco Press IBM Press   New Riders

   QUE   SAMS SAS Sun WILEY